Introduction to Corrections

POLICY, POPULATIONS, AND CONTROVERSIAL ISSUES

Renee D. Lamphere, Kweilin T. Lucas, Timothy J. Holler, and Catherine D. Marcum

SAN DIEGO

Bassim Hamadeh, CEO and Publisher
Alisa Munoz, Project Editor
Susana Christie, Senior Developmental Editor
Abbey Hastings, Production Editor
Emely Villavicencio, Senior Graphic Designer
Greg Isales, Licensing Coordinator
Natalie Piccotti, Director of Marketing
Kassie Graves, Senior Vice President of Editorial
Jamie Giganti, Director of Academic Publishing

3970 Sorrento Valley Blvd., Ste. 500, San Diego, CA 92121

BRIEF CONTENTS

DETAILED CONTENTS

Overview of Corrections

CHAPTER 1

The Evolution of Contemporary Corrections and Philosophies of Punishment

CHAPTER OBJECTIVES

After reading this chapter, you should be able to:

- Discuss the evolution of the U.S. corrections system, from colonial America to today.
- Understand how key historical events shaped the U.S. corrections system.
- Identify the various philosophies of punishment and discuss the similarities and differences between each philosophy.

KEY WORDS

Auburn system

Community-based era

Elmira Reformatory

Evidence-based practices (EBP)

Fair Sentencing Act (2010)

First Step Act (2018)

General deterrence

Industrial prison era

Just deserts model

Lex talionis

Martinson's "nothing works" doctrine

Penn's code

Pennsylvania Prison Society (PPS)

Pennsylvania system

Prison Industry Enhancement Certification Program (PIECP)

Recidivism

Rehabilitative ideal

Restorative justice (RJ)

Selective incapacitation

Specific deterrence

Stocks and pillory

Transportation Act (1718)

Treatment era

Warehousing era

Zebulon Brockway

CASE STUDY: THE INSIGHT PRISON PROJECT AND RESTORATIVE JUSTICE IN PRISONS AND JAILS

As discussed in this chapter, the restorative justice movement aims to help those who commit crime take responsibility for their actions and the harm they caused, while also taking the victim and community into consideration. Restorative justice models have become more prominent in the U.S. corrections system following the warehousing era, in which a record number of people were incarcerated. Restorative justice offers a chance for healing and rehabilitation. One particular restorative justice project out of the state of California, created in 1997, is known as the Insight Prison Project (IPP). The purpose of IPP is to help incarcerated persons grow their emotional and problem-solving skills to help them succeed outside of the prison environment. In addition to aspects of the program aimed at transformation for the offender (e.g., violence prevention programming, yoga, and mindfulness training), victims and survivors also meet with the inmates to allow them to see and understand the harm caused by their criminal actions. Since its inception, IPP has grown to operate in 12 state prisons, one federal prison, and three county jails, helping out incarcerated persons at all levels of confinement. Initial research on restorative justice programs like IPP is promising, showing that these types of programs are effective at reducing recidivism rates and increasing victim satisfaction with the criminal justice process. Specific research on IPP at San Quentin prison found that those in IPP for 6 months or longer had higher levels of self-esteem and decreased levels of aggression (Suttie, 2015). While more research is needed on the effectiveness of restorative justice programs in prison, the existing research is encouraging and suggests that these types of programs have benefits for all those involved.

Questions for Discussion

1. In your opinion, should there be an increased use of restorative justice programs in the United States? What would be the pros of expanding their use? Can you see any drawbacks?

2. Do you think restorative justice programs are appropriate for all types of offenders? What would be the benefits and drawbacks of using these programs for property offenders? Violent offenders?

INTRODUCTION

In 2010, Congress passed the **Fair Sentencing Act** in an attempt to reduce unjust sentencing disparity between crack cocaine and powder cocaine offenses. Prior to the FSA, the Anti-Drug Abuse Acts of 1986 and 1988 allowed for a 100-to-1 ratio of sentences for possession of crack versus possession of powder cocaine. Essentially, possession of 1 gram of crack cocaine mandated the same criminal sentence as possession of 100 grams of powder cocaine. This ratio has resulted in a disparity among those sentenced, with White or Hispanic/Latino individuals making up two thirds of all crack cocaine users and Black individuals constituting more than 80% of federal prison sentences for crack cocaine (American Civil Liberties Union, 2007). Under the Fair Sentencing Act, the 100-to-1 ratio was reduced to 18-to-1; however, at the time it passed it did not apply retroactively to those already serving time.

In December 2018, former President Donald Trump signed into law the Formerly Incarcerated Reenter Society Transformed Safely Transitioning Every Person Act, or **First Step Act**, which retroactively applies the Fair Sentencing Act of 2010, among other provisions. As of April 2019, more than 500 incarcerated persons in federal prisons have been released as a result of the provisions of the First Step Act (Rascoe, 2019). While the First Step Act is certainly a step forward, the fact remains that over 450,000 individuals (or one in five incarcerated people) are serving their sentence for a drug-related offense (Sawyer & Wagner, 2019). Further, while the United States makes up approximately 5% of the world's total population, it is responsible for nearly 25% of the world's prison population (Collier, 2014). The question is, how did the United States get to this point, and where do we go from here?

As will be discussed in this chapter, the road from the creation of modern prisons to today's booming prison system was not straight and narrow; the idea of mass incarceration as we know it today has been a product of changes in sentencing and the prison system in the last 4 decades. In order to understand where we are currently, we must consider the history of the modern U.S. corrections system. In addition to studying the history of the corrections system, it is also of interest to examine the "why" aspect of corrections—that is, why do we sentence people to prison and jail? The following chapter discusses the brief history of the prison system, from colonial America to the present, and provides an overview of different philosophies of punishment.

THE HISTORY AND EVOLUTION OF THE U.S. CORRECTIONS SYSTEM

The U.S. corrections system as it is known today, a place where convicted offenders are sent as a punishment for breaking the law, is a relatively new phenomenon (Banks, 2005). While depictions of imprisonment of criminal offenders have long appeared in historical texts, the prison system of today is very different from early depictions. The idea of prison as a place for segregation and punishment was born in colonial America and has since been replicated in other countries, changing the prison system worldwide (Johnston, 2000; Teeters, 1937). Since the U.S. prison system began almost 200 years ago, it too has undergone a number of significant changes to become the immense, multifaceted structure it is today.

Crime and Early Punishments in Colonial America

Many facets of the criminal justice system can trace their roots back to England, and the corrections system is no different. During the 1600 and 1700s, many crimes in England were punishable by death or banishment. Also during this time period, English settlers were coming to America and needed cheap laborers to help grow the colonies (Ekrich, 1987). In 1717, England passed the **Transportation Act**, allowing judges to send laborers to the American colonies rather than give a death sentence (Coldham, 2007). Between 1718, when the act was passed, and 1775, at the beginning of the American Revolution, more than 30,000 convicted English offenders were sent to work in the American colonies (Ekrich, 1987).

In addition to being heavily influenced by England, punishment in colonial America was also influenced by the Christian Bible. Crime was viewed as a sin, and in order for a person to be absolved of their sin and be right with God, they had to receive a punishment for their crime (Miller, 1986). Prisons as we know them today did not exist in this time period, so many criminals were subjected to physical punishments that were often humiliating in nature (Teeters, 1937). Given the small size of many communities, shame and embarrassment could be wielded as powerful tools to control people's behaviors. Two forms of humiliation that were commonly used in colonial America were the **stocks and pillory**. The stocks were made of heavy wood that had holes cut out for an offender's hands and feet. The pillory was an upright, hinged board with holes for an offender's head and hands. The stocks and the pillory were placed in a public location, and the offender was strapped to either device, unable to move. Over the course of several hours or several days, the offender was subject not only to weather conditions but also to harassment from members of the public. Members of the public were known to throw rotten food at, kick at, and spit on those in the stocks and the pillory (Friedman, 1993). While popular in colonial times, the pillory was reportedly used as late as 1905 in Delaware (Wood & Waite, 1941).

The U.S. prison system of today is a product of a religious group known as the Quakers (Teeters, 1937). The Quakers were an English religious group that faced violent persecution and came to colonial America to escape this and practice their religion freely; however, soon after coming to America, they faced persecution from the Puritan colonists. In an effort to find a place to practice their religion freely, William Penn, an early Quaker and English real estate entrepreneur, founded the colony of Pennsylvania (McKelvey, 1977). The Quakers, who opposed immoral conduct and the taking of human lives, were offended by the harsh physical punishments that existed in the colonies. In 1682, the Pennsylvania legislature enacted a series of statutes to define crimes and their punishments, which are now known as the "Great Law," or **Penn's code.** Under Penn's code, only premeditated murder and treason were punishable by death; all other crimes carried a punishment of fines, hard labor, or imprisonment in a "house of corrections" (McKelvey, 1977; Teeters, 1937).

While great change was made under Penn's code, shortly after William Penn's death in 1718, more conservative factions of the Pennsylvania colony began reintroducing the physical and humiliating punishments of the English criminal codes (Johnston, n.d.). This lasted until around 1775, when the U.S. landscape began to change following the end of the American Revolution. As the population became more mobile, people moved, and cities began to flourish (Lewis, 1922). The increase in population also resulted in increases in job availability, poverty, and crime. These demographic changes also brought about change in people's views on criminal behavior. Rather than being viewed as a product of sin, crime began to be viewed as a product of an individual's environment. Factors such as poor upbringing, inadequate education or lack of education, and alcohol use were now being considered in relation to offender culpability (Teeters, 1937). With this change in thinking came calls for reform, specifically for reform of the harsh English penal codes adopted by the colonies.

One of the biggest catalysts for change came in 1787, when Dr. Benjamin Rush and a group of like-minded prominent citizens met in the Philadelphia home of Benjamin Franklin to discuss the nature and effects of harsh, humiliating punishment. This meeting led to the formation of the Philadelphia Society for Alleviating the Miseries of Public Prisons, known as the **Pennsylvania Prison Society (PPS)** (Johnston, n.d.). In 1788 members of the PPS presented a strategy for punishment reform to the Pennsylvania legislature. Drawing heavily on Quaker philosophy, the reformers proposed that incarceration of an offender could provide an opportunity for penance, and that prisons offered a place for offenders to accept responsibility for their actions and make amends (Teeters, 1937). As it has since its inception over 230 years ago, the PPS continues to advocate for incarcerated persons and their families in the state of Pennsylvania to this day, providing programming and services to thousands of individuals annually (Pennsylvania Prison Society, n.d.).

The Penitentiary and Mass Prison Era

Following calls by the members of the PPS for legal changes, the Pennsylvania legislature passed a bill that called for the building of the first house of penance, or penitentiary, in the United States. In 1790 the Walnut Street Jail opened in Philadelphia, becoming the first state-run prison in the nation (Johnston, n.d.; Teeters, 1937). In what would come to be known as the **Pennsylvania system**, the Walnut Street Jail emphasized the use of solitary confinement and encouraged study of the Bible. The building itself was designed to limit contact with the outside world (it was surrounded by a 20-foot-high wall), as well as contact between incarcerated persons. Silence was enforced at all times under this system. Serious offenders spent the entirety of their day in solitary confinement, while less serious offenders were allowed to work together in shops, performing tasks such as shoemaking and weaving (Lewis, 1922). Under the guidance of the PPS, a vocational school was opened in the facility in 1798 (Johnston, n.d.). The ideals embodied by the Pennsylvania system included separation, silence, rehabilitation, and penitence. By 1818, the Walnut Street Jail faced issues with overcrowding, leading to the building of the Western State Penitentiary in Pittsburgh in 1826 and the Eastern State Penitentiary in Philadelphia in 1829 (Teeters, 1937).

Many states soon adopted and replicated the Pennsylvania system in their own prisons, including Vermont, Massachusetts, Maryland, and Virginia (Lewis, 1922). With the rise in the number of prisons came a rise in prison populations, and some found the constraints of maintaining an environment of solitary confinement in the Pennsylvania system too burdensome. One of the first facilities to depart from this system was a prison in Auburn, New York that opened in 1821. In what would come to be known as the **Auburn system**, the Auburn prison operated on a system of silence, separation, and hard labor. This facility was different from the Pennsylvania system in that it operated as a congregate system, where incarcerated persons lived, worked, and ate together, albeit in silence. The Auburn system also reintroduced the concepts of corporal punishment and shaming for incarcerated persons who violated the rules of the facility (Barnes & Teeters, 1959).

A comparison of the Pennsylvania and Auburn systems reveals similarities and differences. Both systems operated with enforced silence, obedience, and hard labor (Rothman, 1971), but there were a number of key differences between them. One difference was in the construction costs of the facilities; the Auburn system cost less to build because of its simpler facility design (Williams, 1979). The Auburn system was seen as valuable because of the congregate nature of work at these facilities. Profits from prison labor were higher with the Auburn system because the incarcerated persons worked together, meaning they could produce goods more quickly than those working alone in the Pennsylvania system (Rothman, 1971). Consequently, the Auburn system was replicated throughout the United States (Williams, 1979). An interesting fact about these systems is that during the time they were created, representatives from many European nations were sent to the United States to study the two prison systems. While the Auburn system was favored by Americans, the Europeans overwhelmingly supported the Pennsylvania system, as they believed it to be more conducive to reformation for incarcerated persons. As a result of this, the Pennsylvania system was more widely adopted worldwide (Rothman, 1971).

The Reformatory Era

By the end of the Civil War in 1865, the South was left in virtual ruins, particularly from a structural viewpoint, as many cities had been badly damaged at the end of the war. In addition, resources and jobs were scarce in the South due to the influx in population from more than four million freed slaves (Litwack, 1980). Many of these free slaves headed to cities in the North. At the same time there was an influx of Irish, Italian, Jewish, and Chinese immigrants coming to the United States, and many of them flocked to the North. The cities in the North could not absorb all of the new populations, resulting in the creation of slums and ghettos filled with unemployed, homeless people. These areas became breeding grounds for crime and criminal behavior (Blomberg & Lucken, 2000). As crime rates rose, prisons became overcrowded. The strict rules of the Pennsylvania and Auburn systems, which at one point had helped to maintain order, began to dissolve. Prisons became more brutal as those who broke prison rules were treated with severe punishments (Blomberg & Lucken).

While beliefs that immigrants were the cause of crime fueled public opinion during this time period, it was also marked as an era of progressive, scientific thinking. There were experts in the field of criminal justice who adopted a sociological explanation for criminality, believing that criminals could be treated and reformed in the right environment. In Cincinnati, Ohio in 1870, prison reformers from 24 states, Canada, and South America gathered at what is known as the National Prison Congress. The keynote speaker at this conference was a man by the name of **Zebulon Brockway**. Brockway and other key reformers adopted the Declaration of Principles, which included the following elements:

- Religious instruction;
- Opportunities for education;
- Work and vocational opportunities; and
- A plan for supervising convicts post-release. (Brockway, 1910)

Under the umbrella of prison reform and the direction of Zebulon Brockway as superintendent, the **Elmira Reformatory** was built in New York State in 1876 (Banks, 2005). Serving as the nation's first reformatory, Elmira housed male offenders ages 16–30 who were serving their first prison term. The Elmira system was marked by indeterminate sentencing, and incarcerated persons there were classified by three "moral grades" and housed accordingly (Murphy, 1927). Following this three-stage model, an incarcerated person could advance to a higher grade if they followed all prison rules and could be demoted if they failed to follow all the rules. The assumption was that as an incarcerated person advanced to a new moral grade level, they would be further reformed. The final stage, parole, resulted in the incarcerated person being released into the community under the supervision of a parole officer (Blomberg & Lucken, 2000).

Despite the best intentions of Brockway and the Elmira reformers to shape and change the lives of incarcerated persons, overall, the reformatory was not deemed a success (Banks, 2005). Allegations surrounding mistreatment of incarcerated persons by Brockway and other staff resulted in an investigation of the facility by the New York State Board of Charities between 1893 and 1894. The investigation found that the overcrowded facility was understaffed and mismanaged, and that overly harsh methods of treatment were being used to discipline the people incarcerated there (Pisciotta, 1994). Further, it was found that there was an overemphasis on confinement in an effort to maintain deteriorating institutional security, which is not conducive to reform. Also, the supervision of paroled incarcerated persons was ineffective, as many officers were undertrained and overworked (Barnes & Teeters, 1959). Despite the shortcomings of the reformatory era, many of the key principles of this era remain important to the U.S. corrections system, even today.

The Industrial Prison Era

The shortcomings of the Elmira reformatory and of the entire era of reformation for incarcerated persons led to growing public concerns regarding the ability to secure and maintain these individuals. The prison population was continually rising during this time period, and the mounting costs of housing incarcerated persons sparked the idea of utilizing them as a form of cheap labor to offset these costs. Based on the ideals of cheap prison labor, beginning in 1890 and spanning into the mid-1930s, the **industrial prison era** of the U.S. corrections system flourished (Barnes & Teeters, 1959). During this time period, a number of large prisons were built or converted for industrialization, such as Sing Sing Prison in New York and San Quentin Prison in California. According to a report by the American Correctional Association (1986), many of these facilities prospered, resulting in self-sustaining, even self-profiting institutions.

There were certainly a number of correctional officials during the industrial era who were more than content with the profitability of their facilities; however, there was also a growing backlash to prison industry. Many in the general public opposed these industries from their inception, citing the fact that the reduced costs afforded to prison industries resulted in unfair competition for workers and businesses (American Correctional Association, 1986). As a direct result of this opposition, a number of federal laws were passed to restrict prison industry and commerce, such as the Hawes-Cooper Act of 1929 and the Ashurst-Sumners Act of 1935, which prohibited the importation and interstate sale of convict-made goods. Following the passage of these acts and growing economic pressures brought in by the Great Depression, most states had passed statutes to restrict prison-made goods by the mid-1930s.

It is important to note that while the legislative actions of the end of the industrial prison era certainly stifled the prison industry, they did not abolish the industry all together. Under the Justice System Improvement Act of 1979 and the Crime Control Act of 1990, the **Prison Industry Enhancement Certification Program (PIECP)** was created. The PIECP is administered by the Bureau of Justice Assistance and allows for the sale and commerce of prison-made goods by prison industry programs that meet all of the necessary requirements. In addition to being used to offset the costs of prisons, a portion of the money generated by PIECP programs is used for victims' compensation and family support programs. As of March 31, 2019, there were 32 programs participating in the PIECP, generating over $11 million in revenue, with $1.3 million of that going directly to victims' compensation (National Correctional Industries Association, 2019).

The Treatment and Community-Based Eras

Following the era of the Great Depression in the 1930s, the United States experienced a period of economic security in the 1940s that is mainly attributable to the post-war boom created by the end of World War II. In terms of the corrections system, this era was marked by a renewed emphasis on reformation and treatment of incarcerated persons (Barnes & Teeters, 1959). Prison reform became a popular topic for politicians and the media. Known as the **treatment era,** this time period was characterized by beliefs that centered on a medical model of rehabilitation. Under a medical model, an offender is viewed as being "sick," and the "cure" was a matter of finding the right "treatment" for them (Lehman, 1972). Treatments during this time utilized both individual and group therapy approaches, as well as neurosurgery, drug therapy, and aversion therapy, among other types of treatments. A number of states began to use diagnostic centers, where trained medical professionals carefully studied each incarcerated person in terms of their medical, psychological, and criminal history and made recommendations for security-level placements based on these observations. The ultimate goal was to help the offender mature psychologically so that they could develop and take responsibility for their own lives (MacNamara, 1977). Some of the treatments used in this era, particularly the more invasive treatments, were viewed unfavorably by the people receiving the treatment. In addition to the incarcerated persons who complained, a number of academic and legal scholars pointed to a lack of evidence to support the treatment models being imposed (MacNamara, 1977). By the end of the late 1960s, the treatment era by and large came to an end. Regardless, many rehabilitation programs in this era survived, and they continue to thrive in facilities even today.

Despite the many criticisms that marked the treatment era of corrections, the possibility of change for incarcerated persons was not yet abandoned by correctional administrators. There were many who believed that rehabilitation was possible but would not be successful if done in a carceral environment. This belief, combined with added pressures of increasingly overcrowded facilities, marked the beginning of a transition to community corrections in the late 1960s (Scull, 1977). The **community-based era**, sometimes referred to as deinstitutionalization or decarceration, employed a number of mechanisms to keep offenders out of prisons and in their communities. Programs such as halfway houses and work-releases gained considerable popularity during this time period (Williams, 1979).

At the same time that the community-based era was flourishing, there was also emerging research in the 1970s that found diversion programs to be largely ineffective at reducing rates of offending. Little difference was seen between those who participated in diversion programs and those who remained incarcerated (Blomberg & Lucken, 2000). Scientific doubt regarding the effectiveness of rehabilitation came to a head in 1974 with the popular interpretation of a research report done by Robert Martinson and colleagues. Their report, which was a meta-analysis of 231 research studies done between 1945 and 1967 on the effectiveness of correctional rehabilitation programs, found that overall, treatment programs were not effective at reducing offender **recidivism** (Martinson, 1974; Ward, 2009). These results were interpreted, and some would later say misinterpreted, to conclude that "nothing works" in terms of rehabilitation for incarcerated persons. In what is now known as **Martinson's "nothing works" doctrine**, the researchers argued that we did not have the "faintest clue" about how to rehabilitate offenders and reduce recidivism rates. This was not the first time this assertion had been made, but given the context of what was happening with rising rates of public order and violent offenses in the 1970s, this message was readily accepted by policy makers and criminologists (Gendreau et al., 2004). It should also be noted, though, that counter-research to Martinson's acknowledged that many correctional treatment programs failed because they were not therapeutically vigorous, and because the staff that implemented the programs were poorly trained and often did not follow the rules and guidelines they were supposed to when implementing rehabilitation programs (Gendreau & Ross, 1979). While this research is certainly not responsible for the entire downfall of the correctional rehabilitation system, it marks the beginning of a decline in the availability of correctional rehabilitation programs in the United States (Garland, 2001).

The Warehousing Era

In the corrections system, the time period from the 1980s through 2010 was marked by a focus on crime control and mass imprisonment in the United States. Beginning in the late 1970s and early 1980s, the U.S. economy sagged, leaving the nation in a deep state of recession. Nightly news reports of gruesome murders, serial killers, school shootings, and global terrorism infiltrated the American public. Further, reports of high recidivism rates and inaccurate, elaborate depictions of prison life all fueled public opinion that the corrections system was not working. The criminal justice system embraced these perceived failures and countered with a "get tough" approach to criminal offenders (Banks, 2005), which is also referred to as a "tough on crime" approach and associated with a "law and order" approach, in this book and elsewhere. This time period became known as the **warehousing era**, in which the purpose of imprisonment was to protect innocent members of society at all costs, even if that meant completely abandoning the possibility of offender rehabilitation (Herivel & Wright, 2003).

By and large, the warehousing era was driven by the popularity of mandatory minimum sentences, truth-in-sentencing requirements, and "three strikes you're out" (or Three Strikes) laws, as well as by other factors such as increases in parole violations, a drop in the annual release rate of incarcerated persons, and enhanced punishments for drug offenders (Banks, 2005). Beginning in the 1980s, the prison population grew exponentially, reaching an all-time high in the mid-1990s; for example, the number of incarcerated persons in state and federal prisons grew from half a million in 1980 to 1.6 million in 1996 (Blumstein & Beck, 1999). An unfortunate result of the warehousing era has been extreme overcrowding in many U.S. prison facilities. Overcrowding can contribute to problems such as increased misconduct among incarcerated persons, which ultimately affects the security of the facility, offenders, and staff members alike.

The Evidence-Based Era

We are in the process of defining the next era of the U.S. prison system. While many accepted the retributive policies of individual accountability as the rationale for incarcerating so many individuals, the Great Recession in 2009 left a number of states struggling to support large and often overcrowded prison populations. Many states began cutting their corrections budgets in 2009, which may have contributed to a decline in prison populations since that year (Gottschalk, 2010). In an effort to continue to reduce prison expenditures, numerous state legislators and correctional reformers are looking toward **evidence-based practices (EBP)** as a strategy to improve correctional results for incarcerated persons. EBP relies on utilizing scientific research and replicable clinical knowledge to improve correctional outcomes. Outcomes that EBP looks to improve include:

- Incarcerated offender assessment;
- Prison programming;
- Rehabilitation of offenders; and
- Public safety.

Essentially, EBP involves taking a "what works" approach to correctional rehabilitation, basing interventions on scientific evidence and proven strategies. The goal of EBP is to improve outcomes for individual offenders and for the U.S. corrections system as a whole (Serin, 2005).

U.S. Prisons Today

Throughout the world, more than 10.7 million people are held in penal institutions at any given moment. As of 2018 the United States had the largest prison population in the world, accounting for nearly 25% of the world's prison population (Walmsley, 2018). However, it is of interest to note that although the United States leads the world in its number of incarcerated persons, the overall population of the U.S. prison system has declined in recent years. At end of 2019, the total prison population was 1,430,800, representing a decrease of 33,600 incarcerated persons, or 2% of the total prison population, from 2018. At the time of this writing in 2021, the most recently assessed incarceration rate of 419 incarcerated persons per 100,000 U.S. residents is the lowest rate since 1995. Since 2009, the U.S. imprisonment rate has declined 17% overall, more so among Black residents (29% decline) and Hispanic/Latino residents (24% decline). A total of 35 states reported a prison population decrease from 2018 to 2019, with Texas having the greatest decrease (down 5,200), followed by Missouri (down 4,300) and New York (down 3,100). It should also be noted, though, that there were 12 states with increases, with the state of Alabama having the greatest increase (up, 1,500) (Carson, 2020).

Males make up the majority of the U.S. prison population, with females comprising 8% of the total population. Like the male population, the incarcerated female population has also declined in recent years, with a total population decrease of 2,800 incarcerated persons (3%) at year-end 2019. A total of 37 states and the federal government showed decreases in their female prison populations in 2019, with the largest decreases happening in Texas (down 800) and Missouri (down 700) (Carson, 2020).

The imprisonment rate declined in 2019 across all racial demographics. For example, the percentage of both Black and Hispanic/Latino incarcerated persons with a sentence of one year or more decreased 3% between 2018 and 2019, and the White population decreased by 2%. Since 2009, the number of sentenced Black incarcerated persons has declined over 23%. Despite this decrease, it is still of interest to note that more than 1% of all Black adults in the United States are serving a sentence in state or federal prison. The incarceration rate for Black adults (1,446 per 100,000 Black adult U.S. residents) is twice as high as the rate for Hispanic/Latino adults (757 per 100,000 Hispanic/Latino adult U.S. residents) and five times as high as the rate for White adults (263 per 100,000 White adult U.S. residents) (Carson, 2020).

Finally, offense characteristics reveal that more than half (55%) of all incarcerated persons at state-run facilities in 2019 were serving one year or more for a violent offense, with 14% (177,700) serving time for murder or non-negligent manslaughter and 13% (162,700) serving time for rape or sexual assault; the racial makeup regarding each type of violent offense is as follows. Overall, 62% of Black incarcerated persons and 62% of Hispanic/Latino incarcerated persons were serving time for a violent offense, compared to 48% of White incarcerated persons. Regarding murder or non-negligent manslaughter, 19% of all Hispanic/Latino persons in state prison were sentenced for these crimes, compared to 17% of all Black incarcerated persons and 11% of White incarcerated persons. Regarding rape and sexual assault, 40% of those serving time for these crimes were White (65,600), while 22% (35,000) were Hispanic/Latino and 21% (34,800) were Black. In addition to those incarcerated for violent offenses, 46% of those in federal prison were there for drug offenses at the federal level. Approximately 59% of all female federally incarcerated persons were incarcerated for a drug offense, in comparison to 45% of all male federally incarcerated persons (Carson, 2020).

PHILOSOPHIES OF PUNISHMENT

From a legal perspective, a crime is an action (or inaction) that society has deemed wrong by establishing laws that prohibit it. In essence, a crime is an action punishable by law. Some crimes, such as rape and murder, are known as felony crimes, while other crimes, such as traffic offenses, are known as misdemeanor crimes. The federal government, as well as every state in the United States of America, has lists of punishments for specific types of crimes, some of which involve incarceration. These lists are not static in nature; they change over the course of time and history. Sentencing philosophy, or the justification for giving a person a criminal sentence, has also changed over time. These justifications are often entangled in issues relating to religion, morality, and values. As an example of how religion and punishment can intertwine, in early American history, crime was viewed as resulting from sin and punishment was viewed as due to the actions of a sinner. There is not necessarily a "right" or "wrong" reason to punish a person; rather, there are many differing perspectives. While there may be many reasons why a punishment exists, for the purpose of this chapter, five philosophies of punishment will be discussed: retribution, incapacitation, deterrence, rehabilitation, and restoration.

Retribution *least important*

Retribution, the earliest known rationale for criminal punishment, is a sentencing philosophy based on the ancient concept of *lex talionis*, or law of retribution. This is commonly associated with the saying "an eye for an eye, a tooth for a tooth," which implies that if a person commits a crime, they should be punished in a like fashion, where the punishment matches the severity of the crime. For example, if someone breaks someone else's arm, their arm should be broken in return. This is also sometimes referred to as a **just deserts model**, which demands that offenders be punished for their crimes in order to get their "just deserts" (Stohr et al., 2009). An interesting note on the concept of *lex talionis* is that this often-cited justification of "an eye for an eye, a tooth for a tooth" was not intended to make punishments more severe for offenders. Early punishments for wrongdoings were often overly severe; death and exile were commonly imposed for even minor offenses. *Lex talionis* was intended to reduce the severity of punishment for minor offenses. Retribution is viewed as a primary goal of punishment to this day, both in public perception and in politics and policy-making.

Incapacitation   *most important*

The primary purpose of incapacitation is to protect people in society from those who want to commit crime. As a correctional goal, incapacitation seeks to remove offenders from society so that they cannot inflict any further harm on the public while they are incarcerated (Stefanovska & Jovanova, 2017). In fact, the term "incapacitation" is often used interchangeably with the term "community protection" (Pathinayake, 2018). In colonial times, when jails and prisons were first being designed, incapacitation was a primary goal of these facilities (Kifer et al., 2003). More recently, policies based on incapacitation were dominant in the United States in the 1980s and after. These policies resulted in an increase in the prison population since the 1990s, which has also come with a reduction in crime rates following periods of mass incarceration (Stefanovska & Jovanova, 2017). It is important to note, though, that it cannot be determined with accuracy whether this decrease in crime rates is a result of incapacitation or of some other factor (Paternoster, 2010). For example, some studies show that increases in penalty for murder, rape, and physical assault do not reduce the number of these incidents (Stefanovska & Jonanova, 2017).

A key concept regarding incapacitation is the idea of **selective incapacitation**. This concept is based on the premise that a small percentage of offenders are responsible for a greater percentage of crime; therefore, we should identify these offenders and give them longer prison sentences for the protection of the public (Stefanovska & Jovanova, 2017). It is believed that by correctly identifying these particular offenders and imposing lengthier sentences, we can reduce the prison population by decreasing the length of sentence for offenders who do not pose as much risk to society. The key to selective incapacitation is risk assessment, as potential offenders need to be carefully identified, to avoid possible abuse and misclassification.

Deterrence

Deterrence as a model for corrections is based on an understanding of the preventive role of the criminal justice system. In its simplest form, deterrence is the prevention of crime through the threat of punishment (Stohr et al., 2009). Deterrence can be broken down into two categories: specific deterrence and general deterrence. **Specific deterrence** is when an individual offender is punished to be stopped from committing crime. For example, when an individual offender commits murder and receives the death penalty, being put to death specifically deters that person from committing future crimes. **General deterrence** occurs when observers who have not yet committed a crime are deterred from committing that crime because they fear receiving the same punishment as an offender. An example of this would be a potential offender who refrains from committing murder out of fear of the death penalty, after seeing another offender get the death penalty for murder.

Research on the effectiveness of deterrence in the criminal justice system reveals mixed results. For example, research by Dezbakhis et al. (2003) found that the application of the death penalty resulted in 18 lives being saved; however, most findings suggest that the deterrence effect of the death penalty is marginal at best (Paternoster, 2010). In fact, research by Stefanovska and Jovanova (2017) found that severe punishment and long prison sentences did not reduce recidivism rates, but instead increased these rates by 3%. The explanation behind this is that longer sentences result in incarcerated persons losing social contacts in their community, reducing their chances of normal social relations after release from prison and increasing their risk for recidivism. Despite these mixed findings, deterrence as a goal of incarceration remains a top priority for lawmakers and citizens alike in the United States and will likely continue to do so for many years to come.

Rehabilitation ~~MOST IMPORTANT~~

During the early 19th century, the idea that imprisonment itself could reduce crime began to be met with skepticism. Poorly managed institutions, coupled with hard and inhumane conditions, led many to the conclusion that prisons were not reducing crime but putting society at a greater risk, as incarcerated persons who were released from prison would be hardened by the harsh prison environment (Wodahl & Garland, 2009). This shift in thinking was toward what Allen (1981) called the **rehabilitative ideal**. Allen defines the rehabilitative ideal as:

> the notion that a primary purpose of penal treatment is to effect changes in the characters, attitudes, and behavior of convicted offenders, so as to strengthen the social defense against unwanted behavior, but also to contribute to the welfare and satisfaction of others. (1981, p. 2)

It is of interest to note that the rehabilitative ideal does not refer to a specific method of reform, as these methods have varied greatly over time, and our views of these methods have also changed. For example, methods like corporal punishments, religious interventions, and lobotomies are all techniques that have been undertaken in the spirit of rehabilitation (Meranze, 1996). In essence, rehabilitation seeks to bring about change in the offender's behavior, and holds the prison system itself responsible for providing a means to achieve positive changes in behavior. As with deterrence models of punishment, the goal of rehabilitation is to reduce the number of criminal offenses and the rate of recidivism. Strategies such as educational attainment, vocational education, and therapeutic services are all used to rehabilitate incarcerated offenders. As previously discussed, Martinson's "nothing works" doctrine led to a decline and distrust of rehabilitation programming in U.S. corrections; however, there is new and emerging research indicating that effective treatment programs do exist (Ward, 2009). Future research will be needed to provide any definitive conclusions regarding this philosophy of punishment.

Restoration

When a crime occurs there is, of course, immediate harm done to the victim; however, many victims continue to feel the traumatizing physical and emotional effects of a crime long after it occurs. Restoration is a sentencing philosophy that aims to heal the trauma associated with crime victims by bringing together key stakeholders to make the victim "whole again." The key stakeholders in these situations are the offender, the victim, and the community (excluding the state) (Marshall, 1999). Falling under the umbrella of restoration are **restorative justice (RJ)** interventions. RJ can be defined as "a process whereby parties with a stake in a specific offense collectively resolve how to deal with the aftermath of the offense and its implications for the future" (Marshall, 1999, p. 5). RJ interventions focus on creating offender accountability, restoring the community to the state it was in prior to the crime occurring, and meeting the needs of the crime victim. Voluntary participation is emphasized in RJ interventions, as unwilling participants will most likely result in unsatisfied stakeholders (Zehr & Mika, 1997). The use of restoration and RJ interventions is relatively new in the field of criminal justice, especially in comparison to other philosophies of punishment (Armstrong, 2014).

CONCLUSION

The U.S. corrections system is ever evolving. Throughout its history, the system has cycled through many philosophies of punishment; at some points the system has focused on offender rehabilitation while at other points it has focused on incapacitation, and many variations of thought in between these two extremes have manifested themselves through the correctional system. The most recent eras of the corrections system are different than those prior to it because the United States has reached proportions of mass incarceration not previously seen in history. Given the sheer number of incarcerated individuals in the United States, it is important to continue to examine the corrections system at both the systemic and individual levels. As research grows and develops in the field of corrections, differing conclusions regarding the shape and direction of the U.S. corrections system will also continue to emerge. In the meantime, millions of people are impacted by mass incarceration in the United States, and it is not yet clear how current practices will affect individual offenders or the system in the years to come.

DISCUSSION QUESTIONS

1. What is the reason for the 100-to-1 and 18-to-1 (crack-versus-powder) cocaine laws? Why do we continue to see this disparity in sentencing?
2. What are the similarities and differences between the Pennsylvania and Auburn systems? What elements of these systems do we see in our prison system today?
3. How has the U.S. corrections system changed in terms of philosophies of punishment? What historical events coincide with these changes?

APPLICATION EXERCISES

Exercise #1: Advocacy for Incarcerated Persons and the Pennsylvania Prison Society

For this exercise, you will further explore an organization you were introduced to in this chapter, the Pennsylvania Prison Society (PPS). You should visit the PPS website at: https://www.prisonsociety.org/

After visiting this site, answer the following questions:

1. What is the history and mission of the PPS?
2. What is an official visitor, and how can one become an official visitor for the PPS?
3. What types of services are offered by the Prison Reentry Network?
4. What programs and services are offered to family members of incarcerated individuals?

In addition, you should also check out an issue of *Graterfriends*, a newsletter publication that is sponsored by the PPS and written by incarcerated persons. The *Graterfriends* archives can be found at the following link: https://www.prisonsociety.org/archives

Exercise #2: Exploring Your Personal Punishment Philosophy

In this chapter, a number of different philosophies of punishment were discussed. Based on these different philosophies, you should consider your own personal punishment philosophy.

1. What do you think is the most important philosophy of punishment?
2. What do you think is the least important philosophy of punishment?

In addition, you should think about the reasoning behind your particular philosophy of punishment. What about your own personal background influences your personal punishment philosophy? Has anything you've learned about corrections changed your personal punishment philosophy?

REFERENCES

Allen, F. A. (1981). *The decline of the rehabilitative ideal.* Yale University Press.

American Civil Liberties Union. (2007, October 2). *U.S. Supreme Court weighs 100-to-1 disparity in crack/powder cocaine sentencing.* https://www.aclu.org/press-releases/us-supreme-court-weighs-100-1-disparity-crackpowder-cocaine-sentencing

American Correctional Association. (1986). *A study of prison industry: History, components, and goals.* National Institute of Corrections. Retrieved June 15, 2019 from https://www.ncjrs.gov/pdffiles1/Digitization/101050NCJRS.pdf

Armstrong, J. (2014). Rethinking the restorative-retributive dichotomy: Is reconciliation possible? *Contemporary Justice Review, 17*(3), 362–374.

Banks, C. (2005). *Punishment in America: A reference handbook.* ABC-CLIO, Inc.

Barnes, H. E., & Teeters, N. K. (1959). *New horizons in criminology* (3rd ed.). Prentice-Hall, Inc.

Blomberg, T., & Lucken, K. (2000). *American penology: A history of control.* Aldine De Gruyter.

Blumstein, A., & Beck, A. J. (1999). Population growth in U.S. prisons, 1980–1996. *Crime and Justice, 26,* 17–61.

Brockway, Z. R. (1910). The American reformatory prison system. *American Journal of Sociology, 15,* 454–477.

Carson, E. A. (2020). *Prisoners in 2019* (Publication no. NCJ 255115). U.S. Department of Justice, Office of Justice Programs, Bureau of Justice Statistics. https://www.bjs.gov/content/pub/pdf/p19.pdf

Coldham, P. W. (2007). *Emigrants in chains: A social history of the forced emigration to the Americas of felons, destitute children, political and religious non-conformists.* Genealogical Publishing.

Collier, L. (2014). Incarceration nation. *Monitor on Psychology, 45*(9), 56–60.

Dezhbakhsh, H., Rubin, P. H., & Shepherd, J. M. (2003). Does capital punishment have a deterrent effect? New evidence from postmoratorium panel data. *American Law & Economics Review, 5*(2), 344-376.

Ekrich, R. (1987). *Bound for America: The transportation of British convicts to the colonies, 1718–1775.* Clarendon/Oxford University Press.

Fair Sentencing Act of 2010. S.1789 – 111th Congress. (2010).

Formerly Incarcerated Reenter Society Transformed Safely Transitioning Every Person [FIRST STEP] Act. H. Rept. 115-699. (2018).

Friedman, L. M. (1993). *Crime and punishment in American history.* Basic Books.

Garland, D. (2001). *The culture of control: Crime and social order in contemporary society*. University of Chicago Press.

Gendreau, P., French, S. A., & Gionet, A. (2004). What works (what doesn't work): The principles of effective correctional treatment. *Journal of Community Corrections, 13*(3), 4–30.

Gendreau, P., & Ross, R. R. (1979). Effective correctional treatment: Bibliotherapy for cynics. *Crime and Delinquency, 25*, 463–489.

Gottschalk, M. (2010). Cell blocks & red ink: Mass incarceration, the great recession & penal reform. *Daedalus, 139*(3), 62–73.

Herivel, T., & Wright, P. (2003). *Prison nation: The warehousing of America's poor*. Routledge.

Johnston, N. (n.d.). *Prison reform in Pennsylvania*. The Pennsylvania Prison Society. Retrieved June 13, 2019 from http://media.wix.com/ugd//4c2da0_41bed342ea390827839e1ffa4b3dca97.pdf

Johnston, N. (2000). *Forms of constraint: A history of prison architecture*. University of Illinois Press.

Kifer, M., Hemmens, C., & Stohr, M. K. (2003). The goals of corrections: Perspectives from the line. *Criminal Justice Review, 28*(1), 47–69.

Lehman, P. E. (1972). The medical model of treatment: Historical development of an archaic standard. *Crime & Delinquency, 18*(2), 204–212.

Lewis, O. F. (1922). *The development of American prisons and prison customs 1776 to 1845*. J. B. Lyon Company.

Litwack, L. F. (1980). *Been in the storm so long: The aftermath of slavery*. Vintage Books.

MacNamara, D. E. J. (1977). The medical model in corrections. *Criminology, 14*(4), 439–448.

Marshall, T. (1999). *Restorative justice: An overview*. Home Office.

Martinson, R. (1974). What works? Questions and answers about prison reform. *Public Interest, 35*, 22–53.

McKelvey, B. (1977). *American prisons: A history of good intentions*. Patterson Smith.

Meranze, M. (1996). *Laboratories of virtue: Punishment, revolution, and authority in Philadelphia, 1760–1835*. University of North Carolina Press.

Miller, J. C. (1986). *The first frontier: Life in Colonial America*. University Press of America.

Murphy, P. C. (1927). *Behind gray walls*. Caxton Printers.

National Correctional Industries Association. (2019). *PIECP quarterly statistical reports, first quarter 2019 statistical data report*. Retrieved June 15, 2019 from https://nationalcia.org/wp-content/uploads/2019/05/First-Quarter-2019-Statistical-Data-Report-1.pdf

Paternoster, R. (2010). How much do we really know about criminal deterrence? *Journal of Criminal Law & Criminology, 100*(3), 765-824.

Pathinayake, A. (2018). The effectiveness of the objective of incapacitation: Is it a myth? *Journal of Gender, Race, & Justice, 21*(2), 333–366.

Pennsylvania Prison Society. (n.d.). *Who we are*. Retrieved June 13, 2019 from https://www.prisonsociety.org/about_us

Pisciotta, A. (1994). *Benevolent repression: Social control and the American reformatory movement*. University Press.

Rascoe, A. (2019, April 1). 3 months into new criminal justice law, success for some and snafus for others. *National Public Radio*. https://www.npr.org/2019/04/01/708326846/3-months-into-new-criminal-justice-law-success-for-some-and-snafus-for-others

Rothman, D. J. (1971). *The discovery of the asylum: Social order and disorder in the new republic*. Little, Brown and Company.

Sawyer, W., & Wagner, P. (2019, March 19). *Mass incarceration: The whole pie 2019*. Prison Policy Initiative. https://www.prisonpolicy.org/reports/pie2019.html

Scull, A. T. (1977). *Decarceration: Community treatment and the deviant – A radical view*. Prentice Hall.

Serin, R. C. (2005). *Evidence-based practice: Principles for enhancing correctional results in prisons*. National Institute of Corrections. https://nicic.gov/evidence-based-practice-principles-enhancing-correctional-results-prisons

Stefanovska, V., & Jovanova, N. (2017). Deterrence & incapacitation effects of the criminal sanctions. *Journal of Eastern European Criminal Law, 1*, 62–75.

Stohr, M., Walsh, A., & Hemmens, C. (Eds.). (2009). *Corrections: A text/reader*. Sage.

Suttie, J. (2015, June 9). Can restorative justice help prisoners to heal? *Greater Good Magazine*. https://greatergood.berkeley.edu/article/item/restorative_justice_help_prisoners_heal

Teeters, N. K. (1937). *They were in prison: A history of the Pennsylvania Prison Society, 1787–1937*. The John C. Winston Company.

Transportation Act. 4 Geo 1 c. 11. (1717).

Walmsley, R. (2018). *World prison population list* (12th ed.). Institute for Criminal Policy Research. http://www.prisonstudies.org/sites/default/files/resources/downloads/wppl_12.pdf

Ward, S. A. (2009). Career and technical education in United States prisons: What have we learned? *The Journal of Correctional Education, 60*(3), 191–200.

Williams, V. L. (1979). *Dictionary of American penology: An introduction*. Greenwood Press.

Wodahl, E. J., & Garland, B. (2009). The evolution of community corrections: The enduring influence of the prison. *The Prison Journal, 89*(1), 81–104.

Wood, A. E., & Waite, J. B. (1941). *Crime and its treatment: Social and legal aspects of criminology*. American Book Company.

Zehr, H., & Mika, H. (1997). Fundamental concepts of restorative justice. *Contemporary Justice Review, 1*, 47–56.

CHAPTER 2

Correctional Administration

CHAPTER OBJECTIVES

After reading this chapter, you should be able to:

- Describe the roles and responsibilities of correctional administrators.
- Explain how correctional administration has developed historically in the United States during the past century and how it has influenced the current system.
- Discuss the importance of racial and cultural diversity and professionalism in correctional administration.
- Identify contemporary issues that challenge correctional administrators.

KEY WORDS

Assistant warden
Captain
Centralized management
Control model
Correctional administration
Correctional captain
Correctional sergeant
Corrections lieutenant
Corrections officer

De-centralized management
Institutional-level administrator
Regional administrator
Sheriff's sergeant
Stakeholders
Strategic plan
Systemwide administrators
Warden

CASE STUDY: TENT CITY

Using a "tough on crime" approach, a jail in Phoenix, Arizona utilized seven acres of outdoor space to construct an outdoor jail to manage its overcrowded population. The space, known as "Tent City," was highly controversial and was comparable to a modern-day concentration camp. The institution received backlash from many directions for being inhumane, overcrowded, and dangerous. In Tent City, people were subject to serve on chain gangs and were forced to endure inhumane conditions during their incarceration. For example, people served their sentence in both blistering heat (upwards of 130° F) and extreme cold (as low as 41° F) and slept on bunk beds in tents arranged on concrete slabs in gravel lots. Many of the tents had holes in them, which allowed rain and wind to get in, and people complained of flooding and insect and vermin infestations. People were also served food that was valued between 15–40 cents per meal.

The person who created and ran Tent City, Joe Arpaio, was a contentious and outspoken law enforcement officer who styled himself as "America's Toughest Sheriff." Arpaio received a great deal of criticism for misbehavior and mismanagement of Tent City and has been accused of numerous types of misconduct, including racial profiling, abuse of power, misuse of funds, criminal negligence, abuse of suspects in custody, and unlawful enforcement of immigration laws, among others. Arpaio justified his use of Tent City by stating that "jails are intended to be punishment." He is also quoted as saying that "Punishment is for post-conviction only." Tent City operated for 24 years, but after receiving so much public backlash, it closed in 2017. The move to close the facility saved taxpayers approximately $4.5 million in annual payments (Fernández, 2017).

Questions for Discussion

1. In your opinion, why was Tent City allowed to operate for as long as it did?
2. Many of the people incarcerated in Tent City were low-level offenders or people awaiting trial. Should jails be held to a different standard than prisons in terms of punishment? Why or why not?
3. How does the use of extreme measures, like Tent City, reflect societal attitudes regarding incarcerated populations?

INTRODUCTION

The field of corrections is made up of some of the most rapidly growing careers in the United States, and correctional administration has generated a great deal of interest over the years. It is predicted that careers in corrections will continue to flourish and will be heavily influenced by technology in the future. Correctional administration encompasses some of the most challenging and unpredictable occupations in both public and private sectors to date. Therefore, there is a specific need for outstanding headship and innovation in correctional administration, considering the diverse array of challenges correctional administrators face that others in supervisory positions do not (Seiter, 2012).

The following chapter examines correctional management and supervision and discusses the role of correctional administrators in the criminal justice system, as well as the importance of professionalism and diversity in the field. This chapter also outlines organizational hierarchy and correctional systems in both state and federal systems and gives an overview of common policies and administrative regulations. The chapter concludes with a discussion of contemporary issues that challenge correctional administrators, including litigation and constitutional challenges, and the impact of those issues on the operation of the institution.

CORRECTIONAL ADMINISTRATION

Corrections, and the institutions within them, are multifaceted and unique bureaucratic organizations. For correctional institutions to function safely and efficiently, there must be a solid administration in place that consists of professionals who fully understand the complexities of the criminal justice system and the responsibilities their positions demand. **Correctional administration** is a term used to describe the various upper-level management and supervisory positions that exist within the systems of U.S. corrections. Correctional administrators oversee the operations of a correctional institution, such as a jail or prison, including its inhabitants and employers, by planning, organizing, staffing, directing, and controlling the management of the facility. Correctional administrators also partake in the development of goals, objectives, and policy decisions made for the institution, and are largely responsible for serving as leaders and mentors to correctional staff and incarcerated individuals. Correctional administrators also have a responsibility to control media and public relations and represent the institution pending any litigation (Hurley & Hanley, 2010; Seiter, 2012).

Historically, correctional administrators have functioned under various conditions shaped by the overriding philosophies and expectations of society at that time, including penal practices that range from corporal punishment to reintegration and rehabilitation (Seiter, 2012). For example, the leadership and management styles of correctional administrators varied throughout the "tough on crime" era, as there were numerous approaches to achieving reform in unstable correctional institutions (Cerrato, 2014). Overall, however, policy makers, politicians, and criminal justice professionals perpetuated "tough on crime" sentencing practices by moving toward a crime **control model** that focused on incarceration to reduce crime in the community (Mackenzie, 2001). That is, mandatory minimum prison sentences, capital punishment, and sentences of life without the possibility of parole took precedence over rehabilitation. Rather than investing in educational programming, states built more high-security prisons to support the growing prison population, and they capitalized on for-profit correctional institutions (Christenson, 2002). Unit management also become increasingly popular among correctional administrators during the "tough on crime" era. Given the criticism over rehabilitation, rising crime rates, and public fear of crime, correctional administrators focused primarily on incarcerating and incapacitating offenders beginning in the mid-1970s (Mackenzie, 2001).

As the correctional system began to take shape in the 1970s, heavier emphasis was placed on professionalism and the training and competency of correctional officers. As a result, state legislators were encouraged to increase standards for correctional staff and to improve their education and training. During this era, correctional officers also became concerned with improving safety measures and increasing diversity among staff. Although budget constraints have often limited funding for education and training among correctional staff, correctional administrators generally recognize the importance of ensuring that the workforce has the necessary tools to minimize risk and guarantee safe conditions in correctional institutions at both state and federal levels (Hanser, 2021).

FEDERAL AND STATE CORRECTIONAL ADMINISTRATION

To best understand the complexities of correctional administration in the United States, one must consider the differences between federal and state jurisdictions and their systems of correctional management. At the federal level, the Federal Bureau of Prisons (BOP) maintains a Central Office in Washington, DC where prisons are overseen and managed by the director of the BOP. The Central Office to the BOP contains eight service divisions to carry out various responsibilities related to: administration; correctional programs; health services; human resource management; industries, education, and vocational training; information, policy, and public affairs; general counsel; and program review (Hanser, 2021). The service divisions contained within the BOP and their respective responsibilities are detailed in Table 2.1.

The National Institute of Corrections (NIC), an agency under the BOP, consists of a 16-member advisory board that provides policy direction. The NIC is also responsible for training, technical assistance, information services, and policy and program development

Table 2.1 Service Divisions Within the Central Office of the Bureau of Prisons (BOP).

SERVICE DIVISION	RESPONSIBILITIES
Administration	Financial and facility management; budget development and execution; finance; procurement and property; inmate trust fund programs
Correctional Programs	Implements national policies and procedures to ensure safety for incarcerated individuals and correctional staff; encourages programs and activities that promote positive outcomes and work ethic
Health Services	Medical, dental, and psychiatric services; healthcare delivery, infectious disease management, and medical designations
Human Resource Management	Personnel matters (e.g., pay and leave administration, incentive awards, retirement, work-life programs, background investigations, adverse actions, disciplinary actions, performance evaluations)
Industries, Education, and Vocational Training	Educational and vocational training programs
Information, Policy, and Public Affairs	Collects, develops, and shares information to stakeholders (e.g., BOP staff, Department of Justice, Congress, government agencies, the public)
Office of General Counsel	Represents the BOP on legal, policy, and management issues; provide litigation support for inmate litigation; provide legal advice to regional office and prison administrators
Program Review	Provides oversight of BOP program performance and compliance

Note. Adapted from *A Brief Introduction to Corrections,* by R. D. Hanser, 2021, Sage.

assistance to correctional agencies in national, state, and local jurisdictions. The NIC, which is headed by a director appointed by the U.S. attorney general, is an especially important component to the management of federal prisons because it awards funds to support its program initiatives and actively guide correctional policies, practices, and operations nationwide (Hanser, 2021).

The state level of correctional system administration is different from the federal level because states differ from one another regarding the incarceration, rehabilitation, and supervision of offenders. For example, states can combine incarceration, probation, and parole so that all three function within the same agency, or they can utilize separate agencies for each of these elements. There are also variations in states' handling of probation and parole. That is, sometimes these services occur at the state level, whereas other times they are administered in local jurisdictions. Essentially, state policies have developed from historical and legal occurrences; however, more modern organizational arrangements have considered other elements of the department of corrections, such as control of finances and personnel, and flexibility in establishing policies and procedures (Hanser, 2021).

At the local level, correctional systems take the form of county or city jurisdictions. Private institutions can also be utilized at the local level. Most often, local correctional systems, including jails, are county-based and are run by the sheriff's agency. In metropolitan areas, county-level jails are comparable to state institutions, as their populations are much larger than in rural counties. There are also city-level prison systems, which are typically found in large suburbs that require their own adult prison institutions (Hanser, 2021).

There is usually a chief executive officer within a department of corrections, and there are also usually deputies who implement policies to meet the needs of the institution and adhere to the overriding politics that are outlined as a part of a strategic plan. A **strategic plan** is a managerial document that details agency goals and objectives and outlines how they will be achieved. Strategic plans might include the following goals and objectives:

- Provide diversions to traditional incarceration through community supervision and community-based programming.
- Provide secure confinement, custodial care, and support services for incarcerated populations while ensuring public, staff, and offender safety.
- Develop and provide evidence-based rehabilitation and reentry programs to reduce recidivism and produce positive changes in the lives of individuals.
- Assist crime victims and offer a central mechanism for them to participate in criminal justice proceedings.

Typically, goals and objectives outlined on the strategic plan are given oversight by systemwide, regional, or institutional-level administrators. **Systemwide administrators** are executive-level managers who direct the entire system through the state. In comparison, **regional administrators** are found in states where the correctional system is too large, thereby requiring regional divisions of services. Finally, **institutional-level administrators** head specific institutions. For example, the warden is the head administrator of a prison (Hanser, 2021).

CAREERS IN CORRECTIONAL ADMINISTRATION

Like many criminal justice professionals, correctional administrators are promoted over time across various levels. Correctional officers are typically divided into several ranks (listed from lowest to highest on the hierarchy): officer, sergeant, lieutenant, captain, associate warden, deputy warden, chief deputy warden, and warden. The hierarchical order of correctional administration indicates that someone might first gain experience as a member of line staff, where their primary duty is to execute the mission of their specific institution, whether it be an institutional or community-based correctional setting. Those who begin their careers in an entry-level position are employed as corrections officers, probation or parole officers, or corrections counselors. **Corrections officers** can serve various roles within an institution, such as yard officer or tower guard. Generally, however, officers supervise incarcerated people in jails, prisons, and rehabilitative facilities and provide oversight for people who are arrested, awaiting or undergoing trial, or serving sentences.

Supervisors are responsible for oversight of line staff. For example, in a correctional institution such as a state or federal prison, the primary job of a **correctional sergeant**, the second supervisory level in the Sheriff's Correctional Officer series, is to maintain a secure facility and delegate commands to correctional officers. A correctional sergeant is distinguished from a **sheriff's sergeant**, who has peace office powers and rotates between assignments in detention, patrol, and investigations. Conversely, a **corrections lieutenant** is in charge of certain areas of a correctional facility, and of staff and inhabitants of said unit. Lieutenants must also ensure that a shift meets all security standards. Likewise, a **captain**, who also maintains supervisory power, might deal with more large-scale issues, such as cell block inspection and riot control (Seiter, 2012).

The organizational structure of a correctional facility also includes the roles of associate warden, deputy wardens, chief deputy warden, and warden. The position of **warden** is a senior-level leadership position and is the highest career position in which a correctional professional can serve. Wardens are employed at all levels of government and the private sector. For example, they work within the U.S. Department of Justice's Bureau of Prisons, state prisons, and private institutions that are contracted with states. Both prison and jail wardens have several important responsibilities including the supervision of staff and incarcerated populations in respective facilities. Wardens are also responsible for determining staffing needs and allocating resources to ensure that the facility and security equipment are functioning appropriately. Moreover, they ensure staff compliance with laws, rules, policies and procedures, and operation standards. Oftentimes, wardens provide oversight for staff training, and they conduct investigations and take disciplinary action as needed. Finally, wardens are responsible for maintaining budgets and monitoring expenses involving building and grounds, health care, food services, and laundry costs. Many times, wardens work alongside assistant wardens, who provide oversight of daily operations, including staff work assignments and building maintenance. **Assistant wardens** also actively participate in policy decision-making and procedural changes that are directed by the warden. During their career, an assistant warden might also be promoted to serve as a chief deputy warden, whose job is to address large-scale issues such as business management and work-training incentives, or to assume the role of warden when the warden is absent (Hurley & Hanley, 2010).

Like many careers, correctional administration involves standards of conduct, hierarchies, and standardized procedures; however, correctional institutions stand apart amongst other systems of social control, for several pointed reasons. Notably, correctional administrators work in a constantly fluctuating system alongside various **stakeholders** who maintain interest in correctional administration. These groups include various reform associations, legislatures, employee unions, the Department of Corrections and Bureau of Prisons, and the mass media (Stojkovic & Farkas, 2003). While stakeholders have a shared interest in the operation of jails and prisons, external demands can leave them in a state of uncertainty. There is also constant internal and external pressure for correctional administrators to demonstrate effectiveness; stakeholder confidence decreases if jail and prison programs are not successful. Importantly, though, studies have found that many prison programs have been unsuccessful in meeting their goals because of improper implementation, rather than because of poor program design, which further emphasizes the need for effective correctional staff and administration (Hurley & Hanley, 2010).

The demographics of correctional administrators have evolved greatly since the 1980s. Prior to this time, most prisons were found in rural areas and had employed mostly White individuals from local areas. By today's standards, it is important for correctional administrators to reflect the cultural diversity found in broader societies and in the criminal justice system. As such, multiculturalism and diversity are encouraged among staff who manage and supervise jails and prisons. The shift to more diverse populations has allowed the profession to move toward more professional standards in the correctional system. Diversity among correctional administrators is also beneficial because it reflects the diversity found in the correctional population and allows for effective communication as a means of preventing problems and addressing issues. Correctional administrators must demonstrate cultural competence by hiring correctional staff who can break language barriers and share similar customs and beliefs with some of the individuals incarcerated in jails and prisons. Ultimately, diversity helps to mitigate negative effects found in correctional settings and is beneficial to managing the institutions among racial lines (Hanser, 2021).

Correctional administrators conduct their work under one of two types of management. **Centralized management** consists of rigid communication between a small group of people and is reflective of bureaucratic models of prison system management. Centralized management is beneficial because it only involves a handful of people who are fully invested in the decision-making process and operation of an institution. Unfortunately, however, centralized management sometimes results in feelings of empowerment over others within the group, and higher-level management may oversee issues and fail to address them appropriately. Centralized management is appropriate for strategic planning, where long-term goals and objectives span several years. Conversely, **de-centralized management** involves a division of authority in which responsibility and duties are distributed among a supervisory chain. As a result, decisions involve a multitude of people and problems are met at each level of management. De-centralized management styles allow for a quick decision-making process; however, there is less consistency in how problems are solved among supervisors. Still, de-centralized management works well in situations that warrant more narrowly focused planning and situations in which direct interaction occurs between management and correctional staff (Hanser, 2021).

CHALLENGES IN CORRECTIONAL ADMINISTRATION

Correctional administrators face various challenges, given the unique nature of the institutions they are managing and the populations they are supervising. Certainly, the criminal justice system—where billions of dollars are being spent and millions of lives hang in the balance—is complicated and complex. Administrators are ultimately responsible for society's most marginalized populations; their institutions are comprised of massive numbers of uneducated, lower-income individuals, many of whom have mental health problems or substance abuse issues, and a portion of whom have committed violent offenses. Notably, too, people are incarcerated against their will and are not given much support within institutional settings, leaving them to navigate the system with little to no assistance. Regardless of their position, however, correctional administrators have limited power in some circumstances since they are usually restricted by legal proceedings, court decisions, and external demands from interested stakeholders (Hurley & Hanley, 2010; Seiter, 2012).

One of the most significant issues faced by correctional administrators is the overwhelming cost associated with mass incarceration. The U.S. government spends a staggering $182 billion every year on the criminal justice system, with most money associated with the management of jails, prisons, parole, and probation. The remaining funding supports many other areas of the criminal justice system, including law enforcement, the judicial system, public employment, health care, prosecution, indigent defense, civil asset forfeiture, private corrections, construction, familial support, bail fees, commissary, telephone services, interest payments, food, utilities, and private prison profits

(Wagner & Rabuy, 2017). A complete list of government criminal justice spending is found in Table 2.2.

Table 2.2 Government Spending on the Criminal Justice System.

SYSTEM COMPONENT	COST (IN BILLIONS OF $)
Public corrections agencies – *Prisons, jails, parole, and probation*	80.7
Policing – *Criminal law only*	63.2
Judicial and legal – *Criminal law only*	29.0
Public employees	38.4
Health care	12.3
Prosecution	5.8
Indigent defense	4.5
Civil asset forfeiture	4.5
Private corrections	3.9
Construction	3.3
Costs to families	2.9
Food	2.1
Interest payments – *On past construction*	1.9
Utilities	1.7
Commissary	1.6
Bail fees – Only the fees paid to bondsmen	1.4
Telephone calls	1.3
Private prison profits	0.37 ($374 million)
Total	$182 billion

Note. Adapted from *Following the Money of Mass Incarceration*, by P. Wagner & B. Rabuy, 2017, Prison Policy Initiative (https://www.prisonpolicy.org/reports/money.html).

State budgets for correctional spending have quadrupled in the past 20 years, which is largely a result of the 700% state prison population growth since the 1970s. Importantly, however, recent figures exclude extraneous costs such as employee benefits, inmate hospital care, and educational programming (Henrichson & Delaney, 2012; Mai & Subramanian, 2017). Correctional administrators are also challenged by the uncertainty of non-citizen detention facilities. Because the United States has become increasingly reliant on non-citizen detention facilities over the past 4 decades, government spending on detention has grown. For example, in 2018, federal spending on detention reached an all-time high of $3.1 billion compared to $1.8 billion in fiscal year 2010 (Kassie, 2019).

Given these expenditures, it is recommended that states can lower costs without reducing public safety by modifying sentencing, improving efforts to reduce recidivism, and operating correctional institutions more efficiently (Henrichson & Delaney, 2012). Fortunately, state lawmakers have enacted new laws to cut spending and reduce the overall prison population (Mai & Subramanian, 2017). Still, though, the management and operation of correctional institutions is challenged by other issues beyond cost, such as litigation and constitutional issues, as well as staff safety, violence, retention, and advancements in technology. Correctional administrators are also faced with a shift in national politics and changing ideologies that support rehabilitation and decarceration more than punitive measures. Indeed, these challenges should serve as a guide to identify more opportunities to improve the field of corrections.

CONCLUSION

As indicated in this chapter, correctional administration is an essential component to the proper functioning of jails and prisons. As such, elements of correctional administration must include leadership and management, politics and correctional administration, and correctional staff supervision and development. In addition, correctional administration involves collaboration between several individuals who must articulate the mission and values of an institution. Correctional administrators and staff play a unique role in the criminal justice system, largely due to their responsibilities and the issues they encounter on daily basis. Therefore, it is important that people who work in these positions exercise a variety of skills to help them manage politics, human interactions, and the constant array of challenges to the operations of their prisons.

DISCUSSION QUESTIONS

1. Are you interested in a career in correctional administration? Why or why not? Identify the challenges and benefits of this career choice.
2. What are the key features of the federal prison system, compared to state prison systems?
3. How do centralized forms of management differ from decentralized forms of management?
4. Why are racial and cultural diversity and professionalism important aspects of correctional administration?

APPLICATION EXERCISES

Exercise #1: Prison Policy Initiative—Incarceration and Supervision by State

Explore and analyze state punitiveness by visiting the Prison Policy Initiative's incarceration and supervision rates website (https://www.prisonpolicy.org/reports/50statepie.html). The Prison Policy Initiative also presents comprehensive data in the form of a "correctional pie" (https://www.prisonpolicy.org/reports/pie2020.html), a web graphic that details correctional populations and drivers of mass incarceration. This comprehensive view of the correctional system allows readers to gain a strong sense of the complexities of the criminal justice system and can be used to compare state data to determine areas in need of reform.

Exercise #2: The Warden Game

The Warden Game is a "choose your own adventure" game, where you can make decisions as the warden of a prison and be exposed to various key concepts that relate to correctional administration. Take notice of the "adventure" you choose, and briefly summarize your experience. The game can be found using the following link: https://www.waprisonhistory.org/WardenGame/?fbclid=IwAR2Tg_p7uxKnyo1-sGNOaCXxQdnbSX-anwB87QYztFc0XdsJdiOuXPYLhN2g

1. What was the situation you were given in this game? How did you initially respond to this situation? Did your responses change over the course of the game?
2. What were three key concepts (words in yellow) that you learned about while playing this game?
3. What was the ultimate outcome for you in this game? Were you surprised at this outcome?
4. What have you learned from playing this game?

REFERENCES

Cerrato, S. (2014). Achieving reform in unstable correctional institutions: A theoretical perspective – revisited. *Contemporary Justice Review, 17*(2), 273–296.

Christenson, S. (2002). Prisons: History. In J. Dressler (Ed.), *Encyclopedia of crime and justice* (Vol. 3, pp. 1168–1175). Macmillan Reference.

Fernandez, F. (2017). Arizona's 'concentration camp': Why was Tent City kept open for 24 years? *The Guardian.* Retrieved from https://www.theguardian.com/cities/2017/aug/21/arizona-phoenix-concentration-camp-tent-city-jail-joe-arpaio-immigration.

Hanser, R. D. (2014). *Community corrections* (2nd ed.). Sage.

Hanser, R. D. (2021). *A brief introduction to corrections.* Sage.

Henrichson, C., & Delaney, R. (2012). *The price of prisons: What incarceration costs taxpayers.* Vera Institute of Justice. https://www.vera.org/publications/price-of-prisons-what-incarceration-costs-taxpayers

Hurley, M. H., & Hanley, D. (2010). *Correctional administration and change management.* CRC Press.

Kassie, E. (2019, September 24). Detained: How the U.S. built the world's largest immigrant detention system. *The Guardian.* Retrieved from https://www.theguardian.com/us-news/2019/sep/24/detained-us-largest-immigrant-detention-trump.

Mackenzie, D. L. (2001). *Sentencing and corrections in the 21st century: Setting the stage for the future.* National Institute of Justice. https://nij.ojp.gov/library/publications/sentencing-and-corrections-21st-century-setting-stage-future

Mai, C., & Subramanian, R. (2017). *The price of prisons: Examining state spending trends, 2010–2015.* Vera Institute of Justice. https://www.justnet.org/pdf/The-Price-of-Prisons-Examining-State-Spending-Trends-2017.pdf

National Criminal Justice Association. (2019). *Criminal justice system improvement.* https://www.ncja.org/ncja/policy/criminal-justice-reform

Seiter, R. P. (2012). *Correctional administration: Integrating theory and practice* (2nd ed.). Prentice Hall.

The Sentencing Project. (2019). *Issues.* https://www.sentencingproject.org/

Southern Poverty Law Center. (2019). *Criminal justice reform.* https://www.splcenter.org/issues/mass-incarceration

Stojkovic, S., & Farkas, M. A. (2003). *Correctional leadership: A cultural perspective.* Wadsworth Publishing.

Wagner, P., & Rabuy, B. (2017). *Following the money of mass incarceration.* Prison Policy Initiative. https://www.prisonpolicy.org/reports/money.html

CHAPTER 3

Probation, Parole, and Intermediate Sanctions

CHAPTER OBJECTIVES

After reading this chapter, you should be able to:

- Discuss the differences and similarities between probation, parole, and intermediate sanctions.
- Identify and describe the various forms of probation, parole, and intermediate sanctions.
- Identify the decision-making processes of placing someone into community supervision.
- Discuss the positive and negative outcomes of community corrections.

KEY WORDS

Correctional supervision

Probation

Parole

Community corrections

Intermediate sanctions

Federal Probation Act of 1925

Killits decision

John Augustus (1785–1859)

Discretionary release

Sentencing Reform Act of 1984

Truth-in-sentencing

Violent Crime Control and Law Enforcement Act of 1994

Probation officers

Presentence report

      Offender-based

      Offense-based

Parole hearings

Risk assessments

Probation and parole conditions

General conditions

Specific conditions

Parole officers

Technical violation

Revocation

Role conflict

Supervised release

Intensive supervision programs

Net-widening

Drug courts

CASE STUDY: COMPAS

The Department of Corrections in the state of Wisconsin began using the Correctional Offender Management Profiling for Alternative Sanctions tool, or COMPAS, in 2012 (Ferral, 2016). COMPAS is "an automated web-based software package that integrates risk and needs assessment to support criminal justice decision-makers at multiple decision-making junctures in criminal justice" (Brennan & Dieterich, 2018, p. 49). As an assessment tool, COMPAS takes into account static and dynamic risk, as well as the criminogenic needs of a person, in an attempt to predict a person's likelihood of re-offense (Brennan & Dieterich, 2018). That likelihood of re-offense is then used, in combination with a number of other factors, to help determine if a person can remain in the community under supervision, or if they need to be incarcerated (Ferral, 2016). COMPAS is just one of the many risk assessments used in criminal justice processes across the country.

Risk assessments like COMPAS have been praised as an evidence-based tool for decision-making at almost all stages of the justice process. They have also been criticized for their potential inaccuracy and bias. Sentencing decisions made using risk assessments are particularly concerning because there is a belief that sentencing should not be based on future dangerousness, but rather on the crime someone was convicted of committing (Ferral, 2016). These questions came before the Supreme Court of Washington in 2016. The legal argument hinged on both the algorithm that determines a person's level of risk, and the nature of its use as a factor in sentencing (*State of Wisconsin v. Loomis*, 2016). Northpointe, Inc., the company who developed COMPAS, has effectively kept the algorithm a secret, unable to be verified or evaluated. The court ultimately ruled that the use of COMPAS was appropriate in aiding judges in their sentencing decisions, as long as it was not their only consideration. The reluctance of the courts to limit the use of risk assessments likely signals that their use will continue and expand.

(continued)

(continued)

Questions for Discussion
1. What may be some of the benefits and drawbacks to using an automated web-based scoring tool such as COMPAS to try and predict recidivism?
2. Risk assessments are used at nearly every stage of the judicial process from pretrial detention to parole decisions. Are risk assessments appropriate for every stage of the judicial process? Why or why not?

INTRODUCTION

The United States is known worldwide for having the largest prison population of any country. India is populated by over one billion more people than the United States, yet the United States has a prison population 5.5 times larger than that of India (World Prison Brief, 2020). The most disturbing part about that number is that it represents only a small fraction of the people under some form of **correctional supervision**. Correctional supervision refers to custodial authority over a person who has been convicted of a crime by a correctional agency, including any individual in prison or jail and those on probation or parole. The Bureau of Justice Statistics identified over 6.4 million people who were under some form of correctional supervision in 2018 (Maruschak & Minton, 2020).

Probation refers to a suspended sentence of incarceration in which the person serves their time in the community under a set of defined conditions. **Parole** is a conditional early release from confinement that allows the person to serve the remainder of their sentence in the community. Probation and parole are also both forms of a larger group of community-based sanctions called **community corrections**. Because of the way the U.S. system of government is set up, the federal, state, and local governments can legally operate as relatively autonomous, or self-directed, entities; this concept recurs throughout this text. Therefore, the ways in which people enter onto probation and parole, as well as the conditions they must adhere to and the length of time they remain under those conditions, can vary greatly.

Incarcerating every person for every crime, even the most minor violations, would be an impractical and unsustainable model due to the sheer volume of people that would need to be incarcerated. American society has also deemed that simply placing someone on probation may not be enough to secure the safety of the community, or to rehabilitate and ultimately deter that person from committing further crime. Officials have tried to remedy this issue by developing other correctional methods, known as intermediate sanctions. **Intermediate sanctions** are forms of punishment that fall somewhere between traditional probation and incarceration. Intermediate sanctions allow governments to respond to criminality in a way that is more proportional to the severity of the crime committed and that does not place an additional burden on our jail and prison systems (Tonry & Lynch, 1996).

This chapter examines the sanctions that exist outside of, or in combination with, traditional incarceration. It begins by exploring probation and parole separately, focusing on their development, their application by the courts, and the magnitude of their use. Because each of these options is further divided by its differing applications across the country, the multitude of programs and the ways these sanctions are carried out are also described. Next, the chapter discusses the roles of probation and parole officers and the conditions applied to individuals under their oversight. This section includes a critical discussion of the impact of technical violations on the criminal justice system and on the people serving their time in the community. The chapter culminates with a brief discussion of what criminological research suggests about the impact of probation, parole, and intermediate sanctions on individuals and on the criminal justice system as a whole, including a look toward the future of community corrections.

PROBATION: A BRIEF HISTORY

The development of probation in the United States as a sentencing option was not something debated behind the walls of state or federal legislatures; rather, it can be traced back to one man, **John Augustus (1785–1859)** (Labrecque, 2017). Augustus routinely showed up to court hearings and asked the court to exercise its discretion for defendants prior to their sentencing. He believed that persons, particularly those who committed public order crimes like public intoxication, should have the opportunity to turn their lives around. While he was not paid or hired by anyone, Augustus detailed his first 10 years of "work" as the nation's first probation officer in a report he published himself (Augustus, 1852; Panzarella, 2002). In this report, Augustus gives the first account of what the duties and purposes of a probation officer should be.

> It is generally known that my time has been wholly developed to the unfortunate, in seeking out the wretched who have become victims of their passions and subjects of punishment by law, and that my mission has been to raise the fallen, reform the criminal, and so far as my humble abilities would allow, to transform the abode of suffering and misery to the home of happiness. (1852, p. 2)

In some ways, Augustus played the role of both defense attorney and probation officer. Although he would not advocate for guilt or innocence, he would stand and advocate to the court on behalf of those convicted of a crime. What was different about this form of "probation" was that it "was not an alternative sentence in place of imprisonment, nor a suspended sentence" like we see today, but rather a testing period that could impact the eventual sentence imposed (Panzarella, 2002, p. 40). Augustus's ideas of rehabilitation and reform aided "nearly 2,000 men, women and children," including alcoholics, juvenile offenders, and prostitutes (Labrecque, 2017, p. 7; Panzarella, 2002).

Though he was later coined the "Father of Probation," Augustus was not someone who set out to gain recognition for his actions, but he was the type of person who believed from the start of his career that rehabilitation was an option for some people (Labrecque, 2017; Panzarella, 2002). The passage quoted above shows how Augustus exposed the court to a contemporary conceptual idea of reform. He truly believed that caring for loved ones, and creating a happy home had the power to reform people, and that this could only happen if they were free. Augustus's actions created precedent within the courts that still stands today, including fines based on a person's ability to pay and the granting of a grace period for attempted reform prior to possible incarceration (Panzarella, 2002). In 1878, the model developed by John Augustus led to the creation of the first ever paid probation officer position in the country, in his home state of Massachusetts (de Courcy, 1910).

Expanding the Use of Probation

As is the case with many criminal justice policies, once states see the success of another state's efforts, they quickly follow suit. By 1909, with several states already authorizing the use of probation, especially in the juvenile justice system, Congress began introducing bills that included the ability to provide suspended sentences through the use of probation (de Courcy, 1910). The formalization of the federal probation program would not come until 1925, and it did not happen without pushback (Globokar & Toro, 2017). A number of factors contributed to the eventual passing of the **Federal Probation Act of 1925**. These included the ***Killits* decision** by the Supreme Court in 1916, which "disallowed the practice of suspension of sentence among federal judges," leaving the door open for a legislative challenge to the decision (Globokar & Toro, 2017, p. 538). The progressiveness of Congress in 1925 and the exponential growth of the federal prison system during Prohibition have also been cited as reasons for the eventual passage of the Federal Probation Act (Globokar & Toro, 2017).

The relative stability in incarceration rates between the 1930s and the 1970s provided the same stability within the probation population (Mackenzie, 2001). The War on Drugs was, and still is, an obvious catalyst to the exponential growth of incarceration rates that started in the early 1970s. However, the shifting of penal ideology away from the rehabilitation that had up to this point characterized correctional options, including probation, is also consistently attributed to the "Martinson report," or Martinson's "nothing works" doctrine, previously discussed in Chapter 1. Martinson (1974) questioned the effectiveness of correctional programming aimed at reducing recidivism (Weisburd et al., 2017, p. 416). The report, which never attempted to discount rehabilitative models completely, was picked up by politicians on both sides of the political aisle, as well as by criminological and sociological researchers. The mantra of "nothing works" consequently drowned out all other reasonable attempts to understand Martinson's work, which pointed to needed changes in how rehabilitation was approached at the time (Cullen et al., 2009).

The impact of Martinson's report was felt across the criminal justice system at all levels. The report helped to strengthen belief in the necessity of "law and order"/"get tough on crime" approaches, which have been the backbone of political campaigns ever since. It is no coincidence, then, that soon after the report was released, the United States saw steep rises in both incarceration rates and probation rates. As Mackenzie (2001) points out:

> From 1980 to 1997, the national correctional population rose from 1.8 million to 5.7 million, an increase of 217 percent. During the same period, the probation population grew by 191 percent; parole, 213 percent; and the number of prisoners, 271 percent. By 1998, more than 4.1 million adult men and women were on probation or parole, and there were 1,705 probationers and 352 parolees per 100,000 adults in the population. (p. 2)

The number of people on probation rose rather consistently from then on, until the first decreases were seen in 2008. Kaeble (2018) notes: "The probation population increased from 2000 to 2007, followed by average annual decreases of 2% from 2008 to 2016" (p. 3). Declining probation rates have helped to drive down the community supervision population as a whole, and in 2018 they were the lowest they have been since 1998 (Kaeble & Alper, 2020). The majority of states (37) saw reductions in both crime rates and their community corrections population during this time. The belief is that correctional reforms, including using evidence-based practices and prioritizing resources for high-risk offenders, helped contribute to these declines (Pew Research Center, 2018). While these numbers seem promising, Jones (2018) tempers expectations by noting that these decreases have been largely driven by just a few states (4), and that several states (16) actually saw increases in their probation populations.

As of 2018 there were 4.4 million people in community supervision, or 1 in every 58 adults (Kaeble & Alper, 2020; Pew Research Center, 2018). That includes 3,540,000 on probation, or 80% of the total community supervision population (Kaeble & Alper, 2020). The estimated annual cost of probation to states is over $4.7 billion (Wagner & Rabuy, 2017). The Pew Research Center (2018) has also reported on the demographics of both probationers and parolees. The report indicates that the overwhelming majority of individuals are male and White. However, specific demographic rates show a disproportionate number of Black individuals under community supervision. Among individuals on probation and parole in 2016, 1 in 23 were Black while 1 in 81 were White. Regarding criminality, 8 in 10 individuals were being supervised following conviction for a non-violent offense (Pew Research Center, 2018). Disparities in the racial makeup of individuals on probation may be, in part, attributable to disparities in whether probation is offered as a sentencing option.

Probation Decision

The suspended sentence of imprisonment, or probation, is one of the most widely used criminal sentences throughout the country. There are a number of reasons why a person may be given a suspended sentence, and the expectation is that the seriousness of the criminal offense is the first, and primary, factor considered by judges. This may be the case for jurisdictions that rely predominantly on mandatory minimum sentences and sentencing guidelines. Currently, half of all states use such sentencing guidelines, which mandate sentences, including probation, with room for minor deviation (Lawrence, 2015). However, no matter the sentencing model used by a state, much of the work in determining who should be free to be supervised in the community and who should be incarcerated comes from individual probation officers themselves.

Probation officers are licensed officials who provide community supervision of individuals who have been given a suspended sentence of imprisonment by the court. Because probation officers are officers of the court, their duties often go beyond community supervision. Once a person has been convicted of a crime, especially one that could carry a term of imprisonment, courts generally ask a probation officer to complete a presentence report. A **presentence report** is compiled during a presentence investigation into the actual criminal offense, the defendant's prior record, and the defendant's background characteristics. This report is then used by a judge to make a determination on the sentence for that defendant.

Jurisdictions that rely on indeterminate models of sentencing, which value some level of rehabilitation use an **offender-based report** (Macallair, 2002). These reports tend to place more emphasis on understanding the defendant's version of the criminal event and on their amenability to rehabilitation (Macallair, 2002). An examination of items like their relationships, employment status, military service, and financial records can indicate their suitability for remaining in the community throughout the duration of their sentence. By contrast, **offense-based reports** are used in determinate sentencing jurisdictions and tend to focus more on making sure that sentencing guidelines are adequately adhered to (Macallair, 2002). While these reports traditionally included extensive processes of investigation, the growing caseload demand on probation officers and the move toward more calculable methods of risk analysis have made these processes much shorter and less personal (Lawrence, 2015; MacDonald & Baroody-Hart, 1999). This has also led many jurisdictions to use one group of probation officers to develop the reports and another group to supervise the completion of a probation sentence (MacDonald & Baroody-Hart, 1999). Based on that presentence report, judges are better able to make the decision to grant an appropriate sentence of probation, incarceration, or both.

PAROLE: A BRIEF HISTORY

The pairing of probation and parole, in texts such as this, is often seen as intuitive because both are sanctions carried out within the community. There are, however, some stark differences in the application of the two forms of community supervision. Parole is seen as being more serious, as the person on parole has been convicted of a felony offense, and they have already spent time incarcerated. While felony probation is an option in some jurisdictions, not all people on probation have been convicted of a felony offense. Parole is also not granted at the front end of the justice process, like probation. Probation is granted as part of someone's sentence, whereas a parole decision takes place after a period of incarceration and is granted by a parole board. **Parole boards** are panels that oversee the eligibility and early release of people who are incarcerated. The differences and similarities between the two methods will be discussed further below. First, it is necessary to explore the historical and conceptual development of parole as a part of the correctional system.

The conceptual roots of parole, like nearly everything in the U.S. criminal justice system, stretch all the way back to the common law system established in England (Petersilia, 2009). In addition to having English origins, the system of parole that would eventually become standard in the United States also developed from a combination of correctional practices from Australia and Ireland, and from the correctional systems in Pennsylvania and Auburn that were discussed in Chapter 1 (Witmer, 1925). These practices meshed together at the nation's first reformatory, the Elmira Reformatory (see Chapter 1).

As also discussed in Chapter 1, Zebulon Brockway (1827–1920) is known as one of the earliest prison reformers, and his efforts culminated in his position as superintendent of the Elmira Reformatory. As a part of his duty, Brockway brought with him penal reform concepts that had been informing his work in corrections up to this point. One of his greatest contributions was the development of the indeterminate sentencing model, which essentially simultaneously created the need for a system of parole (Petersilia, 2009; Witmer, 1925). Thus, the history of parole is indistinguishable from the development of the indeterminate sentencing model.

Brockway, and other penal reformers of the time, pushed for indeterminate sentencing because unreformed persons were automatically being let out at the expiration of their sentences as a result of determinate sentencing (Witmer, 1925). Indeterminate sentencing and parole would give justice systems the ability to test a person's readiness for release. As Brockway states:

> No man, be he judge, lawyer, or layman, can determine beforehand the date when imprisonment shall work a reformation in any case, and it is an outrage upon society to return to the privileges of citizenship those who have proved themselves dangerous and bad by the commission of crime, until a cure is wrought and reformation reached. (Witmer, 1925, p. 320)

Brockway's beliefs, and the eventual implementation of these systems, earned him the nickname the "Father of Parole." In 1907 his ideas led to "New York [becoming] the first state to formally adopt all of the components of a parole system: indeterminate sentences, a system for granting release, postrelease supervision, and specific criteria for parole revocation" (Petersilia, 2009, p. 57).

The Federal Government's movement toward a system of parole was all but simultaneous with the adoption of parole in New York. A report by Hoffman (2003) on behalf of the United States Parole Commission details the movement toward a federal system of parole. In 1910, undoubtedly influenced by the penal reform movement taking place, federal legislation established the first instances of parole for federal inmates. Another 20 years would pass before the formation of a federal Board of Parole in 1930 (Hoffman, 2003). Expansion of the state and federal systems of parole continued until 1942, when all 50 states had developed processes for granting parole (Petersilia, 2009).

Expanding the Use of Parole

As states and the Federal Government began using parole more regularly, rates of discretionary release increased a moderate 28% between 1940 and 1977 (Petersilia, 2009). **Discretionary release** refers to the decision by a paroling board to release the individual from confinement prior to the expiration of their maximum sentence. This is different from **mandatory release**, which is the release of a person from confinement and onto parole as mandated by law rather than by a parole board. Discretionary releases outpaced mandatory releases for a long period of time, but between 1976 and 1999, discretionary releases fell by over 40% (Travis & Lawrence, 2002). This means that by 1999, parole boards were granting release in less than a quarter of all cases. The shift away from discretionary release was driven by several factors including the War on Drugs, growing crime rates, and "get tough on crime" political posturing (Ditton & Wilson, 1999; Mackenzie, 2001).

During the late 1970s and early 1980s, due to calls for harsher punishment of criminal offenders, sentencing practices and policies that contributed to the early release of convicted persons were regularly challenged. The factors listed above had the effect of changing the narrative of rehabilitation and reform on which parole was built. In 1984, the Federal Government effectively dismantled the systems of probation and parole that had operated somewhat autonomously up to that point with the passing of the **Sentencing Reform Act of 1984** (Doyle, 1996). Doyle (1996) discusses the implications of this change:

> As a consequences [sic], federal defendants who upon conviction might have once enjoyed the prospect of a suspended sentence and who would have been eligible for parole after serving a third of their sentences now have no chance for parole or a suspended sentence and will have [to] serve at least 85% of the term to which they are sentenced even with exemplary prison behavior. (p. 2)

At the same time, states had also begun to adopt similarly punitive attitudes and policies toward parole. These policies would eventually come to be known as **truth-in-sentencing laws**.

Beginning in 1984, when the state of Washington adopted standardized sentencing guidelines, truth-in-sentencing laws spread rapidly throughout the country. Truth-in-sentencing was a direct and swift response to the indeterminate model of sentencing that dominated the early efforts of prison reform. The discretion of release under indeterminate models of sentencing rested squarely on the shoulders of parole boards (Dinton & Wilson, 1999). At the same time, there were a number of options available to persons with determinate sentences that decreased their time incarcerated (Travis & Lawrence, 2002). These included "good-time reductions for satisfactory prison behavior, earned-time incentives for participation in work or educational programs, and other time reductions to control prison crowding" (Dinton & Wilson, 1999, p. 2). Within the indeterminate sentencing model, the public saw what they believed was the indiscriminate release of dangerous felons. The natural response was to push for sentencing guidelines that would ensure convicted persons spent the majority of their sentence incarcerated.

The Federal Government solidified the move to more determinate models of sentencing by passing the **Violent Crime Control and Law Enforcement Act of 1994**. The act would eventually house the Violent Offender Incarceration and Truth-in-Sentencing grant programs, which would provide federal money to states for expansion of their correctional systems (Sabol et al., 2002). The grant programs required states to show that their sentencing policies for violent offenders had them serving at least 85% of their imposed sentence, which is considered the threshold for truthfulness in criminal sentencing (Dinton & Wilson, 1999; Sabol et al., 2002). As a result, a number of states adopted federal truth-in-sentencing recommendations, and some went as far as completely abolishing their systems of parole.

By 1999, 41 states and Washington, DC contributed to truth-in-sentencing changes, including 14 states that completely abolished the use of parole as a release option (Dinton & Wilson, 1999; Sabol et al., 2002). Even with the changes in sentencing models that limited the use of parole for violent offenses, the increase of the correctional population overall also increased the use of parole overall. Between 2000 and 2016, the number of people on parole nationwide grew by over 20% (Kaeble, 2018). Unlike probation numbers, parole numbers have continued to increase, and in 2018 there were nearly 878,000 people on parole (Kaeble & Apler, 2020).

There have since been efforts made to undo, or to minimize the impact of, truth-in-sentencing laws. It should also be noted that determinate and indeterminate models of sentencing, as well as the processes of parole, are jurisdictionally specific and can vary greatly from one state to the next. Currently, only 16 states rely almost exclusively on determinate sentencing options, while the remaining 34 continue to make use of paroling authorities (Rhine et al., 2018). As was discussed in Chapter 1, the First Step Act (2018) has begun to ease the restrictions on good-time credits implemented under the Sentencing Reform Act of 1984 while also making changes to federal sentencing guidelines. These changes will undoubtedly impact the number and rates of persons on parole at the federal level.

Parole Decision

The decision to place someone on parole is conceptually similar to that of putting someone on probation, but the two processes are very different. First, as discussed earlier, paroling decisions are made by paroling authorities (known as parole boards) rather than by judges. Several states have terminated their use of parole boards, while "the remaining states range from having a system of presumptive parole—where when certain conditions are met, release on parole is guaranteed—to having policies and practices that make earning release almost impossible" (Renaud, 2019, para. 2). Parole boards are somewhat of a mystery in the criminal justice system because their processes often happen behind closed doors, their members can come from outside the system, and they have a wide range of discretion (Renaud, 2019; Rhine et al., 2015; Schwartzapfel, 2015).

Parole hearings are held by parole boards to aid in the decision-making process of granting parole. At these hearings, both advocates of the person seeking parole, and those individuals who would like to see the person remain incarcerated, are able to attend and voice their opinions. These opinions are taken into consideration with a number of other factors including the seriousness of the offense, the person's criminal history, the length of time they have been incarcerated, and their mental health (Caplan, 2007; Tewksbury & Connor, 2012). Additionally, two of the most important factors in parole decisions are how well the person has served their time, which is known as institutional behavior, and whether they pose a risk to the community (Caplan, 2007; Rhine et al., 2015).

Institutional behavior during incarceration is believed to be indicative of how well a person will respond to being back in the community, and what level of risk they pose to the community through recidivism (Caplan, 2007). Institutional records from correctional facilities are typically easy to obtain, and prison staff may even be asked to give accounts of a person's behavior while serving their time. Institutional behavior is a concrete example for parole boards to look at during decision-making, but there is also a large push in criminal justice reform for the use of actuarial assessments called risk assessments, which may not be as straightforward.

Risk assessments are statistical tools that help criminal justice officials analyze a person's level of dangerousness and their risk of re-offense. They are tools that can be used at almost any part of the criminal justice process, from making a bail decision to determining the level of supervision someone should receive while out on parole. A variety of risk assessment tools have been developed to analyze demographic, socio-economic, and other social and personal factors, to score a person's level of risk. Individuals are placed into categories of low, medium (moderate), or high risk for criminal behavior. From the perspective of paroling authority, those who pose the lowest risk of re-offense are more likely to receive a favorable parole decision.

As previously discussed, parole was abolished at the federal level for anyone convicted of a federal crime after 1987 (United Sates Department of Justice, 2015). The Federal Government now primarily uses a system known as supervised release. **Supervised release** is conceptually similar to parole, but it is actually an additional sentence imposed on top of a federal prison sentence (Office of General Counsel, 2019). The sentencing judge, rather than a federal parole board, stipulates the time required on supervised release following a person's period of confinement (Office of General Counsel, 2019). At any level of government, once someone is deemed eligible to be placed on probation, parole, or supervised release, the next step is determining what conditions they face while under community supervision.

CONDITIONS OF PROBATION AND PAROLE

There are a number of similarities in the conditions of community supervision at every level. However, each jurisdiction has the ability to determine its own set of conditions that apply to individuals under community supervision. Conditions normally fall within two categories: general conditions and specific conditions. **General conditions** apply to every person put on probation or parole, regardless of their crime. **Specific conditions** (sometimes referred to as *special conditions*) are unique to that individual and are often determined by the type of crime they committed and their rehabilitative needs.

One of the most important conditions to a person on probation or parole is their supervision requirement. This can range from having no supervision at all, meaning the person simply completes their sentence without further criminal activity, to intensive supervision, which requires the person to be available to their probation or parole officer 24 hours a day, 7 days a week.

General guidelines typically include:

- Limiting travel outside of the state;
- Notifying a probation officer of any residential changes;
- Holding or attempting to secure employment;
- Submitting to random drug and alcohol screenings;
- Not possessing a weapon; and
- Paying any and all fees/fines related to conviction or supervision expenses.

Special conditions of probation are specific to each jurisdiction and require the court to make a determination based on the offense a person has committed, the risk they pose to the community, and the best methods for addressing their rehabilitation. These conditions can center on any number of rehabilitative programs that a person must complete, and can also include additional fines, fees, or other forms of victim restitution that the court deems necessary. For example, the Administrative Offices of the United States Courts (2016) detail 20 separate special conditions that may be provided at the federal level. The conditions can include additional substance abuse treatment and testing, acquisition of mental health services, limited associations and contacts with certain persons, gambling-related conditions, community service requirements, and even computer and internet restrictions. The task of making sure that all of these conditions are met falls squarely on the shoulders of probation and parole officers.

PROBATION AND PAROLE OFFICERS

Parole officers are licensed officials who supervise the conditions of parole for individuals released from prison. Unlike their counterparts in probation, who derive their authority from the court, parole officers derive their authority from the parole board. Also, parole and probation officers have differing levels and types of reentry work that they must consider. Whereas probation officers may be dealing with individuals who spent 45 days in a county jail before returning to the community, parole officers could be working with people who have spent decades behind bars. The nuances of the reentry process, and the specific roles of officers in reentry, will be further discussed in Chapter 5: Reentry and Reintegration.

Probation and parole officers have an enormous amount of responsibility, as they do not have the comfort of knowing that the people they oversee will be locked down at the end of every night like those who are incarcerated. This means that officers always have to be prepared to work, no matter the time or day. Handling individuals convicted of crimes, some of which are serious and violent, especially in the case of parole officers, can be extremely dangerous, traumatic, and personally exhausting, but also very rewarding. The primary responsibilities of probation and parole officers can be described as boiling down to two things: control and support (Barnes & Mowen, 2020). This is not to minimize their role, but rather to note that many of their responsibilities can be linked to controlling the movements of persons (some more, some less) in the community, while offering the support necessary for those persons to remain crime-free.

Over time, control and support have each dominated the models employed by probation and parole officers, but most officers now incorporate both control and support as community corrections strategies (Schaefer & Williamson, 2017). This combined approach includes meeting regularly with the probationer or parolee, coordinating treatment plans and schedules for needed treatment programming, completing drug and alcohol screenings, supporting active employment, maintaining electronic monitoring if necessary, submitting reports to the court or parole board, and coordinating mental health services if needed, among many other tasks.

One of the most controversial positions that a probation or parole officer can be put in is that of issuing a technical violation. **Technical violations** of probation and parole do not consist of new crimes committed, but rather of violations of the conditions of community supervision. The penalty for a technical violation for probationers can be to serve out the remainder of their original sentence incarcerated. Those on parole may suffer a **parole revocation** and be re-incarcerated for the remainder of their sentence as well. Technical violations can include failing a drug or alcohol screening, missing treatment appointments, not paying fines, and not communicating in an appropriate manner with a probation or parole officer. The Council of State Governments Justice Center (2019) reports: "Technical violations … account for nearly one quarter of all state prison admissions," which costs the system $2.8 billion (p. 1). These numbers, although specific to prisons, seem to indicate that the nation's jails could also be filled with technical violators (Sawyer et al., 2020). Some actors in the criminal justice system are concerned that high levels of technical violations can be both counter-productive to the mission of community corrections and burdensome to probation and parole officers, who either have to confront someone's violation formally or ignore it and allow them to remain in the community.

The issue described above highlights questions about the true role of a probation or parole officer. Considerable questions arise from conflicts that may be experienced—between officers, and within or between departments—because of the differing philosophical approaches an officer can take in carrying out their duties (Allard et al., 2003). **Role conflict** occurs when probation and parole officers must balance enforcement activities with the welfare of the community and of the individuals they supervise. For example, should an officer choose the strict enforcement of a minor technical violation and risk the individual's revocation, or choose to handle it informally and allow the person to continue on in community supervision? Officers must also weigh this decision against department policy and what they believe is best for the individual, while doing everything they can to keep the community safe. The true impact of this conflict is hard to determine, but it is clear that it adds to the exhaustion and burnout experienced by probation and parole officers (Allard et al., 2003).

Probation and parole officers have fallen victim to disturbing trends also seen in other parts of the criminal justice system. These include increasing caseloads and decreasing financial and personal support (Denney et al., 2020). The National Institute of Justice (Finn & Kuck, 2003) detailed issues related to probation and parole officer stress. High caseloads, excessive paperwork, and the pressure of meeting deadlines can cause officers to take increased amounts of sick time and can also place a strain on interpersonal relationships, as the stress is often brought home with the officer (Finn & Kuck, 2003). Additionally, high levels of stress and conflict can directly impact how officers do their jobs, calling into question their ability to protect both themselves and the communities they serve. When stress levels and exhaustion are ignored, the cost to probation and parole departments can be enormous, as officers become less efficient and less careful in carrying out their responsibilities, putting themselves and the community at risk.

The stress of probation and parole officers also has a direct impact on those they oversee. Officers who have to handle excessive numbers of cases could be more "concerned with administration and compliance rather than intervention" (Schaefer & Williamson, 2017, p. 454). This forces officers to worry less about developing relationships and encouraging the overall success of their clients, and more about checking boxes to ensure departmental compliance. The introduction of additional sentencing options, or intermediate sanctions (discussed below), has only added to their duties, as they often become responsible for overseeing the conditional completion of those programs as well.

INTERMEDIATE SANCTIONS

As discussed earlier, the decision to imprison someone or place them on probation is a difficult one. Judges who get it wrong could potentially release a dangerous person into the community or incarcerate someone who should not have their freedom taken away. Beyond these somewhat philosophical concerns, the practical concerns levied by the expansion of the criminal justice system and the cost of corrections over the last 50 years have forced officials to look for sentencing options that fall somewhere between probation and incarceration (Petersilia & Deschenes, 1994; Tonry & Lynch, 1996). These options have become known as intermediate sanctions or alternative sanctions. Intermediate sanctions allow those who may otherwise be incarcerated to be supervised in the community. During the 1980s and 1990s, when the prison boom was especially high, the belief was that intermediate sanctions could be a way to mediate the growth of the prison population while better managing criminal offenders and correctional budgets (Caputo, 2004). Intermediate sanctions keep a person's pro-social attachments to the community in place. Ongoing employment and continuing familial support are beneficial to the reduction of recidivism, and these attachments can better remain intact if a person is supervised in the community but are severed if that person is incarcerated.

Intermediate punishments offer a number of sentencing options that vary in both supervision levels (including possible short periods of incarceration) and conditions for completion. Options include intensive supervision programs, house arrest, electronic monitoring, boot camp, shock probation, community service, fines and restitution, halfway houses, and day reporting centers (Caputo, 2004). Among the most popular forms of intermediate sanctioning are intensive supervision programs. **Intensive Supervision Programs** (ISPs) are essentially more stringent forms of probation that "fill the gap between traditional probation and incarceration by serving as tougher punishments with stricter controls over offenders than traditional probation could provide" (Caputo, 2004, p. 35).

ISPs as intermediate sanctions were born out of the "get tough on crime" movement of the late 20th and early 21st centuries. At this point, and for the first time in its history, the responsibility of probation and parole became "establishing prison-like controls over offenders in the community" rather than rehabilitation or treatment (Paparozzi & Gendreau, 2005, p. 447). This was the dominant model of ISPs for a number of years, but at the time of this writing in 2021, they have started to revert to their rehabilitative roots and now often include both supervision and treatment modalities (Hyatt & Barnes, 2017). Research indicates that deterrence-based ISPs, which focus primarily on supervision, are less effective in reducing recidivism than those with a treatment-centered, "human service approach" (Lowenkamp et al., 2010, p. 374).

Caputo (2004) notes that there are typically three ways ISPs are used: as a diversion from incarceration through probation, as a form of early release through parole, or as an "enhancement tool" for people already sentenced to probation (p. 39). The flexibility of intensive supervision also allows programs to target the individuals they think would benefit most. Thus, while many programs have chosen to target persons who are considered low-risk, others choose to use it for the moderate- to highest-risk persons who they believe can still be managed in the community (Paparozzi & Gendreau, 2005).

The state of Pennsylvania offers a number of intermediate sanctions including the State Intermediate Punishment (SIP) program and a motivational boot camp program (Pennsylvania Department of Corrections, 2021). The SIP program uses periods of both incarceration (which could also include the motivational boot camp) and community-based treatment in order to support the rehabilitation of persons convicted of nonviolent, drug-related offenses. According to the Pennsylvania Department of Corrections (2021):

> Under SIP, theinmate will serve a flat sentence of 24 months, at least seven of which will be served in in-prison, (four of them in a therapeutic community), a minimum of two months in a community-based therapeutic community and a minimum of six months in outpatient treatment. (para. 4)

Over 3,000 individuals have graduated from the SIP program since its inception in 2005 (Bucklen et al., 2017). The program boasts recidivism rates that are nearly 10% lower than those of non-participants in the program, as well as savings of nearly $34,000 per program participant (Bucklen et al., 2017). Beginning in February 2020, the program was rebranded as the State Drug Treatment Program, bringing it, at least in name, closer to a treatment modality and farther from a program built for deterrent supervision.

Technological advancements in the tracking of individuals have helped to expand the use of intermediation sanctions. Electronic Monitoring (EM) has been used since the 1980s and has advanced from simply tagging people who stray too far from home to using Global Positioning Systems (GPS) to pinpoint their movements anywhere in the world (Belur et al., 2020). EM has proven versatile because it can be used for individuals convicted of almost any type of crime, including sex offenses. While EM has shown that it can substantially reduce recidivism rates, many of the other stated goals of intermediate sanctions may not be met by this form of supervision, as individuals still experience numerous barriers to employment and increased strain on their interpersonal relationships (Bales et al., 2010).

Intermediate sanctions have become a staple of sentencing options across the country. The variety of programs, which includes specialty courts such as drug courts, mental health courts, and veterans courts, indicates that the criminal justice system is looking for alternatives to incarceration in order to handle all types of criminality. **Drug courts** are a rapidly expanding sentencing option for individuals with substance abuse problems. Drug courts have the flexibility and resources to provide a better rehabilitative model for combatting substance abuse than traditional courts do. They also have the potential to decrease costs to the criminal justice system by helping to reduce repeat offending and institutional overcrowding. There is concern, however, that diversion to drug courts, and to other forms of intermediate sanctions, is being used for individuals who do not benefit from them (Griffin et al., 2018). It is also argued that intermediate sanctions have, in effect, cast a larger system of correctional control over people who would otherwise receive normal probationary measures or simple fines for their convictions.

The expansion of correctional control over the criminal population is known as **net-widening** and may be increasing costs to the criminal justice system, rather than decreasing them as intended (Tonry & Lynch, 1996). Net-widening occurs when intermediate sanctions are used for individuals who would benefit less from their services. When net-widening occurs, the cost to the courts and the correctional systems is increased, and those who would benefit from intermediate sanctions most are never even provided the option.

CONCLUSION

Probation, parole, and intermediate sanctions have developed as reform responses to the methods of incarceration that dominated early justice efforts. Their use has fluctuated over time, with various supervision options falling in and out of favor. The decision to place someone on community supervision is not easy to make, due to the number of variables that are unknown. Judges and parole boards cannot predict with any real accuracy the personal and social conditions that will be faced by individuals under supervision. However, the number of people under community supervision and the push to deinstitutionalize the correctional system in general stand to potentially increase the use of community corrections.

Generally speaking, community correctional options have not produced the outcomes that were anticipated. The Vera Institute of Justice (2013) paints a grim picture of what will result if changes to community corrections are not made:

> While community supervision clearly costs less than incarceration, in many instances, the low cost is a result of large caseloads and a lack of key services. Without funds sufficient to ensure that people are receiving appropriate and individualized supervision, communities may see high failure rates, increased victimization, and delayed rather than avoided costs as understaffed agencies return probationers and parolees to costly jail and prison beds on technical violations of probation or parole conditions or rules. ... (p. 8)

The lack of empirical support for community supervision as a method to reduce recidivism places it directly in the crosshairs of correctional reformers (Bonta et al., 2011). The push has already begun for probation and parole officers to become better educated in the use of evidence-based practices that produce more appropriate and sustainable outcomes for participants. This includes understanding and utilizing cognitive behavioral treatments and the risk-needs-responsivity model, both of which will be examined in Chapter 5 (Pearson et al., 2016).

DISCUSSION QUESTIONS

1. How do you think the job of a probation or parole officer might be different from that of a police officer?

2. Should technical violations of probation and parole be used as cause to re-incarcerate someone?

3. What could be the long-term impacts of net-widening?

APPLICATION EXERCISES

Exercise #1: Local Intermediate Sanctions

Do some searching on the intermediate sanction programs that take place in your local area through your county's website. If your county does not list or describe any intermediate sanctions, expand your search to your state. What intermediate sanctions are there? How are they carried out? What conditions must participants meet in order to complete the program? What happens once they complete the program? Next, look at the research on those types of intermediate sanctions. What does the research say about their effectiveness? Finally, based on your research, put together a presentation you could make to your local probation/parole officials, arguing for either the expansion or the reduction and replacement of these programs.

Exercise #2: Probation/Parole Conditions

Examine the conditions of probation and parole in your local area. What are some of the general and specific conditions that are used? Do those conditions focus more on supervision or on social support and treatment? Are there ways that you think these conditions could be altered to provide better outcomes? Find out how these conditions are relayed to individuals on probation and parole. Consider creating a pamphlet that can be placed at probation and parole offices to help people navigate their community corrections experience.

REFERENCES

Administrative Office of the United States Court. (2016). *Overview of probation and supervised release conditions.* https://www.uscourts.gov/sites/default/files/overview_of_probation_and_supervised_release_conditions_0.pdf

Allard, T. J., Wortley, R. K., & Stewart, A. L. (2003). Role conflict in community corrections. *Psychology, Crime & Law, 9*(3), 279–289.

Augustus, J. (1852). *A report of the labors of John Augustus for the last ten years, in aid of the unfortunate: Containing a description of his method of operations: Striking incidents, and observations upon the improvement of some of our city institutions, with a view to the benefit of the prisoners and of society.* Wright and Hasty, Printers.

Bales, W., Mann, K., Blomberg, T., Gaes, G., Barrick, K., Dhungana, K., & McManus, B. (2010). *A quantitative and qualitative assessment of electronic monitoring.* National Institute of Justice. https://www.ojp.gov/pdffiles1/nij/grants/230530.pdf

Barnes, K. J., & Mowen, T. J. (2020). Examining the parole officer as a mechanism of social support during reentry from prison. *Crime & Delinquency, 66*(6–7), 1023–1051.

Belur, J., Thornton, A., Tompson, L., Manning, M., Sidebottom, A., & Bowers, K. (2020). A systematic review of the effectiveness of the electronic monitoring of offenders. *Journal of Criminal Justice, 68*, 1–18.

Bonta, J., Bourgon, G., Rugge, T., Scott, T. L., Yessine, A. K., Gutierrez, L., & Li, J. (2011). An experimental demonstration of training probation officers in evidence-based community supervision. *Criminal Justice and Behavior, 38*(11), 1127–1148.

Brennan, T., & Dieterich, W. (2018). Correctional Offender Management Profiles for Alternative Sanctions (COMPAS). In J. P. Singh, D. G. Kroner, J. S. Wormith, S. L. Desmarais, & Z. Hamilton (Eds.) *Handbook of recidivism risk/needs assessment tools* (pp. 49–75). John Wiley & Sons.

Bucklen, K. B., Bell, N., & Lategan, D. (2017). *State intermediate punishment program: 2017 performance report*. Pennsylvania Department of Corrections. https://www.cor.pa.gov/About%20Us/Statistics/Documents/Reports/2017%20SIP%20Annual%20Final.pdf

Caplan, J. (2007). What factors affect parole: A review of empirical research. *Federal Probation Journal, 71*(1), 1–8.

Caputo, G. (2004). *Intermediate sanctions in corrections*. University of North Texas Press.

The Council of State Governments Justice Center. (2019). *Confined and costly: How supervision violations are filling prisons and burdening budgets*. https://csgjusticecenter.org/wp-content/uploads/2020/01/confined-and-costly.pdf

Cullen, F. T., Smith, P., & Lowenkamp, C. T. (2009). Nothing works revisited: Deconstructing Farabee's *Rethinking Rehabilitation*. *Victims and Offenders, 4*, 101–123.

de Courcy, C. A. (1910). The probation system of Massachusetts. *The Yale Law Journal, 19*(3), 187–192.

Denney, A. S., Copenhaver, A., & Schwendau, A. (2020). Predicting health and wellness outcomes for probation and parole officers: An exploratory study. *Criminal Justice Policy Review, 31*(4), 573–591.

Ditton, P. M., & Wilson, D. J. (1999). *Truth in sentencing in state prisons*. U.S. Department of Justice, Office of Justice Programs, Bureau of Justice Statistics. https://bjs.gov/content/pub/pdf/tssp.pdf

Doyle, C. (1996). *Truth in sentencing: Summary of implicated state laws* [Report]. American Law Division, Congressional Research Service.

Federal Probation Act of 1925. H.R. 5195 (1925)

Ferral, K. (2016, July 13). Wisconsin Supreme Court allows state to continue using computer program to assist in sentencing. *The Capital Times*. https://madison.com/ct/news/local/govt-and-politics/wisconsin-supreme-court-allows-state-to-continue-using-computer-program-to-assist-in-sentencing/article_7eb67874-bf40-59e3-b62a-923d1626fa0f.html#:~:text=COMPAS%2C%20which%20stands%20for%20Correctional, using%20the%20program%20in%202012

Finn, P., & Kuck, S. (2003). *Addressing probation and parole officer stress.* National Institute of Justice. https://www.ojp.gov/pdffiles1/nij/grants/207012.pdf

Globokar, J. L., & Toro, M. (2017). The politics of punishment: A study of the passage of the 1925 Federal Probation Act. *Journal of Offender Rehabilitation, 56*(8), 534–551.

Griffin, O. H., III, Woodard Griffin, V., Copes, H., & Dantzler, J. A. (2018). Today was not a good day: Offender accounts of the incidents that led to their admission to drug court. *Criminal Justice Studies, 31*(4), 388–401.

Hoffman, P. B. (2003). *History of the federal parole system.* United States Parole Commission. https://www.justice.gov/sites/default/files/uspc/legacy/2009/10/07/history.pdf

Hyatt, J. M., & Barnes, G. C. (2017). An experimental evaluation of the impact of intensive supervision on high-risk probationers. *Crime & Delinquency, 63*(1), 3–38.

Jones, A. (2018). *Correctional control 2018: Incarceration and supervision by state.* Prison Policy Initiative. https://www.prisonpolicy.org/reports/correctionalcontrol2018.html

Kaeble, D. (2018). *Probation and parole in the United States, 2016.* U.S. Department of Justice, Office of Justice Programs, Bureau of Justice Statistics. https://www.bjs.gov/content/pub/press/cpus16pr.pdf

Kaeble, D., & Alper, M. (2020). *Probation and parole in the United States, 2017–2018.* U.S. Department of Justice, Office of Justice Programs, Bureau of Justice Statistics. https://www.bjs.gov/content/pub/pdf/ppus1718.pdf

Lawrence, A. (2015). *Making sense of sentencing: State systems and policies.* National Conference of State Legislatures. https://www.ncsl.org/documents/cj/sentencing.pdf

Labrecque, R. M. (2017). Probation in the United States: A historical and modern perspective. In O. H. Griffin III & V. H. Woodward (Eds.), *Handbook of corrections in the United States* (pp. 155–164). Routledge.

Lowenkamp, C. T., Flores, A. W., Holsinger, A. M., Makarios, M. D., & Latessa, E. J. (2010). Intensive supervision programs: Does program philosophy and the principles of effective intervention matter? *Journal of Criminal Justice, 38,* 368–375.

Macallair, D. (2002). The history of the presentence investigation report. In J. Dressler (ed.), *Encyclopedia of crime and justice* (2nd ed., pp. 1149–1453). Macmillan Reference USA.

MacDonald, S. S., & Baroody-Hart, C. (1999). Communication between probation officers and judges: An innovative model. *Federal Probation, 63*(1), 42–50.

Mackenzie, D. L. (2001). *Sentencing and corrections in the 21st century: Setting the stage for the future.* U.S. Department of Justice. https://www.ncjrs.gov/pdffiles1/nij/189106-2.pdf

Maruschak, L. M., & Minton, T. D. (2020). *Correctional populations in the United States, 2017–2018.* U.S. Department of Justice, Office of Justice Programs, Bureau of Justice Statistics. https://www.bjs.gov/content/pub/pdf/cpus1718.pdf

Martinson, R. (1974). What works? Questions and answers about prison reform. *The Public Interest, 35,* 22–54.

Office of General Counsel. (2019). *Supervised release.* U.S. Sentencing Commission. https://www.ussc.gov/sites/default/files/pdf/training/primers/2019_Primer_Supervised_Release.pdf

Panzarella, R. (2002). Theory and practice of probation on bail in the report of John Augustus. *Federal Probation, 66*(3), 38–42.

Paparozzi, M., & Gendreau, P. (2005). An intensive supervision program that worked: Service delivery, professional orientation, and organizational supportiveness. *The Prison Journal, 85*(4), 445–466.

Pearson, D. A. S., McDougall, C., Kanaan, M., Torgesrson, D. J., & Bowels, R. A. (2016). Evaluation of the Citizenship evidence-based probation supervision program using a stepped wedge cluster randomized control trial. *Crime & Delinquency, 62*(7), 899–924.

Petersilia, J. (2009). *When prisoners come home.* Oxford University Press.

Petersilia, J., & Deschenes, E. P. (1994). Perceptions of punishment: Inmates and staff rank the severity of prison versus intermediate sanctions. *The Prison Journal, 74*(3), 306–328.

Pennsylvania Department of Corrections. (2021). *State intermediate punishment.* https://www.cor.pa.gov/Inmates/Pages/SIP.aspx

Pew Research Center. (2018). *Probation and parole systems marked by high stakes, missed opportunities.* https://www.pewtrusts.org/-/media/assets/2018/09/probation_and_parole_systems_marked_by_high_stakes_missed_opportunities_pew.pdf

Renaud, J. (2019). *Grading the parole release systems of all 50 states.* Prison Policy Initiative. https://www.prisonpolicy.org/reports/grading_parole.html

Rhine, E., Petersilia, J., & Reitz, K. R. (2015). Improving parole release in America. *Federal Sentencing Reporter, 28*(2), 96–104.

Rhine, E., Watts, A., & Reitz, K. R. (2018, April). *Parole boards within indeterminate and determinate sentencing structures.* Robina Institute of Criminal Law and Criminal Justice, University of Minnesota. https://robinainstitute.umn.edu/news-views/parole-boards-within-indeterminate-and-determinate-sentencing-structures

Sabol, W. J., Rosich, K., Kane, K. M., Kirk, D., & Dubin, G. (2002). *Influences of truth-in-sentencing reforms on changes in states' sentencing practices and prison populations.* U.S. Department of Justice. https://www.ncjrs.gov/pdffiles1/nij/grants/195161.pdf

Sawyer, W., Jones, A., & Trolio, M. (2020) *Technical violations, immigration detainers, and other bad reasons to keep people in jail.* Prison Policy Initiative. https://www.prisonpolicy.org/blog/2020/03/18/detainers/

Schaefer, L., & Williamson, H. (2017). Probation and parole case management as opportunity-reduction supervision. *Journal of Offender Rehabilitation, 56*(7), 452–472.

Schwartzapfel, B. (2015). *Nine things you probably didn't know about parole.* The Marshall Project. https://www.themarshallproject.org/2015/07/10/nine-things-you-probably-didn-t-know-about-parole

Sentencing Reform Act of 1984, 18 U.S. Code § 3553 (1984)

State of Wisconsin v. Loomis, 881 N.W.2d 749 (Wis. 2016)

Tewksbury, R., & Connor, D. P. (2012, June/July). Predicting the outcome of parole hearings. *Corrections Today*, 54–56.

Tonry, M., & Lynch, M. (1996). Intermediate sanctions. *Crime and Justice, 20*, 99–144.

Travis, J., & Lawrence, S. (2002). *Beyond the prison gates: The state of parole in America.* Urban Institute. http://webarchive.urban.org/UploadedPDF/310583_Beyond_prison_gates.pdf

United States Department of Justice. (2015). *How parole works.* https://www.justice.gov/uspc/how-parole-works

Vera Institute of Justice. (2013). *The potential of community corrections: To improve communities and reduce recidivism.* https://www.prisonpolicy.org/scans/vera/potential-of-community-corrections.pdf

Violent Crime Control and Law Enforcement Act of 1994, H.R.3355 (1994)

Wagner, P., & Rabuy, B. (2017). *Following the money of mass incarceration.* Prison Policy Initiative. https://www.prisonpolicy.org/reports/money.html

Weisburd, D., Farrington, D. P., & Gill, C. (2017). What works in crime prevention and rehabilitation: An assessment of systematic reviews. *Criminology and Public Policy, 16*(2), 415–449.

Witmer, H. (1925). The development of parole in the United States. *Social Forces, 4*(2), 318–325.

World Prison Brief. (2020). *Highest to lowest – prison population total.* https://www.prisonstudies.org/highest-to-lowest/prison-population-total

CHAPTER 4

Incarceration

CHAPTER OBJECTIVES

After reading this chapter, you should be able to:

- Compare and contrast jails, prisons, and non-citizen detention facilities.
- Define mass incarceration and give examples of how it affects U.S. corrections.
- Evaluate reform efforts that aim to reduce or eliminate mass incarceration.
- Describe life in prison, utilizing various aspects from the reading.
- Discuss policy implications concerning overcrowding, solitary confinement, and communicable diseases.

KEY WORDS

Commissary

Extended confinement units

Incarceration

Institutional corrections

Jail

Marion model

Mass incarceration

Maximum-security prison

Medium-security prison

Minimum-security prison

Non-citizen detention facilities

Nutraloaf

Overcrowding

Prison

Prison labor

Secure housing units

Shock incarceration

Solitary confinement

Special housing units

Split sentence

Supermax prisons

Weekend confinement

CASE STUDY: RICHARD DELISI

On December 8th, 2020, Richard DeLisi, 71, was released from South Bay Correctional Facility in Palm Beach, Florida after spending 31 years in prison. DeLisi, who had been incarcerated since 1989, was convicted on charges of racketeering, trafficking in cannabis, and conspiracy and had been sentenced to 90 years in prison for his role in smuggling more than 100 pounds of marijuana from Colombia into Florida. According to the Last Prisoner Project, a nonprofit organization that advocates for the release of incarcerated people convicted of marijuana charges, DeLisi was serving the longest sentence in the nation for a nonviolent marijuana crime. Several factors were related to his early release, including health concerns and the nonviolent nature of his crime. Importantly, too, marijuana laws have changed dramatically since DeLisi's conviction.

In December 2020, the U.S. House of Representatives approved legislation that would decriminalize marijuana and seek to correct injustices stemming from the War on Drugs. If passed, the Marijuana Opportunity Reinvestment and Expungement (MORE) Act would remove marijuana from the Category I substance classification mandated by the Controlled Substances Act and would eliminate criminal penalties for individuals who manufacture, distribute, or possess marijuana. Prior convictions would also be removed or expunged, and review hearings would be held for marijuana offenses at the federal level. Finally, the act would authorize sales tax on marijuana products to create revenue for poor communities and would fund services to provide job training, legal aid, and substance abuse treatment. The move marks the first time a chamber of Congress has voted on federal marijuana decriminalization.

Questions for Discussion
1. Discuss the implications of Richard DeLisi's sentence. Do you believe his sentence was fair? Why or why not?
2. What challenges might arise if the Senate passed the MORE Act? Do the benefits outweigh the costs?

INTRODUCTION

Incarceration refers to the imprisonment or confinement of an individual following a criminal conviction by a judicial authority (Batten, 2011). According to this philosophy, when a person is incapacitated to this degree, they are removed from mainstream society to reduce harm through restraint and separation, thereby giving purpose to institutional settings (Zimring & Hawkins, 1995). As mentioned in Chapter 1, the United States has the highest incarceration rate in the world, with 2.3 million Americans, or 655 people per 100,000 residents, incarcerated in jails or state or federal prisons (American Civil Liberties Union, 2020b; Kaeble & Cowhig, 2018). The United States also incarcerates thousands of undocumented men, women, and children in the world's largest immigration detention system (Detention Watch Network, n.d.).

The United States holds only 5% of the global populace, yet it imprisons nearly 25% of the world's incarcerated people. Although there was a slight decrease in the correctional population between 2016 and 2017, the United States continues to surpass the incarceration rates of other developed countries. Much of the growth in U.S. imprisonment rates has occurred during the past 4 decades. In fact, prison and jail populations in the United States have increased 700% since the late 1970s (American Civil Liberties Union, 2020b; Kaeble & Cowhig, 2018). The massive influx of the correctional populace has put tremendous strain on the criminal justice system, creating various issues; among them are environmental, personal, and economic problems. In addition, high imprisonment rates, coupled with racial prejudices, have perpetuated social inequalities, racial disparities, and concentrated incarceration among marginalized populations (Garland, 2001; Wakefield & Wildeman, 2016).

The following chapter gives an overview of the role that incarceration plays in corrections and details the institutional settings included in adult corrections. The chapter also discusses social, political, and economic factors that have aided mass incarceration over a 4-decade period, including punitive laws and policies and heavier utilization of life sentences for individuals convicted of crimes. This chapter also gives insight into life in prison and discusses various elements including prison-issued clothing, cells and dormitories, involuntary labor, meals and commissary, phone calls, and visitation. The chapter concludes with a discussion of contemporary issues that continue to challenge modern standards for incarceration including overcrowded conditions, solitary confinement, and communicable diseases.

INSTITUTIONAL CORRECTIONS

Institutional corrections include the incarceration and rehabilitation of individuals who have been convicted of criminal offenses, as well as the confinement of persons suspected of a crime who are awaiting trial or adjudication. While the underlying philosophy of incapacitation remains the same across correctional settings, each institution differs, according to the populations in which they serve and their purpose within the larger criminal justice system. Adult correctional institutions in the United States include jails, state and federal prisons, and non-citizen detention facilities.

Jails

Jails serve several functions in the criminal justice system. A **jail** is a confinement facility that is used to house people who are being detained or held in lawful custody, as well as people who are at various stages of the criminal justice process (Hanser, 2021). At the time of this writing in 2021, recent figures suggest that approximately 631,000 people are incarcerated in local jails across the United States (Sawyer & Wagner, 2020). Importantly, however, 10–14 million people funnel in and out of jail facilities annually, due in part to transient populations. As such, jails are responsible for managing more people in any given year than prisons, which are typically made up of more stable, long-term populations (Hanser, 2021).

According to the Bureau of Justice Statistics (2000), jail populations consist mostly of: young, uneducated, lower-income people; mentally ill individuals; and substance abusers. Because this diverse population presents a host of issues, facilities must also grapple with illiteracy, general medical conditions, communicable diseases, gangs, sexual violence, and suicide ideation (Hanser, 2021; Stohr & Walsh, 2021). Males comprise most jail populations (89%); however, figures show that the incarcerated female population (11%) is growing at a much faster rate. While males are more likely to be incarcerated for violent offenses, females are incarcerated for drug crimes at a higher frequency than males. In addition, females are more likely to have experienced physical or sexual abuse or rape prior to their admission to jail. Disparities also occur across racial lines. That is, in the United States, Black people are more likely than White, Hispanic/Latino, or Asian American people to serve time in jail (Beck, 2000; Flynn, 2002). It is important to note, however, that much of the variance in the nation's jail population can be explained by various factors including court practices, differences in law enforcement, alternatives to incarceration, and public opinion (Flynn, 2002).

Because of the many purposes that jails serve, there is a constant flow of people coming into and leaving the facility (Hanser, 2021). For example, jails house people awaiting trial or other court proceedings such as conviction or sentencing. People who are and are not eligible for bail, as well as people who cannot pay bail because of little or no income, are found in jails, as are people who have violated the terms of their probation or parole and who absconded correctional supervision. Jails are also used to incarcerate mentally ill individuals or juveniles awaiting transfer to another institution and persons wanted by military or federal authorities. Finally, jails hold people for short periods of time following convictions of lesser offenses or misdemeanors, such as those serving a sentence of one year or less (Flynn, 2002).

There are several specialized types of jail sentences that help to mitigate the negative effects of short-term incarceration. These specialized jail sentences—weekend confinement, shock incarceration, and split sentences—are generally reserved for people awaiting adjudication or those charged with minor or petty crimes who are subject to a less restrictive form of custody. **Weekend confinement** refers to confinement that is restricted to weekends or times when the individual is not working in the community.

Conversely, **shock incarceration** refers to a short-term incarceration, followed by a specified term of community supervision. Shock incarceration aims to curb recidivism through deterrence, by exposing individuals to the reality of incarceration. The specialized sentence is most often utilized for juveniles and first-time offenders. In some cases, people are given a **split sentence**, in which they are sentenced to a specified term and then serve the remainder of their sentence on probation. Usually, people must serve at least half of their original sentence before being supervised in the community. This type of sentence has helped to alleviate overcrowded jails and often plays a role in plea bargaining (Hanser, 2021).

There are an estimated 3,134 local and county jails in the United States managed by county sheriffs and city police (Sawyer & Wagner, 2020). To put this number into perspective, the total number of local and county jails in the United States exceeds the total number of degree-granting colleges and universities nationwide (Ingraham, 2015). Jails are classified by the number of people they hold and are categorized as small, medium, large, or mega-sized. The type of jail varies by jurisdiction, but most jails in the United States are classified as small; they typically contain less than 50 beds, and many are in rural county jurisdictions. Rural jails face additional challenges that larger, better-funded jails do not, including lack of funding, limited training for staff, and limited access to important provider services (e.g., physician services, nonemergency medical services, rehabilitative programming, and psychoeducational programming) because of geographic location (Hanser, 2021). In comparison, mega-jails contain more than 1,000 beds, thus serving larger populations. Florida has the most mega-jails in the nation (17), followed by California (15), Texas (13), and New York (12) (Flynn, 2002). Jails in metropolitan areas face unique challenges because they are tasked with operating facilities for sizeable and diverse populations while also providing more extensive services to manage substance abuse, mental health, and medical issues (Hanser, 2021).

Both short-term and long-term jail facilities have booking areas where intakes occur. Correctional staff who work in the booking area must be well-trained and equipped because of the influx of people coming and going, who present various issues. Emotions and stress levels can be high during booking, and large numbers of people who are booked into jail suffer from mental illness, substance abuse issues, or both. In addition, many are under the influence of drugs and alcohol during their intake (Kerle, 1999). Correctional staff often address challenges faced in the booking area by utilizing a holding cell to alleviate chaos, supervise at-risk individuals, and allow time for detoxification. Importantly, too, the risk of suicide is greater in jails than in prisons, particularly within the first 48 hours after someone is booked into the jail facility, especially if they are under the influence of drugs or alcohol. For this reason, it is essential that staff accurately assess risk factors and classify individuals accordingly when they are first brought into the facility (Hanser, 2021).

Staff and correctional administrators who are employed in jails are met with many responsibilities and are often provided with a variety of training programs. However, training standards vary from state to state, and staff often learn through trial and error. Jail training standards usually dictate that jail staff should be diverse and representative of the population in their area. In addition, jail staff should have knowledge about different cultures and maintain linguistic skills that allow them to communicate with ethnically diverse populations. Female staff must also manage challenges that male staff might not face. For example, female staff are more likely to be subject to higher levels of disrespect and harassment than males. Unfortunately, jail staff in local jurisdictions are not paid high wages for their work, compared to correctional staff in state facilities and law enforcement officials. For various reasons, turnover rates are high among jail staff, although the position does serve as a good starting point for other career opportunities. Correctional administrators have addressed these issues by providing more staff training, increasing employment qualifications, and encouraging higher pay and benefits to help the profession evolve and increase professionalism (Hanser, 2021).

Government bodies and correctional administrators are also finding innovation in the form of podular jail designs and community jails. Podular designs in jail settings allow for direct supervision. If implemented correctly, the new generation of jail pods will reduce long-term costs, create a safer environment for both staff and inhabitants, provide jail staff with more opportunities for development, and create more amenities. Relatedly, community jails are organized so that individuals who are involved with programming during their incarceration can continue those services once they are released. Community jails serve to assist people who are engaged in educational programs, drug and alcohol counseling, or mental health programming. These developments have allowed jails to expand their treatment options, reduce reoffending, and meet the needs of people in disadvantaged communities. As such, they are likely to be defining features for jails moving forward (Stohr & Walsh, 2021).

Prisons

A **prison** is a correctional institution that houses people who have been convicted of serious offenses and sentenced for longer periods of time. The length of a prison sentence varies and is often determined by the nature and seriousness of the offense, as well as the defendant's personal and criminal history. The specifics of someone's correctional placement depend on several factors as well. Once a judge considers all the elements of the case, they determine the specifics of the sentence, including in which setting time will be served. For example, a person can be incarcerated at a minimum-, medium-, maximum-, or super-maximum security level prison after they are sentenced (Batten, 2011).

Security measures vary greatly from one prison facility to another. Typically, policies and preventive strategies are dictated by the security level of the institution (Andrus & Richards, 2005). **Minimum-security prisons** utilize dormitory-style housing and have limited to no fencing around the institution's perimeter. The facilities have less staff than higher-security institutions do, and certain areas of the prison are not as heavily patrolled by armed guards. For example, people incarcerated in minimum-security prisons are not typically supervised while they are showering or participating in recreational activities. Minimum-security prisons are also career- and program-oriented, and they sometimes offer opportunities for people to participate in off-site work programs. In addition, they facilitate public works like farming or roadway systems, in which people work on community projects such as roadside litter cleanup or conservation efforts during their incarceration (Hanser, 2021).

Medium-security prisons utilize greater internal controls and have a higher staff-to-incarcerated-person ratio than minimum security facilities do. Medium-security prisons use both cell-type housing and dormitories with lockers and communal toilets and showers. Medium-security prisons also feature strengthened perimeters and offer minimal supervision over internal movements and the population of inhabitants (Federal Bureau of Prisons, n.d.; Hanser, 2021). Like minimum-security prisons, medium-security prisons offer career and treatment programming and recreational activities, and there are more opportunities to move throughout the facility than in more secure facilities (Hanser, 2021).

Maximum-security prisons utilize highly secured perimeters including walls and reinforced fences, and a high staff-to-incarcerated-person ratio, to gain close control of those who inhabit the space (Federal Bureau of Prisons, n.d.). Maximum-security prisons also utilize cameras and sensors, floodlights, electric fencing, and watchtowers that house armed guards, to supervise the surrounding area. People who are incarcerated in maximum-security prisons may be housed in either a single- or double-person cell that is operated from a remote-controlled station. It is also common for inhabitants to have access to programming, recreational activities, and time in the exercise yard (Hanser, 2021).

Supermax prisons are reserved for people who are deemed as being the most dangerous and troublesome to supervise (Haney, 2005). Thus, supermax facilities provide the highest level of prison security by featuring highly restrictive housing units within a secure facility. People who are incarcerated in supermax facilities have little to no contact with other people, apart from prison guards. The use of supermax facilities began to rise in the mid-1990s as states began to adopt the **Marion model** of prison design, fashioned after the United States Penitentiary, Marion (USP Marion), which created higher security classification for troublesome inmates. At least 36 states adopted the Marion model by adding a supermax unit to their facilities, or by building new, more secure prisons within their state. In some cases, different terms were used in place of "supermax," including

special housing units (SHUs) or **extended confinement units** (ECUs). Since the construction of supermax units, correctional administrators have grappled with several constitutional challenges that concern problems with both the operations of and legal criteria for these units (Hanser, 2021).

State and Federal Prisons

State prisons house people convicted of state-level felonies, while federal institutions are reserved for people convicted of violating federal or military laws. There are 110 federal prisons in the United States, containing an estimated population of 175,116 people. In comparison, there are 1,833 state prisons nationwide, containing an estimated population of 1,291,000 people (Sawyer & Wagner, 2020). Louisiana had the highest incarceration rate in 2019, followed by Oklahoma, Mississippi, Arkansas, and Arizona. The lowest incarceration rates were recorded in Maine, Massachusetts, Minnesota, New Hampshire, Rhode Island, and Vermont (Carson, 2020).

Incarceration rates include both state and federal prison populations. According to the Bureau of Justice Statistics (BJS), 1,430,800 people, or 419 per 100,000 U.S. residents, were incarcerated in state and federal prisons by the end of 2019. The numbers represent a 3% decrease from 2018, when 1,464,400 people, or 432 per 100,000 U.S. residents, were incarcerated. Overall, incarceration rates have dropped 17% since 2007 and 2008, when rates peaked at 506 sentenced people per 100,000 U.S. residents for both years. Recent statistics indicate that 2019 was the 11th consecutive year in which the prison population decreased. In addition, 2019 boasted the lowest incarceration rate in 24 years (since 1995). For some states, like Texas and Missouri, changes in laws on nonviolent offenders' parole eligibility might explain the declining prison population. New York, Illinois, Pennsylvania, and Florida also saw large declines in incarceration rates in 2019 (Carson, 2020). Table 4.1 depicts the combined state and federal imprisonment rates per 100,000 U.S. residents, between 1989 and 2019, based on data from the BJS.

The most recent data on state and federal prison populations indicate that by the end of 2019, males made up 92% of the U.S. prison population. Almost half (47%) of sentenced individuals were between 25 and 39 years old. In addition, Black males (1,446 per 100,000 black adult U.S. residents) were incarcerated at five times the rate of White males (263 per 100,000 White adult male U.S. residents) and almost two times the rate of Hispanic/Latino males (757 per 100,000 Hispanic/Latino adult male U.S. residents). In comparison, Black females (83 per 100,000 black female U.S. residents) were incarcerated at 1.7 times the rate of White females (48 per 100,000 White female U.S. residents), and Hispanic/Latina females were incarcerated at 1.3 times the rate of White females (63 per 100,000 Hispanic/Latina female U.S. residents). According to the BJS, the highest Black-to-White racial disparity of any age group occurred

Table 4.1 Combined State and Federal Imprisonment Rates per 100,000 U.S. Residents, 1978–2019.

YEAR	ALL AGES	AGE 18+	YEAR	ALL AGES	AGE 18+
1978	131	183	2000	470	632
1979	133	185	2001	470	630
1980	138	191	2002	477	639
1981	153	211	2003	483	645
1982	170	232	2004	487	649
1983	179	243	2005	492	655
1984	187	254	2006	501	666
1985	201	272	2007	506	670
1986	216	293	2008	506	669
1987	230	311	2009	504	665
1988	246	331	2010	500	656
1989	274	369	2011	492	644
1990	295	398	2012	480	626
1991	311	420	2013	479	624
1992	330	446	2014	472	613
1993	360	486	2015	459	595
1994	389	526	2016	450	583
1995	411	556	2017	442	570
1996	427	577	2018	432	556
1997	444	599	2019	419	539
1998	463	623			
1999	476	640			

Note. From *National Prisoner Statistics, 1978–2019*, U.S. Department of Justice, Office of Justice Programs, Bureau of Justice Statistics, 2020 (https://www.bjs.gov/content/pub/pdf/p19.pdf).

among Black males between the ages of 18 and 19, who are 12 times as likely to be incarcerated as their White counterparts in the same age group (Carson, 2020). Researchers point to several factors that contribute to these racial disparities, including implicit bias, structural disadvantage, and policies and practices (McCoy, 2002; Yingling, 2009). In addition, Black males experience a disproportionate number of arrests for drug offenses and comprise a greater percentage of the prison population than they represent in the general population (Yingling, 2009). Table 4.2 depicts the percentage of sentenced individuals under state correctional authority, both male and female, by most serious offense and race.

Table 4.2 Percentage of Sentenced Individuals Under State Correctional Authority by Serious Offense and Race.

		WHITE	BLACK	HISPANIC/LATINO
Violent		48.3%	61.9%	61.6%
	Murder	10.7	17.3	19.2
	Negligent manslaughter	1.4	0.9	1.2
	Rape/sexual assault	16.6	8.5	12.7
	Robbery	6.9	19.1	9.9
	Aggravated/simple assault	9.3	12.3	13.5
	Other	3.4	3.9	4.9
Property		21.8%	13.2%	14.9%
	Burglary	10.6	7.9	7.1
	Larceny/theft	5.1	2.6	3.1
	Motor-vehicle theft	0.9	0.5	1.4
	Fraud	2.6	1.1	1.7
	Other	2.6	1	1.6
Drug		16.3%	12.7%	10.5%
	Possession	5.1	3	1.7
	Other	11.3	9.7	8.8
Public order		12.8%	11.9%	12.6%
	Weapons	2.9	6	4.2
	DUI/DWI	2.4	0.7	3.1
	Other	7.4	5.1	5.2
Other		0.7%	0.4%	0.4%

Note. From Percent of sentenced prisoners under the jurisdiction of state correctional authorities, by most serious offense, sex, and race or ethnicity, December 31, 2018, U.S. Department of Justice, Office of Justice Programs, Bureau of Justice Statistics, 2020 (https://www.bjs.gov/content/pub/pdf/p19.pdf)

Most people convicted at the federal level are serving time for drug offenses (46%), most often for drug trafficking, whereas a portion are incarcerated for weapons charges (18%), violent offenses (8%), and immigration charges (5%) (Carson, 2020; Sawyer & Wagner, 2020; Walmsley, 2019). In comparison, most people in state correctional institutions are incarcerated for violent, drug, or property offenses, whereas a small portion are incarcerated for public order offenses or other convictions. Violent offenders made up 55% of all people sentenced to state prisons at the end of 2018, and an estimated 14% of sentenced individuals were serving time for murder or non-negligent manslaughter. In addition, 13% were incarcerated for rape or sexual assault. By the end of 2018, 58% of males were serving time in state prisons for a violent offense, compared to 38% of females. Property offenses represented 16% of the state prison population, whereas 14% were sentenced for drug offenses. Females made up most of the population sentenced for drug (26%) or property (24%) offenses (Carson, 2020). Table 4.3 depicts the percentage of sentenced individuals under the jurisdiction of state correctional authorities, by most serious offense and sex.

Table 4.3 Percentage of Sentenced Individuals Under State Correctional Authority by Serious Offense and Sex.

		ALL	MALE	FEMALE
Violent		55.5%	57.9%	38%
	Murder	14.2	14.6	12
	Negligent manslaughter	1.5	1.4	2.8
	Rape/sexual assault	13	14.1	2.5
	Robbery	12.4	13	7.5
	Aggravated/simple assault	10.9	11.2	8.9
	Other	3.5	3.5	4.3
Property		16%	15.6%	24.4%
	Burglary	8.5	8.8	6.8
	Larceny/theft	3.1	2.8	7.6
	Motor-vehicle theft	0.8	0.8	1
	Fraud	1.8	1.5	6.5
	Other	1.8	1.7	2.5
Drug		14.1%	13.4%	25.7%
	Possession	3.7	3.4	8.5
	Other	10.4	10	17.2

(continued)

Table 4.3 Percentage of Sentenced Individuals Under State Correctional Authority by Serious Offense and Sex.   *(continued)*

		ALL	MALE	FEMALE
Public order		12.3%	12.6%	11.1%
	Weapons	4.6	4.9	2
	DUI/DWI	1.7	1.7	2.5
	Other	5.9	6	6.6
Other		0.6%	0.6%	0.9%

Note. From Percent of sentenced prisoners under the jurisdiction of state correctional authorities, by most serious offense, sex, and race or ethnicity, December 31, 2018, U.S. Department of Justice, Office of Justice Programs, Bureau of Justice Statistics, 2020 (https://www.bjs.gov/content/pub/pdf/p19.pdf)

Non-Citizen Detention Facilities

The United States also utilizes 218 **non-citizen detention facilities** to house non-U.S. citizens who are determined to need custodial supervision (Sawyer & Wagner, 2020). According to the American Immigration Council (2020), non-U.S. citizens can be detained by one of several government entities, including the Department of Homeland Security (DHS), the Department of Health and Human Services (HHS), or the Department of Justice (DOJ). The U.S. Customs and Border Protection (CBP) and Immigration and Customs Enforcement (ICE) agencies are each governed by the DHS. Most people detained by these agencies are at or near the border; however, some people are also detained within the interior of the country or at airports (American Immigration Council, 2020).

Immigration detention emerged in the United States in the early 1980s, during the War on Drugs era. During this time, the Immigration and Naturalization Act (1952) was amended by Congress to mandate that non-citizen be detained, without a hearing or investigation, if they had been convicted of certain criminal offenses. By the 1990s, detention became the primary means of immigration enforcement. Following the terrorist attacks on September 11, 2001, immigration was viewed as a national security issue; as a result, detention facilities were used to house more and more non-citizens. More recently, law enforcement officials have implemented nationwide community raids, and policies that protected immigrants have been eliminated. As a result, the number of non-citizens being held in detention facilities has grown exponentially.

According to the Detention Watch Network (n.d.), nearly 360,000 people were incarcerated in non-citizen detention facilities in 2016. These numbers include documented and undocumented people, asylum seekers, women, and children (Detention Watch Network, n.d.).

While non-citizens await their immigration status or the possibility of deportation, they are typically incarcerated in one of 200 facilities across the country, many of which are contracted between government officials or county jails and privately run institutions—primarily the GEO Group or Corrections Corporation of America/CoreCivic (Detention Watch Network, n.d.). The immigration system itself is vast, largely due to the agreements held between ICE and correctional providers and to the overflow in the population. As a result, the system has gone through various changes and has been restructured multiple times to improve federal oversight and management (Hanser, 2021).

Non-citizen detention facilities have been scrutinized for a multitude of civil rights violations. Investigations have shown that occupants of non-detention facilities are exposed to a variety of abuses, including medical abuse/neglect, nutrition issues, prolonged detention, legal issues, hunger strikes, solitary confinement, family abuse, and cleanliness issues. In addition, people have complained about physical issues, access issues, worker issues, religious issues, the lack of phone access, and problems with sexual abuse (Freedom for Immigrants, 2018). There are also reports of over 100 people dying under the custody of immigration officials (Detention Watch Network, n.d.). Under the Trump administration, the number of detention facilities grew, and measures were enforced to target people at the U.S.–Mexico border who were fleeing instability and violence in their homelands and seeking asylum in the United States (Kassie, 2019). As a result, Trump's immigration policies were heavily criticized for being overtly punitive, for unfairly targeting people seeking asylum in the United States, and for invoking violence (Fritze, 2019).

Investigations concerning standards of care indicate that more needs to be done to provide better medical and mental health services in non-citizen detention facilities. In addition, it has been suggested that staff be adequately trained to maintain effective communication with youth and build meaningful rapport with them, to alleviate negative consequences of incarceration. Moreover, facilities must provide educational services to youth who are being detained in non-citizen facilities. It is important to note, too, that non-citizen detention facilities should not resemble prison settings. Since most individuals who are in custody are not charged with criminal offenses, the facilities should be fashioned in a way that reflects more civil detention (Hanser, 2021).

MASS INCARCERATION

Mass incarceration, also known as mass imprisonment, hyper-incarceration, or the carceral state, is a phenomenon taking place in the United States in which rates of incarceration (in jails, prisons, detention centers, etc.) are comparatively and historically extreme. Mass incarceration has several defining features and is a complex occurrence. For example, mass incarceration comprises the wide range of policies, practices, and institutions that affect individuals and communities both prior to and following incarceration. Finally, mass incarceration is defined by the concentration of imprisonment rates in communities of color. Even though racial disparities in the system are evident and problematic, it is also true more generally that mass incarceration is a significant issue which highlights Americans' overreliance on incarceration as a means of punishment for crime. While some scholars argue that vast cultural shifts contribute to mass incarceration in the United States (Beckett, 1997; Garland, 2001; Simon, 2007), most observe that the dramatic increase and disparity in imprisonment rates can be explained by political changes, stricter laws, greater levels of enforcement, and punitive sentences (Beckett, 1997; Blumstein & Beck, 1999; Jacobs & Helms, 2001; Mauer, 1999; Tonry, 1996).

The shift in imprisonment rates can be tracked using statistical data from past decades. From 1930 to 1972, the United States experienced a relatively stable incarceration rate. During that time, the jail and prison populations were comprised of 93–137 incarcerated people per 100,000 in the population (Blumstein & Beck, 1999). However, beginning in the 1980s, the prison populace increased dramatically; since 1980, the incarceration rate for drug offenses has risen from 40,900 in 1980 to 176,300 in 2019. The most current statistics show that 14.1% of all sentenced prisoners under state jurisdiction are there for drug offenses. The rapid growth can be traced to strict, government-enforced policies that aimed to tackle illegal drug use, most notably three-strike laws, and mandatory minimum sentences (Carson, 2020; James, 2004; Zeng, 2019). Beginning in the 1980s, this period, known as the War on Drugs era, resulted in policies that have had a devastating impact on poor communities and produced sentencing disparities across racial groups. For example, in 2020, nearly 80% of people in federal prison and nearly 60% of people in state prison for drug offenses were Black or Hispanic/Latino (Drug Policy Alliance, 2020).

Mass incarceration and overcriminalization have spread deeply into the U.S. economy. It is estimated that the U.S. government has spent upwards of $87 billion dollars on jails and prisons in recent years, with state government, not federal government, making up most of the spending. This amount represents a 1,000% increase in spending since 1975, when spending was closer to $7.4 billion (Equal Justice Initiative, 2020). Alarmingly, however, annual spending might total upwards of $182 billion if policing and court costs, and costs paid by families to support incarcerated loved ones, are considered (Prison Policy Initiative, 2017). Because jails and prisons do not definitively improve public safety and because incarceration destabilizes communities, families, and the lives of individuals, it is well worth the time and effort to invest in reforming these institutions. This can be done by increasing the availability of parole and improving its services, offering community-based programs, including substance abuse treatment, and reinvesting money in other social institutions that will improve public safety in the long term (Equal Justice Initiative, 2020).

According to the Prison Policy Initiative, ending mass incarceration, or at least improving the system, will require society and the criminal justice system to make drastic changes. For example, officials should concentrate more effort on serious crimes than on drug offenses and should stop incarcerating people for non-threatening behaviors. There should also be less reliance on privatized services (e.g., telephone services, medical care, and commissary) so that the costs associated with incarceration do not burden vulnerable people and their families. Prison labor should also be given more regulation and over-sight, and exploited workers should be given more rights and protections. Finally, more attention should be given to violence prevention, social investment, and alternatives to incarceration that address the root causes of crime (Sawyer & Wagner, 2020).

PRISON LIFE

It is estimated that approximately 600,000 people are admitted to state prisons per year. Before beginning their sentence, people must first go through a process known as intake, or processing, at a central facility. While the intake processes vary depending on the institution (e.g., state vs. federal prison), measures typically include photographing and fingerprinting the individual, taking inventory of their personal items, and identifying any group affiliations they might have. Intake also includes a series of systemic and highly structured measures that are carried out over several days to evaluate an individual's level of risk and security requirements, medical needs, and mental health. This information is used to classify people and to recommend housing, cell assignments, work assignments, and programming. Once a person is classified, they are sent to a long-term facility to be admitted. Upon arrival at the prison to which they were assigned, people participate in an orientation session where they learn about various elements of prison life, including the rules of the facility, individual responsibilities, educational and recreational programs, treatment services, and daily procedures (Hardyman et al., 2004).

Clothing

People are first issued prison clothing during their orientation. Prison clothes serve a symbolic purpose and create uniformity. Following early industrialization, black-and-white striped uniforms first originated within the Auburn system (previously discussed in Chapter 1). The striped clothing represented prison bars and made people more recognizable if they escaped from an institution. Once the stripes began to be associated with chain gangs, institutions moved to using solid-colored clothes, with colors ranging from gray to denim blue, khaki, and orange. In some states, different-colored garments are based on custody levels or are used in detention situations or transfers between institutions (Beam, 2010). Prison clothing, by design, is used to reduce individuality and freedom of expression among the correctional population. Prison clothes have also been used to degrade incarcerated people. For example, in Arizona, corrections officials required people to wear pink underwear and sandals, stating that it helped to prevent the theft of certain types of clothing. Because incarcerated people do not have a lot of flexibility with their clothing, they express themselves in other creative ways, such as by crossing their shoelaces or adorning their uniforms with trinkets (Fox, 2017).

Cells and Dormitories

State prisons typically use cells and dormitories to house large numbers of people on any given day. To deal with overcrowding, institutions also use double bunks, as well as overflow space such as dayrooms, classrooms, and offices. A typical prison dormitory is designed to hold large numbers of people; however, they often hold twice their capacity. Some dormitories have partitions, while others have rows of bunk beds separated by about 4 feet, or metal lockers. Because of the extremely close conditions and the inability to supervise everyone at once, dormitories pose significant safety problems, especially at night. In comparison, a prison cell typically measures 60 square feet (approximately 6' x 8') and usually holds one or two people. Each cell usually contains a bed, a cabinet, shelving, a table, a chair, and a toilet/sink combination. Sanitary conditions in prisons vary; however, they are usually dirty and unsanitary and have insufficient infrastructure, so it is common to see water leaks and infestations (Human Rights Watch, 1991).

Prisons can also be unbearably hot, particularly in the southern regions of the United States. There are at least 13 states that lack universal air conditioning in their prisons, including Alabama, Arizona, Florida, Georgia, Kansas, Kentucky, Louisiana, Mississippi, Missouri, North Carolina, South Carolina, Texas, and Virginia. Without access to air conditioning, people in prison are at risk of suffering from significant health problems such as dehydration and heat stroke. Many people, particularly mentally ill individuals and older people, both of whom make up a significant portion of the prison population, are especially vulnerable to heat-related illnesses. Temperatures inside prisons can often exceed outside temperatures, and incarcerated people do not usually have easy access to cold water, shade, and fans to remedy the heat. Concerningly, several people have already died in prison from heat-related illnesses (Jones, 2019).

Involuntary Labor

When people are incarcerated in both state and federal prisons, large portions of their days are spent working and supporting prison industries. **Prison labor** is a term that refers to the forced labor done by incarcerated people in a prison. This requirement stems from the 13th Amendment to the Constitution, which forbids slavery and involuntary servitude but includes a clause that permits involuntary servitude "as punishment for crime." Essentially, this means that incarcerated people can be forced to work as punishment for their crimes. Typically, people are paid extremely poor wages for their service, and in some cases, they are not compensated at all (Benns, 2015).

Over the decades, prison labor has expanded dramatically. Incarcerated people can work as a part of in-house operations or through convict-leasing partnerships with for-profit businesses; they can provide services to mining and agricultural industries, corporations, or call centers (Benns, 2015). Most incarcerated people work in custodial, maintenance, grounds-keeping, or food-service jobs within the prison. According to recent figures from the Prison Policy Initiative, incarcerated people are paid an average of 86 cents an hour. Other than a few exceptions, prisons in Alabama, Arkansas, Florida, Georgia, and Texas do not pay people for their labor at all. The problem of prison labor exacerbates people's inability to support themselves, both during their incarceration and after they are released (Sawyer, 2017).

Meals

The U.S. Supreme Court has ruled that incarcerated people have a right to an adequate diet and that meals must be tailored to meet people's religious and medical needs. State laws, local policies, and court decisions impose nutritional guidelines in state prisons; therefore, food services in state institutions vary dramatically and do not meet federal standards (Bosworth & Thomas, 2005). Moreover, prisons do not adhere to regular health inspections because they are not considered to be food establishments (Camplin, 2017). While the American Correctional Association (ACA) mandates that menus be reviewed by a licensed dietician, some institutions require low-fat diets or menus based on caloric numbers. In addition, although the ACA recommends that prisons serve three meals a day, it does not require this, and it is not uncommon for incarcerated people to be served only twice. Incarcerated people have complained for years that prison meals are not sufficient, but administrators continue to feed them at the lowest cost possible, resulting in small, low-calorie meals being served, oftentimes through private contractors (Santo & Iaboni, 2015).

Prison food is problematic for other reasons as well, including how and when meals are distributed. Incarcerated people are served their first meal as early as 6:00 a.m., with about 14 hours between meals. The allotted time for meals is brief, and people are only given a half an hour to retrieve their food and eat it. Most kitchens and dining rooms are also unsanitary. Poor ventilation and human conditions cause kitchen workers to perspire in the food, and they can taint the food with their saliva or feces. People who are in segregation units are served food on carts, and there is no way for them to know who prepared their meal and how (Bosworth & Thomas, 2005).

The law dictates that food may not be used to punish incarcerated people. In some institutions, however, people are served prison loaf, also known as **nutraloaf**, if they act violently or do not adhere to the rules of the institution. Nutraloaf, as its name implies, is a nutritionally adequate combination of the ingredients of a regular meal, mashed together and served as a loaf. For example, nutraloaf can consist of hot dogs, potatoes, and beans, but institutions can use their own variations and often use reheated leftovers (Bosworth & Thomas, 2005). It is unclear how many prisons utilize nutraloaf, but there are at least 12 states that serve it. There are also reports of people being served nutraloaf multiple times a day for weeks. The monotony of the same meal can be psychologically damaging and can cause people to stop eating altogether. As a result, people have brought claims and lawsuits against correctional institutions. Administrators report that they use nutraloaf sparingly, but there is no official tracking system to determine how prevalent the practice is (Barclay, 2014).

Commissary

The prison **commissary** plays an important role in a person's stay in prison. A commissary is a store within a correctional institution where people can purchase various items. Accessibility of prison commissaries and pricing policies vary by institution. The choice of available products varies as well. Typically, a commissary carries necessities, snacks, clothing, radios, writing instruments, stamps, condiments, phone cards, ingredients, and sometimes over-the-counter medication. Some states also offer digital sales in the form of music and electronic messaging for people who can afford to purchase tablets and MP3 players. Most money goes toward food and hygiene products as opposed to luxury items. Many people rely on their small labor earnings to afford items in the commissary, and the poorest people spend little to nothing there. Those with a support system also depend on their families, who are overwhelmingly poor, to put money into their accounts so that they can purchase items from the commissary, including phone cards that can be used to call home (Bosworth & Thomas, 2005; Raher, 2018).

Phone Calls

Phone calls from prison are essential to maintain contact with family members and legal representatives. Unfortunately, however, prison phone calls cost a great deal of money for incarcerated people and their families because phone companies gain revenue by charging correctional institutions high phone rates. Fortunately, many costs have been capped, and most state prisons have lowered their rates for in-state calls. Still, phone companies charge people with hidden fees that can stack up quickly (Wagner & Jones, 2019). For example, in Washington, incarcerated people pay $1.65 for a 15-minute phone call, whereas people in Connecticut or Kentucky pay $4.87 and $5.70, respectively. The prison phone market is controlled by only two companies, Global Tel Link and Securus Technologies, who make an estimated $1.2 billion annually. Nearly 60% of their earnings are paid back to the state, which is largely why legislators hesitate to restructure the prison phone market (Pipia, 2019; Smith, 2019).

Visitation

It is important for incarcerated people to maintaining contact with their family members, who provide valuable support during and after incarceration. In addition, people who have more contact with their families in prison are less likely to be re-incarcerated (Shanahan & Agudelo, 2012). Parent–child visitation also helps to mitigate the risks that parental incarceration poses for millions of children. Research has shown that contact visits are the most beneficial for strengthening family relationships. High-security institutions can be especially traumatic for visitors, though, because they involve invasive searches of both adults and children (Boudin et al., 2013; Poehlmann-Tynan, 2015). In addition, the prison environment and correctional staff are generally unwelcoming to visitors (Cramer et al., 2017).

While visitation is standard in many correctional institutions, it can also be part of a family strengthening program. Typically, visitation takes on various forms including video conferencing, in-person visitation with or without contact, or extended family visits. Visitations also vary in frequency and length, depending on the program. While some institutions allow multiple visits each week, others only allow one or two visits every few weeks. Despite the number of opportunities for visitation that are made available, schedules can be especially taxing for families who travel long distances or out of state to the institution (Cramer et al., 2017).

CONTEMPORARY ISSUES

Given the complexity of the system and the wide array of negative effects that incarceration has on individuals, families, and communities, it would be difficult to discuss all the issues that relate to incarceration within the scope of this chapter. However, several contemporary problems that significantly impact the functioning of correctional institutions and could result in financial hardships and civil rights violations are worth noting: overcrowding, solitary confinement, and the transmission of communicable diseases.

Overcrowding

Mass incarceration has created overcrowded conditions of confinement. The dramatic increase in the correctional population, coupled with institutions that function at or beyond full capacity, is known as **overcrowding**. It has been widely accepted that overcrowded conditions in both jails and prisons are the result of criminal justice policy, not of increased crime rates. Correctional institutions have historically functioned above full capacity and failed to adhere to minimum space requirements (Penal Reform International, n.d.). According to the Bureau of Justice Statistics, in 2019, prisons in seven states and the Federal Bureau of Prisons (BOP) maintained a custody population that was equal to or greater than the capacity of the institution. In addition, the minimum number of prison beds was exceeded in 21 states and the BOP. Overall, Iowa (119%), Nebraska (115%), Idaho (110%), Colorado (107%), and Washington (105%) had the highest custody populations at year-end 2019. Likewise, the BOP maintained a custody population that was 10% higher than it was intended to hold (Carson, 2020).

Because correctional institutions absorb large numbers of people from transient and diverse populations, the system is rife with problems (The Sentencing Project, 2019). Overcrowded conditions are especially concerning because they create a dangerous environment that puts correctional staff and incarcerated people at risk. Overcrowding also hinders institutions from functioning properly (Flynn, 2002). For example, overcrowded conditions compromise program effectiveness, educational and vocational training, and recreational activities (McCain et al., 1976; Paulus & McCain, 1983). In addition, when freedom of movement is restricted and people are given longer periods of confinement without access to recreational activities, they can fill their time with violence and deviant behavior, creating an environment that is not conducive to rehabilitation. Densely populated spaces can also have a significant effect on a person's stress and psychological well-being and can contribute to, or exacerbate, mental health problems, self-harm, and suicide (Penal Reform International, n.d.).

Modest progress has been made to reduce overcrowding at the state level, albeit slowly. For example, in 2011, the California Supreme Court ordered the state to reduce its burdensome prison population, maintaining that overcrowded conditions are a violation of the Eighth Amendment, which prohibits against cruel and unusual punishment. Prior to the ruling, California state prisons were housing more than 30,000 people in dormitory-style rooms, gyms, or hallways filled to the brim with double or triple bunk beds (Liptak, 2011). The overcrowded conditions led to prison riots among the prison population, in which hundreds of people were injured (Prison Legal News, 2010; Stateman, 2009). Since this time, however, California has made significant progress, and by the end of 2019 it had released more people from prison than any other state (Carson, 2020).

Traditionally, suggestions to reduce overcrowding include the construction of more prisons and greater utilization of early-release programs. Neither of these strategies, however, can address population reductions in the long term (MacDonald, 2018). A recent study conducted by the Urban Institute determined that state and federal governments can alleviate prison overcrowding and save billions of dollars by implementing a series of policy changes that address the root of mass incarceration. These changes include cutting fixed sentences for drug offenses and retroactively applying laws to reduce the disparity between crack and powder cocaine sentences. Other recommendations were to allow early-release credits for people who participate in rehabilitation programming and to give judges greater discretion over sentencing. Finally, the study stated that policies should make a concentrated effort to lower the truth-in-sentencing requirement and release more elderly individuals from custody (Knafo, 2013).

Solitary Confinement

The demand for more secure institutions and segregated units stems from the exponential growth in the jail and prison populace over recent decades, as well as the heightened policies that appear "tough on crime" (Hannem-Kish, 2005; Riveland, 1999). **Secure housing units** (SHUs), also commonly referred to as special housing units, restricted housing units, or intensive management units, are meant to provide extremely high levels of security for high-risk correctional populations and are maintained independently or as a separate housing unit within larger facilities. People in segregated units are supervised with strengthened measures to control both contraband and the individuals held within the unit. They also have extremely limited access to rehabilitation and educational programming and are rarely allowed visitors or phone calls. In some cases, too, people in solitary confinement are banned from having radios, art supplies, or reading materials in their cells (Dodson, 2015; Kiebala & Rodriguez, 2018). **Solitary confinement** refers to the practice in which people are isolated in closed cells measuring between 6×9 or 8×10 feet for upwards of 22 to 24 hours each day, rendering them almost entirely free of human contact for days, weeks, months, or, in extreme circumstances, years. It is common for people to be given 1 hour for exercise and for them to be shackled anywhere they are escorted, such as the shower (Kiebala & Rodriguez, 2018). While solitude was historically used as a means of rehabilitating people who were under correctional supervision (e.g., in the Pennsylvania system or separate system discussed in Chapter 1), today it is mostly used as a punitive measure to control incarcerated people or to separate individuals (Dodson, 2015).

Most state prisons and local jails contain a unit where people are held in solitude. There are also several supermax prisons that are composed solely of solitary confinement cells, including Pelican Bay State Prison in California and the federal ADX Florence in Colorado (Kiebala & Rodriguez, 2018). Correctional institutions usually refer to solitary confinement using other terms that are based on the justification for segregation. For example, disciplinary segregation, or punitive segregation, is an approach that uses solitary confinement as punishment for anyone who violates institutional rules or is found guilty of a serious offense during their incarceration. Conversely, administrative segregation is utilized in situations that require protection for the overall security of the institution (Hannem-Kish, 2005). Typically, SHUs house people with a history of violent behavior, people who have assaulted other people during their incarceration, people who attempt to escape from confinement, or people who disrupt the functioning of the facility. In some instances, protective custody is used to protect individuals from being victimized by groups or people in the general population who threaten to cause them harm (Haney, 2005; Hannem-Kish, 2005; Riveland, 1999). Involuntary protective custody is commonly used for vulnerable populations, including juveniles and LGBTQ individuals. Regardless of variations in terminology, the practice entails a deliberate effort to limit social contact for a determinate or indeterminate period (Kiebala & Rodriguez, 2018).

There is no national database that records the number of people held in solitary confinement in the United States because: states vary in the use of the practice, there are limitations to data collection, and there are differences in how states determine what constitutes solitary confinement. Recent estimates, however, suggest that there are at least 80,000 people in solitary confinement on any given day. Moreover, the BJS estimates that about 448,000 people were held in solitary confinement at some point in 2012. People of color are over-represented in solitary confinement compared to the general population. In addition, they are shown to receive longer terms in solitary than White people for the same disciplinary infractions (Kiebala & Rodriguez, 2018).

A myriad of longstanding research has explored the negative consequences associated with solitary confinement, particularly among vulnerable populations such as mentally ill individuals and people assigned to death row. There is also evidence to suggest that solitary confinement can negatively impact the psychology of a person and that exposure to such conditions poses risks to mental health. For example, time spent in solitary confinement can contribute to perceptual distortions, hallucinations, hypersensitivity, and paranoia, and cause a litany of other psychopathological conditions such as anxiety, nervousness, anger, violent fantasies, heart palpitations, and trouble sleeping (Haney, 2005; Kiebala & Rodriguez, 2018; Riveland, 1999). Moreover, a class-action lawsuit filed against the BOP and officials at ADX Florence supermax prison in 2012 revealed that individuals developed severe psychological problems and began to engage in self-harm after years of solitary confinement at ADX Florence (Kiebala & Rodriguez, 2018).

The punitive practices of solitary confinement have been condemned by the American Psychiatric Association, the National Commission on Correctional Health Care, and the National Alliance on Mental Health. Professional and advocacy organizations contend that the treatment is cruel and inhumane and a violation of the Eighth Amendment (Hannem-Kish, 2005; Kiebala & Rodriguez, 2018; Riveland, 1999). Advocates of reform generally argue that solitary confinement works counter to the growing movement for change and to the already-established public health functions that exist to prevent violence and minimize psychological hazards. In addition, keeping a person incarcerated in solitary confinement for one year costs an estimated $75,000, which is three times more than it costs to incarcerate them at a regular maximum-security prison. Despite these concerns, correctional institutions across the country continue to rely on solitary confinement as a means of control and punishment, with only a handful of states (Colorado, North Dakota, Washington, California, and New York) working to eliminate solitary confinement or develop policies to reduce its use (Kiebala & Rodriguez, 2018).

Communicable Diseases

Blood-borne and airborne pathogens are of serious concern for jails and prisons because communicable diseases affect incarcerated people, correctional staff, and the outside community simultaneously. Oftentimes, correctional staff grapple with hepatitis A, B, and C, HIV/AIDS, tuberculosis, measles, and rubella (Berzofsky et al., 2015). Typical procedures dictate that jails and prisons be prepared for the transmission of communicable diseases with a written plan that details facility operations, distribution of personal protective equipment, vaccination delivery, and staff training. Importantly, however, there are still areas of the system that need improvement (Hanser, 2021).

In late 2019, the world was struck with an unprecedented crisis in the form of the COVID-19 pandemic, leading officials to scramble for ways to protect the lives of people incarcerated in jails and prisons. According to the Centers for Disease Control and Prevention (CDC), people who have contracted COVID-19 have reported displaying a wide range of symptoms ranging from mild symptoms to severe illness. COVID-19 is a contagious respiratory illness that is spread mainly through close contact. People who are infected but do not show symptoms can also spread it to others (Centers for Disease Control and Prevention, 2021). As of January 7, 2021, more than 433,000 incarcerated people and correctional staff have been infected with COVID-19, and at least 1,960 people have died after being infected. The virus continues to spread at an extraordinary rate across the country (Equal Justice Initiative, 2021).

Communicable diseases can have devastating impacts on the operation of jails and prisons. As the COVID-19 pandemic has revealed, incarcerated populations face a greater risk of sickness and death because institutional settings are not conducive to social distancing and do not offer opportunities for quarantine, which leads to a higher risk of infection among incarcerated populations and correctional staff. In addition, health care in jails and prisons is of limited or poor quality, and the facilities are overflowing with vulnerable populations, including older adults, who make up a larger share of the populace (Equal Justice Initiative, 2021). Officials have responded to the public health crisis by adopting strategies to protect vulnerable people, reducing the burden on the healthcare system, protecting essential correctional staff from illness, and slowing the spread of the virus (Wagner & Widra, 2020). For example, officials have reduced prison admissions, eliminated unnecessary face-to-face contact for justice-involved people, and released people from jail where possible. Officials have also eliminated medical co-pays for treatment, making correctional healthcare more humane and efficient, and have either reduced or eliminated the cost of phone and video calls for incarcerated people and their families (Prison Policy Initiative, 2020).

CONCLUSION

Incarceration is one of the main methods of punishment and rehabilitation utilized in U.S. corrections. This chapter provided an overview of institutional corrections and described current incarceration rates and details of jail and prison populations. In addition, the chapter considered the problems associated with mass incarceration and provided insight into contemporary issues that will challenge the criminal justice system for years to come. As was discussed, the United States has maintained a per-capita incarceration rate that exceeds those of other modern nations, and there are 2.2 million people currently serving time in jails and prisons across the country. Mass incarceration has also been costly to individuals and communities and is a large source of government spending. Incarceration is also counterproductive to crime reduction, and it exacerbates social inequalities and racial disparities. Certainly, reforming the system presents a multitude of issues to consider, and only time will tell how the United States will respond to mass incarceration and the issues that stem from it.

DISCUSSION QUESTIONS

1. Describe the major characteristics of jails, prisons, and non-citizen detention facilities. How are they similar? How are they different?
2. What impact have drug laws had on incarceration rates in the United States? What policy changes can be made to reduce mass incarceration?
3. What element of prison life do you find to be the most problematic and why?
4. What problems emerge from overcrowding, solitary confinement, and the transmission of communicable diseases in correctional institutions?

APPLICATION EXERCISES

Exercise #1: A Closer Look at the War on Drugs

The War on Drugs has had a devastating impact on communities and has subsequently led to harsher laws that targeted drug offenders, leading to a massive influx of the correctional population. In this activity, students are encouraged to take a closer look at the War on Drugs by examining the social history of the most popular drugs in the United States. The following website provides a starting point for doing so: https://www.pbs.org/wgbh/pages/frontline/shows/drugs/buyers/socialhistory.html

- Research and present a brief history of the criminal justice system's handling of illegal drugs (e.g., alcohol, amphetamines, cocaine, LSD, marijuana, opium/heroin, tobacco).
- Data and policy implications can be creatively presented in many ways, including through infographics, podcasting, documentary films, graphical depictions, and other visual displays of information.

Exercise #2: Prison Recipes

- During their incarceration, many people adopt or create their own meals, using various types of foods and condiments that are available to them in the commissary. Many recipes are easily found online. Research which foods incarcerated people have regular access to in the commissary and create a list. What types of food are most sold in the commissary?
- Then, create your own recipe using ingredients from your list to share with your classmates. As a group, discuss how prison recipes can have a negative impact on an incarcerated person's health and well-being. What are the negative factors? What are the positive factors?

Exercise #3: Surviving Solitary—6 x 9 Virtual Experience

Consider what it is like to spend 23 hours a day in a cell measuring 6 × 9 feet for extended periods of time by visiting the following weblink to a virtual reality experience of solitary confinement: https://www.theguardian.com/world/ng-interactive/2016/apr/27/6x9-a-virtual-experience-of-solitary-confinement

- Following the activity, summarize the experience in a brief essay to share with your peers, recording reactions and critical takeaways.
- Then, as a larger group, discuss common themes that emerged from the experience.

REFERENCES

Alper, M., Durose, M. R., & Markman, J. (2018). *2018 update on prisoner recidivism: A 9-year follow-up period (2005–2014)*. U.S. Department of Justice, Office of Justice Programs, Bureau of Justice Statistics. https://www.bjs.gov/content/pub/pdf/18upr9yfup0514.pdf

American Civil Liberties Union. (2020b). *Mass incarceration*. https://www.aclu.org/issues/smart-justice/mass-incarceration

American Immigration Council. (2020, January 2). *Immigration detention in the United States by agency*. https://www.americanimmigrationcouncil.org/research/immigration-detention-united-states-agency

Andrus, T., & Richards, S. C. (2005). State prison system. In M. Bosworth (Ed.), *Encyclopedia of prisons and correctional facilities* (Vol. 2). Sage.

Bailey, D. S. (2003). Alternatives to incarceration. *Monitor on Psychology, 34*(7), 54.

Barclay, E. (2014, January 2). *Food as punishment: Giving U.S. inmates 'the loaf' persists.* NPR. https://www.npr.org/sections/thesalt/2014/01/02/256605441/punishing-inmates-with-the-loaf-persists-in-the-u-s

Batten, D. (2011). *Gale encyclopedia of American law* (Vol. 5, 3rd ed.). Gale.

Beam, C. (2010, December 3). *Orange alert: When did prisoners start dressing in orange?* Slate. https://slate.com/news-and-politics/2010/12/when-did-prisoners-start-dressing-in-orange.html

Bureau of Justice Statistics. (2020). *National Prisoner Statistics, 1978–2019.* U.S. Department of Justice, Office of Justice Programs. Retrieved from https://www.bjs.gov/content/pub/pdf/p19.pdf

Bureau of Justice Statistics, (2020), *Percent of sentenced prisoners under the jurisdiction of state correctional authorities, by most serious offense, sex, and race or ethnicity, December 31, 2018,* U.S. Department of Justice, Office of Justice Programs. Retrieved from https://www.bjs.gov/content/pub/pdf/p19.pdf

Beck, A. J. (2000). *Prison and jail inmates at midyear 1999.* U.S. Department of Justice, Office of Justice Programs, Bureau of Justice Statistics. https://bjs.gov/content/pub/pdf/pjim99.pdf

Beckett, K. (1997). *Making crime pay: Law and order in contemporary politics.* Oxford University Press.

Benns, W. (2015, September 21). *American slavery, reinvented.* The Atlantic. https://www.theatlantic.com/business/archive/2015/09/prison-labor-in-america/406177/

Berzofsky, M., Maruschak, L. M., & Unangst, J. (2015). *Medical problems of state and federal prisoners and jail inmates, 2011–12.* U.S. Department of Justice, Office of Justice Programs, Bureau of Justice Statistics. https://www.bjs.gov/content/pub/pdf/mpsfpji1112.pdf

Blumstein, A., & Beck, A. J. (1999). Population growth in U.S. prisons, 1980–1996. In M. Tonry & J. Petersilia (Eds.), *Crime and justice: A review of research—Prisons* (Vol. 26, pp. 17–62). University of Chicago Press.

Bosworth, M., & Thomas, J. (2005). Food. In M. Bosworth (Ed.), *Encyclopedia of prisons and correctional facilities* (Vol. 2, pp. 330–333). Sage.

Boudin, C., Stutz, T., & Littman, A. (2013). Prison visitation policies: A fifty-state survey. *Yale Law & Policy Review, 32,* 149–189.

Breen, C. D. (2014). Three-strikes laws. In B. A. Arrigo (Ed.), *Encyclopedia of criminal justice ethics* (Vol. 2, pp. 934–936). Sage Reference.

Camplin, E. (2017). *Prison food in America.* Rowman & Littlefield.

Carson, E. A. (2021). *Prisoners in 2019.* U.S. Department of Justice, Office of Justice Programs, Bureau of Justice Statistics. https://www.bjs.gov/content/pub/pdf/p19.pdf?utm_content=p19errata&utm_medium=email&utm_source=govdelivery

Centers for Disease Control and Prevention. (2021). *COVID-19.* https://www.cdc.gov/coronavirus/2019-nCoV/index.html

Cramer, L., Goff, M., Peterson, B., & Sandstrom, H. (2017). *Parent-child visiting practices in prisons and jails: A synthesis of research and practice.* Urban Institute. https://www.urban.org/sites/default/files/publication/89601/parent-child_visiting_practices_in_prisons_and_jails.pdf

Detention Watch Network. (n.d.). *Immigration detention 101.* https://www.detentionwatchnetwork.org/issues/detention-101

Dodson, K. D. (2015). Solitary confinement. In B. A. Arrigo (Ed.), *Encyclopedia of criminal justice ethics* (Vol. 2, pp. 884–886). Sage.

Drug Policy Alliance. (2020). *Race and the drug war.* https://www.drugpolicy.org/issues/race-and-drug-war

Equal Justice Initiative. (2021, January 7). *Covid-19's impact on people in prison.* https://eji.org/news/covid-19s-impact-on-people-in-prison/

Equal Justice Initiative. (2020). *Criminal justice reform.* https://eji.org/criminal-justice-reform/

Federal Bureau of Prisons. (n.d.). *About our facilities.* https://www.bop.gov/about/facilities/federal_prisons.jsp

Flynn, E. E. (2002). Jails. In J. Dressler (Ed.), *Encyclopedia of crime and justice* (Vol. 2, pp. 851–862). Macmillan.

Fox, J. (2017). Uniformity rules: Prisoners often try to customize their uniforms but does stripping individuality make rehabilitation more difficult? *Index on Censorship, 45*(4), 50–53.

Freedom for Immigrants. (2018). *Detention by the numbers.* https://www.freedomforimmigrants.org/detention-statistics

Fritze, J. (2019, August 8). *Trump used words like 'invasion' and 'killer' to discuss immigrants at rallies 500 times: USA Today analysis.* USA Today. https://www.usatoday.com/story/news/politics/elections/2019/08/08/trump-immigrants-rhetoric-criticized-el-paso-dayton-shootings/1936742001/

Garland, D. (2001). Introduction: The meaning of mass imprisonment. In D. Garland (Ed.), *Mass imprisonment: Social causes and consequences.* Sage.

Grassian, S. (1983). Psychopathological effects of solitary confinement. *American Journal of Psychiatry, 140*(11), 1450–1454.

Haney, C. (2005). Supermax prisons. In M. Bosworth (Ed.), *Encyclopedia of prisons and correctional facilities* (Vol. 2, pp. 928–934). Sage.

Hannem-Kish, S. (2005). Solitary confinement. In M. Bosworth (Ed.), *Encyclopedia of prisons and correctional facilities* (Vol. 2, pp. 909–912). Sage.

Hanser, R. D. (2021). *A brief introduction to corrections.* Sage.

Harding, D. J., Morenoff, J. D., Nguyen, A. P., & Bushway, S. D. (2017). Short- and long-term effects of imprisonment on future felony convictions and prison admissions. *PNAS, 114*(42), 11103–11108.

Hardyman, P. L., Austin, J. A., & Peyton, J. (2004). *Prisoner intake systems: Assessing needs and classifying prisoners.* U.S. Department of Justice. https://s3.amazonaws.com/static.nicic.gov/Library/019033.pdf

Human Rights Watch. (1991). *Prison conditions in the United States: A Human Rights Watch report.* https://www.hrw.org/sites/default/files/reports/US91N.pdf

Immigration and Nationality Act of 1952, Pub. L. No. 82–414, 66 Stat. 163 (1952) (codified as amended at 8 U.S.C. §§ 1101–1537)

Ingraham, C. (2015, January 6). *The U.S. has more jails than colleges. Here's a map of where those prisoners live.* The Washington Post. https://www.washingtonpost.com/news/wonk/wp/2015/01/06/the-u-s-has-more-jails-than-colleges-heres-a-map-of-where-those-prisoners-live/

Jacobs, D., & Helms, R. (2001). Toward a political sociology of punishment: Politics and changes in the incarcerated population. *Social Science Research, 30,* 171–194.

James, D. J. (2004). *Profile of jail inmates, 2002.* U.S. Department of Justice, Office of Justice Programs, Bureau of Justice Statistics. https://www.bjs.gov/content/pub/pdf/pji02.pdf

Jones, A. (2019, June 18). *Cruel and unusual punishment: When states don't provide air conditioning in prison.* Prison Policy Initiative. https://www.prisonpolicy.org/blog/2019/06/18/air-conditioning/

Jonson, C. L. (2010). Incarceration and recidivism. In F. T. Cullen and P. Wilcox (Eds.), *Encyclopedia of criminological theory* (Vol. 1, pp. 465–469). Sage Reference.

Kaeble, D., & Cowhig, M. (2018). *Correctional populations in the United States, 2016.* U.S. Department of Justice, Office of Justice Programs, Bureau of Justice Statistics. https://www.bjs.gov/content/pub/pdf/cpus16.pdf

Kassie, E. (2019, September 24). *Detained: How the U.S. built the world's largest immigrant detention system.* The Guardian. https://www.theguardian.com/us-news/2019/sep/24/detained-us-largest-immigrant-detention-trump

Kerle, K. (1999). Short term institutions at the local level. In P. M. Carlson & J. S. Garrett (Eds.), *Prison and jail administration: Practice and theory* (pp. 59–65). Aspen.

Kiebala, V., & Rodriguez, S. (2018). *FAQ.* Solitary Watch. https://solitarywatch.org/facts/faq/

Knafo, S. (2013, November 8). *10 ways to reduce prison overcrowding and save taxpayers millions.* Huffington Post. https://www.huffpost.com/entry/prison-overcrowding_n_4235691

Liptak, A. (2011, May 23). *Justices, 5-4, tell California to cut prisoner population.* New York Times. https://www.nytimes.com/2011/05/24/us/24scotus.html?pagewanted=all

MacDonald, M. (2018). Overcrowding and its impact on prison conditions and health. *International Journal of Prisoner Health, 14*(2), 65–68.

Mauer, M. (1999). *Race to incarcerate.* The New Press.

Mauer, M. (2018, November 5). *Long-term sentences: Time to reconsider the scale of punishment.* The Sentencing Project. https://www.sentencingproject.org/publications/long-term-sentences-time-reconsider-scale-punishment/

Mauer, M., & Nellis, A. (2018). *The meaning of life: The case for abolishing life sentences.* The New Press.

McCain, G., Cox, V. C., & Paulus, P. B. (1976). The relationship between illness complaints and degree of crowding in a prison environment. *Environment and Behavior, 8*, 283–290.

McCoy, C. (2002). Sentencing: Mandatory and mandatory minimum sentences. In J. Dressler (Ed.), *Encyclopedia of crime and justice* (Vol. 4, pp. 1443–1447). Macmillan.

Nellis, A. (2016, June 14). *The color of justice: Racial and ethnic disparity in state prisons*. The Sentencing Project. https://www.sentencingproject.org/publications/color-of-justice-racial-and-ethnic-disparity-in-state-prisons/

Paulus, P. B., & McCain, G. (1983). Crowding in jails. *Basic and Applied Social Psychology, 4*(2), 89–107.

Penal Reform International. (n.d.). *Overcrowding*. https://www.penalreform.org/issues/prison-conditions/key-facts/overcrowding/

Pipia, L. (2019, December 31). *Many families struggle to pay for phone calls with loved ones in U.S. prisons*. NBC News. https://www.nbcnews.com/news/us-news/many-families-struggle-pay-phone-calls-loved-ones-u-s-n1107531

Poehlmann-Tynan, J. (2015). Children's contact with incarcerated parents: Summary and recommendations. In J. Poehlmann-Tynan (Ed.), *Springer briefs in psychology. Children's contact with incarcerated parents: Implications for policy and intervention* (pp. 83–92). Springer International Publishing.

Prison Legal News. (2010, March 15). *California prison erupts, hundreds hurt in riot, multiple causes cited*. https://www.prisonlegalnews.org/news/2010/mar/15/california-prison-erupts-hundreds-hurt-in-riot-multiple-causes-cited/

Prison Policy Initiative. (2017, January 25). *Following the money of mass incarceration*. https://www.prisonpolicy.org/reports/money.html

Prison Policy Initiative. (2020, June 10). *Responses to the COVID-19 pandemic*. https://www.prisonpolicy.org/virus/virusresponse.html

Raher, S. (2018). *The company store: A deeper look at prison commissaries*. Prison Policy Initiative. https://www.prisonpolicy.org/reports/commissary.html

Rhodes, W., Gaes, G., Kling, R., & Cutler, C. (2017). *The relationship between prison length of stay and recidivism: A study using regression discontinuity with multiple break points*. U.S. Department of Justice, Office of Justice Programs, Bureau of Justice Statistics. https://www.ncjrs.gov/pdffiles1/bjs/grants/251410.pdf

Riveland, C. (1999). *Supermax prisons: Overview and general considerations*. U.S. Department of Justice. https://www.prisonpolicy.org/scans/NIC_014937.pdf

Santo, A., & Iaboni, L. (2015). *What's in a prison meal?* The Marshall Project. https://www.themarshallproject.org/2015/07/07/what-s-in-a-prison-meal

Sawyer, W. (2017, April 10). *How much do incarcerated people earn in each state?* Prison Policy Initiative. https://www.prisonpolicy.org/blog/2017/04/10/wages/

Sawyer, W., & Wagner, P. (2020). *Mass incarceration: The whole pie 2020*. Prison Policy Initiative. https://www.prisonpolicy.org/reports/pie2020.html

The Sentencing Project. (2019). *Fact sheet: Trends in U.S. corrections.* https://www.sentencingproject.org/wp-content/uploads/2016/01/Trends-in-US-Corrections.pdf

The Sentencing Project. (2020, February 20). *People serving life exceeds entire prison population of 1970.* https://www.sentencingproject.org/publications/people-serving-life-exceeds-entire-prison-population-1970/

Shanahan, R., & Agudelo, S. V. (2012). *The family and recidivism.* Vera Institute of Justice. https://www.prisonpolicy.org/scans/vera/the-family-and-recidivism.pdf

Simon, J. (2007). *Governing through crime: How the war on crime transformed American democracy and created a culture of fear.* Oxford University Press.

Smith, C. (2019, May 24). *While prisoners struggle to afford calls to their families, states are making a profit. This must stop now.* Time. https://time.com/5595475/prison-phone-calls-connecticut-law/

Stateman, S. (2009, August 14). *California's prison crisis: Be very afraid.* Time. http://content.time.com/time/nation/article/0,8599,1916427,00.html

Stohr, M. K., & Walsh, A. (2021). *Corrections: From research, to policy, to practice* (2nd ed.). Sage.

Tonry, M. (1996). *Malign neglect: Race, crime, and punishment in America.* Oxford University Press.

Wakefield, S., & Wildeman, C. (2016). *Children of the prison boom: Mass incarceration and the future of American inequality.* Oxford University Press.

Walmsley, R. (2019). *World Prison Brief.* Institute for Criminal Policy Research. http://www.prison-studies.org/world-prison-brief

Wagner, P., & Jones, A. (2019). *State of phone justice: Local jails, state prisons and private phone providers.* Prison Policy Initiative. https://www.prisonpolicy.org/phones/state_of_phone_justice.html

Wagner, P., & Widra, E. (2020, March 27). *Five ways the criminal justice system could slow the pandemic.* Prison Policy Initiative. https://www.prisonpolicy.org/blog/2020/03/27/slowpandemic/

Yingling, J. (2009). Mandatory minimums. In H. T. Greene & S. L. Gabbidon (Eds.), *Encyclopedia of race and crime* (Vol. 2, pp. 471–473).

Zeng, Z. (2019). *Jail inmates in 2017.* U.S. Department of Justice, Office of Justice Programs, Bureau of Justice Statistics. https://www.bjs.gov/content/pub/pdf/ji17.pdf

Zimring, F. E., & Hawkins, G. (1995). *Incapacitation: Penal confinement and the restraint of crime.* Oxford University Press.

CHAPTER 5

Reentry and Reintegration

CHAPTER OBJECTIVES

After reading this chapter, you should be able to:

- Describe the need for reentry-based services that support reintegration into the community.
- Identify and discuss the criminogenic needs of people coming out of prisons and jails.
- Describe what makes reentry processes and programs evidence-based.
- Describe the risk-need-responsivity model of intervention.
- Recognize the need for collaborative efforts of reentry that include practitioners, researchers, and legislators.

KEY WORDS

Revolving door of criminal justice
Reentry
Reentrants
Reintegration
Cost-benefit analysis
Criminogenic
        Needs
Criminal desistance

Risk-need-responsivity model
Static risk factors
Dynamic risk factors
        General responsivity
        Specific responsivity
Silo effect
Continuity of care
Reentry coalitions

CASE STUDY: THE ALLEGHENY COUNTY JAIL COLLABORATIVE

High rates of recidivism have exposed the need for comprehensive reentry and reintegration services that can provide a continuation, or continuity, of care from incarceration to the community. In 2000, Allegheny County, Pennsylvania, which includes the city of Pittsburgh and a number of its surrounding suburbs, was experiencing rates of recidivism over 71% (Allegheny County Department of Human Services, 2021). The response was the formation of the Allegheny County Jail Collaborative (ACJC). The ACJC is a network of criminal justice and community service personnel, from both government and nonprofit agencies, overseeing one of the most comprehensive reentry and reintegration strategies in the country.

The ACJC provides medium- to high-risk individuals with needs-based services from the time they enter the jail system through their release into the community. Reentry services within the jail include cognitive behavioral therapy, drug and alcohol rehabilitation, GED prep, vocational training, job readiness programming, and family support courses. Adult Probation Community Resource Centers throughout the county help to provide continued reentry services to over 300 reentrants annually. The collaborative has been serving the county for over 20 years and is proven to be effective in two critical areas: cost savings and recidivism reduction. ACJC programming is estimated to provide $6 of cost savings for every $1 spent in correctional funding. This produces a total cost savings for the county of $5.3 million annually (Yamatani, 2008). Two separate evaluations of ACJC programming show its success in limiting recidivism. Yamatani (2008) found a 50% reduction in recidivism for reentrants, while the Urban Institute found that the collaborative reduced recidivism by 24% and significantly prolonged the time to rearrest (Willison et al., 2014). Programs that recognize the need for reentry services, from the moment someone is arrested through their successful reintegration, are a necessary tool in combatting mass incarceration.

Questions for Discussion

1. How might the needs of rural reentrants be similar to or different from the needs of those returning to urban areas?
2. What groups or individuals need to buy in to reentry programming in order for it to be effective? Why?

INTRODUCTION

As previously discussed, almost 7 million people in the United States are currently incarcerated or under some form of correctional supervision in the community. Of those, the U.S. Department of Health and Human Services (2020) estimates that "Each year, more than 600,000 individuals are released from state and federal prisons. Another 9 million cycle through local jails" (para. 1). These numbers are not surprising, given the incarceration binge that continues to impact correctional systems across the country. What is concerning about the population of people who have been imprisoned is that over two thirds of them will be rearrested within the span of 3 years (Alper et al., 2018; U.S. Department of Health and Human Services, 2020).

After the first three years post-release, the rate of rearrests continues to grow as people get farther out from their release date. In fact, between 2005 and 2014, it was estimated that 83% of state prisoners were rearrested (Alper et al., 2018). To add to this dismal picture, among the 401,288 people released in 2005, there were an average of "5 arrests per released prisoner" (p. 1). Criminal justice researchers refer to this arrest, incarceration, and release cycle, which occurs unceasingly for many people, as the **revolving door of criminal justice**. A great deal of effort has gone into understanding what drives these high rates of relapse, or recidivism.

High recidivism rates demonstrate that the criminal justice system is not working, regardless of which philosophical approach to punishment is used to explain how the system operates (see Chapter 1). From a deterrence standpoint, high recidivism rates show that people experiencing incarceration are not specifically deterred by the threat of further incarceration. From a rehabilitation perspective, the legacy of the Martinson (1974) report still rings true, as rehabilitative prison programming rarely translates into "real world" success for the person who committed a crime or into any form of restoration for the people who were harmed by that crime. Retribution, although initially somewhat satisfied by a prison sentence, is all but negated if the person who was imprisoned later victimizes someone else or continues to negatively impact society in any way. Even the idea of simply incapacitating people to limit the amount of crime on the streets is hard to justify, as we know that prisons can cultivate criminal thinking and even add to criminal opportunity (Stemen, 2017). The failure to prevent further criminality is not easily attributable to one policy or process, as it has been a gradual and collective effort.

Preventing criminal activity in its entirety is not a realistic goal, as social interaction will inevitably lead people into conflict with legally acceptable behavior. However, as the criminal justice system is largely reactionary, those of us who work within it can determine how that criminal conflict should be handled, and what our goals should be in responding to those people who perpetrate crime. This means developing an understanding of how the law itself can impact the likelihood of re-offense, including how justice procedures often negatively affect the psychological, social, and physical well-being of the people in the system, making it more likely that they will be unable to resist criminal activity. Preventing crime also requires a criminal justice system that takes a proactive approach and recognizes that the "choice" to commit crime is rarely a choice at all, but rather a complex set of interrelated and inseparable phenomena (Haney, 2020).

One of the most important processes we can examine, to try and understand why people continue to commit crime, is reentry. **Reentry**, in its most basic element, is the process of returning from confinement to the community. Reentry occurs in a number of ways; it can happen when a person completes their entire sentence, or when they are placed on community supervision to complete the remainder of their sentence, as discussed in Chapter 3. Reentry also facilitates a deeper process of reintegration. **Reintegration** is the process by which a person is reintroduced to society and also becomes a productive member of society. Many people think of the reentry and reintegration process as something that occurs at the end of a prison or jail sentence. In actuality, the ability to properly reintegrate someone into society starts with the law. Voting laws, right-to-work laws, and housing discrimination laws can all be seen as starting points for successful reentry that can either facilitate or obstruct reintegration.

Beyond the macro, or top-down, approach of considering how legislation impacts reentry, it is necessary to take a micro approach and examine the social and interpersonal effects that incarceration can have on someone. This issue extends beyond the criminal justice system and affects society and culture at large. Therefore, even general members of society who are not a part of the criminal justice system must take an active role in acknowledging and addressing reentry concerns. Knowing that incarceration can have extremely negative effects on a person's life, how can we anticipate and mitigate the damage that is done to their relationships, employability, mental health, parenting skills, and social skills? How do we remain attentive to the variable needs of men, women, and youth in the criminal justice system? Who is responsible for ensuring that reentry is carried out properly? This chapter will explore the necessity of reentry and reintegration research, planning, and implementation. This includes examining evidence-based practices that provide the best chance for the successful reintegration of **reentrants,** or those individuals who were formerly incarcerated.

THE NEED FOR REENTRY

Because the eradication of criminal activity from society is an impossibility, all we can do is attempt to control it to the best of our ability. Assessments of whether the criminal justice system adequately controls criminality usually rely on political associations and personal biases (good or bad) regarding people who have committed crime. However, the best indicators of effectiveness—which avoid personal bias—are the rates of crime and recidivism and the estimated costs of crime to society. For example, the Center for

Economic Advisors (CEA) (2016) reported that between 1980 and 2014, the U.S. incarceration rate grew by 220%, costing over $270 billion in 2016 alone. During that same period, violent crime rates decreased by 39% and property crime rates decreased by 52% (CEA, 2016). Some may see the decreasing rates of criminality as a sign of success, while others may indicate the steadily increasing costs of incarceration as a criminal justice failure.

Unfortunately, the enormous economic and social costs of crime to society cross all political and personal boundaries and warrant attention from all sides. It is extremely difficult to estimate the amount of money spent on criminal justice, but these calculations must be made in order to assess fiscal responsibility in the use of taxpayer monies. One way to understand the fiscal impact of crime is through cost-benefit analysis. **Cost-benefit analysis** attempts to determine "the worth of a program" or policy (Roman, 2004, p. 257). The problems with using a cost-benefit approach involve defining which costs and benefits to examine, and deciding how to tangibly measure both.

Downey & Roman (2014) identify two criticisms of cost-benefit analyses. The first involves attempts to place a value on crime and victimization. Trying to quantify what it means to be a victim is not only impossible, but likely unethical as well. How can the pain someone feels when their loved one is murdered be quantified? The second criticism is that a good portion of the costs and benefits involved can only be approximated. The value of things like a criminal justice practitioner's time, or how much crime and victimization have been prevented, are inherently inaccurate (Downey & Roman, 2014). The cost of a home robbery may be extensive from the perspective of the homeowner or tenant, but from the perspective of researchers, it may represent only a few thousand dollars in criminal justice costs and therefore not warrant as much attention.

Beyond the ground-level costs of crime, policy makers must also decide if implementing and funding specific policies will be effective, often by producing estimates of what Heaton (2010) calls the "tangible and intangible costs of crime" (p. 2). Heaton elaborates:

> Tangible costs involve direct financial costs to individuals, businesses, or government from out-of-pocket expenditures or lost productivity. They include such costs as property loss, medical treatment, and lost productivity for victims; crime-prevention expenditures by businesses; and expenditures for offender adjudication and incarceration by government entities. These costs can typically be measured using accounting or other expenditure data. Intangible costs involve lost quality of life resulting from fear of crime or the psychological effects of victimization. (2010, p. 2)

No matter the approach that policy makers take to quantify the costs and benefits of reentry, there is little doubt that crime and justice are expensive to American society (Ostermann & Caplan, 2016).

Ostermann & Caplan (2016) attempted to examine the cost of recidivism among former inmates of a New Jersey prison between 2005 and 2007. The study identified over 30,000 individuals with a total of 42,382 arrests occurring within 3 years of their release. The authors found that 56.32% of those released were rearrested within 3 years, which is similar to data reported at the national level. Their results indicated that those reentering society cost the state of New Jersey $2.5 billion. Other findings point to the fact that those released on parole cost the state $68,000 for new crimes, while those released without supervision cost the state $102,000. Lastly, through an examination of the risk level of criminal offenders, the authors found that placing correctional emphasis on the most high-risk offenders would likely produce cost savings over placing emphasis on all offenders including low-risk offenders (Ostermann & Caplan, 2016).

Studies like the one above show that incarceration, and the rehabilitative programming that takes place inside and outside of prisons, is not having the desired effect of either reducing recidivism or reducing the cost to the criminal justice system. In fact, due to the net-widening effect (see Chapter 4), the increased use of custodial sanctions produces a higher cost to the criminal justice system than that of using non-custodial programming (Cullen et al., 2011). Cullen et al. (2011), through an extensive review of prison-based research, also found that prisons have no real deterrent effect on inmates and that prisons may actually be **criminogenic**, meaning they can produce further criminality. That is, low-risk offenders who are incarcerated may actually "experience increased recidivism" (p. 605). Based on findings like these, the criminal justice system has a responsibility to simply do better. From a reentry and reintegration standpoint, the greatest benefit would come from reducing the continued criminal activity of people who have already been convicted of a crime.

Determining the best approach to limiting a person's criminal involvement requires looking beyond the mostly tangible variables discussed above and trying to understand the deeply personal, and sometimes troubling, experience that is incarceration. Derrick Mobley (2010) recounts his time within the criminal justice system in Philadelphia, Pennsylvania. He notes that his reentry process did not begin until a parole date had been set, and that "A few weeks of intensive reentry instruction is woefully inadequate preparation when juxtaposed to several months or years of perpetual exposure to pervasive criminal mentalities while incarcerated" (p. 572). One of his biggest obstacles was obtaining employment, even though he held multiple degrees including a doctoral degree. Thus, the very things that could prevent him from continuing in his criminality were ill-conceived, improperly managed, and potentially criminogenic (Mobley, 2010).

Derrick Mobley's time incarcerated is not unique; the ills of prison, and the inability of criminal justice systems to adequately prepare someone for their reentry into society, are well documented. It was undoubtedly Martinson's (1974) report that catapulted the problematic nature of rehabilitative and reentry programs into the spotlight, but the conservative shift in punishment that would follow placed this issue on the back burner. The last 2 decades have seen a renewed sense of interest in prisoner reentry. As Petersilia (2004) notes, "Between 2001 and 2004, the federal government allocated over $100 million to support the development of new reentry programs in all 50 states" (p. 4). This is also likely why there has been an abundance of "what works" research taking place across the country. The renewed focus on reentry has provided numerous studies, guides, and evaluations that can move criminal justice toward an effective framework for doing reentry well.

Conceptualizing Successful Reentry

If it has not yet become clear, the variability in every aspect of the criminal justice system makes it difficult to draw concrete conclusions about almost everything that goes on within it. The same holds true for reentry processes. Even defining what reentry is, in order to study or evaluate it, continues to be cause for debate (Petersilia, 2004). Some scholars define reentry in the broad sense, seeing it as an inevitability that nearly all inmates will be faced with; others define it more narrowly, focusing on specific programmatic outcomes that link prison and community treatment (Petersilia, 2004). Definitional issues unfortunately plague the outcome measures of reentry as well.

A common theme throughout reentry-based research has been the use of recidivism data as the sole indicator of success (Butts & Schiraldi, 2018). From basic measures such as rearrest within the first 6 months, to more complex survival data that track how long an individual is in the community before recidivating, various types of data have been used to argue proof of reentry effectiveness. However, these measures often fall short of truly capturing the positive effects of reentry. In some cases, the data "may even be harmful, as it often reinforces the racial and class biases underlying much of the justice system" (Butts & Schiraldi, 2018, p. 2). This has also left many jurisdictions with the expectation that the first thing they must do in order to implement effective reentry strategies is to develop a definition of reentry. However, the need to develop this definition can often stalemate any progress toward reentry, and this should not become a prerequisite for developing reentry strategies.

Researchers have begun to argue for a movement away from a strict reliance on recidivism data and toward reliance on the more complete indicators of criminal desistance. **Criminal desistance** is the transition a person goes through until they stop criminally offending completely (Laub & Sampson, 2001). Criminal desistance can be seen as a more complete indication of a person's successful progress toward a crime-free life. Kazemian (2015) suggests that "A recidivism-focused approach disregards changes and progress exhibited in other behavioral, cognitive and social outcomes" and that "desistance should extend beyond offending outcomes, and include variables such as improvements in mental health and thinking styles, social bonds and integration, and other behaviors" (p. 2).

The process of desistance also means that even if someone recidivates, they may still be desisting from crime. If a person imprisoned for armed robbery is released from prison and commits a petty theft, a measure of recidivism (which does not distinguish between crimes) will indicate a failure of the reentry process. However, from a criminal desistance perspective, that person may well be on their way toward ceasing criminal activity altogether. In this framework, it is not beneficial for the system of reentry to sensationalize small failures or relapses of criminality. Rather than focusing on the failures of people reentering society, "A desistance framework encourages justice agencies to promote and monitor positive outcomes" (Butts & Schiraldi, 2018, p. 9). The wealth of evidence that has been established in the literature on rehabilitation, reentry, recidivism, and criminal desistance provides a framework of policies, programs, and practices that are likely to contribute to the success of reentrants.

Reentry Approaches

As discussed in Chapter 1, one of the major movements in criminal justice has been toward that of evidence-based practices. The phrase "evidence-based practice" (EBP), while newly adopted by the criminal justice system, has been used within scientific fields of study for years. In medicine, where the term originated, the introduction of EBPs meant moving away from decision-making models that relied on intuition and clinical experience and toward models of scientific evaluation and understanding (Zimmerman, 2013). EBPs are widely regarded as having the greatest impact on reentry outcomes and have become the "gold standard" in reentry processes. The National Institute of Corrections (2020) defines evidence-based practices in criminal justice as:

> The objective, balanced, and responsible use of current research and the best available data to guide policy and practice decisions, such that outcomes for consumers are improved. An evidence-based approach involves an ongoing, critical review of research literature to determine what information is credible, and what policies and practices would be most effective given the best available evidence. (para. 1)

One EBP that is now widely regarded as a cornerstone of proper reentry procedures is the **risk-need-responsivity model** (RNR), which was developed in 1990 by several scholars from Canada (Andrews et al., 2011). The RNR approach views reentry as a process and emphasizes the steps that need to be taken in order for a person to be successful once they are released from confinement. Specifically, RNR emphasizes the importance of using risk and needs assessments to understand an individual offender's specific criminogenic issues and triggers, which can lead to reoffending. The RNR model uses validated screening and assessment tools to identify the most appropriate levels of supervision, services, and treatment for each offender. The benefit of using this model is that it can help policy makers, administrators, and practitioners effectively allocate resources, deliver services, and successfully manage corrections interventions, in order to have the greatest impact on public safety and recidivism. A vast amount of research indicates that the proper implementation of RNR principles in a diverse range of settings (e.g., jails, prisons, probation, and parole) can significantly reduce recidivism rates (Andrews & Bonta, 2007; Bonta & Andrews, 2007; Latessa et al., 2010).

RISK

The risk principle of the RNR model attempts to match the intensity of an offender's interventions to their level of risk for future criminal activity. In this approach, it is of particular importance to identify the high-risk offenders, as higher-risk groups generally pose a significantly greater risk of recidivism (Latessa & Lowenkamp, 2006). Research indicates that prioritizing supervision and services for individuals at a moderate or higher risk of re-offending leads to a more significant reduction in recidivism among these offenders (Clement et al., 2006; Lowenkamp et al., 2006). Conversely, intensive interventions for individuals who are at a low risk of recidivism can be counterproductive and may actually increase their likelihood of criminal behavior, not to mention misuse resources (Andrews & Dowden, 2006).

In order to ensure that an offender receives the amount of intensive supervision and intervention that corresponds to their risk level, it is imperative that trained personnel establish an offender's risk level through the use of reliable and valid screening and assessment tools. Empirically based assessment tools help identify the risk factors most strongly associated with future criminal activity. Assessment tools also identify an offender's specific needs that, if unaddressed, can make it difficult for them to benefit from a particular intervention. These assessment instruments help determine both placement and programming decisions (e.g., supervision levels for adults on probation and parole). Most importantly, they can guide subsequent placement in the most appropriate treatment programs, before and during the time period in which an offender reenters the community. A number of assessment tools have been validated for use in reentry. Although these tools will not be focused on in depth, Andrews et al. (2011) note that one in particular, the Level of Service assessment, along with its component pieces, is the assessment tool which most closely follows the RNR principles.

Researchers have placed empirically based risk factors into two categories: **static risk factors** that are unable to be changed, such as the age at first offense or gender, and **dynamic risk factors** or criminogenic factors, which can be changed through appropriate interventions. The following dynamic risk factors have been empirically shown to significantly affect recidivism rates (Bonta & Andrews, 2007).

- **Antisocial Personality Pattern:** individuals who are adventurous and pleasure-seeking, possess weak self-control, and are restlessly aggressive and irritable.
- **Procriminal Attitudes:** those who have rationalizations supportive of crime and who hold negative attitudes toward the law and justice systems.
- **Social Supports for Crime:** those who have a close association with criminal friends and are somewhat isolate from law-abiding individuals.
- **Substance Abuse:** those who abuse alcohol &/or other drugs
- **Family and/or Marital:** those with poor familial relationships, including inappropriate and inconsistent parental monitoring and disciplining.
- **School and/or Work:** those with low levels of performance and satisfaction in school and/or work.
- **Prosocial Recreational/Leisure Activities:** those with low involvement and satisfaction in prosocial activities.

NEED

The need principle of the RNR model suggests that case management should prioritize the core "criminogenic needs" as evidenced by the dynamic risk factors listed above. Those dynamic factors can be translated into needs that can be effectively treated through services, supervision, and supports. Research indicates that the greater the number of criminogenic needs addressed through interventions, both in the correctional facility and in the community, the more positive impact the interventions will have on lowering recidivism rates (Andrews & Bonta, 2007; Andrews et al., 2006; Bourgon & Armstrong, 2005). Most of the criminogenic needs addressed in these interventions are measured in the aforementioned assessments, which include: history of antisocial behavior, procriminal attitudes, antisocial personality (e.g., low self-control), pro-criminal associates, social/achievement issues (e.g., education, employment, and housing), family/marital relationship issues (e.g., poor parenting skills), lack of leisure/recreational activities and pursuits, and substance abuse (Andrews & Bonta, 2010; Andrews & Dowden, 2007; Looman & Abracen, 2013).

RESPONSIVITY

The responsivity principle of the RNR model is arguably the most important, as it attempts to fold high-quality EBPs into the reentry process. Once risk and criminogenic needs are assessed, often by parole/probation officers or reentry specialists, a reentry plan is developed that includes the programming necessary to address a person's risk and need factors (or the *response*). The responsivity principle also includes two parts, general and specific responsivity. **General responsivity** refers to the utilization of interventions that have had the greatest impact on reentrants, which are "those based on cognitive, behavioral, and social learning theories" (Smith et al., 2009, p. 154). **Specific responsivity** refers to the pairing of reentrants with treatment programs and services that support their individual characteristics as well, including those listed outside of the criminogenic needs above, such as temperament or criminal motivation (Smith et al., 2009). Being responsive to the needs and risks of reentrants by coupling them with appropriate reentry services and programs can also be one of the most difficult things to do.

When jurisdictions are struggling to adequately manage criminal populations, they may also be unable to provide a large array of evidence-based services to reentrants. Beyond that, probation and parole officers are often the same people who must translate risk and needs assessments into workable reentry plans that can produce sustainable outcomes, while simultaneously monitoring the progress of reentrants. The importance of these officers' work should not be understated, as they have an enormous amount of responsibility in ensuring that EBPs are properly carried out (Viglione, 2017). Yet, they are consistently asked to manage larger caseloads with less and less resources (Bonta et al., 2011). In addition to relying on the officers themselves, providing extensive reentry services necessitates a collaborative and supportive approach from legislators, researchers, and practitioners alike (Burke, 2008).

SUPPORTING EVIDENCE-BASED REENTRY

Supporting the development and implementation of EBPs, in both correctional facilities and the community, often requires a restructuring of the "silo effect" that tends to take hold throughout criminal justice agencies (Borakove et al., 2015). The **silo effect** simply refers to the fact that criminal justice agencies and departments primarily focus their attention inward, limiting the collaboration and sharing of data across agencies. Borakove et al. (2015) describe the effects of the silo effect on justice:

> For many jurisdictions, the desire to break down the silos is strong, but the knowledge of how to do so is lacking. Policies and practices are entrenched and those within the system are left operating within the confines of "it's just the way it is." (p. 3)

When criminal justice agencies become complacent about doing reentry their own way, it can become a barrier to the development and implementation of EBPs that can improve the quality of reentry. According to Borakove et al. (2015), jurisdictions that have created a "culture of collaboration," where all agencies are working toward a common goal, are improving "fairness and equality, increasing access to justice, and reducing the misuse and overuse of jails" (p. 3). One of the most important places to break down silo walls is in probation and parole departments.

A great deal of the work that goes on in reentry occurs through probation and parole departments. Many departments have now begun placing officers who are trained in reentry practices inside prisons and jails, allowing for better avenues of communication. This also gives them the opportunity to facilitate the reentry planning process, with the help of correctional officials on the inside and service providers on the outside. Doing so provides a level of continuity of care. **Continuity of care** is the process of tying programs from correctional facilities together with community-based programs, to ensure there is no lapse in treatment. Unfortunately, departments across the country are still lacking this ability, due to fiscal or ideological issues. Training (and in some cases transforming) probation and parole departments and officers at all levels to be better overseers of EBPs is imperative to a reentry process (Bond & Gittell, 2010; Burke, 2008).

Probation and parole departments at all levels have been one of the driving forces in places where collaborative efforts of reentry have been realized. Throughout Pennsylvania, county probation and parole departments have helped to develop county reentry coalitions. **Reentry coalitions** are groups of criminal justice reentry stakeholders, including county officials, service providers, criminal justice agencies, and reentrants themselves. Several counties have also included local university researchers in their reentry coalitions in order to better develop strategies for EBP evaluation and implementation. The work of reentry coalitions at the county level is supported by the state through the Pennsylvania Commission on Crime and Delinquency (PCCD) and the Pennsylvania Reentry Council (PARC). PCCD offers grants and information-sharing opportunities to support EBPs and other reentry processes throughout Pennsylvania's 67 counties. PARC was established in May 2017 in order to provide a direct link between county reentry coalitions and state policy makers, including the attorney general and the governor. Over 30 counties currently utilize reentry coalitions, each of which reports to PARC regularly, allowing them to directly influence criminal justice legislation.

The link between state policy makers in Pennsylvania and those working in reentry has exposed a harsh reality for returning citizens: The law is not on their side, and it typically does not favor their successful reintegration. The law does not support those convicted of a crime, especially a felony crime. A litany of legal barriers to reentry exists in employment, licensing, voting, legal services, record expungement, substance abuse treatment, and many other areas. These barriers also represent the same dynamic need factors that have been discussed within the RNR model. Without addressing the legislative and legal barriers to reentry, reentrants will continue to be unsuccessful in remaining crime-free. Thankfully, in 2019, over 150 laws were passed to help eliminate the barriers to reentry (Love & Schlussel, 2020). One of the dynamic need areas that has been most problematic for reentrants is that of obtaining housing.

The process of procuring housing is often complicated by a number of factors: the scarcity of affordable and available housing, legal barriers and regulations (depending on conviction), prejudices that restrict tenancy (especially for sex offenders or those convicted of drug offenses), strict eligibility requirements for federally subsidized housing, and the fact that many families may not allow offenders to return home upon their release (Lutze et al., 2014). The lack of housing availability has consequences for both the convicted person and the community: Research indicates that reentrants who do not have stable housing arrangements are more likely to commit crimes and return to prison than those with stable housing arrangements (Metraux & Culhane, 2004). Researchers have identified three key factors that affect successful reentry in regard to housing: (1) the accessibility of housing, (2) increasing available housing units for returning offenders, and (3) neighborhood revitalization (Cortes & Rogers, 2010). A number of states are currently addressing the accessibility of housing by passing legislation that bars discrimination based on criminal conviction (Love & Schlussel, 2020).

Another area of recent legislative improvement involves employment opportunities for convicted persons. The relationship between employment and recidivism has been studied extensively, and it has been found that employment issues can precede criminal involvement and are exacerbated by a criminal conviction (Tripodi et al., 2010). While the research is mixed on what type of employment is most beneficial, the general consensus is that reentrants with gainful employment fare better than their counterparts, yet finding that employment can be extremely difficult (Duwe, 2015; Ramakers et al., 2017; Tripodi et al., 2010). Couloute and Kopf (2018) reported that "the unemployment rate for formerly incarcerated people was 27.3% compared with just 5.2% unemployment for their general public peers" and that the jobs they were likely to receive were mostly insecure jobs (para. 7).

Thirty-five states and the federal government have attempted to reconcile some of these problems through legislative actions like "ban the box" and "fair chance" laws, which no longer allow employers to inquire about a person's criminal record on the application (Avery & Lu, 2019). This gives reentrants more of an opportunity to make it to the interviewing stage, where they have a much better chance of securing employment after explaining their criminal conviction. In Pennsylvania, after pressure from PARC and member organizations, Governor Tom Wolf signed legislation in 2020 that creates new standards for the 255 occupations that require licenses to practice. Laws that once allowed a license to be denied because the applicant lacked "good moral character" have been revamped, to provide licensing agencies with a wider latitude in granting occupational licenses (Collateral Consequences Resource Center, 2020). The ability of legislatures to influence the outcomes of reentry and reintegration is something that should be front-and-center in any discussion of reentry processes moving forward.

EVIDENCED-BASED EXAMPLES

As is hopefully evident from the discussion of the RNR model above, this approach to reentry is not simply a "blueprint" that counties or states can plug inmates into. Rather, the RNR model is a set of guiding principles and a form of EBP that can be referenced as reentry policies, programming, and procedures are developed and selected. As mentioned, those that match most closely with the RNR approach tend to produce better and more consistent results. Table 5.1 identifies a number of resources, both nonprofit and governmental, that house evidence-based research and programming.

Table 5.1 EBP Resources and Clearinghouses.

Blueprints for Violence Prevention	www.colorado.edu/cspv/blueprints
Campbell Collaboration	www.campbellcollaboration.org
Coalition for Evidence-Based Policy: Social Programs that Work	www.evidencebasedprograms.org
Cochrane Collaboration	www.cochrane.org
Department of Education: What Works Clearinghouse	ies.ed.gov/ncee/wwc
Evidence-Based Practices for Substance Abuse Disorders	adai.washington.edu/ebp
Office of Juvenile Justice and Delinquency Prevention: Model Programs Guide	www.ojjdp.gov/mpg
Pacific Northwest Evidence-Based Practice Center	www.ohsu.edu/evidence-based-practice-center
Substance Abuse and Mental Health Services Administration: Evidence-Based Practices Resource Center	www.samhsa.gov/ebp-resource-center
Society for Prevention Research	www.preventionresearch.org
Washington State Institute for Public Policy	www.wsipp.wa.gov
National Institute of Corrections	nicic.gov/evidence-based-practices-ebp www.nicic.gov/evidence-based-practices-criminal-justice-system-annotated-bibliography

(continued)

Table 5.1 EBP Resources and Clearinghouses.   *(continued)*

National Institute of Justice	www.crimesolutions.ojp.gov/
Center for Court Innovation	www.courtinnovation.org/areas-of-focus/evidence-based-practices
Office of Criminal Justice Services (Ohio)	www.ocjs.ohio.gov/ebp.stm#gsc.tab=0
Juvenile Justice Information Exchange	www.jjie.org/hub/evidence-based-practices/

Note. Adapted and expanded from "Issues in defining and applying evidence-based practices criteria for treatment of criminal-justice involved clients," by M. L. Pendergrast, 2011, *Journal of Psychoactive Drugs, 43*(S1), pp. 10–18.

CONCLUSION

Correcting criminal behavior is not an easy task, but it is one that falls squarely on the criminal justice system. The complexity of human behavior means that individuals could be committing crime for any number of reasons. Factors like poverty, lack of education, experiences of trauma, and substance abuse, among others, are not mutually exclusive; when compounded, they can make the reentry and reintegration process that much more difficult. Couple those issues with a lack of institutional support from local, state, and federal legislatures, and it is easy to understand why exponentially high rates of recidivism continue.

Recent responses to criminality have begun to move away from the "lock them up and throw away the key" mentality that produced harsh criminal sanctions over the last 5 decades. Evidence-based approaches that are well thought out, collaborative, comprehensive, and sensitive to the litany of needs of persons convicted of a crime are taking shape across the country. These have been supported by legislative actions in nearly all 50 states, and by the Federal Government. As we move further toward a rehabilitation and reintegration mindset, criminal justice practitioners must become well-versed in EBPs and the RNR model, as the success of reentrants will continue to depend on the criminal justice system's ability to balance safety with effective intervention.

DISCUSSION QUESTIONS

- Who do you think has the most important role in ensuring that a person does not recidivate and why?
- How can the criminal justice system better support individuals who are attempting to reintegrate into society?
- What are some of the ways we can begin to break down the "silos" that can hinder criminal justice reform?

APPLICATION EXERCISES

Exercise #1: Supporting Local Reentry

A lot of the work that is done in reentry is done at the local level. Reentrants coming out of prisons and jails have long lists of needs to help them acclimate to society. Contact your local prison or jail and inquire about the reentry process in your area. Be sure to ask about programs that are currently being offered, and if there are areas where community support could be offered. Think about starting a program, like a clothing drive for reentrants going on job interviews, or providing informational sessions about drug and alcohol services in the local community. The options are endless, and your support can make all the difference in someone's life.

Exercise #2: Reentry Informational

As a class, or as individual groups within a class, determine what you believe to be the most pressing need of returning citizens in your local community. Is it supportive housing? Substance abuse treatment? Employment opportunities? Explore further what the research says about that need. Examine your local policies on these issues. Examine the clearinghouses listed above and the programs they offer. Prepare an informational presentation for criminal justice officials, or for inmates themselves, on the benefits of developing similar evidence-based practices in your community.

REFERENCES

Andrews, D. A., & Bonta, J. (2007). The risk-need-responsivity model of assessment and human service in prevention and corrections: Crime-prevention jurisprudence. *The Canadian Journal of Criminology and Criminal Justice, 49*(4), pp. 439–464.

Andrews, D. A., & Bonta, J. (2010). Viewing offender assessment and rehabilitation through the lens of the risk-need-responsivity model. In: F. McNeil, P. Raynor, & C. Trotter (Eds.) *Offender supervision: New directions in theory, research and practice* (pp. 19–40). Willan Publishing.

Andrews, D. A., & Dowden, C. (2006). Risk principle of case classification in correctional treatment: A meta-analytic investigation. *International Journal of Offender Therapy and Comparative Criminology, 50*(1), 88–100.

Andrews, D. A., & Dowden, C. (2007). The risk-need-responsivity model of assessment and human service in prevention and corrections: Crime-prevention jurisprudence. *Canadian Journal of Criminology and Criminal Justice, 49*(4), 439–464.

Andrews, D. A., Bonta, J., & Wormith, J. S. (2006). The recent past and near future of risk and/or need assessment. *Crime & Delinquency, 52*(1), 7–27.

Andrews, D. A., Bonta, J., & Wormith, J. S. (2011). The risk-need-responsivity (RNR) model: Does adding the good lives model contribute to effective crime prevention? *Criminal Justice and Behavior, 38*(7), 735–755.

Alper, M., Durose, M. R., & Markman, J. (2018). *2018 update on prisoner recidivism: A 9-year follow-up period (2005–2014)*. U.S. Department of Justice. https://www.bjs.gov/content/pub/pdf/18upr9yfup0514.pdf

Avery, B. & Lu, H. (2019). *Ban the box: U.S. cities, counties, and states adopt fair hiring policies*. National Employment Law Project. https://www.nelp.org/publication/ban-the-box-fair-chance-hiring-state-and-local-guide/

Bond, B. J., & Gittell, J. H. (2010). Cross-agency coordination of offender reentry: Testing collaboration outcomes. *Journal of Criminal Justice, 38*(2), 11–129.

Bonta, J., & Andrews, D. A. (2007). *Risk-Need-Responsivity model for offender assessment and rehabilitation*. Public Safety Canada. https://www.publicsafety.gc.ca/cnt/rsrcs/pblctns/rsk-nd-rspnsvty/rsk-nd-rspnsvty-eng.pdf

Bonta, J., Bourgon, G., Rugge, T., Scott, T. L., Yessine, A. K., Gutierrez, L., & Li, J. (2011). *Criminal Justice and Behavior, 38*(11), 1127–1148.

Borakove, M. E., Wosje, R., Cruz, F., Wickman, A., Dibble, T., & Harbus, C. (2015). *From silo to system: What makes a criminal justice system operate like a system*. MacArthur Foundation. https://warrencopa.com/wp-content/uploads/2018/08/JMI_From-Silo-to-System-30-APR-2015_FINAL.pdf

Bourgon, G., & Armstrong, B. (2005). Transferring the principles of effective treatment into a "real world" prison setting. *Criminal Justice and Behavior, 32*(1), 3–25.

Burke, P. B. (2008). *TPC reentry handbook: Implementing the NIC transition from prison to the community model*. National Institute of Corrections. https://s3.amazonaws.com/static.nicic.gov/Library/022669.pdf

Butts, J. A., & Schiraldi, V. (2018, March). *Recidivism reconsidered: Preserving the community justice mission of community corrections*. Program in Criminal Justice Policy and Management, Harvard Kennedy School. https://www.hks.harvard.edu/sites/default/files/centers/wiener/programs/pcj/files/recidivism_reconsidered.pdf

Center for Economic Advisors. (2016). *Economic perspectives on incarceration and the criminal justice system*. https://obamawhitehouse.archives.gov/sites/whitehouse.gov/files/documents/CEA%2BCriminal%2BJustice%2BReport.pdf

Clement, M., Schwarzfeld, M., & Thompson, M. (2011). *The national summit on justice reinvestment and public safety: Addressing recidivism, crime, and corrections spending*. Council of State Governments Justice Center. https://bja.ojp.gov/sites/g/files/xyckuh186/files/media/document/csg_justicereinvestmentsummitreport.pdf

Collateral Consequences Resource Center. (2020). *Pennsylvania expands access to 255 licensed occupations for people with a record*. https://ccresourcecenter.org/2020/07/14/pennsylvania-expands-access-to-255-licensed-occupations-for-people-with-a-record/

Cortes, K., & Rogers, S. (2010). *Reentry housing options: The policymakers' guide.* Council of State Governments Justice Center. https://bja.ojp.gov/sites/g/files/xyckuh186/files/Publications/CSG_Reentry_Housing.pdf

Couloute, L., & Kopf, D. (2018). *Out of prison & out of work: Unemployment among formerly incarcerated people.* Prison Policy Initiative. https://www.prisonpolicy.org/reports/outofwork.html

Cullen, F. T., Jonson, C. L., & Nagin, D. S. (2011). Prisons do not reduce recidivism: The high cost of ignoring science. *The Prison Journal, 91*(3), 48S–65S.

Downey, M., & Roman, J. K. (2014). *Cost-benefit analysis: A guide for drug courts and other criminal justice programs.* National Institute of Justice. https://www.ncjrs.gov/pdffiles1/nij/246769.pdf

Duwe, G. (2015). The benefits of keeping idle hands busy: An outcome evaluation of a prisoner reentry employment program. *Crime & Delinquency, 61*(4), 559–586.

Haney, C. (2020). *Criminality in context: The psychological foundations of criminal justice reform.* American Psychological Association.

Heaton, P. (2010). *Hidden in plain sight: What cost-of-crime research can tell us about investing in police.* RAND. https://www.rand.org/content/dam/rand/pubs/occasional_papers/2010/RAND_OP279.pdf

Kazemian, L. (2015). *Straight lives: The balance between human dignity, public safety, and desistance from crime.* Research & Evaluation Center, John Jay College of Criminal Justice. https://johnjayrec.nyc/2015/08/24/kazemian2015/

Latessa, E., Brusman Lovins, L., & Smith, P. (2010). *Follow-up evaluation of Ohio's community based correctional facility and halfway house programs—outcome study.* Center for Criminal Justice Research, University of Cincinnati. https://www.uc.edu/content/dam/uc/ccjr/docs/reports/project_reports/2010%20HWH%20Executive%20Summary.pdf

Latessa, E. J., & Lowenkamp, C. (2006). What works in reducing recidivism? *University of St. Thomas Law Journal, 3*(3), 521–535.

Laub, J. H., & Sampson, R. J. (2001). Understanding desistance from crime. *Crime and Justice, 28*, 1–69.

Looman, J. & Abracen, J. (2013). The risk need responsivity model of offender rehabilitation: Is there really a need for a paradigm shift? *International Journal of Behavioral Consultation and Therapy, 8*(3–4), 30–36.

Love, M., & Schlussel, D. (2020). *Pathways to reintegration: Criminal records reforms in 2019.* Collateral Consequences Resource Center. https://www.prisonlegalnews.org/media/publications/Collateral_Consequences_Resource_Center_-_Pathways_to_Reintegration_Criminal_Record_Reforms_in_2019.pdf

Lowenkamp, C. T., Latessa, E. J., & Holsinger, A. M. (2006). The risk principle in action: What have we learned from 13,676 offenders and 97 correctional programs? *Crime & Delinquency, 52*(1), 77–93.

Lutze, F. E., Rosky, J. W., & Hamilton, Z. K. (2014). Homelessness and reentry: A multisite outcome evaluation of Washington State's reentry housing program for high risk offenders. *Criminal Justice and Behavior, 41*(4), 471–491.

Metraux, S., & Culhane, D. P. (2004). Homeless shelter use and reincarceration following prison release. *Criminology & Public Policy, 3,* 139–160.

Mobley, D. K. (2010). A personal perspective on reentry services. *Dialectical Anthropology, 34*(4), 571–574.

Martinson, R. (1974). What works? Questions and answers about prison reform. *The Public Interest, 35,* 22–54.

National Institute of Corrections. (2020). *Evidence-based practices.* https://nicic.gov/evidence-based-practices-ebp

Ostermann, M., & Caplan, J. M. (2016). How much do the crimes committed by released inmates cost? *Crime & Delinquency, 62*(5), 563–591.

Pendergrast, M. L. (2011). Issues in defining and applying evidence-based practices criteria for treatment of criminal-justice involved clients. *Journal of Psychoactive Drugs, 43*(S1), 10–18.

Petersilia, J. (2004). What works in prisoner reentry? Reviewing and questioning the evidence. *Federal Probation, 68*(2), 4–8.

Ramakers, A., Nieuwbeerta, P., Van Wilsem, J., & Dorkzwager, A. (2017). Not just any job will do: A study on employment characteristics and recidivism risks after release. *International Journal of Offender Therapy and Comparative Criminology, 61*(16), 1795–1818.

Roman, J. (2004). Can cost-benefit analysis answer criminal justice policy questions, and if so, how? *Journal of Contemporary Criminal Justice, 20*(3), 257–275.

Smith, P., Gendreau, P., & Swartz, K. (2009). Validating the principles of effective intervention: A systematic review of the contributions of meta-analysis in the field of corrections. *Victims and Offenders, 4,* 148–169.

Stemen, D. (2017). *The prison paradox: More incarceration will not make us safer.* Vera Institute of Justice. https://www.vera.org/downloads/publications/for-the-record-prison-paradox_02.pdf

Tripodi, S. J., Kim, J. S., & Bender, K. (2010). Is employment associated with reduced recidivism? The complex relationship between employment and crime. *International Journal of Offender Therapy and Comparative Criminology, 54*(5), 706–720.

U.S. Department of Health and Human Services. (2020). *Incarceration & reentry.* https://aspe.hhs.gov/incarceration-reentry

Viglione, J. (2017). Acceptability, feasibility, and use of evidence-based practices in adult probation. *Criminal Justice and Behavior, 44*(10), 1356–1381.

Willison, J. B., Bieler, S. G., & Kideuk, K. (2014). *Evaluation of the Allegheny County jail collaborative reentry programs: Findings and Recommendations.* Urban Institute.

Zimmerman, A. L. (2013). Evidence-based medicine: A short history of a modern medical movement. *American Medical Association Journal of Ethics, 15*(1), 71–76.

Correctional Populations

CHAPTER 6

Constitutional Rights of Incarcerated Persons

CHAPTER OBJECTIVES

After reading this chapter, you should be able to:

- Explain how the "hands-off" and "hands-on" approaches taken by the Supreme Court differ, and how these approaches impacted incarcerated persons' rights.
- Recognize the various constitutional amendments that apply to incarcerated persons' rights and the key constitutional challenges facing incarcerated persons.
- Identify key pieces of legislation that relate to incarcerated persons' rights, and understand how this legislation has impacted their right to find redress through the court system.

KEY WORDS

Bivens doctrine

Constitutional torts

Eighth Amendment

Federal Torts Claim Act (FTCA)

Fifth Amendment

First Amendment

14th Amendment

Fourth Amendment

Habeas corpus

"Hands-off" approach

"Hands-on" approach

Hunger strike

Injunctive relief

Legal correspondence

The Prison Litigation Reform Act (PLRA)

Standards Relating to the Legal Status of
      Prisoners

CASE STUDY: DISABILITY RIGHTS IN CALIFORNIA PRISONS

The California Department of Corrections & Rehabilitation (CDCR) is responsible for housing incarcerated persons in the state of California. In recent years, a number of lawsuits have been filed against the CDCR on behalf of disabled persons who felt their rights were being violated. One particular group that has helped in filing these suits is the Prison Law Office. The first suit filed by the Prison Law Office was a class-action lawsuit in 1994, on behalf of those with disabilities who were in CDCR custody. The lawsuit alleged that access to programming and services for disabled prisons was not equal, both during their incarceration and while they were on parole. The court ruled in favor of the plaintiffs and found the CDCR was violating the Americans with Disabilities Act, forcing the CDCR to improve accommodations (Prison Law Office, 2021).

More recently, the Prison Law Office filed a motion in regard to the safe housing of incarcerated persons with disabilities during the COVID-19 pandemic. A motion was filed in July 2020 stating that the CDCR placed persons with disabilities at the California Institution for Men in inaccessible settings. The claim is that those individuals with significant underlying health conditions were housed in crowded dormitories, resulting in many of them getting infected with COVID-19. A California judge issued an order requiring the CDCR to create and maintain housing for the purposes of medical isolation and quarantine (Prison Law Office, 2021). It should be noted that in addition to cases regarding disability laws, the Prison Law Office also litigates in cases regarding the condition of county jails, immigration detention, and rights for those serving life without parole. More information on the litigation this group is involved with is at the following link: https://prisonlaw.com/major-cases/

Questions for Discussion

1. What accommodations do you think should be made for disabled incarcerated persons? What can be done to make sure access to programming and services is equal for all incarcerated persons?

2. Do you think that prison facilities should be required to maintain separate areas for isolation and quarantine of incarcerated persons with airborne diseases like COVID-19? What are the benefits of doing this? What are the potential drawbacks of doing this?

INTRODUCTION

In July 2013, over 30,000 incarcerated persons in California went on a **hunger strike**, which is prolonged refusal to eat, to protest the state's use of maximum-security prisons and solitary confinement (Carroll, 2013). After two months of the hunger strike, California prison officials obtained a federal court order allowing them to force-feed those protesting. This created a rift in the medical community, in which some medical experts argued that force-feeding incarcerated persons against their will, particularly those with "do not resuscitate" orders, was medically inappropriate (Kim, 2015). While the hunger strike ended before any force-feeding was conducted, the question over the appropriateness of force-feeding methods still looms. Further, this leads to bigger questions regarding the constitutional rights of incarcerated persons in the United States.

A question that may come to mind is: "What rights do incarcerated persons have?" In the United States, the most important source of incarcerated persons' rights is the Constitution of the United States, with the Supreme Court having the final say in regard to these rights (Cripe, 1997). Over the past half-century, there have been thousands of court cases involving incarcerated persons grieving over correctional operations, and the majority of these cases are on the basis of constitutional rights violations (Mitchell, 2003). The purpose of this chapter is to explore the constitutional rights of incarcerated persons, highlighting the ways in which the Constitution has been historically interpreted in regard to the rights of incarcerated persons.

INCARCERATED PERSONS' RIGHTS AND THE "HANDS-OFF" APPROACH

As stated, over the past 50 years, the American courts system has become more involved in matters related to the constitutional rights of incarcerated persons. Prior to the prison reform movement of the 1970s, the courts took what is known as a **"hands-off" approach** when dealing with prisons and the cases of incarcerated persons. Simply put, the courts did not want to interfere with how incarcerated persons were treated, as the prevailing philosophy during this time period was that the warden and those who ran prisons were in charge of controlling the people incarcerated there, not the judicial system (Cripe, 1997). Change came in the 1960s and 1970s when women's rights and civil rights came to the forefront of American politics, and this change ultimately trickled down into the corrections system (Herson, 1990). Politicians, particularly liberal politicians, had an increased concern for the quality of life around them, including the quality of life for those who were incarcerated. Several cases of injustice in prison caught the attention of young reform lawyers, such as an Alaskan prison where 40 incarcerated persons shared 20 beds, one toilet, and one shower. In another case from Arkansas, it was discovered that incarcerated persons were being administered electrical shocks as punishment, without any form of hearing to determine if the incarcerated persons were in violation of prison regulations (Collins, 1990). When cases like these came to light, it was evident that the court system needed to get involved, essentially ending the "hands-off" approach that had prevailed prior to these cases.

INCARCERATED PERSONS' RIGHTS AND THE "HANDS-ON" APPROACH

While the Federal Civil Rights Acts was passed in 1871, civil rights regarding litigation for incarcerated persons did not come to light until the 1960s and 1970s, beginning what is known as the **"hands-on" approach** (Collins, 1990). According to Title 28 of the Federal Bureau of Prisons, incarcerated persons are afforded the following rights:

1. The right to expect that as a human being you will be treated respectfully, impartially, and fairly by all personnel.
2. The right to be informed of the rules, procedures, and schedules concerning the operation of the institution.
3. The right to freedom of religious affiliation and voluntary religious worship.
4. The right to health care, which includes nutritious meals, proper bedding and clothing, a laundry schedule, an opportunity to shower regularly, proper ventilation for warmth and fresh air, a regular exercise period, toilet articles, and necessary medical and dental treatment.
5. The right to visit and correspond with family members and friends and correspond with members of the news media in keeping with department rules and institution guidelines.
6. The right to unrestricted and confidential access to the courts by correspondence.
7. The right to legal counsel from an attorney of your choice.
8. The right to participate in the use of law libraries and reference materials to assist in resolving legal problems.
9. The right to reading materials for educational purposes and enjoyment.
10. The right to participate in education, vocational training, and employment as far as resources are available.
11. The right to use your monetary funds as one pleases, if in compliance with security and good order of the institution. (Cripe, 1997, pp. 180–182)

Further, in 1977, the American Bar Association (ABA) created the **Standards Relating to the Legal Status of Prisoners**. These standards cover the rights of incarcerated persons throughout the entire criminal justice process, from arrest to post-conviction. Some of the rights not specifically mentioned by the Federal Bureau of Prisons but mentioned in the ABA standards include:

1. The right to employment, including furlough, work release programs, and private enterprises.
2. Entitlement to compensation for employment that is comparable to a free person doing the same duties outside of prison. This includes all privileges guaranteed by the Occupational Safety and Health Act (OSHA).
3. The right to medical services, including physical, dental, and psychological services. This includes a screening of incarcerated persons at the time of intake for communicable diseases, and immediate, emergency treatment of these diseases.
4. The right to prenatal and postnatal care for incarcerated females. (American Bar Association, 1977, pp. 387–397)

Following the Federal Bureau of Prisons and ABA standards set forth in the 1970s, many states drafted their own rules and regulations regarding the rights of incarcerated persons. For example, Massachusetts added more provisions for incarcerated persons, such as allowing them to express themselves via clothing and hairstyling, and to wear religious medallions that are not considered contraband (Krantz, 1983). Massachusetts was one of many states that created standards for the rights of incarcerated persons, some of which are still seen today.

In the "hands-on" era, the courts sought to find a balance between the fundamental individual rights of incarcerated persons and the needs of the institution housing them. As with other aspects of the criminal justice system, the courts used what is known as a "balancing test" to determine these rights, taking into consideration the balance between the importance of protecting rights and the need to restrict certain rights in a correctional setting (O'Brien et al., 1981). There are many amendments to the Constitution that relate to the rights of the incarcerated (i.e., the first, fourth, fifth, sixth, eighth, and 14th). While these rights have always been afforded to incarcerated persons, it was not until the "hands-off" approach ended that the individual grievances of incarcerated persons began to be heard. The following sections explore each of the aforementioned amendments and their effect on incarcerated persons in the United States.

Freedom of Speech, Visitation, and Religion

The **First Amendment** deals with issues relating to the freedom of speech and the freedom of religion (U.S. Const. amend. I). One of the first issues brought before the Court was that of correspondence, mainly dealing with who incarcerated persons could correspond with, and what right prison officials had to read their correspondence. As discussed by

Palmer (2010), reading and inspection of incarcerated persons' mail serves two purposes: prevention of the smuggling of contraband, and detection of plans for illegal activity, such as escape attempts from prison. However, the court system has been critical of administrators' refusal to mail correspondence that does not contain contraband or other illegal details. For example, in *Procunier v. Martinez* (1974), incarcerated persons challenged the constitutionality of regulations censoring their mail, saying that the state regulations violated their First Amendment rights to free speech. The Court found the state regulation to be unconstitutional and said that speech can only be restricted to maintain government security, and that incarcerated persons can only be stopped from communicating to the extent it is necessary to protect governmental interests (Cripe, 1997). In *McNamara v. Moody* (1979), the administrators of a prison facility were found guilty of violating an incarcerated person's constitutional rights by refusing to mail a letter to his significant other. In this case, the court held that censorship must be limited to concrete violations such as importing contraband or planning an escape or a riot. In the case of *Palmigiano v. Garrahy* (1977), the court ruled that the reading of outgoing mail by prison officials was unnecessary and in violation of the First Amendment, unless pursuant to a search warrant (Krantz, 1983).

Ten years later, in the case of *Turner v. Safley* (1987), the issue before the court was whether officials were justified in preventing incarcerated persons from corresponding with other incarcerated persons at different facilities. The Supreme Court upheld a lower court ruling, saying that these practices were justifiable for the purpose of maintaining prison security (Cripe, 1997). Generally speaking, prison officials may not censor incarcerated persons' speech because of unwelcome opinions; rather, they must show that censorship is needed to maintain the security interests of a facility, and that this censorship is no greater than that needed to protect the facility's interests (Krantz, 1983).

Another type of correspondence that falls under the First Amendment is **legal correspondence** between an incarcerated person and their attorney. Along with their right to access the courts, incarcerated persons have a right to correspond with an attorney concerning topics such as the validity of their conviction and issues regarding the constitutionality of the conditions of their detention (Palmer, 2010). This right remains even if the details of what they are communicating are critical of the prison administration and staff. The right to consult with legal counsel extends beyond contacting individual members of the ABA and also applies to contacting legal rights organizations such as the American Civil Liberties Union (ACLU). The courts have weighed in on the issue of legal correspondence between incarcerated persons and attorneys. The case of *Wolff v. McDonnell* (1974) surrounded the practice of a detention facility where all mail, including legal correspondence, was read and inspected. The Supreme Court ruled that legal correspondence could be opened and checked for contraband, but should not be read, and that the inspection should take place in front of the addressee (i.e., the incarcerated person) (Sisk et al., 2019).

Another issue that relates to the First Amendment is the freedom of visitation. According to Mitchell (2003), "visitation is the most vocalized First Amendment complaint that [incarcerated persons] have" (p. 251). Visitation is important to incarcerated persons, as confinement without regular outside contact will make the transition back into the community post-incarceration that much more difficult (Krantz, 1983). For a long time the Supreme Court did not weigh in on visitation for incarcerated persons, as it believed that prison administration problems were best solved by prison authorities (Palmer, 2010). In the case of *Block v. Rutherford* (1984), the Los Angeles County jail system was prohibiting contact visits for pretrial detainees and their spouses and loved ones. The Supreme Court upheld the regulation, stating that there was no constitutional requirement for contact visits (Cripe, 1987). Further, in *Jordan v. Wolke* (1978), the Seventh Circuit Court of Appeals ruled that officials who created a blanket refusal to allow contact visits between incarcerated persons and family did not violate any constitutional rights as long as the refusal was not intended as punishment, but rather as a rationale related to the goal of maintaining order and security in the prison facility (Palmer, 2010). Overall, the courts have viewed matters related to prison visits as falling under the umbrella of internal prison administration, but that does not permit the discriminatory application of visiting regulations; for example, denying visitation because of an offender's or a visitor's race would be considered discrimination under the 14th Amendment.

An additional source of complaint for incarcerated persons regarding the First Amendment is the freedom of religion. The courts have recognized the difficulty in applying the freedom of religion to incarcerated persons. For example, in *Gittlemaker v. Prasse* (1970), the courts pointed out that supplying every incarcerated person with a member of the clergy and religious service of their choice is different than providing a facility for worship or having clergy visit an institution (Palmer, 2010). One of the first Supreme Court cases to address this issue, *Cruz v. Beto* (1972), involved a Buddhist incarcerated person who was not allowed to have a Buddhist religious advisor or share his beliefs with other incarcerated persons. In fact, when trying to share his beliefs, he was punished and placed into solitary confinement (Mitchell, 2003). The Supreme Court determined that if the religious activities of one group are allowed in a facility, that facility must be prepared to allow other similar activities of other religions (Cripe, 1997). Since this ruling, many prison administrators have made certain changes to their policies on their own, to avoid further lawsuits. For example, some prisons now have menus that indicate items made from pork for those who are Muslim, or prepare meals with separate utensils to follow strict Jewish food preparation customs (Mitchell, 2003).

A more recent ruling on freedom of religion was made in *Holt v. Hobbs* (2015), where the Supreme Court unanimously ruled that when the Arkansas Department of Corrections deemed the beard of an incarcerated Muslim person potentially dangerous, it violated the man's constitutional rights to freedom of religion. In the opinion written by Justice Samuel Alito, it was asserted that the hair on the man's head and his clothing were more plausible places to hide contraband, but the department did not make incarcerated persons go around bald or naked; therefore, why would a beard be forced to be shaved off? (Wolf, 2015). With similar cases coming forth in the future and the potential for changing of justices, it will be of interest to see how the Supreme Court weighs in on issues of religion in prison in the time ahead.

Freedom From Illegal Search and Seizure

In terms of the **Fourth Amendment**, most violations that incarcerated persons claim regard their right to be protected from illegal search and seizure (U.S. Const. amend. IV). Historically, the courts have given correctional administrators and officials vast discretion to search incarcerated persons and their cells without a warrant; however, there are limitations, as incarcerated persons are protected from being arbitrarily harassed or unreasonably searched (Mitchell, 2003; O'Brien et al., 1981). Palmer (2010) argues that the unpredictability of random cell searches may be the most effective weapon that prison officials have in the never-ending fight against contraband. Without searches and seizures—that is, if incarcerated persons retained a total right to privacy in their cells—it would be nearly impossible for prison officials to prevent the introduction of weapons and goods into the prison environment.

As discussed by Mitchell (2003), searches in prison typically fall under two categories: searches of living quarters, and searches of an individual. In the case of *Hudson v. Palmer* (1984), an administrative policy was under question after it allowed "shakedown searches" of incarcerated persons' cells for contraband. The Court sided with the prison officials and their policy, explicitly stating that the Fourth Amendment does not apply to a prison cell (Mitchell, 2003). On the other side, the courts have ruled that some searches and seizures of property are unconstitutional in nature, such as those that violate the right to possess legal and religious materials (Palmer, 2010). In *Bonner v. Coughlin* (1976), the Seventh Circuit of the United States Court of Appeals awarded an incarcerated person damages for the illegal seizure of his copy of his trial transcripts. In regard to searches of individuals, the Supreme Court ruled in *Bell v. Wolfish* (1979) that no probable cause or individual suspicion is needed for incarcerated persons to be subjected to a body-cavity search following a visitation. Prison officials can conduct body-cavity searches on less than probable cause, as long as the searches are not done in an abusive manner (Palmer, 2010). The searches, however, must be conducted by a same-sex officer and be performed professionally and in a private area (Cripe, 1997).

Prison Discipline and Due Process

The right to due process is guaranteed under the Fifth and 14th Amendments (U.S. Const. amend. V; U.S. Const. amend. XIV). The **Fifth Amendment** protects those incarcerated at the federal level, and state and local incarcerated persons are protected by the **14th Amendment** (Cripe, 1997). The majority of cases that deal with these amendments are those cases disputing discipline of incarcerated persons. Discipline in prison can end an incarcerated person's shot at parole, land them in solitary confinement, or cause them to lose privileges and recreation, making individuals feel they should be afforded some level of due process in regard to discipline (Mitchell, 2003).

The Supreme Court case of *Wolff v. McDonnell* (1974), discussed earlier in relation to the First Amendment, was a landmark case involving a person incarcerated in a state prison in Nebraska who filed actions in federal court alleging he had been denied due process in a prison disciplinary hearing. The Court found that incarcerated persons have due process rights when they are facing serious sanctions for misconduct. These rights include:

1. Advance written notice of charges being filed again them, with at least 24 hours' notice before appearing before the disciplinary board.
2. A written statement as to the reasons for the disciplinary hearing.
3. The right to call witnesses and present documentary evidence in their defense.
4. The right to legal assistance, whether that be another incarcerated person or a staff member, if the charged incarcerated person is illiterate or the case is very complex.
5. The prison disciplinary board must be impartial. (*Wolff v. McDonnell*, 1974)

It should also be noted that in 1995, the Supreme Court changed the *Wolff* ruling, stating that prison disciplinary actions do not deprive an incarcerated person of liberty and do not require due process unless the sanctions will add to a sentence or go beyond the conditions of the original sentence (Cripe, 1997). Further, the courts have decided that a penal system can assign an individual to any facility within the agency without providing due process, including transferring incarcerated persons across state lines and international boundaries (Mitchell, 2003)

Freedom From Cruel and Unusual Punishment

When an incarcerated person claims their **Eighth Amendment** rights have been violated, they are discussing that amendment's protection against cruel and unusual punishment

(U.S. Const. amend. VIII). While the Constitution does not explicitly state what is meant by "cruel and unusual," society's definition has changed over time. The Supreme Court has stated that a punishment is cruel and unusual if "it is greatly disproportionate to the offense for which it has been imposed or if it goes far beyond what is necessary to achieve a sentencing aim, even if that aim is justified" (Cripe, 1997, pp. 228–229). One practice that has gained traction over the years as a potential violation of the Eight Amendment is the use of solitary confinement. The idea of isolation alone is not a constitutional issue; the use of isolation as a means of protecting the general prison population and preventing disobedience, disorder, and escapes has long been validated by the federal court system (Palmer, 2010). It is when the conditions of the isolation are disproportionate to the offense involved, or are used for improper means, that it becomes a violation of the Eight Amendment.

The courts have declared that when an incarcerated person is moved from the general population to administrative segregation (i.e., solitary confinement), the following rights must be given to them:

1. A written statement of reasons for the change of status.
2. A fair hearing within 72 hours.
3. A right to be represented by counsel if the issue is complex or the incarcerated person is illiterate or otherwise incapable of defending themselves.
4. A right to present witnesses and evidence, unless doing so would jeopardize institutional safety.
5. A written copy of the decision, including references to evidence relied upon to make the transfer decision. (Knight & Early, 1986)

Another topic that has been discussed in recent years, especially in light of mass incarceration, is that of overcrowding. Overcrowding has not yet been declared unconstitutional, in and of itself (Mitchell, 2003; Palmer, 2010). The court's rationale behind this decision is that overcrowding is not something done to the incarcerated person with the intent to punish them. As discussed by Palmer (2010),

> "Constitutional treatment of human beings who are confined ... does not depend upon the willingness or the financial ability of the state to provide decent penitentiaries, especially when the legislature has had ample opportunity to provide for the state to meet its constitutional responsibilities." (p. 274)

Further, while overcrowding on its own does not violate the Eight Amendment, situations where it results in unsanitary conditions or high levels of violence may constitute a violation.

Medical treatment, particularly lack of proper medical treatment, is another claim that falls under cruel and unusual punishment. As discussed by O'Brien et al. (1981), "Under local, state, and federal law, correctional facilities are required to provide adequate medical treatment to [incarcerated persons] in their custody" (p. 49). In *Priest v. Cupp* (1976), the court explained that prohibitions against cruel and unusual punishment do not guarantee that an incarcerated person will be cured of all real or imagined medical disabilities while in custody, but rather that they will be afforded the care, in the form of diagnosis and treatment, that is reasonably available under the circumstances of their confinement and medical condition (Palmer, 2010). Incarcerated persons do not have a reasonable expectation to have flawless medical services provided to them during their period of incarceration. The Supreme Court has ruled that more than mere negligence must be proven to support an Eighth Amendment violation, and the test set out in *Estelle v. Gamble* (1976) is a "deliberate indifference to serious medical needs" test (O'Brien et al., 1981, p. 49).

STATUTORY RIGHTS OF INCARCERATED INDIVIDUALS

When an incarcerated person's rights have been violated, the most popular remedy available is **injunctive relief**. This comes in the form of restrictive injunctions, which order a defendant to stop doing things they have wrongfully been doing. The other remedy available is a mandatory injunction, which requires a defendant to begin doing things they should have been doing all along (Mitchell, 2003). Also available to incarcerated persons are **constitutional torts**, in which an incarcerated person claims that they were injured or suffered harm because of the wrongful actions of another person, and that these injuries were caused by a violation of their constitutional rights. In constitutional torts, the injured party is usually asking for monetary compensation, and must show "negligence, gross or wanton negligence, or intentional wrong" (O'Brien et al., 1981, p. 116).

Section 1983 of Title 42

Title 42, Section 1983 under the U.S. Code of the Civil Rights Act has been in existence since the time of the Civil War (Mitchell, 2003). In the 1960s the Supreme Court interpreted Section 1983 as a legal remedy for citizens to sue state and local government officials when their policies or actions fell below the minimum standards set forth in the Constitution. In *Monroe v. Pape* (1961), the Court extended the Act by declaring that those incarcerated in prisons and jails could also use Section 1983 to challenge the conditions of their incarceration. It should be noted that Section 1983 only allows one to sue for actions taken "under the color of state law." This requirement, however, does not mean that the action had to have been legal under the state law in order for it to be "under color of" state law. In a Section 1983 suit, an incarcerated person can sue over a one-time action (e.g., physical assault by a guard), or over a pattern of actions (e.g., a pattern established over time in which a guard deliberately fails to act in response to physical assault from other incarcerated persons). A Section 1983 suit cannot be used to sue a private citizen without any connection to the government; for example, an incarcerated person cannot use it to sue another incarcerated person who assaults them because they do not work for the government. However, the incarcerated person who was attacked could use Section 1983 to sue a guard for failure to protect them from the attack. In another issue connected to this, the Supreme Court has not yet made a firm decision regarding whether private prison guards can be sued in the same manner as state prison guards. In *Giron v. Corrections Corporation of America* (1998), an incarcerated woman was raped by a guard at a private prison and filed a Section 1983 suit. The Court held that the guard was performing a "traditional state function" and was therefore "under color of state law" (Center for Constitutional Rights, 2010).

Bivens *Doctrine*

As discussed, Section 1983 or Title 42 only applies at the state and local level; if an incarcerated person wishes to bring a lawsuit against a federal employee, it is done under what is known as a *Bivens* **Doctrine**. This stems from the Supreme Court case *Bivens v. Six Unknown Federal Narcotics Agents* (1971), where the Court asserted that if someone's legal rights have been violated, it is their right to sue for these violations in order to make good on the wrong done to the individual (Knight & Early, 1986; Pereyra, 2019). As discussed by Pereyra (2019), *Bivens* claims have not fared well in the Supreme Court, and since 1980 the Court has cut back on the availability of *Bivens* remedies where they exist. In fact, in the more recent case of *Ziglar v. Abbasi* (2017), the Supreme Court held that unlawfully detained incarcerated persons post-9/11 did not have a *Bivens* claim against federal officials, furthering the belief that the claim is no longer critical in safeguarding incarcerated persons' rights (Pereyra, 2019).

The Federal Torts Claim Act

Applying only to those incarcerated at the federal level, the **Federal Torts Claim Act (FTCA)** allows for monetary compensation of incarcerated persons who suffer from negligent or abusive acts by correctional officers. It should be noted, though, that the causes of negligence or wrongdoing are narrow, so claims made under the FTCA have not been a notable source of incarcerated persons' rights (Knight & Early, 1986). Also, under the FTCA, an incarcerated person may petition to challenge their conviction and incarceration in the jurisdiction where their original case was heard. An incarcerated person may only file this one time following a conviction.

An additional right of incarcerated persons is that of *habeas corpus*, where an incarcerated person asks the court to review the circumstances surrounding their incarceration. Once it is filed, the court can dismiss the case, or have a hearing to determine the merit of the case presented. If the conditions of confinement are deemed illegal by the court, the incarcerated person is released from prison (Mitchell, 2003). All *habeas corpus* cases are first sent to state court, where all branches of the state court system must first be exhausted before the case moves to federal court. In *Brown v. Allen* (1953) the court determined that once a *habeas corpus* claim has been denied by a district court, the petitioner may appeal to the U.S. appellate court, and if necessary to the Supreme Court (Knight & Early, 1986).

The Prison Litigation Reform Act

Since the 1960s, the number of civil rights lawsuits by incarcerated persons has grown in the United States. In the 1960s only a few hundred such suits were filed in the federal court system; by 1996, over 41,000 suits were being filed annually (Palmer, 2010). Most of the suits (over 70%) were deemed to have no merit. The costs and judicial resources associated with many of these frivolous suits became a heavy burden on the federal court system, where upwards of 15% of the cases federal judges heard were lawsuits brought by incarcerated persons. The judicial response to these suits was excessive in some cases; the court overextended its power by doing things like ordering the release of incarcerated persons to relieve overcrowding, which was a common source of complaints by incarcerated persons (Palmer, 2010). In response to these events, **The Prison Litigation Reform Act (PLRA)** was passed in 1996.

The PLRA has a few purposes. First, it limits judicial power to order the release of incarcerated persons to relieve overcrowding. Any release of incarcerated persons must be ordered by a three-judge panel, and the court must find clear and convincing evidence that overcrowding, and overcrowding alone, is the cause of the federal rights violation, and must also find that no other remedy will correct the problem (Palmer, 2010). The PLRA also made it more difficult for incarcerated persons to file lawsuits in federal court. Under the PLRA, an incarcerated person must exhaust ALL administrative remedies (i.e., prison grievance procedures), or the case will be dismissed in federal court (ACLU, 2002). The PLRA also places restrictions on the waiver of filing fees for indigent incarcerated persons, something that happened regularly prior to the passing of the PLRA. Under the new law, an incarcerated person must pay a partial fee to file, based upon the availability of funds in their account. These fees must be paid even if the court dismisses the case; however, no incarcerated person may be denied filing because of no funds being available (ACLU, 2002). Also under the PLRA, an incarcerated person may not sue the United States or an agent or employee for emotional injury unless it is accompanied by a physical injury (Palmer, 2010).

As discussed by Schlanger (2015), the impact of the PLRA on prison litigation has been substantial. Following the passing of the PLRA in 1996, there was a sharp decline in filings in 1996 and 1997, and that number continued to decrease over the next decade. The number plateaued around 2005, where it remains, in the range of 20,000–25,000 case filings per year. The PLRA not only made it more difficult for incarcerated persons to bring forward civil rights cases, but also made the cases that did come forward harder to win (Booker, 2016). In looking at cases from 1988–2012, Schlanger (2015) noted a decrease in settlements, as well as a decrease in victories at trial. Notably, there was also an increase in pre-trial victories, which means that defendants are settling fewer matters and going to trial less often. While more research is needed to discover the true impacts of the PLRA, what is clear is that "litigation has receded as an oversight method in American corrections [and] it is vital that something take its place" (Schlanger, 2015, p. 171).

CONCLUSION

The answer to the question of what rights incarcerated persons have is complex, as offenders do have rights, but in a much different capacity than they have outside of a prison environment. As cases continue to make their way through the court system, the landscape of incarcerated persons' rights will continue to change and grow in any number of directions. Changes to the litigation process, such as the PLRA, have brought with them their own set of unique challenges that ultimately shape the rights of incarcerated persons. Continued research on the impact of changes to the litigation process for incarcerated persons is needed in order for researchers to understand the true impact of this legislation. While the courts continue to debate key issues related to incarcerated persons' rights, millions of incarcerated individuals will hang in the balance as their rights are clarified and modified over time.

DISCUSSION QUESTIONS

1. What are your thoughts on hunger strikes by incarcerated persons? Should officials be able to force-feed incarcerated persons who are on a hunger strike, and at what point should they be allowed to do so? How could force-feeding be seen as a possible violation of an incarcerated person's First Amendment rights?

2. Do you consider overcrowding to be a violation of an incarcerated person's constitutional rights? Under what conditions, if any, does overcrowding become a violation of rights in your opinion? Give specific examples of how other factors can combine with overcrowding to make it unconstitutional.

3. What impact has The Prison Litigation Reform Act (PLRA) had on incarcerated persons in the United States? Do you think the PLRA should remain as it is, or do you believe it needs modifications moving forward?

APPLICATION EXERCISES

Exercise #1: Explore an Incarcerated Persons' Rights Organization

There are many incarcerated persons' rights organizations advocating on behalf of incarcerated persons in the United States. For this exercise, you will explore an existing organization to learn more about how they are advocating for incarcerated persons' rights. Choose one of the following organizations to explore:

- American Correctional Association
- American Civil Liberties Union
- Human Rights Watch
- The Sentencing Project
- Equal Justice Initiative
- Criminal Justice Policy Foundation

Once you pick an organization, answer the following questions:

1. What are the origins of the organization? When, where, and why was it formed?
2. What is the mission of this organization?
3. How does the organization advocate for incarcerated persons' rights? What are the key issues that the organization advocates for?
4. What is some recent news regarding the organization?

Exercise #2: An In-Depth Look at Lawsuits by Incarcerated Persons

For this exercise, you should utilize an internet search browser to find two examples of lawsuits by incarcerated persons: one that was deemed frivolous by the courts, and one lawsuit with merit. Be sure to copy the hyperlink for the lawsuits you find. You should then answer the following questions.

1. Briefly explain the lawsuit you picked and the constitutional grounds on which the rights violation claims were made. Be sure to use terminology from this chapter when discussing the constitutional grounds under which the claims were made.
2. If you could create a policy for lawsuits by incarcerated persons, what would it look like? That is, in your ideal world, what rights to litigation should incarcerated persons have? Be sure to support your opinion with information you learned in this chapter.

REFERENCES

American Bar Association. (1977). *Standards relating to the legal status of prisoners.* American Bar Association.

American Civil Liberties Union. (2002). Know your rights: The Prison Litigation Reform Act (PLRA). https://www.aclu.org/sites/default/files/images/asset_upload_file79_25805.pdf

Bell v. Wolfish, 441 U.S. 520 (1979)

Bivens v. Six Unknown Federal Narcotics Agents, xxx (1971)

Block v. Rutherford, 468 U.S. 576 (1984)

Bonner v. Coughlin, 657 F.2d 931 (1976)

Booker, M. (2016, May 5). 20 years is enough: Time to repeal the Prison Litigation Reform Act. Prison Policy Initiative. https://www.prisonpolicy.org/blog/2016/05/05/20years_plra/

Brown v. Allen, 344 U.S. 443 (1953)

Carroll, R. (2013, July 9). *California prisoners launch biggest hunger strike in state's history*. The Guardian. https://www.theguardian.com/world/2013/jul/09/california-prisoners-hunger-strike

Center for Constitutional Rights. (2010). *The jailhouse lawyer's handbook* (5th ed.). Center for Constitutional Rights and the National Lawyers Guild.

Civil Right Act. 42 U.S.C. § 1983. (1871).

Code of Federal Regulations, Title 28 (Judicial Administration). 28 CFR 541.12 (Inmate Rights and Responsibilities). (2003).

Collins, W. C. (1990). *Correctional law for the correctional officer.* St. Mary's Press.

Cripe, C. A. (1997). *Legal aspects of corrections management.* Aspen Publishers, Inc.

Cruz v. Beto, 405 U.S. 319 (1972) Estelle v. Gamble, 429 U.S. 97 (1976)

Federal Torts Claims Act. Title IV, 60 Stat. 812, 28 U.S.C. Part VI, Chapter 171 and 28 U.S.C. § 1346. (1946).

Giron v. Corrections Corporation of America, xxx (1998)

Gittlemaker v. Prasse, 428 F.2d 1 (1970)

Herson, L. J. (1990). *The politics of ideas: Political theory and American public policy.* Waveland Press, Inc.

Holt v. Hobbs, 574 U.S. 352 (2015)

Hudson v. Palmer, 468 U.S. 517 (1984)

Jordan v. Wolke, 593 F.2d 772 (1978)

Kim, H. G. (2015). Applying international human rights laws to force-feeding prisoners: Effort to create domestic standards in the United States. *Global Business & Development Law Journal, 28*(2), 389–410.

Knight, B. B., & Early, S. T. (1986). *Prisoners' rights in America.* Nelson-Hall Publishers.

Krantz, S. (1983). *Corrections and prisoners' rights.* West Publishing Company.

McNamara v. Moody, 606 F.2d 621 (1979)

Mitchell, D. (2003). Prisoners' constitutional rights. *Criminal Justice Studies, 16*(3), 245–264.

Monroe v. Pape, 365 U.S. 167 (1961)

O'Brien, E., Fisher, M., & Austern, D. T. (1981). *Practical law for correctional personnel: A resource manual and a training curriculum.* West Publishing Group.

Palmer, J. W. (2010). *Constitutional rights of prisoners* (9th ed.). Matthew Bender & Company, Inc.

Palmigiano v. Garrahy, 443 F. Supp. 956 (1977)

Pell v. Procunier, 417 U.S. 817 (1974).

Pereyra, J. (2019). Ziglard v. Abbasi and its effect on the constitutional rights of federal prisoners. *Journal of Criminal Law & Criminology, 109*(2), 395–421.

Priest v. Cupp, 24 Or. App. 429 (1976)

Prison Law Office. (2021). *Litigation.* Retrieved March 22, 2021 from https://prisonlaw.com/major-cases/

Prison Litigation Reform Act (PLRA). 42 U.S.C. § 1997e. (1996).

Procunier v. Martinez, 416 U.S. 396 (1974)

Schlanger, M. (2015). Trends in prisoner litigation as the PLRA enters adulthood. *UC Irvine Law Review, 5*, 153–178.

Sisk, G., King, M., Beitzel, J. N., Duffus, B., & Koehler, K. (2019). Reading the prisoner's letter: Attorney-client confidentiality in inmate correspondence. *Journal of Criminal Law & Criminology, 109*(3), 559–632.

Turner v. Safley, 482 U.S. 78(1987)

U.S. Const. amend. I.

U.S. Const. amend. IV.

U.S. Const. amend. V.

U.S. Const. amend. VIII.

U.S. Const. amend. XIV.

Wolf, R. (2015, Jan 20). *Supreme Court upholds religious rights of prisoners.* USA Today. https://www.usatoday.com/story/news/nation/2015/01/20/supreme-court-prisoner-beard-muslim-religion/19916823/

Wolff v. McDonnell, 418 U.S. 539 (1974).

Ziglar v. Abbasi, 137 S. Ct. 1843 (2017)

CHAPTER 7

Prison Culture

CHAPTER OBJECTIVES

After reading this chapter, you should be able to:

- Define prison culture using examples and context.
- Define the prisonization process and indicate which factors contribute to the process.
- Compare the deprivation and importation models to explain prison culture.
- Examine the prevalence of sexual victimization in a prison setting.
- Discuss current legislation used to combat sexual victimization in prison.

KEY WORDS

Contraband

Deprivation model

Importation model

Inmate code

National Standards to Prevent, Detect, and Respond to Prison Rape

Pains of imprisonment

Prison argot

Prison culture

Prison gang

Prisonization

Prison Rape Elimination Act (PREA)

Pseudo-families

Sub rosa economy

Substantiated allegations

Survey of Sexual Victimization

Total institution

Unfounded allegations

Unsubstantiated allegations

CASE STUDY: EXTENDED FAMILY VISIT PROGRAM

The state of Washington allows eligible incarcerated persons to apply for the Extended Family Visit Program. This program allows the incarcerated male or female and his/her immediate family member(s) to spend time in a private housing unit. The intention of these visits is to support individuals by helping them to build sustainable relationships that are important to reentry and provide better home life for the reentering person. In addition, participating in the Extended Family Visit Program can provide incentive for those serving long-term sentences to maintain positive behavioral choices, reducing violent infractions (including those involving sexual assault). Importantly, however, few states have found success with conjugal visitation programs.

Questions for Discussion

1. In your opinion, would conjugal visitation programs reduce sexual assault rates in prison? Why or why not?
2. Why do you believe other states have been hesitant in permitting the implementation of these programs? Are there detriments to their use?

INTRODUCTION

A separate culture exists within prisons, and its etiology is entirely different from the that of a community setting. Even though most people will never serve time in an institutional setting, they generally learn over time that prison is a "bad place" and that the experience can be life-altering. Prison life is depicted through various means including crime-related media, relationships with former or currently incarcerated individuals, and personal life experience. Opportunities to gain firsthand exposure to prison culture are extremely limited because prisons are far removed from the daily lives of most people. In addition, because they are such strictly controlled environments, the only people with access to prisons are those who work at the institution, those approved to visit, and those who are incarcerated. The media provides a wealth of prison imagery and insight into prison life; however, the media is known to present inaccurate portrayals of crime and punishment (Cecil, 2015). Therefore, it is important to note that prison culture and the socialization of incarcerated populations to staff and administration align with specific elements that are unique to institutional facilities.

This chapter discusses various aspects of prison culture to enhance readers' understanding of what life is like for people who are incarcerated in prisons. The chapter begins with a discussion of the socialization process that people experience when they are first sent to prison, including the theoretical underpinnings that aim to describe the origin of prison subcultures. It then details some of the major developments that have shaped today's system and gives insight about aspects of incarceration that shape the prison culture, including language, contraband, and the sub rosa economy. This chapter also examines the prevalence of sexual victimization in a prison setting and the differences in victimization for male and female populations. Finally, the chapter concludes with an overview of current legislation passed by the government to address sexual victimization that occurs in correctional institutions.

PRISON CULTURE

The lives of incarcerated people are constantly regulated in prison, with their sleeping, eating, and activity times on a strict schedule. Moreover, people who are incarcerated in higher security facilities are monitored 24 hours a day, including during times when they use bathrooms and participate in recreational activities. Certainly, prison operations differ according to the varying security levels, and a person's schedule is dictated by their classification status. Goffman (1961) coined the term **"total institutions"** to describe prisons, which means that all activities occur according to rigid rules and regimented schedules. In addition, incarcerated people share every aspect of their daily and personal lives with others who inhabit the facility. Because interactions with family and friends are often limited, or even non-existent, incarcerated people become dependent on each other in multiple ways (Hensley, Castle & Tewksbury, 2003).

The dynamics of social relationships, the significant loss of individual liberties, the mental anguish, and the highly secure yet potentially dangerous environments make prison culture unique among other cultures that exist in society. Indeed, an individual who is incarcerated in prison experiences a different lifestyle compared to those who live on the "outside." Although prisons regulate a person's physical existence during their incarceration, individuals are in control of their own values, norms, and beliefs, which are applied to their routine behaviors. Like their counterparts in the community, incarcerated people share their emotional and mental selves with others as a coping strategy to navigate their current circumstances. In general, incarcerated people often feel like outcasts because of their criminality. Therefore, others who share similar experiences may support their deviant beliefs and foster a sense of community and commiseration, creating a bonded group simply based on the fact they share the experience of incarceration. The term **prison culture** is used to refer to the values, norms, and beliefs of people who are incarcerated. It is well documented that prison culture prominently influences the lives of incarcerated individuals, as well as their families and communities (Bondesson, 1989; Irwin, 1980; Sykes, 1958).

When someone is brought into a facility, they participate in a process in which they adjust and adapt to the radical shift in lifestyle of the prison environment and assimilate to the norms, customs, and underlying behavioral expectations of the prison community (Austin, 2005; Einat & Einat, 2000). This process, known as **prisonization**, was first conceptualized by Donald Clemmer (1940), who was one of the first researchers to conduct a general study of the prison setting and examine "the folkways, mores, customs, and general culture of the penitentiary" (Clemmer, 1940, p. 299). In studying prison culture, Clemmer (1940) recognized that not all people experience prisonization to the same degree and that personality types and the length of sentence a person serves, as well as their relationships with loved ones outside of prison and their desire to isolate themselves from others, contribute to prisonization. For example, people who participate in programming have been found to exhibit lower measures of prisonization than people who are in more restricted institutional settings. People who maintain healthy relationships with others in the community, and people serving shorter sentences, experience prisonization to lesser degrees. Conversely, people who lack support and are serving longer sentences exhibit higher measures of prisonization (Clemmer, 1940; Dobbs & Waid, 2005). According to Irwin (1980), groups in prison are distinguished by behavioral patterns that classify their level of prisonization. For example, someone who is "jailing" is thoroughly prisonized, whereas someone who is "playing the system" might participate in prison programming to look as though they are rehabilitated. Lastly, people who are "gleaning" make genuine attempts to better themselves while they are incarcerated. When these groups interact, they introduce norms and beliefs to each other, creating a cultural structure within the prison (Austin, 2005; Irwin, 1980).

Because the values of the prison population contradict many societal values, people who adapt to prison must alter their behaviors to adhere to the "inmate code." The **inmate code** is a set of norms, rules, and expected patterns of behavior among the incarcerated populace that outline which behaviors are and are not acceptable. For example, while violence is generally unacceptable in the community, it can be encouraged and rewarded in prison (Austin, 2005; Clemmer, 1940; Dobbs & Waid, 2005). The inmate code is reflective of the hierarchy and leadership that exist among groups of incarcerated people. In addition, the inmate code creates solidarity among incarcerated individuals and opposition toward correctional staff (Austin, 2005; Clemmer, 1940; McCorkle & Korn, 1962). The primary rule for people to abide by when they are serving time in prison is to "do your own time" by ignoring others and not causing trouble. The inmate code also dictates that people do not involve correctional staff when problems arise and that they never snitch, exploit others, or interfere in other people's affairs. These rules and standards have become central to the prisonization process and are highly influential on daily life in prison (Inderbitzin, 2005).

Since Clemmer's (1940) study on the prison community, scholars have continued to examine the role of deprivation and loss of liberties in prison culture (Sykes, 1958). Throughout their attempts to explain how the prison culture is fostered, two main theoretical explanations, the deprivation and importation models, have emerged as dominating themes. The **deprivation model** explains prison culture and individual conduct as a product of the deprivations, or the loss of liberty, that people experience while they are incarcerated. In other words, the deprivation of certain choices and freedoms leads people to react in certain ways (McManimon, 2005; Sykes, 1958). According to Gresham Sykes (1958), a person experiences specific losses following incarceration, known as "**pains of imprisonment**." These losses can be organized into five main categories:

1. Loss of autonomy and self-sufficiency;
2. Loss of goods and services;
3. Loss of heterosexual relationships;
4. Loss of liberties associated with those who are not incarcerated (e.g., ability to create desired schedules); and
5. Loss of a sense of security and protection from harmful attacks.

More recently, the pains of imprisonment have been expanded to include feelings of powerlessness, meaninglessness, normlessness, detachment, and alienation (Austin & Irwin, 2001). Certainly, prison life removes a person's ability to enjoy these liberties and essentially limits their ability to make choices in so many daily decisions. As a result, the coping mechanism for these deprivations may entail an amended set of values and norms, some of which may be inappropriate and/or illegal. In addition, the limited pool of individuals that one can have a relationship with may influence adapted preferences or attractions. Not only are incarcerated people limited to participating in relationships with only members of the same sex, but the pool is also further limited to those in that specific facility (Marcum et al., 2012).

Critics of the deprivation model argue that exogenous factors such as individual characteristics and prior experiences also contribute to the prison culture (Austin, 2005; Irwin & Cressey, 1962). According to the **importation model**, prison populations consist of subcultures that extend from those found within the community; incarcerated people bring in their own lifestyle norms, beliefs, and personal values when they are incarcerated, and they act accordingly (Irwin & Cressey, 1962). In other words, the criminal code that exists outside of prison is brought into the institution by people who have already developed values and attitudes that manifest in prison. Therefore, the prison culture originates from conflicting group norms and values (Austin, 2005; Dobbs & Waid, 2005). For example, people who practice Catholicism prior to serving a prison sentence will continue to practice and invest in the beliefs of the Catholic faith while they are incarcerated. The same idea applies to people who are members of gangs or who are predisposed to violent behavior, as well as people who are dedicated to family and community service. All of these affiliations come into the facility and are part of the persona of the person who is incarcerated. As a result, these influences permeate the prison culture (Irwin & Cressey, 1962).

Today, penologists recognize that people's experiences with prison are best described by a combination of concepts from the deprivation model and the importation model (McManimon, 2005). That is, both individual and environmental factors impact prison culture (Dobbs & Waid, 2005). It is also generally accepted that prison populations consist of several subgroups, with competing ideologies, that have evolved over time due to political stratification, growth of racial minority populations, and an influx of gangs in prison. The contemporary prison system has evolved significantly over recent decades, and correctional institutions are now held to higher standards due to civil rights and litigation (McManimon, 2005). However, other problematic circumstances that affect the overall culture in an institution, such as overcrowding, violence, and racial issues, persist in prisons today (Austin, 2005).

PRISON SUBCULTURES

Subcultures exist within the larger prison population, just as they do in the community. Subcultures share common characteristics, histories, experiences, and interests that make them distinct from other groups in mainstream culture. Early research has helped to identify several types of prison groups, consisting of people who shared similar backgrounds and criminal behaviors. For example, based on his observations of both the formal and informal social structures of the prison community, Caldwell (1956) identified groups that included: influential people who had committed notorious crimes; individuals who strictly adhered to the inmate code; people who secretly furnished alcohol and narcotics to others; thieves; gamblers; skilled laborers; religionists; homosexuals; weapons manufacturers; and nudists. In his work, the researcher recommended that correctional administrators utilize a scientific classification of incarcerated people, comprehensive educational programs, and social group activities to assist with custodial and rehabilitative programs (Caldwell, 1956).

Part of the development of a unique prison subculture is the development of a language affiliated with incarceration experiences. Groups in prison communicate to each other using a special language known as slang, or **prison argot**, as well as through gestures (Hensley et al., 2003a; O'Brien, 2009). These types of communication enable incarcerated people to differentiate themselves from others, help to facilitate social interactions and relationships, and enhance a sense of belonging to a subculture (Einat & Einat, 2000). Use of prison argot also allows people to feel more in control of their environment and to communicate more privately, with less detection of any potentially deviant plans that may be developing. Moreover, language is a principal element of prisonization that develops and perpetuates the inmate code (Hensley et al., 2003b). Essentially, prison argot represents yet another adaptation for coping with the deprivations of prison life (Goffman, 1961). According to Einat and Einat (2000), the use of prison argot performs six functions:

1. Affirms membership in the prison subculture;
2. Relieves the feeling of rejection from peers on the outside;
3. Develops relationships with other incarcerated persons;
4. Identifies acceptance by other incarcerated persons, as only they are allowed to use the language;
5. Allows for secrecy; and
6. Expresses the uniqueness afforded by distinct words.

In summary, prison argot allows individuals to justify acceptance into the prison subculture, while giving the incarcerated person the satisfaction of communicating without detection by correctional officers.

Prison Gangs

Prison gangs are prevalent in many, if not all, correctional institutions. While the definition of a **prison gang** varies, this term generally refers to groups that threaten or disrupt the prison environment through criminal activity and rule violations. Gang membership often depends on race, geography, political affiliation, and religious beliefs. For example, several prison gangs exist across racial lines, including the Aryan Brotherhood, the Black Guerrilla Family, La Nuestra Familia, and the Mexican Mafia. Street gangs such as the Bloods, Crips, Latin Kings, and Vice Lords are also incarcerated in prisons across the country. While there are various reasons why someone might join a prison gang, it is generally recognized that the group helps to satisfy the need for belonging and acceptance, and that prison gangs share common ideologies (Cantora, 2014). Another element that defines prison subcultures, particularly prison gangs, is tattoos, a form of body art that acts as a symbolic expression of identity. Tattooing is generally prohibited in prison because tattoos are often given using handmade machines and needles, which poses significant health risks. Sometimes, incarcerated people even tattoo others using pieces of glass. Prison gangs often use tattoos to signify group membership and criminal specialty, and to identify hierarchical structure (Sullivan, 2005).

Prison gangs create problematic conditions and are often the source of violence and racial tensions that impact the operation of the entire prison system. In addition, prison gangs are known to orchestrate criminal enterprises involving drug distribution, prostitution, gambling, and violence (Cantora, 2014). Oftentimes, gangs are directly involved in the **sub rosa economy,** which is a term used to describe the prison underground economy and the exploitive nature of the sexual activity that is inextricably linked to the prison culture. Like the black market, the sub rosa economy involves the illicit exchange of goods and services among incarcerated populations. A prison's sub rosa economy is a major concern to correctional administration and staff because it lays a foundation for various types of economic victimization; further, because it occurs underground, they are often not aware of what is going on between people. Gangs can also manipulate others and attempt to control the flow of canteen goods and contraband. **Contraband** includes any item an incarcerated person possesses that was not directly issued to them by the institution or purchased through appropriate channels. Examples of common contraband include food, clothing, magazines, cell phones, drugs, alcohol, or weapons. Obviously, some contraband is more dangerous than other kinds and poses a serious risk to the incarcerated population and correctional staff (Santos, 2005).

Often, correctional officers attempt to intervene by separating groups and individuals within the prison, or by sending them to another institution. Another strategy is to house gang members of the same group together, to control their activity and prevent conflicts with other groups (Cantora, 2014). In addition, staff must make conscious steps to identify gang members and to determine affiliation. Although this is difficult to do based purely on the racial composition of the group, staff seek to identify gang members' similar mannerisms, language, and style of dress (Ross, 2009).

SEXUAL VICTIMIZATION IN PRISON

Males and females adapt to institutionalization in different ways. For example, women are generally more drawn to relationships for their emotional and companionship aspects. This is not to say that sex cannot be a part of these relationships, but that the core of these relationships concerns establishing a connection with another person (Marcum, 2013). It is important to note that sexual relationships in any correctional facility are not permitted. However, despite these restrictions, research indicates that incarcerated individuals do participate in consensual sexual relationships. Hensley et al. (2002) found that younger incarcerated persons and those with longer sentences were more likely to participate in these relationships. Ironically, many incarcerated females who participate in same-sex relationships in prison do not identify as gay outside of prison, referring to this conduct as "gay for the stay." Incarcerated females are often motivated to participate in these relationships because of economic manipulation, pressure, boredom, or simple loneliness.

Some incarcerated females who play the masculine role are called "studs," while those who adhere to feminine roles are referred to as "femmes." Despite stereotypical assumptions that masculine females would be more dominant and aggressive, there are conflicting findings. For example, Alarid (2000) suggested that some femmes are more likely to act as the predator. On the other hand, Trammell (2009) asserted that some studs acted as a dominating force and controlled weaker women. Conversely, Keys (2002) found that there was no power differential between the two roles. Regardless of the mixed research, there is overall agreement that incarcerated females can be sexually coerced via verbal coercion, harassment, or physical exhibition. Incarcerated males, on the other hand, utilize sexual relationships as a method of domination and protection, and prison argot is used to designate the sexual hierarchy of males. One of the first studies of male prison sex was performed in 1934 by Joseph Fishman (as cited in Hensley, Wright, Tewksbury, & Castle 2003). At the top of Fishman's sexual hierarchy were the most aggressive inmates, or the "wolves." These men used sex to dominate and victimize less powerful, more feminine males, who were referred to as "fairies." These types of men were classified as lower on the hierarchy because they were highly vulnerable and more likely to be victimized.

Donaldson (2001) furthered the research by separating the less powerful, passive group of male inmates into more specific categories. Those labeled as "queens" were not as respected as the wolves, but they held higher positions on the hierarchy because they submitted to a natural role of the passive counterpart. These men also displayed feminine characteristics, assuming the role of a woman in the relationship. On the other hand, "punks" or "jailhouse turnouts" were viewed as cowards because they were too weak to protect themselves. In turn, they were often victims of forced sex. According to Donaldson (1993), these men were generally younger, first-time offenders who were smaller in stature; according to Kirkham (1971), they assumed a status similar to that of a prostitute. Dumond (2000) supported these findings via a study that found that typical victims of male sexual assault in prison were young, white property or drug offenders with small statures. In addition, victims often exhibited mental illness or disabilities, no gang affiliation, and admitted homosexual sexual orientation, and had often been convicted of sex crimes (Dumond, 2000).

Prevalence of Sexual Victimization and Policy Responses

Sexual victimization in prisons and jails has historically been recognized as a prevalent yet underreported occurrence (Dumond, 2000; Hensley et al. 2003a; Struckman-Johnson & Struckman-Johnson, 2000). While this issue was recognized as early as the 1930s (Fishman, 1934), the first valid and reliable study of incidence rates was not published until 1968 (Davis, 1968, as cited in Tewksbury & Connor, 2013). In his groundbreaking study, Davis interviewed over 3,300 incarcerated people and 570 correctional staff in Philadelphia jails and found that in a 2-year period, over 2,000 sexual assaults had occurred, while more than 60,000 people had passed through the system. Following Davis's (1968) work, research on prison sexual violence became more rigorous. For example, in 1980, Lockwood conducted a study on institutional violence in New York State prisons. The incarcerated people he interviewed described varying levels of sexual victimization, ranging from completed sexual assault to verbal harassment. In a separate study, Bowker (1980) supported Lockwood's finding that violence was a frequent part of prison life, but found that violence was also used by older incarcerated individuals who promised protection in exchange for sexual favors. Furthermore, no matter the specific incident of violence, the researchers agreed that sex was used either to demonstrate strength and dominance, or to obtain desired goods (Bowker, 1980; Lockwood, 1980). Later studies have also found that most sexual assaults occurred during the daytime in housing units, but also in bathrooms or dorms (Austin et al., 2006). In addition, sexual assault has also been found to occur as payment for debts (Fleischer & Kreinert, 2006).

Since 1980, a barrage of scholarly research has indicated that sexual victimization in correctional institutions is a growing problem (Beck & Johnson, 2012; Listwan & Hanley, 2012; Rantala, 2018; Wolff et al., 2006). Sexual victimization in the prison setting can occur in a variety of ways, and researchers have asserted that the number of known victimizations is woefully less than the real number. Victims of sexual assault often do not report their victimization, whether incarcerated or not, because of shame or fear of retaliation by the offender. In addition to these commonalities, incarcerated people do not report their victimization because they are fearful that the assault will negatively affect their reputation, and they do not want to admit socially undesirable behaviors (Gaes & Goldberg, 2004). Since many individuals do not identify as homosexual outside of prison, admitting sexual assault by a member of the same sex can be a humiliating experience and can demonstrate weakness. Furthermore, many incarcerated people do not understand the parameters that define sexual assault (Fowler et al., 2010). As a result of many of these factors and other contributing issues, official reports of sexual victimization in prison are lower than actual occurrences (Calhoun & Coleman, 2002; Hensley et al., 2002; Owen et al., 2014).

There has been a collective push for better government policies to combat and prevent these behaviors. One of the most notable changes was a piece of legislation passed by the Federal Government in the early 21st century, implemented with the intention of cracking down on this rampant violation of people supervised by our corrections system. The **Prison Rape Elimination Act (PREA)** (2021) was signed into law in 2003 by President George W. Bush after unanimous support was shown by both parties of Congress (Bureau of Justice Statistics, 2004). PREA is a zero-tolerance federal policy passed with the intention of improving sexual safety in correctional facilities (Kubiak et al., 2017). PREA requires annual data collection and reporting of sexual victimization of incarcerated people by the Bureau of Justice Statistics. It also provides funding for research and programs, as well as increased severity of punishment for perpetrators of sexual victimization, whether the perpetrator is a member of staff or an incarcerated person (Lauger, 2020).

Another requirement of PREA is development of a national standard of sexual victimization, so that occurrences can be measured more accurately and proactive and reactive policies can therefore be better developed. In June 2012, the Department of Justice published the **National Standards to Prevent, Detect, and Respond to Prison Rape**. Numerous issues were addressed by this document, including providing definitions of terms related to sexual abuse; planning of preventative measures; planning of responsive measures; training and education of all persons in a correctional facility; and reporting and investigating allegations of sexual abuse. In addition, the Survey of Sexual Violence, which was used to measure victimization in correctional facilities, was later renamed the **Survey of Sexual Victimization** in 2013 and updated in multiple ways. That is, questions were added to capture sexual harassment and the inclusion of transgender and intersex characteristics. Table 7.1 provides uniform definitions for sexual behaviors as defined by the Bureau of Justice Statistics.

Table 7.1 Definitions of Sexual Acts in Correctional Facilities.

Inmate-on-inmate sexual victimization	Nonconsensual sexual acts or abusive contact with victim without consent
Nonconsensual sexual acts	Most serious forms of victimization
	Contact between penis and the vulva
	Contact between the mouth and the penis, vulva, or anus
	Penetration of the anal or genital opening of another person
Abusive sexual contact	Less serious forms of victimization
	Intentional touching of genitals, anus, breast, thigh, buttocks, or groin
Staff-on-inmate sexual victimization	Sexual misconduct or harassment perpetrated by any correctional staff member
Staff sexual misconduct	Any consensual or nonconsensual sexual behavior toward inmate by staff, including consensual romantic relationships
	Intentional touching of genitals, anus, breast, thigh, buttocks, or groin
	Any sexual act that is attempted, completed, threatened, or requested
	Indecent exposure, invasion of privacy, or voyeurism

(continued)

Table 7.1 Definitions of Sexual Acts in Correctional Facilities.   *(continued)*

Staff sexual harassment	Repeated verbal comments or gestures of a sexual nature to an inmate
	Demeaning or suggestive comments regarding an inmate's gender or sexuality
	Repeated profane or obscene gesture or language

Note. Adapted from *Sexual Victimization Reported by Adult Correctional Authorities, 2012–15 (*NCJ 251146), by R. Rantala, 2018, July, U.S. Department of Justice, Office of Justice Programs, Bureau of Justice Statistics (https://www.bjs.gov/content/pub/pdf/svraca1215.pdf).

Indeed, sexual victimization in correctional facilities can take multiple forms, but it is often categorized as inmate-on-inmate or staff-on-inmate. As described above, incarcerated persons who offend in this manner are generally more physically or mentally dominant. Staff sexual misconduct may include a perpetrator who is more physically or mentally dominating than their victim but can also include individuals who utilize their position of authority to dominate an incarcerated person (Dumond, 2000; Siegal, 2001). This type of misconduct can take multiple forms: coercing an individual into sexual behavior, including actual rape; inappropriate language or degradation; intrusive searches; threat of force or use of force; and the use of goods and privileges. In addition to these manipulative and/or illegal behaviors, staff may also participate in consensual sexual relationships with incarcerated persons based on amorous feelings. A continuum of sexual coercion that occurs between staff and an incarcerated person is depicted in Table 7.2.

Table 7.2 Continuum of Sexual Coercion: Staff-on-Inmate.

- Proclamation of love and seductive behaviors
- Inappropriate comments
- Requests for sexual contact
- Voyeurism and flashing
- Abuse of searching authority
- Exchange of sexual behaviors
- Sexual intimidation
- Sexual activity without physical violence
- Sexual activity with physical violence

Note. Adapted from *Critical Issues Impacting Women in the Justice System: A Literature Review*, by B. Owen, J. Pollock, J. Wells, & J. Leahy, 2014, National Institute of Corrections (https://nicic.gov/sites/default/files/033010.pdf)

Piecora (2014) found that in cases involving staff-on-inmate sexual assaults, 98% of the sexual victimization incidences among incarcerated females involved a male perpetrator. Further, Kubiak et al. (2018) found that incarcerated females were more likely to be victimized by male correctional staff than by female staff. Therefore, it is important to specifically note that interaction with male staff can have a profoundly detrimental effect on incarcerated females. Because many incarcerated females have previously experienced sexual abuse by males, they are often hesitant to report victimization (Miller, 2010). As most correctional facility staff are men, females may be searched or restrained by males. Even though the staff are completely within their right to perform these actions, the practice can be traumatizing to survivors of sexual violence (Pollock, 2002).

As a result of PREA, the Bureau of Justice Statistics (BJS) now publishes an annual report on the rate of sexual victimization in adult correctional facilities. The report provides information on various levels of determined events as previously defined by the BJS (Rantala, 2018). For example, a **substantiated allegation** is an event that was investigated and determined to have occurred, and an **unfounded allegation** is an event that was investigated and determined not to have occurred. Lastly, an **unsubstantiated allegation** is a situation in which the investigation indicated that evidence was insufficient to determine if the event occurred. Some of the most recently published data on sexual victimization in adult correctional facilities found that among the 1.92 million incarcerated persons polled in 2015, there were 24,661 allegations of sexual violence. About 58% of these allegations involved staff-on-inmate victimization. Of all of these allegations, only 8% (n = 1,473) were substantiated based on completed investigations. Furthermore, there was an increase in allegations of sexual victimization from 2011 to 2015; this increase is assumed to be related to the release of the National Standards to Prevent, Detect, and Respond to Prison Rape. During this time range, the number of allegations in prisons increased by 180% (from 6,660 allegations in 2011 to 18,666 allegations in 2015). The number of substantiated incidents of sexual victimization increased by 63% (from 902 substantiated incidents in 2011 to 1,473 substantiated incidents in 2015) (Rantala, 2018).

Owen et al. (2014) asserted that for PREA to succeed, correctional facilities must recognize that violence and safety practices are different for incarcerated males and females and that relationships have different meanings between the sexes. In addition, the execution of sexual violence can differ between the sexes. Therefore, prevention and intervention techniques should take a more comprehensive approach based on each facility, rather than being broadly implemented policies. Notably, individual states have also adopted plans to reduce victimization in their jurisdictions. After the implementation of Texas's "Safe Prisons Program," an initiative that promoted the use of a broader definition of sexual victimization in correctional facilities and encouraged reporting, the number of reported assaults increased dramatically (Austin et al., 2006).

Increased rates of sexual victimization in correctional facilities also highlight concerns about the long-term health effects of sexual victimization on incarcerated persons. It is well established that unprotected sex can result in transmission of viruses and bacteria, potentially causing HIV/AIDS, gonorrhea, hepatitis, or syphilis. Small cells and staff shortages can influence high risk rates of sexual victimization and acquisition of sexual diseases (Stewart, 2007). Studies have also shown that incarcerated males are especially susceptible to contracting diseases compared to non-incarcerated individuals (Senkowski et al., 2016; Subramanian et al., 2016). Education on methods of disease contraction is a key to prevention, and research has indicated that condom use in correctional facilities decreases the likelihood of infection (Butler et al., 2013). However, condoms are not normally provided to incarcerated persons. Correctional facilities have safety concerns about regular distribution of condoms, and they lack support for resource allocation for these purchases (Williams et al., 2018). Conjugal visitation has also been found to have positive effects for incarcerated persons, potentially decreasing depressive symptoms, administrative infractions during incarceration, and recidivism. However, very few states allow for conjugal visitation, limiting the ability to fully explore its effectiveness on the reduction of sexually transmitted diseases (D'Alessio et al., 2013; De Claire & Dixon, 2017; Einat & Rabinovitz, 2012; McElreath et al., 2016).

CONCLUSION

This chapter offered an in-depth look at what it is like to be incarcerated in a prison, and gave context to the prison culture to enhance understanding of what life and relationships are like in correctional facilities. Certainly, there are many challenges present for incarcerated people that relate directly to the environment and its inhabitants, which can dramatically impact the experiences that people have during their incarceration. As paradoxical as it might seem, the liberties that people surrender when they are incarcerated are also the qualities that are necessary for community reintegration. Therefore, the culture within a prison setting can also impact a person's success in reentering society. Fortunately, albeit slowly, wide-scale policy changes have occurred to soften experiences and create training programs for security and staff to positively influence the prison culture. For example, PREA and additional pieces of state legislation have enhanced punishments for offenders of sexual victimization, whether the offending party is an inmate or a staff member, and correctional facilities are now required to report all incidents on a yearly basis. However, more resources need to be funneled into the system to create safer environments for inhabitants.

DISCUSSION QUESTIONS

1. Which do you believe best explains the development of a prison subculture: the deprivation model or the importation model? Justify your decision.

2. What impact do prison gangs have on prison culture? How can correctional institutions control prison gangs?

3. The masculinity and femininity demonstrated by a person can range throughout a fluid scale, and this is demonstrated by the roles taken by inmates in a correctional facility. Explain how these different levels of masculinity and femininity can change the status level and role of an inmate in a male or female facility.

4. Why is it difficult for incarcerated people to maintain relationships with their families while they are serving their sentence in prison?

APPLICATION EXERCISES

Exercise #1: Researching Prison Gangs – Virtual Poster Presentations

This chapter gives students an opportunity to research different prison gangs and create a virtual poster that summarizes their findings. Poster templates can be found online and can be easily uploaded to various virtual learning platforms.

Exercise #2: Efforts by the States to Curb Sexual Victimization

Choose one state in the United States and find the following information about that state:

1. Current rate of sexual victimization in correctional facilities in that state; and
2. Comparison of the state's rate of sexual victimization compared to the national level.

In addition, investigate efforts being made at the state level to address sexual victimization in correctional facilities. Do these efforts go above and beyond PREA? How do these efforts compliment PREA, and are they effective?

Exercise #3: Develop a Program for Implementation in a Female Facility

Many female inmates claim that they participate in same-sex relationships in prison not because of sexual preference, but because of the need for companionship and emotional connection. However, a host of issues can emerge from romantic relationships in prison, including violence. Develop a program for implementation in a female facility that is created with the intention of allowing women to form and maintain friendships in a positive setting. This program should involve prosocial activities and the ability to develop positive bonds.

REFERENCES

Alarid, L. (2000). Sexual assault and coercion among incarcerated women prisoners: Excerpts from prison letters. *The Prison Journal*, 80(4), 391–406.

Austin, A. (2005). Prisonization. In M. Bosworth (Ed.), *Encyclopedia of prisons and correctional facilities* (Vol. 2, pp. 765–767). Sage.

Austin, J., & Irwin, J. (2001). *It's about time: America's incarceration binge* (3rd ed.). Wadsworth.

Austin, J., Fabelo, T., Gunter, A., & McGinnis, K. (2006). *Sexual violence in the Texas prison system.* The JFA Institute. https://www.ojp.gov/pdffiles1/nij/grants/215774.pdf

Beck, A., & Johnson, C. (2012). *Sexual victimization reported by former state prisoners, 2008* (NCJ 237383). U.S. Department of Justice, Office of Justice Programs, Bureau of Justice Statistics. https://www.bjs.gov/content/pub/pdf/svrfsp08.pdf

Bondesson, U. (1989). *Prisoners in prison societies.* Transaction.

Bowker, L. (1980). *Prison victimization.* Elsevier North Holland.

Bureau of Justice Statistics. (2004). *Data collections for the Prison Rape Elimination Act of 2003.* U.S. Department of Justice, Office of Justice Programs. https://www.bjs.gov/content/pub/pdf/dcprea03.pdf

Butler, T., Richters, J., Yap, L., & Donovan, B. (2013). Condoms for prisoners: No evidence that they increase sex in prison, but they increase safe sex. *Sexually Transmitted Infections, 89*(5), 377–379.

Caldwell, M. G. (1956). Group dynamics in the prison community. *Journal of Criminal Law and Criminology, 46*(5), 648–657.

Calhoun, A., & Coleman, H. (2002). Female inmates' perspectives on sexual abuse by correctional personnel: An exploratory study. *Women & Criminal Justice, 13*(2/3), 101–124.

Cantora, A. (2014). Prison gangs. In B. A. Arrigo (Ed.), *Encyclopedia of criminal justice ethics* (Vol. 2, pp. 707–709).

Cecil, D. K. (2015). *Prison life in popular culture: From "The Big House" to "Orange is the New Black."* Lynne Rienner Publishers.

Clemmer, D. (1940). *The prison community.* Christopher.

D'Alessio, S. J., Flexon, B., & Stolzenberg, L. (2013). The effect of conjugal visitation on sexual violence in prison. *American Journal of Criminal Justice, 38*, 13–26.

Davis, A. J. (1968). Sexual assaults in the Philadelphia prison system and sheriff's vans. *Trans-Action, 6*(2), 8–16.

De Claire, K., & Dixon, L. (2017). The effects of prison visits from family members on prisoners' well-being, prison rule breaking, and recidivism: A review of research since 1991. *Trauma, Violence, and Abuse, 18*, 185–199.

Dobbs, R. R., & Waid, C. A. (2005). Prison culture. In M. Bosworth (Ed.), *Encyclopedia of prisons and correctional facilities* (Vol. 2, pp. 719–723). Sage.

Donaldson, S. (2001). A million jockers, punks, and queens. In D. Sabo, T. Kupers, & W. London (Eds.), *Prison masculinities* (pp. 118–126). Philadelphia, PA: Temple University Press.

Dumond, R. (2000). Inmate sexual assault: The plague that persists. *The Prison Journal, 80*(4), 407–414.

Einat, T., & Einat, H. (2000). Inmate argot as an expression of prison subculture: The Israeli case. *The Prison Journal, 80*(3), 309–325.

Einat, T., & Rabinovitz, S. (2012). A warm touch in a cold cell: Inmates' views on conjugal visits in a maximum-security women's prison in Israel. *International Journal of Offender Therapy and Comparative Criminology, 57,* 1522–1545.

Fishman, J. F. (1934). *Sex in prison: Revealing sex conditions in American prisons.* National Library Press.

Fleischer, M., & Krienert, J. (2006). *The culture of prison violence.* National Institute of Justice.

Fowler, S. K., Blackburn, A. G., Marquart, J. W., & Mullings, J. L. (2010). Inmates' cultural beliefs about sexual violence and their relationship to definitions of sexual assault. *Journal of Offender Rehabilitation, 49*(3), 180–199.

Gaes, G., & Goldberg, A. (2004). *Prison rape: A critical review of the literature* [Working Paper]. National Institute of Justice. https://www.researchgate.net/publication/252520860_Prison_Rape_A_Critical_Review_of_the_Literature

Goffman, E. (1961). *Asylums: Essays on the social situation of mental patients and other inmates.* Doubleday Anchor.

Hensley, C., Castle, T., & Tewksbury, R. (2003). Inmate-to-inmate sexual coercion in a prison for women. *Journal of Offender Rehabilitation, 37,* 77–87.

Hensley, C., Tewksbury, R., & Koscheski, M. (2002). The characteristics and motivations behind female prison sex. *Women & Criminal Justice, 13*(2/3), 125–139.

Hensley, C., Wright, J., Tewsbury, R., & Castle, T. (2003). The evolving nature of prison argot and sexual hierarchies. *The Prison Journal, 83,* 289–300.

Inderbitzin, M. (2005). Inmate code. In M. Bosworth (Ed.), *Encyclopedia of prisons and correctional facilities* (Vol. 1, pp. 472–474). Sage.

Irwin, J. (1980). *Prisons in turmoil.* Little, Brown.

Irwin, J., & Cressey, D. (1962). Thieves, convicts, and the inmate subculture. *Social Problems, 54,* 590–603.

Keys, D. P. (2002). Instrumental sexual scripting: An examination of gender-role fluidity in the correctional institution. *Journal of Contemporary Criminal Justice, 18*(3), 258–278.

Kirkham, G. (1971). Homosexuality in prison. In J. M. Henslin (Ed.), *Studies in the sociology of sex.* Appleton-Century-Crofts.

Kubiak, S. R., Brenner, H., Bybee, D., Campbell, R., Cummings, C., Darcy, K. M., & Fedock, G. (2017). Sexual misconduct in prison: What factors affect whether incarcerated women will report abuse committed by prison staff? *Law and Human Behavior, 41,* 361–374.

Kubiak, S. R., Brenner, H., Bybee, D., Campbell, R., & Fedock, G. (2018). Reporting sexual victimization during incarceration: Using ecological theory as a framework to inform and guide future research. *Trauma, Violence, and Abuse, 19,* 94–106.

Lauger, A. (2020). *PREA data collection activities, 2020.* U.S. Department of Justice, Office of Justice Programs, Bureau of Justice Statistics. https://www.bjs.gov/index.cfm?ty=pbdetail&iid=6886

Listwan, S., & Hanley, D. (2012). *The prison experience and reentry: Examining the impact of victimization on coming home.* National Institute of Justice.

Lockwood, D. (1980). *Prison sexual violence.* Elsevier.

Marcum, C. D. (2013). Examining prison sex culture. In C. Marcum & T. Castle (Eds.), *Prison sex: Myths and realities.* Lynne Rienner Press.

Marcum, C. D., Hilinski, C., & Freiburger, T. (2012). Examining the correlates of male and female inmate misconduct. *Security Journal, 27*(3), 284–303.

McCorkle, L. W., & Korn, R. (1962). Resocialization within walls. In N. Johnston, L. Savitz, & McElreath, D. H., Doss, D. A., Jensen, C. J., III, Wigginton, M. P., Mallory, S., Lyons, T., Williamson, L., & Jones, D. W. (2016). The end of the Mississippi experiment with conjugal visitation. *The Prison Journal, 96*(5), 752–764.

McManimon, P. F., Jr. (2005). Deprivation. In M. Bosworth (Ed.), *Encyclopedia of prisons and correctional facilities* (Vol. 1, pp. 223–226). Sage.

Miller, K. (2010). The darkest figure of crime: Perceptions of reasons for male inmates to report sexual assault. *Justice Quarterly, 27,* 692–712.

National PREA Resource Center. (2021). Prison Rape Elimination Act. Available at: https://www.prearesourcecenter.org/about/prison-rape-elimination-act

National Standards to Prevent, Detect, and Respond to Prison Rape, 28 C.F.R. §115 (2012)

O'Brien, J. (2009). Prison culture. In E. Gunnison (Ed.), *Encyclopedia of gender and society* (Vol. 2, pp. 677–681). Sage.

Owen, B., Pollock, J., Wells, J., & Leahy, J. (2014). *Critical issues impacting women in the justice system: A literature review.* National Institute of Corrections. https://nicic.gov/sites/default/files/033010.pdf

Piecora, C. (2014, September). *Female inmates and sexual assault.* Jurist: Legal News & Research. http://jurist.org/dateline/2014/09/christina-piecora-female-inmates.php

Pollock, J. (2002). *Women, prison & crime.* Wadsworth.

Rantala, R. (2018, July). *Sexual victimization reported by adult correctional authorities, 2012–15* (NCJ 251146). U.S. Department of Justice, Office of Justice Programs, Bureau of Justice Statistics. https://www.bjs.gov/content/pub/pdf/svraca1215.pdf

Ross, J. I. (2009). Prison gangs. In S. L. Gabbidon (Ed.), *Encyclopedia of race and crime* (Vol. 2, pp. 657–659). Sage.

Santos, M. (2005). Contraband. In M. Bosworth (Ed.), *Encyclopedia of prisons and correctional facilities* (Vol. 1, pp. 160–162). Sage.

Senkowski, V., Norris, K., McGaughey, A., & Branscum, P. (2016). A review of the effectiveness of HIV sexual risk prevention interventions in adult prison inmates. *Journal of Correctional Healthcare, 22*(4), 309–321.

Siegal, N. (2001). Sexual abuse of women inmates is widespread. In M. Wagner (Ed.), *How should prisons treat inmates? Opposing viewpoints.* Greenhaven Press.

Stewart, E. C. (2007). The sexual health and behaviour of male prisoners: The need for research. *The Howard Journal*, *46*(1), 43–59.

Struckman-Johnson, C., & Struckman-Johnson, D. (2000). Sexual coercion rates in seven Midwestern prison facilities for men. *The Prison Journal*, *80*(4), 379–390.

Subramanian, Y., Khan, M. N., Berger, S., Foisy, M., Singh, A., Woods, D., Pyne, D., & Ahmed, R. (2016). HIV outcomes at a Canadian remand centre. *International Journal of Prisoner Health*, *12*(3), 145–156.

Sullivan, M. (2005). Tattooing. In M. Bosworth (Ed.), *Encyclopedia of prisons and correctional facilities* (Vol. 2, pp. 947–949). Sage.

Sykes, G. M. (1958). *The society of captives: A study of maximum-security prisons*. Princeton University Press.

Trammell, R. (2009). Values, rules, and keeping the peace: How men describe order and the inmate code in California prisons. *Deviant Behavior*, *30*(8), 746–771.

United States Department of Justice. (2019). *Investigation of Alabama's state prisons for men*. Department of Justice. https://www.splcenter.org/sites/default/files/documents/doj_investigation_of_alabama_state_prisons_for_men.pdf

Williams, S. P., Myles, R. L., Sperling, C. C., & Carey, D. (2018). An intervention for reducing the sexual risk of men released from jails. *Journal of Correctional Health Care*, *24*, 71–83.

Wolff, N., Blitz, D., Shi, J., Bachman, R., & Siegel, J. (2006). Sexual violence inside prisons: Rates of victimization. *Journal of Urban Health: Bulletin of the New York Academy of Medicine*, *83*(5), 835–848.

CHAPTER 8

Correctional Programming

CHAPTER OBJECTIVES

After reading this chapter, you should be able to:

- Explain the concept of the principle of least eligibility and how it affects the resources allocated for correctional programming.
- Discuss the factors considered in the classification process.
- Identify the multiple types of correctional programming.
- Identify the benefits and risks of each category of correctional programming.

KEY WORDS

Cognitive skill building
Confrontation therapy
Contract labor system
Correctional programming
Educational programs
Deliberate indifference
Group therapy
Lease system
Piece price system
Principle of least eligibility
Prison maintenance

Psychotherapy
Public account system
Reality therapy
Recreational programming
Rehabilitative programs
Sex offender programs
Social therapy
Substance abuse programs
Therapeutic communities
Vocational programs

CASE STUDY: GIRL SCOUTS BEYOND BARS

Over 60% of women who are incarcerated have at least one child. The majority of these children are raised by another family member, often a grandparent or a relative other than the father, while the mother is in prison or jail. It is difficult for the incarcerated mother to maintain bonds and regular communication with her children, and this can have an especially harmful effect on young girls. These girls can experience depression and withdrawal, and may exhibit frustration via aggressive behavior or substance use.

In 1992, the Girl Scouts of Central Maryland and the National Institute of Justice formed a partnership and developed Girl Scouts Beyond Bars (GSBB) to give girls age 5 through 17 the opportunity to build and maintain relationships with their incarcerated parents. Since 2003, this program has been funded by the Office of Juvenile Justice and Delinquency Prevention, and it can now be found all over the country. GSBB allows girls to attend regular troop meetings with their mothers in the correctional facility, as well as special activities and even sleepovers. This encourages the strengthening of bonds between daughters and their incarcerated mothers, with the hope of positive emotional and mental health for both parties.

Questions for Discussion

1. In your opinion, would participating in GSBB have a positive effect on recidivism for the women who participate? Why or why not?
2. How do you feel the scouts might be affected by this consistent interaction with their mothers in a correctional facility? Are there potential negative consequences?

INTRODUCTION

State and federal correctional facilities have been offering correctional programming for decades, but support for these programs has wavered depending upon the correctional philosophy of the era. As discussed in previous chapters, Robert Martinson's (1974) study on correctional programming infamously asserted that "nothing works," shifting the emphasis away from the rehabilitation used in the mid-20th century and toward targeting resources to fund punitive punishment in the 1980s and 1990s. However, in the early 21st century, the field shifted again toward a belief that programming could be effective at improving life within a facility, as well as reducing recidivism.

Gendreau et al. (2004) argued that correctional intervention could be very effective if an incarcerated person's risk of recidivating, personal characteristics, and responsivity were examined individually. Furthermore, if a risk-need-responsivity (RNR) model is used, incarcerated persons (particularly those with high risk) could have much lower recidivism rates (Andrews & Bonta, 2010). While criminal history is a high predictor of future criminality (Caudy et al., 2013) and cannot be changed (i.e., it is a **static factor**), **dynamic factors** such as lack of education and substance addiction can be addressed and improved. Analysis of multiple studies has found that the correctional interventions that are carefully planned with an RNR basis, rather than being chosen because they are cheapest to run or most appealing to the public, will have the most success in reducing recidivism (Duwe & Clark, 2015).

Despite empirical evidence demonstrating that crime reduction for incarcerated persons has guided the development and implementation of correctional programming in use today, many members of society are not supportive of providing individuals with "extras" during incarceration. The **principle of least eligibility** asserts that individuals should receive the minimum benefits and services required by law during their incarceration (Sieh, 1989). This mantra, held by many members of society, is based on the belief that persons who have committed crime should not be entitled to anything beyond food, shelter, and basic care (i.e., they should not receive beneficial services and programs that may not necessarily be available to those who have not broken the law). While the general public supports both rehabilitation of incarcerated persons and successful reentry practices, many see correctional programming as an extravagant expense that rewards criminal behavior, confirming the stereotype of the "country club prison."

The fate of the original Pell Grant program is a classic example of the repercussions of applying the principle of least eligibility (Mastrorilli, 2016). Pell Grants provided college loans to inmates, accompanied by repayment rules that were beneficial to individuals reentering society after incarceration. In 1994, Senator Kay Bailey Hutchinson (R) of Texas argued that providing college courses to incarcerated persons cost taxpayers $2 million and prevented 100,000 students from attending institutions of higher education. Despite the fact that this information was wrong (of the four million grants awarded that year, only 23,000 went to inmates), and that research indicated educational programs were one of the strongest predictors of decreased recidivism, the Pell Grant was quashed (Clear et al., 2019; Mastrorilli, 2016).

As we move well into the 21st century, more Americans are recognizing the importance of educational programming for rehabilitation and success, which is very encouraging for our correctional population. In 2017, the United States Department of Education introduced the Second Chance Pell Pilot Program, with the intent of measuring the impact of these grants for inmate college students (Douglas-Gabriel, 2016; Mastrorilli, 2016). Sixty-seven institutions of higher education have agreed to participate for 3 years, with an expectation of enrolling 12,000 eligible students. The Higher Education Act's Grants for

Youth Offenders program, targeting individuals under age 25 with less than 5 years to serve, has also contributed millions of dollars in funding to fuel the success this program is hoped to have.

It is encouraging that public awareness of the benefit and effectiveness of correctional programming as a whole is increasing. However, providing enough funds to meet the needs of incarcerated persons is still an uphill battle. Many prison programs have long waiting lists, due to the supply-and-demand ratio. Many incarcerated persons are unable to enroll in classes that would be useful to them before they are released. The purpose of this chapter is to examine the various types of programming available to incarcerated persons, as well as the limitations and benefits associated with each program. Before these categories are explored, the process of determining which programming is suitable for each inmate must be explained.

CLASSIFICATION AND PROGRAMMING PLACEMENT

Participation in prison programming is not a privilege automatically afforded to inmates upon entry to a facility. Incarcerated persons must participate in the process of **classification**, in which individuals are assigned to a level of facility security and treatment programming based on thorough assessment and testing (National Institute of Corrections, n.d.). Introduced by Zebulon Brockway at the Elmira Reformatory in the latter part of the 19th century, classification involves psychological and educational testing to determine the needs and deficiencies of an incarcerated person. (Zebulon Brockway and the Elmira Reformatory were previously discussed in Chapters 1 and 3.) Classification also includes an analysis of past criminal history, and of administrative infractions during any past incarceration, to evaluate the security level (and restrictions) required for an offender. At the end of the process, an incarcerated person is placed in a specific facility and enrolled in (or placed on the waiting list for) the suggested correctional programming.

Correctional programming is structured activity that is offered to individuals under correctional supervision, for their benefit; it provides skills that will hopefully improve the success of their reentry. There are five categories of correctional programming: 1) industrial; 2) maintenance; 3) medical; 4) recreational; and 5) rehabilitative. The following sections discuss the background of each category, as well as its current implementation.

It is important to note that the classification process does not occur only during the entrance into a prison facility. Incarcerated persons' cases are regularly reviewed (every 6–12 months), so that they can be reclassified. For instance, an incarcerated person who has demonstrated the ability to be a model inmate and has not posed a security risk may be moved to a different facility and given more programming privileges. Conversely, an incarcerated person who continues to earn administrative infractions for certain behaviors may lose access to programming or be moved to an elevated security level. While many states require an incarcerated person to enroll in specific programming, such as GED courses or drug therapy, other programming is considered a privilege and can be taken away.

INDUSTRIAL PROGRAMMING

Our correctional roots have a long history of using labor as a core component of punishment. Labor was long viewed as an essential part of the reformation process for lawbreakers, as it teaches the value of hard work and its benefit of it (e.g., sense of self-worth, ability to purchase goods and services). In addition, labor was seen as a way to pass the time during the long days of incarceration, as well as a method to "pay back" the government for providing an incarcerated person with shelter, food, and safety. Even today, the state and federal governments profit greatly from the use of incarcerated persons for labor. They can pay incarcerated individuals a fraction of what it would cost them to employ non-incarcerated individuals, and have a captive group constantly able to fill a need without the cost of hiring practices. According to Sawyer (2017), the average wage for an incarcerated person is $0.63 per hour. However, incarcerated persons who work for state-owned businesses earn approximately twice as much as individuals who work for the prison system.

As has been noted previously, the early American penitentiary system was heavily influenced by England and was specifically influenced by the Quaker belief in the importance of repentance for sins through hard work and meditation (Krisberg et al., 2019). Penitentiaries built under the Pennsylvania system in the 19th century kept incarcerated persons in solitary confinement constantly. At approximately the same time, institutions built under the Auburn system, or congregate system, allowed individuals out of their cells during the day for hard labor with other inmates (though they were still not allowed to interact and communicate with non-incarcerated persons). Records from as early as 1819 indicate that boots and shoes were produced in the state prison in Auburn, New York.

As time passed, private employers recognized the benefit of contracting out incarcerated persons to make goods for sale, and they exploited inmate labor through various methods. In the **contract labor system**, employers provided the materials and machinery to the incarcerated persons and then sold the goods on the open market. The **piece price system** set a price for the goods made with the materials provided by the contractor. Lastly, contractors maintained laborers and worked them up to 16 hours per day in the **lease system**, which was often seen with early chain gangs in the South. All of these systems paid the incarcerated persons nothing for their labor, with the government and contractors profiting. Corruption was not unusual in these situations, with bribes offered and wardens profiting (Krisberg et al., 2019).

In the late 19th century, labor leaders and reformers lobbied for the prohibition of contract labor by incarcerated persons. In response to the criminalization of contract labor, states like Minnesota and Wisconsin instituted **public account systems**. These states began making twine in the prisons by purchasing the materials and using labor by incarcerated persons. Oklahoma had particular success with the program, reducing the cost of twine for farmers and earning profits that paid for over 60% of prison operation costs. Unfortunately, corrupt behavior began again, and private industry stopped cooperating when the prison began making more profit than those companies.

The 20th century saw a consistent rollercoaster of change in regard to the perception and use of prison labor. In 1929, Congress passed the Hawes-Cooper Act (previously discussed in Chapter 1), followed by additional pieces of legislation in 1935 and 1940 that outlawed incarcerated-person-made goods from interstate commerce (Fields, 2005). By 1940, all states had followed suit. However, at the initiation of World War II, President Franklin Roosevelt ordered the government to reinstate goods production in state and federal prisons for the military effort. President Harry Truman revoked the order after pressure from labor unions.

It was not until the Nixon administration that the tide began to turn regarding the use of the prison industry. In 1973, the National Advisory Commission on Criminal Justice Standards and Goals reported that most incarcerated persons did not engage in productive work during incarceration (National Legal Aid & Defender Association, 2017). Congress lifted the ban on interstate sale of prison-made goods and encouraged the improvement of the prison industry in 1979. In addition, the Law Enforcement Assistance Administration (LEAA) allotted funding for seven states to develop industry programs in their prison facilities. Although this would again implement a relationship of free labor versus prison labor, the following standards were implemented for these programs, to help avoid corruption and abuse:

1. Reasonable wage (dependent on the job, with some close to federal minimum wage);
2. Designated schedule for inmate employees;
3. Productivity standards akin to private industry;
4. Hiring and firing standards;
5. Self-sufficient operations; and
6. Goal of postrelease job placement.

By the end of the 20th century, almost 20 states were participating in prison industry production, and that number has only grown. Prison industries offer a variety of goods and services, including clothing, furniture, and agricultural products.

Today, there are two main methods used by states when they utilize the prison industry. In order to diminish resentment and competition between prison and private industry, states that use a **state-use system** only sells their goods and services to state agencies (Lovely, 1913). This system, the most common form of prison industry, allows states to purchase some goods more cheaply for their institutions without competing with the open market. Some states purchase a multitude of materials for their public schools from the prison industry, such as desks, milk, and vegetation for school meals. Uniforms for government employees are also made in the prison industry, as well as license plates for all licensed drivers in multiple states. While the state-use system can be financially beneficial for the state budget, it also has downfalls. Skills acquired in the prison industry are often outdated and specific to the prison industry, therefore not transferable to the labor market outside of prison. With the boom of technology and changing trade skills, a proficient incarcerated person may be unable to compete with other skilled individuals (without a criminal history) when seeking a job after release.

The **public works and ways system**, another method used by states to utilize the prison industry, is seen frequently in the 21st century. Incarcerated persons are hired to work for the state on construction and maintenance projects outside the prison, such as building repair, bridge construction or repair, and pothole repair. After release, these skills are extremely beneficial and helpful for obtaining a job in maintenance, construction, or public works.

Most incarcerated persons prefer to participate in the prison industry, and there are often more willing participants than positions available. Incarcerated persons earn money that can be used for commissary or saved for basic needs after release from prison. The prison industry allows individuals to have a sense of purpose and hopefully to learn skills that will benefit them when they are released, allowing them more autonomy. Lastly, it gives them the opportunity to leave the cell block and interact with other inmates. While there are always social benefits that equate to these positions, there is also the opportunity for corruption (as discussed in Chapter 15).

MAINTENANCE PROGRAMS

Much like any other agency that utilizes a structure to house operations, a correctional facility also requires regular maintenance. These facilities, often housing hundreds of people, are like a mini-city, providing many of the services a city does: mail delivery, food preparation, landscaping, building and road maintenance, and more. As a result, it is necessary to employ dozens of individuals to maintain a correctional facility. It is more economical to hire incarcerated persons to provide **prison maintenance** than it is to contract out workers or maintain more staff. Furthermore, it allows for a system of reward and punishment, providing incentives for incarcerated persons to perform their jobs appropriately so as to climb the hierarchy of preferred assignments.

There are a variety of prison maintenance jobs, ranging in prestige and responsibility (Zoukis, 2017). The positions most coveted are those linked to access to power, as well as mobility through the facility. For example, incarcerated persons who perform clerical work in the administrative building with the warden and the warden's staff often have access to private records. Information can be a priceless commodity, and these employed incarcerated individuals can receive goods and favors for accessing information about other people who are incarcerated, such as their risks and needs, programming, and infractions. In addition, those people who are awarded clerical jobs have gained the trust of the administration and are viewed as low-risk. They generally work in a temperature-controlled office at a comfortable desk, and may have access to extra snacks and preferable schedules; these conditions compare favorably to the work conditions of an incarcerated individual who cuts grass in the hot sun.

Any prison maintenance assignments that provide access to goods and services are appealing to incarcerated individuals as a method of obtaining and transporting contraband. Individuals who work in commissary or have kitchen duty can steal unauthorized food or toiletries for use or trade. Positions in areas where items have to be delivered or returned, such as library books or laundry, create potential for passing notes or other goods to incarcerated persons across the facility. Individuals who are given authority to act as a "handyman" have access to tools and can move about the facility, fixing broken lights or clogged toilets. While the punishment for participating in this unauthorized behavior can result in the removal of the position, the benefit is gaining favor amongst the incarcerated population.

The least desired position is janitorial work, but most incarcerated individuals begin their job placement here and move up the chain if they demonstrate trustworthiness. In order to run well, correctional facilities must be cleaned on a daily basis, with tasks often required multiple times a day. The floors in the cafeteria must be swept and mopped after each meal. All bathroom facilities must be cleaned, and trash must be emptied and taken to dumpsters. These tasks may be boring and sometimes even unappetizing (especially when they require dealing with human waste and fluid), but consistent performance demonstrates an incarcerated person's ability to do more challenging tasks.

MEDICAL

In 1973, J.W. Gamble was incarcerated in Texas when he was injured by a 600-pound bale of cotton that fell on him during his work at a textile mill. After complaining of stiffness and pain, he was examined, given two pain pills, and sent to his cell. When he was released for light work, Gamble refused to report for duty, stating that his back pain was as severe as on the day of the injury. He was placed in administrative segregation, as punishment, for several weeks. In February 1974, Gamble filed a *pro se* complaint, accusing the prison of cruel and unusual punishment based on Eighth Amendment protections. In *Estelle v. Gamble* (1976), previously discussed in Chapter 6, the Supreme Court of the United States ruled in favor of Gamble, stating that incarcerated persons are entitled to the same standard of medical care as individuals who are not incarcerated. In addition, the Court stated that incarcerated persons who file suit against inadequate medical care must demonstrate **deliberate indifference** in order to show unconstitutional treatment.

Estelle v. Gamble (1976) should not be interpreted as saying that incarcerated persons have the right to be taken to the top medical providers in the country to address their needs. However, the case does assert that incarcerated persons deserve basic health care and that if they are diagnosed with an illness or disorder, they should be treated appropriately. As these men and women are the responsibility of the state or federal government and do not have the ability to pay for health care services or obtain health insurance, it is the responsibility of the government to provide care. With that being said, the cost of medical care for correctional facilities is quite high, due to the plethora of health issues that accompany that population.

Prison facilities generally have a full-time staff of nurses, along with either a full-time or part-time physician available for checkups and examinations. Prisons also have a pharmacy to dispense medications for spontaneous medical issues, or for long-term diagnosis care. However, an incarcerated person who needs to see a specialist or has an emergency will be transported to a local hospital by correctional staff. It is important to note that, except in cases of life-threatening emergency, medical care may not occur as quickly in prison as it does outside prison. Incarcerated persons are seen based on the availability of the staff, and this may delay care that could be received more quickly at an urgent care or emergency room facility. In addition, some states charge co-pays to see a physician, which can deter impoverished incarcerated persons from seeking medical treatment (Hatton et al., 2006).

Lifestyle choices are a huge contributor to health. Incarcerated persons often bring in high rates of pre-existing conditions to prison, or acquire diseases while in prison (Bruswanger et al., 2009). Infected needles used for drug use and tattoos are a frequent contributor to hepatitis C and HIV. Another culprit for these diseases is unprotected sex, which also increases the transmission of other sexually transmitted diseases and the rate of unplanned pregnancy.

Incarcerated persons also have a variety of illnesses and issues found in the general population, such as epilepsy, cancer, and the common cold. A correctional facility can be an incubator for germs, and as inmates do not generally have regular access to fresh fruits and vegetables, nutritional options are limited, and inmate health is often not in prime state. Poor nutrition and hygiene practices can cause expensive dental problems, Type 2 diabetes, and other preventable illnesses. As the majority of individuals were of low-income status before incarceration, regular health care was not an option or a choice. Therefore, inmates bring with them a variety of health issues that must be addressed.

Another unpreventable predictor of health issues is aging, and prisons have an increased population of older adults. Due to harsh sentencing policies from the 1980s and 1990s, especially for drug offenders, individuals are serving much longer sentences and spending their "golden years" incarcerated. According to Clear et al. (2019), it is expected that approximately 20% of the prison population will soon be composed of individuals 50 or older. Health care for these individuals is often more expensive due to the medication, increased risk of long-term ailments, and mobility requirements.

Mortality rates have also increased for incarcerated persons, especially those who are 50 or older. Long-term incarceration can be extremely degrading to one's health, especially for older individuals. According to Mumola (2007), mortality rates for individuals over the age of 55 are 50 times greater than those of younger incarcerated persons. Deaths in prison increased by 4% between 2012 and 2013 (3,357 deaths to 3,479 deaths), with 89% of those deaths being illness-related (Noonan, 2015).

Lastly, although this does not pertain to physical health issues, the majority of incarcerated persons have been diagnosed with a mental illness. This can range from mild depression to violent schizophrenia, and between all the mental health conditions, a lot of time and financial resources are needed for treatment and regular medication. According to Bronson (2017), 24% of incarcerated persons in prisons and 31% of individuals incarcerated in jails reported having a major depressive disorder. Furthermore, 26% of persons in jail and 14% of persons in prison met the standard for serious psychological distress within 30 days, with prescription medication being the most common treatment.

RECREATION

In addition to all the benefits for reformation and reentry that prison programming provides, it also provides the benefit of occupying time. The old adage "idle hands are the devil's workshop" impresses the need to keep people busy, with the goal of maintaining control and safety, in a correctional facility. When an incarcerated person is not working or participating in some sort of programming, their down time spent in a cell or cell block is not as productive. This opens up the opportunity for them to get involved in nefarious and illegal activities. Providing alternative prosocial options, such as **recreational programming**, allows energy to be channeled in a positive way.

Recreation in a correctional facility can entail a variety of choices. Individuals can participate in athletics, such as basketball or baseball. Weight training is an option frequently seen in correctional facilities, as well as card-playing or board games. Activities involving art, music and drama are also available in many prisons.

Participation in any type of recreational activity can allow incarcerated persons to meet others who share similar interests and to form friendships. It also teaches teamwork and mediation skills and, essentially, teaches people how to behave appropriately in a social environment. However, like any type of programming in a correctional facility, recreation presents security risks. Socialization with other incarcerated persons opens up opportunities to pass contraband and plan vengeful activities against other people. It is not unusual for competitive athletics to flare tempers, and this may result in physical altercations or violent attacks. Prison recreation requires constant supervision and careful management, which can be extremely difficult due to the huge disparity seen in the incarcerated-person-to-staff ratio.

REHABILITATIVE

The goal of **rehabilitative programs** is to provide treatment, not punishment, to incarcerated persons. These programs aim to improve the person, and to teach skills and provide resources that will aid successful reintegration upon release. This category of correctional programming has several subcategories, all of which address a deficit in an inmate's life or character that is a result of environment, lack of resources, or family circumstances, to name a few.

Educational and Vocational Programs

Research has consistently indicated that employment is a key factor in predicting successful reintegration of individuals leaving prison. Simply having a criminal record makes it difficult to obtain employment, and not meeting the educational requirements makes it even more difficult. Approximately two thirds of incarcerated individuals do not have a high school diploma, and two fifths do not even have a general equivalency diploma (GED), indicating the demand for **educational programs**. In addition, many professions require certain skill sets that can be learned at vocational schools, but incarcerated persons often do not have access to these **vocational programs**. Past research has indicated that participation in these programs is significantly associated with early release from incarceration, as well as a decrease in recidivism (Wilson et al., 2000). This section will explore these programs.

Educational programs in correctional facilities have long waiting lists for admittance, as the majority of incarcerated individuals have low educational achievement. Many states require incarcerated persons who have not completed the eighth grade to be assigned to full-time educational programming. The curriculum focuses on math, basic reading, and English skills that will allow these individuals to meet GED standards. Research has indicated that individuals who participate in prison education programs are more than 40% less likely to recidivate after release, with even better success for those who participate in college-level courses (Steurer et al., 2010).

Although these programs can be very helpful to offenders, there are problematic issues that may be encountered. Learning disabilities are linked to delinquency, and many incarcerated persons have learning disabilities; as younger students, they often remained undiagnosed and/or did not receive the appropriate therapies in school. These students have limited academic abilities, which may have caused frustration associated with learning. It may be difficult to get these individuals to cooperate with instructors, due to past trauma from childhood. In addition, many students require educational materials well below their age and maturity. A 25-year-old incarcerated person may have a fourth grade reading level, but the books on that level focus on interests and ideas that are not generally appealing to a grown adult.

Vocational programs are those that teach skills that can be used in the workplace. Popular vocational programs include cosmetology and barbering, auto mechanic training, woodworking, and clerical programs. Other programs teach bricklaying and agricultural skills (Coppedge & Strong, 2013). However, the main problem with these programs is that the available worker pool is already past capacity, so it can be difficult to obtain a job upon release, especially with a criminal record. Some prisons offer very marketable skills with higher opportunity for hire, such as plumbing, welding, and denture building and repair.

Even with the appropriate skill set, reentering offenders may also need instruction on appropriate attitudes and behaviors to succeed in the workforce. Many individuals need help preparing a resume and cover letter, as well as proper interview responses. Punctuality and collegiality are important for employment success, as well as adherence to and respect of authority.

Psychological Programs

As mentioned in the section on medical programs, mental illnesses are prominent in the inmate population. It was not until the medical model era of the 1930s that the diagnosis and treatment of physical and mental health issues was recognized as an important method of inmate classification. The resources dedicated toward evaluation and treatment of incarcerated persons with mental illness became more of a mainstay in U.S. correctional facilities due to evidence that routine mental health care was effective in reducing violence and maintaining stable behavior (Stohr et al., 2013). However, as we are solidly in the 21st century, there is much debate about attributing criminal behavior solely to mental health factors. A multitude of factors have been found to be predictive of offending in addition to mental illness, including environmental factors, predisposition to violence, and peer influence. With that being said, the large proportion of incarcerated persons who suffer from mental illness supports the demand for associated correctional programming, using the various approaches discussed in this section.

According to the National Institute of Health (2016), **psychotherapy** is considered "talk therapy." Rather than using medical means, psychotherapy uses a variety of techniques to help guide a person through the discussion and discovery of emotions. In addition, this therapy (which can be one-on-one or group) can assist someone through determining why behaviors are performed. This type of therapy is one of the more common forms used by individuals outside of prison, with the person in counseling visiting a therapist on a regular basis and paying per visit. Due to the expense, and to debate over whether it is actually useful to offenders, this type of therapy is often not used in prison. Rather than addressing feelings, therapy in prison focuses on problems occurring in real time, such as broken bonds with family or reentry challenges (Clear et al., 2019).

If incarcerated persons participate in therapy that addresses emotions and feelings, **group therapy** is used. This is a more efficient and cost-effective method of therapy, but it also allows individuals to interact with others in therapy, discuss opinions on behaviors and thoughts, and confront each other. Colleagues in crime are often the most likely to call out another offender for justifying behavior, or simply lying, and they tend to be the most accurate in doing so. There are several types of group therapies used in prison, including cognitive skill building, confrontation therapy, and reality therapy.

Cognitive skill building therapy (also referred to as cognitive behavioral therapy) works to change the thought patterns of the offender's brain with the intention of helping them to make better prosocial choices (Mayo Clinic, n.d.). Many offenders are raised in environments where violence and criminality are promoted and expected; therefore, it is difficult for their minds to consider alternative options. Cognitive skill building teaches offenders to consider more positive options when stressful situations arise, and to understand the results. For instance, if a person is confronted by an aggressive individual, the therapy teaches methods to cope, back away, and decelerate the situation. This type of therapy has found success with offender populations if the situations are reflective of true group experiences (Ward et al., 2007).

Confrontation therapy is a discussion of the consequences of criminal behavior. Generally performed in a group, this can become quite a heated conversation, as individuals are confronted on rationalizing their behaviors and often feel led to defend themselves. Related to confrontation therapy is **reality therapy**, which emphasizes living a crime-free lifestyle in order to lead a better life. It focuses on the consequences of breaking the law, not allowing an offender to rationalize behaviors. This form of therapy has been shown to be effective for setting goals (Arnold, 2015).

Therapeutic communities (TCs), often considered a **social therapy**, are also utilized in correctional facilities. These groups focus on prosocial attitudes and behaviors, providing guidance on maintaining a crime-free lifestyle, and are often part of substance abuse treatment plans. TCs implement reward and punishment. This can be difficult for many incarcerated persons, as they have not been exposed to a background of discipline and consequence. TCs are separated from the rest of the general population in order to foster an environment of positivity and non-violent attitudes (Stohr et al., 2013).

Religious Programs

The First Amendment guarantees citizens of the United States the freedom to practice religion. Constitutional rights are somewhat conditional, based on safety concerns and the requirements of the facility, but the ruling of *Cruz v. Beto* (discussed in Exercise #2 and in Chapter 6) cemented the requirement of providing a reasonable opportunity to practice worship. A wide range of faiths can be found in prison, as can be found in the general public, and the proportion of individuals in a prison who follow a particular religion is often dependent on geographical location. For instance, there is a larger Catholic following in the Northeast, while Native American practices are more prominent in the Southwest.

Religious practice, although a constitutional right, does have limitations in a prison setting. For instance, a facility does not have to provide every religious leader possible for the wide variety of faiths practice. A chaplain can be hired to represent all faiths and assist with worship. In addition, religious artifacts only have to be provided as long as they are not a security risk, and justification must be given when not provided to the incarcerated person (*McFaul v. Valenzuela*, 2012). Dietary practices based on religious faith have also been addressed by the court system. If reasonable accommodations can be made, courts have ruled that facilities should provide religious meals to practicing inmates and should not require inmates to eat food that goes against their religious beliefs (*Koger v. Bryan*, 2008; *Moorish Science Temple of Amer., Inc. v. Smith*, 1982).

While research is mixed regarding the long-term effectiveness of religious programming on recidivism, there is evidence that it is helpful during incarceration. It provides opportunity for meditation and for peaceful time in a safe place, and it also provides confidantes in the form of spiritual leaders and like-minded inmates. Furthermore, it provides a positive outlet that helps people who are incarcerated maintain ties with family and friends, which decreases their participation in violence.

Sex Offender Programs

The term "sex offense" encompasses a broad range of offenses, including indecent exposure, prostitution, sexual abuse of a child, and attempted rape. Giving the same label to a large group of individuals who have committed a wide continuum of crimes is problematic when treatment is being developed for these offenders—one size does not fit all. Curriculum for these treatment programs must be customized for each individual and their behavior (Stohr et al., 2013). The programs used in the past have demonstrated varying levels of success in reducing recidivism. Furthermore, some offenders may recidivate not with sex offenses, but with other types of criminality.

Sex offender programs focus on a variety of topics. Programs for child sex abusers teach offenders how to approach inappropriate sexual arousals and potentially prevent those feelings. Curriculum for violent sex offenders discusses methods of managing impulsivity and neutralizing anger. The majority of sex offender programs, no matter the target, address issues with handling intimacy, utilizing prosocial behaviors, and managing emotions. Sex offender programs also explore an offender's past history of abuse, as many are also past victims of sexual abuse.

Substance Abuse Programs

Drug and alcohol abuse is an extremely prominent problem with offenders, as up to two thirds of incarcerated persons (dependent upon the jurisdiction) have a substance abuse issue. Approximately 50% of individuals are under the influence of a substance at the time of arrest, causing detox to be a huge problem for jails. The necessity for **substance abuse programs** in correctional facilities is blatant, and the waiting list for participation is long. Most facilities have some version of Alcoholics Anonymous, Narcotics Anonymous, and other specialized programs.

Despite the need for this programming, the recidivism rate for substance abuse program participants is often high if the program does not have the proper components. Simply dealing with physical addiction or psychological addiction does not provide enough tools to resist the temptation to use drugs or alcohol. According to Clear et al. (2019), studies have indicated that the most effective substance abuse programs have the following components:

1. Treatment should be phased, and should include 6–12 months in residence;
2. Privileges in residential treatment should be earned gradually, based on achievements in the program;
3. Multiple treatments should be used to address the various issues associated with addiction;
4. Plans for reentry should be coordinated with residential and community stakeholders; and
5. The program participant should undergo therapy and regular drug testing post-release.

Supporters of the principle of least eligibility have argued that the expenses of implementing these intense programs cannot be justified for offenders, especially when so many who are not incarcerated cannot afford such programs. However, the long-term benefits of reduction in both recidivism and relapse are proof of the effective change that occurs.

CONCLUSION

Our corrections system has a large catalog of options that can be offered to incarcerated persons, all designed with the intention of providing the inmate with skills to hopefully succeed during reintegration. However, this offering of programming is dependent on the financial resources available to the jurisdiction that provides the staff and programming materials.

DISCUSSION QUESTIONS

1. As a prison programming advocate, how would you effectively argue for resources for these programs?
2. What are the pros and cons of providing vocational and industrial training to inmates?
3. Offenders who fall under the category of substance abuser have a high recidivism rate, and programming can be difficult to develop. In your opinion, what types of therapies would be the most beneficial?

APPLICATION EXERCISES

Exercise #1: New Leash on Life

The state of North Carolina offers the "New Leash on Life" program in several of its minimum- and medium-security state custody facilities. Partnering with local animal shelters and rescues, the program pairs inmate trainers and dogs, and the animals spend 8–12 weeks living with the inmate. The inmate teaches the animal obedience, house training, and positive socialization, and then the dog can be placed with a family. This program has an approximate 93% rate for successful adoption placement, and the inmate can earn an apprenticeship certificate, which can be used to obtain employment after release.

How can this program, and those like it that teach transferable employment skills, reduce the recidivism rate of offenders? What other benefits can such programs provide?

Exercise #2: *Cruz v. Beto*

Fred Cruz was sentenced to 50 years in prison in 1961 for robbery by assault. Cruz contested his innocence and filed a pro se appeal to his robbery charge, earning him the reputation of a troublemaker. He was placed in the "Ellis Unit," a solitary confinement unit in Texas, until he agreed to drop the lawsuit. Cruz wrote to a Buddhist minister, Reverend Hogen Fujimoto, to request information on Buddhism. This landed him back in solitary with a diet of bread and water, as well as a small meal. Despite the facility's oppressive actions against him, Cruz filed another lawsuit on behalf of himself and other inmates who claimed religious oppression. The main claims included that he was denied use of the prison chapel, access to religious materials, and contact with his religious adviser.

The Supreme Court case *Cruz v. Beto* (1972) ruled that inmates should have "reasonable opportunity to pursue their religious faith." This was interpreted as a requirement that correctional facilities should provide a common space for all inmates to use to practice recognized religions. Spiritual leaders should be provided to lead religious worship and give counsel, though at some facilities inmates are asked to lead worship for certain faiths. For instance, if there is not a large Islamic population in an area surrounding a prison and access to an Imam is difficult, an inmate may provide guidance. In addition, the ruling also required the correctional facility to provide reasonable artifacts for worship, such as the Bible or Quran. Items that are considered dangerous (e.g., sharp objects, fire, etc.) are not allowed into the facility, even if they are considered items of worship for a religion.

How can participation in religious programming benefit an individual inmate, as well as the facility as a whole? Conversely, how can this type of programming negatively influence a prison community?

REFERENCES

Andrews, D. A., & Bonta, J. (2010). Rehabilitating criminal justice policy and practice. *Psychology, Public Policy, and Law, 16*, 39–55.

Arnold, M. (2015). *Reality therapy.* CRC Health. https://www.crchealth.com/types-of-therapy/reality-therapy/

Bronson, J. (2017). *Indicators of mental health problems as reported by prisoners and jail inmates, 2011–2012.* U.S. Department of Justice, Office of Justice Programs, Bureau of Justice Statistics. https://www.bjs.gov/index.cfm?ty=pbdetail&iid=5946

Brunswanger, I., Krueger, P., & Steiner, J. (2009). Prevalence of chronic medical conditions among jail and prison inmates in the USA compared with the general population. *Journal of Epidemiology and Community Health, 63*(11), 912–919.

Caudy, M. S., Durso, J. M., & Taxman, F. S. (2013). How well do dynamic needs predict recidivism? Implications for risk assessment and risk reduction. *Journal of Criminal Justice, 41*, 458–466.

Clear, T., Reisig, M., & Cole, G. (2019). *American Corrections* (12th edition). Cengage Publishing.

Coppedge, R., & Strong, R. (2013). Vocational programs in the Federal Bureau of Prisons: Examining the potential of agricultural education programs for prisoners. *Journal of Agricultural Education, 54*(3), 116–125.

Cruz v. Beto, 405 U.S. 319 (1972)

Douglas-Gabriel, D. (2016, June 24). *12,000 inmates to receive Pell Grants to take college classes*. Washington Post. https://www.washingtonpost.com/news/grade-point/wp/2016/06/24/12000-inmates-to-receive-pell-grants-to-take-college-classes/?noredirect=on&utm_term=.02d2c82d503c

Duwe, G., & Clark, V. (2015). Importance of program integrity: Outcome evaluation of a gender-responsive, cognitive-behavioral program for female offenders. *Criminology & Public Policy, 14*, 301–328.

Estelle v. Gamble, 429 U.S. 97 (1976)

Fields, C. (2005). Hawes-Cooper Act 1929. In M. Bosworth (Ed.), *Encyclopedia of prisons and correctional facilities* (Vol. 1, pp. 395–397). Sage.

Gendreau, P., French, S., & Gionet, A. (2004). What works (what doesn't work): The principles of effective correctional treatment. *Journal of Community Corrections, 13*, 4–6.

Hatton, D., Kleffel, D., & Fisher, A. (2006). Prisoners' perspectives of health problems and healthcare in a US women's jail. *Women's Health, 44*(1), 119–136.

Koger v. Bryan, 523 F.3d 789, 801 (7th Cir. 2008)

Krisberg, B., Marchionna, S., & Hartney, C. (2019). *American corrections: Concepts and controversies* (2nd Ed.). Sage.

Lovely, C. (1913). The state-use system. *The annals of the American academy of political and social science, 46*, 138–141.

Martinson, R. (1974). What works? Questions and answers about prison reform. *The Public Interest, 34*, 22–54.

Mastrorilli, M. (2016). With Pell Grants rising: A review of contemporary education literature on prison post-secondary education. *Journal of Correctional Education, 67*(2), 44–60.

Mayo Clinic. (n.d.) *Cognitive behavioral therapy*. https://www.mayoclinic.org/tests-procedures/cognitive-behavioral-therapy/about/pac-20384610

McFaul v. Valenzuela, 684 F.3d 564, 575–77 (5th Cir. 2012)

Moorish Science Temple of Am., Inc. v. Smith, 693 F.2d 987, 990 (2nd Cir. 1982)

Mumola CJ.(2007). *Medical Causes of Death in State Prisons, 2001–2004*. Washington, DC: Bureau of Justice Statistics. Available at http://www.bjs.gov/content/pub/pdf/mcdsp04.pdf

National Institute of Corrections. (n.d.). *Prison classification*. https://nicic.gov/prison-classification

National Institute of Health. (2016, November). *Psychotherapies*. https://www.nimh.nih.gov/health/topics/psychotherapies/index.shtml

National Legal Aid & Defender Association. (2017). *National advisory commission on criminal justice standards and goals, the defense (1973)*. http://www.nlada.org/defender-standards/national-advisory-commission

Noonan, M. (2015). *Deaths in local jails and state prisons increased for third consecutive year*. U.S. Department of Justice, Office of Justice Programs, Bureau of Justice Statistics. https://www.bjs.gov/content/pub/press/mljsp0013stpr.cfm

Sawyer, W. (2017). *How much do incarcerated people earn in each state?* Prison Policy Initiative. https://www.prisonpolicy.org/blog/2017/04/10/wages/

Sieh, E. (1989). Less eligibility: The upper limits of penal policy. *Criminal Justice Review, 3*(2), 159–183.

Steurer, S., Linton, J., Nally, J., & Lockwood, S. (2010). *The top-nine reasons to increase correctional education programs.* Rifuture.org. http://www.rifuture.org/wp-content/uploads/top-nine-reasons-to-increase-corr-ed-programs.pdf

Stohr, M., Walsh, A. & Hemmens, C. (2013). *Corrections: A text/reader* (2nd Ed.). Sage.

Ward, T., Mesler, J., & Yates, P. (2007). Reconstructing the risk-need-responsivity model: A theoretical exploration and evaluation. *Aggression and Violent Behavior, 12*, 208–228.

Wilson, D., Gallagher, C., & Mackenzie, D. (2000). A meta-analysis of corrections-based education, vocation, and work programs for adult offenders. *Journal of Research in Crime and Delinquency, 37*(4), 347–368. https://doi.org/10.1177/0022427800037004001

Zoukis, C. (2017, September). *Inmate work assignments in federal prison.* Zoukis Prisoner Resources. https://www.prisonerresource.com/work-assignment/inmate-work-assignments-federal-prison/

CHAPTER 9

Female Populations

CHAPTER OBJECTIVES

After reading this chapter, you should be able to:

- Identify the exclusive characteristics of incarcerated female populations and understand how these characteristics impact their incarceration experience.
- Understand the physical and mental health conditions faced by incarcerated female populations and recognize the illnesses that are distinctive to these offenders.
- Discuss the incarceration environment for female incarcerated populations and the unique experiences they face while incarcerated.
- Identify the key programming needs of female incarcerated populations, as well as the barriers to their successful reentry after prison.

KEY WORDS

Accompanied offenders

Adultification

Co-offending

Coerced offenders

Female sex offenders (FSOs)

Intimate partner abuse

Prenatal care

Sexually transmitted infections (STIs)

Shackling

Trauma-focused treatment

CASE STUDY: WOMEN'S PRISON NURSERY PROGRAMS

The bond between a newborn child and the new mother is something that is important for both the well-being of the mother and the growth and development of the child. In recognizing the importance of this bond, some prisons are allowing mothers to raise their children behind bars. One of these programs is the Wee Ones Nursery Program in Indiana, which was founded in 2008. Women in this program have their own dormitory and are separated from other incarcerated persons. The program accepts low-level offenders with less than 30 months to serve after giving birth. Accommodating up to 33 mothers at a time (making it the largest prison nursery in the United States), the program offers education about prenatal care and child development as well as opportunities to participate in substance abuse programming. A recent study of the Wee Ones Nursery program found that those in the program are about half as likely to return to prison after release, when compared to mothers who were not in the program. In addition to receiving assistance while in prison, mothers in the program also work with a transition team after release to continue things like drug treatment, vocational education, and health care (Becker, 2020). Despite the success of this particular program, prison nursery programs are relatively rare, with less than a dozen currently being offered in the United States.

Questions for Discussion

1. In your opinion, what are the strengths of prison nursery programs? Can you see any drawbacks in the use of these programs?
2. Should there be more prison nursery programs in the United States? If yes, what can be done to increase the use of prison nursery programs? How would you market these programs to key stakeholders if you were proposing starting a new program?

INTRODUCTION

In 2013, Netflix released the now-popular television show *Orange is the New Black* (OITNB). The main character of OITNB is Piper Chapman, who is based on the real-life individual Piper Kerman. Kerman was incarcerated for 13 months on charges stemming from a federal drug offense. She wrote a book titled *Orange Is the New Black: My Year in a Women's Prison*, which is the basis for the Netflix series (Terry, 2016; Kerman, 2011). The series, based loosely on Kerman's biography, gives the viewer a glimpse into the lives of women living in a prison. Issues related to victimization, mental health, addiction, and oppression are explored in the series (Blake, 2016). While viewed by some as sensational, OITNB has raised awareness regarding the plights of incarcerated women. How much of this show is true? What issues do incarcerated women face in prison? What is life like for women after incarceration? These are all questions that will be answered in this chapter.

The purpose of this chapter is to discuss the incarceration experience for incarcerated female populations. First, the chapter discusses the characteristics of incarcerated females, breaking down these characteristics by offense and offender type. Next, it explores the unique physical and mental health issues facing incarcerated females. The incarceration experience is also discussed, touching on specific topics such as the presence of pseudo-families and the trials faced by incarcerated mothers. Programs for incarcerated women and the reentry process for this population are also examined. Overall, this chapter explores the incarcerations process for women, from their experiences prior to prison through their reentry and all points in between, giving a basic overview of who incarcerated female populations are and the challenges they face both in and out of prison.

EXPERIENCES OF FEMALE OFFENDERS PRIOR TO INCARCERATION

Before examining the characteristics of incarcerated females, it is important to try and understand the experiences of this population prior to incarceration. The research on the pathways to prison for female offenders is limited, particularly for women serving lengthier prison sentences (Leigey & Reed, 2010). The research that does exist suggests that females enter prison as survivors of many types of traumatic experiences. Incarcerated women are more likely to experience sexual abuse when compared to both women in the general population and incarcerated men (Belknap, 2003). The perpetrator of this sexual abuse is most likely a male relative, and more than one third of incarcerated women report marital rape prior to incarceration (Leigey & Reed, 2010). Physical abuse is also common, with anywhere from 23%–55% of incarcerated women experiencing this type of abuse prior to the age of 18. The statistics regarding physical abuse get bleaker in the case of adulthood victimization rates, which are upwards of 75% or more for incarcerated women. Further, physical abuse of incarcerated women appears to be the result of ongoing events rather than a single incident (Owen & Bloom, 1995). Incarcerated women are also more likely to experience **intimate partner abuse**. For example, in a sample of incarcerated women studied by O'Keefe (1998), 98% of the sample reported being pushed, grabbed, or shoved by an intimate partner. This type of abuse results in a loss of self-identity and self-esteem for these female victims, something that is only of further detriment to them upon incarceration (Richie, 1996; Leigey & Reed, 2010).

In addition to the abuse suffered by incarcerated females, they are also more likely than male offenders to be lacking in social and emotional support systems in both adulthood and childhood. For example, research by McClellan et al. (1997) found that incarcerated women were less likely to be raised by biological parents and were more likely to run away as a child when compared to incarcerated men. They were also more likely to report that a close family member was addicted to drugs or alcohol, and more than half reported having an incarcerated family member. Many incarcerated females describe serious financial issues prior to incarceration and are more likely to be unemployed than incarcerated males. Because of this, incarcerated females are also more likely to be dependent on public assistance such as welfare (Daly, 1994). For some, even public assistance is not enough, as anywhere from 5%–32% report being homeless prior to incarceration (Cook et al., 2005; Owen & Bloom, 1995).

CHARACTERISTICS OF INCARCERATED FEMALES

At year-end 2019, there were approximately 107,955 women incarcerated at state and federal prisons in the United States (Carson, 2020). The number of incarcerated females, who make up 8% of the total prison population, decreased by 2,800 women between 2018 and 2019, representing a 3% decrease in the total population. A total of 32 states and the Federal Bureau of Prisons had declines in female populations, with the largest declines in Texas (down 800 incarcerated women) and Missouri (down 700 incarcerated women). The incarceration rate for women is 77 per 100,000 U.S. residents, while the overall incarceration rate is 1,025 per 100,000 U.S. residents (Carson, 2020). In addition to the state and federal populations, there are over 100,000 women in local jails, and over 6,500 female youth are incarcerated, bringing the total number of incarcerated women in the United States to over 230,000 at the time of this writing (Kajstura, 2019).

Females in Jails

In looking specifically at the impact of jail facilities on incarceration, it is astounding that nearly 25% of all women who are incarcerated are awaiting trial and have not yet been convicted of a crime. This number increases in jail facilities, where upwards of 60% of women are awaiting trial. Further, state and federal agencies often pay local jails to house additional incarcerated persons, and an estimated 12,500 women are in jail because of these housing arrangements. Further, while prison and jail populations are declining, between 2016 and 2017, the number of women in jail grew by more than 5%, despite declines overall. Interestingly, in this same time period, the arrest rate for women declined by 0.7%, meaning that new arrests do not seem to explain the increase of female offenders in jail. More research and data are needed to fully understand the increase in this population (Kajstura, 2019).

Female Youth Offenders

There are over 6,500 girls in juvenile detention facilities throughout the United States. Of these girls, approximately 600, or almost 10%, are there for status offenses, such as running away or truancy. Among male youth offenders, only 3% are incarcerated for status offenses. These numbers are particularly troublesome when one considers the fact that many status offenses result as a response to abuse; for example, a girl may run away from home because she is being abused there. Further, girls of color and LGBTQ youth are disproportionately locked away in juvenile facilities, with Black girls making up 35% of the confined population and Hispanic/Latina girls making up 19%, while White girls account for 38%. Additionally, 40% of girls in the juvenile justice system are LGBTQ, compared to less than 14% of boys (Kajstura, 2019). In an effort to explain gender differences among justice-involved youth, Epstein et al. (2017) suggest that society holds girls to a stricter code of conduct than boys, and that Black girls in particular deal with issues related to **adultification**. Adultification is the perceived belief (or misbelief) that youth are older, and more culpable for their actions, when compared to their peers. This can ultimately lead to more frequent contact with the justice system, and to harsher consequences resulting from that contact. It is important to recognize this bias, as it can result in youth of color having to shoulder added burdens that are beyond their control.

Female Drug Offenders

As was previously discussed in Chapter 4, the War on Drugs in the United States led to more people serving time for drug-related offenses. Further, Three Strikes laws and truth-in-sentencing laws led to longer, mandated sentences for drug offenders. In 2015 more than 15% of those in state prison and half of those in federal prison were incarcerated for a drug crime (Carson & Anderson, 2016). The changes to the correctional population because of the War on Drugs resulted in drastic changes in the female population, especially in comparison to their male counterparts. For example, roughly 25% of females incarcerated in state prison are there for drug crimes, compared to 15% of incarcerated males. Federally, 59% of females and 49% of males were incarcerated for drug charges. Of these women, most were convicted of nonviolent offenses and reported problems with substance abuse at the time of their offense (Bloom et al., 2004). As discussed by Carter (2019), females' crimes are more likely to be driven by addiction, with most incarcerated women reporting having used drugs at some point in their lives. In fact, 40% of incarcerated females reported being under the influence of drugs at the time of the arrest for which they were incarcerated, compared to 32% of incarcerated males (Bloom et al., 2004).

Female Sex Offenders

Much of the research on sex offenders focuses on male sex offenders (MSOs); however, there is a greater need to understand **female sex offenders (FSOs)** because the number of these offenders may be higher than first thought (Cortoni et al., 2017; R. Williams et al., 2019). The limited research on FSOs suggests that they are more likely to have a history of sexual and/or physical victimization (Wijkman et al., 2010). Also, FSOs are more likely to suffer from mental health and drug and alcohol problems (Muskens et al., 2011; Wijkman et al., 2010). A study by Freeman & Sandler (2008), which compared 390 FSOs with 390 MSOs from New York State, found that MSOs had a greater number of convictions, both for sexual and non-sexual offenses, and MSOs were more likely to offend against females. A more recent study of over 800,000 sex offenders found that FSOs and MSOs were similar in many respects; they offended more in their homes, they were likely to be acquainted with their victims, they were more likely to offend against victims of the opposite sex, and they seldom injured the victim during the offense (K. S. Williams & Bierie, 2015). In this same study, some differences did emerge: FSOs were more likely to have a male accomplice when committing their crime, and they were more likely to offend against their own children.

Female Co-Offending

While most offenses are committed by just one offender, it is estimated that anywhere from 10%–20% of all offenses are committed by more than one offender (D'Alessio & Stolzenberg, 2010). **Co-offending** occurs when a crime is committed with one or more accomplices (VanMastrigt & Farrington, 2010). As discussed by Becker and McCorkel (2011), mixed-gender (i.e., male-female) co-offending appears to influence men and women differently, with women who have male peers being more likely to commit violent offenses. This greater influence on females is seen across demographic characteristics such as age and race (Zimmerman & Messner, 2010). Pettersson (2005) argues that this increase can be explained by the gendered interaction dichotomy of the "dominant male/submissive female." This notion is supported by the fact that women often express submissive behavior in the context of co-offending relationships, suggesting that gender roles influence the occurrence of violence in these relationships (Heimer & DeCoster, 1999; Terranova & Vandiver, 2014).

In addition to the research on mixed-gender co-offending for violent offenses, there has also been a considerable amount of research on co-offending FSOs and MSOs (Budd et al., 2015; Mathews et al., 1989, 1991; Miller & Marshall, 2019; Nathan & Ward, 2001; Saradjian & Hanks, 1996; R. Williams et al., 2019). This research has identified two subsets of FSOs who co-offend: coerced offenders and accompanied offenders. The **coerced offenders** are more likely to offend only in the presence of a male co-offender, and often have high levels of emotional dependency toward their coercer (Mathews et al., 1991; Gannon & Rose, 2008). FSOs who are coerced offenders, though, are still active participants in the offending, typically victimizing their own children, most likely their daughter (Atkinson, 1996). The other subset, **accompanied offenders**, are not coerced into offending, and may initiate the sexual abuse themselves (Mathews et al., 1991).

Research has also compared solo FSOs with those who have a male co-offender (Budd et al., 2017; Comartin et al., 2018). Females with co-offenders are more likely to offend against a female victim when compared to solo FSOs. They are also more likely to offend against family members and are more likely to have more than one victim (Vandiver, 2006). Gillespie and colleagues (2015) found that co-offending FSOs had more environmental factors preceding their offense, such as having a romantic partner who was a sex offender. Co-offenders were also more likely to exhibit antisocial behaviors. Budd and colleagues (2015) also studied female co-offending and found that co-offending FSOs were more likely to have a stranger as a victim, caused more injuries, and used weapons more often in the commission of their sex offense. More research is needed on co-offending by FSOs, as understanding this population has implications for the risk assessment, management, and rehabilitation of these offenders.

PHYSICAL HEALTH OF INCARCERATED FEMALES

When considering the physical health of incarcerated female offenders, it is important to first understand the health risks these populations face pre-incarceration. Some of these risks include addiction, trauma, homelessness, and the burden of a variety of diseases (Alves et al., 2016; Harner & Riley, 2013). For many incarcerated women, these pre-incarceration risks are mixed with the carceral environment, resulting in a variety of health outcomes. For some women, prison is an environment that promotes better health through measures such as diagnosis and treatment of diseases, and preventative health interventions. For other women, the prison environment has a negative impact on their health, as experiences such as exposure to violence, isolation, and overcrowding can exacerbate health problems from their lives pre-incarceration (Alves et al., 2016).

Looking specifically at the physical health conditions that impact incarcerated females, one area that must be addressed is gynecological health. Women who are incarcerated are more likely to suffer from gynecological issues such as irregular menstrual bleeding and vaginal discharge (National Commission on Correctional Health Care [NCCHC], 2020). For example, Allsworth and colleagues (2007) found that more than one third of incarcerated women experienced abnormal menstrual bleeding, and many women reported having inadequate access to feminine hygiene products. Another issue specific to incarcerated women is their increased risk of cervical and breast cancer. Much of this risk can be attributed to lack of screening for these issues prior to and during incarceration (NCCHC, 2020). Also, women entering prison have higher rates of **sexually transmitted infections (STIs)**, with one study reporting that one third of women tested positive for STIs at admission (Willers et al., 2008). Further, when compared to incarcerated men, incarcerated women have a greater prevalence of diseases such as hypertension, diabetes, and hepatitis (Binswanger et al., 2009). The NCCHC (2020) recommends standards that correctional institutions should maintain when it comes to women's health services, and a major component of these standards involves providing comprehensive diagnostic and treatment services to address the unique health needs of incarcerated female offenders.

FEMALE OFFENDERS AND MENTAL HEALTH

The mental health of incarcerated female offenders is important to discuss, as incarcerated persons, in general, are 2–4 times more likely to have mental health problems when compared to community-dwelling individuals (McPhail et al., 2012). In looking specifically at female offenders, a nationally representative study of over 2,000 female offenders found that approximately 40% of the sample had depression, 24% were bipolar, and 17% had anxiety-related disorders (Aday et al., 2014). Other studies corroborate these findings, showing that anywhere from 20%–50% of incarcerated females suffer from mental health problems (Aday & Dye, 2019; Lynch et al., 2014). Incarcerated females also suffer from mental health problems at a greater rate when compared to incarcerated men, at the federal (61% vs. 41%), state (73% vs. 55%), and local jail (75% vs. 63%) levels (James & Glaze, 2006). When trauma, sexual abuse, and lack of access to health services all come into play, they can exacerbate the onset and continuation of mental health problems for female offenders (Bloom & Covington, 2009; James & Glaze, 2006). Consequently, factors such as undiagnosed and untreated mental disorders and unhealthy lifestyles have led to higher rates of incarceration for women (Carter, 2019).

Mental Health and Elderly Female Offenders

In 2015 there were more than 15,000 female offenders over the age of 50 being housed in U.S. prisons (Carson & Anderson, 2016). In addition to their physical health ailments, these elderly offenders also suffer from a number of mental health problems (Aday & Dye, 2019; Fedock, 2016; Leigey & Hodge, 2012). Depression is one of the most prevalent forms of mental health disorders among incarcerated women (Leigey & Hodge, 2012), and this is especially true for elderly incarcerated females, where the rates range from 10%–50% (Curtice et al., 2003; Murdoch et al., 2008; Strupp & Willmott, 2005). One study of older incarcerated women found that 30% of those aged 50 and older had mental health problems, while 65% of those 65 and older had the same problems (Sterns et al., 2008). While these numbers are significant, one must also keep in mind that they may actually be low, as many mental health problems among incarcerated women go undetected and untreated (Aday & Dye, 2019).

Since the number of elderly incarcerated female offenders who have mental health problems is so high, it is important to understand the risk factors that lead to depression and other problems among this population. As discussed by Aday & colleagues (2014), there is debate over whether the depression these women feel is influenced by the prison environment, or whether it is pre-existing and brought into the prison environment by the women. The deprivation model (previously discussed in Chapter 7), which is grounded in the classical work of Goffman (1961) and Sykes (1958), focuses on how the harsh and restrictive environment of a prison results in maladaptation among incarcerated persons (i.e., anxiety, depression, suicide, etc.). On the other side, the importation model focuses on the pre-prison experiences of incarcerated individuals and how those experiences affect their current mental health status. Rather than looking at the deprivation and importation models as an either/or situation, recent research has combined models to get a more holistic view of mental health disparities among incarcerated women (Armour, 2012; Dye et al., 2014; Aday & Dye, 2019). In their study of these two models among elderly incarcerated females, Aday and Dye (2019) found that both importation and deprivation models were related to depression among participants.

THE INCARCERATION EXPERIENCE FOR FEMALE OFFENDERS

As discussed by Einat and Chen (2012), most researchers of female prison life agree that the realities of prison are harsh, and are characterized by "persistent surveillance, a stringent schedule, and suppression of individuality" (pp. 108–109). This is often referred to as the "pains of imprisonment" (Chesney-Lind & Rodriguez, 1983), as previously discussed in Chapter 7. Many women are faced with the reality that they have to modify their attitudes and beliefs about the world if they are going to survive the prison environment. Upon entry, women are expected to quickly learn the values and norms of the prison environment, as abuse of the norms can result in harsh punishment for violators (Einat & Chen, 2012). Therefore, the prison experience is often a dynamic process of learning, adapting, and coping for female offenders (Carlen & Tombs, 2006).

Pseudo-Families

When a woman is incarcerated, she is often learning to adapt to an environment where she is exposed to things she otherwise would not be exposed to. For example, this may be a woman's first time being in a close environment with women from different cultural backgrounds, or her first time abiding by strict rules such as when to eat and sleep. Research shows that men and women act differently in the incarcerated environment, with women being more likely to be relational when compared to men (Harner, 2004; Kolb & Palys, 2018). To help cope with this environment, some women become involved in pseudo-families as a means of coping with the stress of incarceration and the separation from their own families outside of prison, as previously discussed in Chapter 7 (Propper, 1982; Severance, 2004). Some women join these families because they are deprived of heterosexual relationships while incarcerated, and they use pseudo-families to have a sexual relationship.

As discussed by Jones (1993), for most women in pseudo-families, it is less about sex and displaying sexuality and more about the love and support that comes from these relationships. This notion is supported by more current research by Kolb & Palys (2018), who found in their sample of formally incarcerated women who were in pseudo-families that the primary reason women reported joining the families was for a sense of belonging and emotional support. Many of these women were not close with family prior to incarceration, so they did not have outside visits; because of this, they formed new relationships to meet their emotional needs in prison. Kolb & Palys (2018) also found that these families offered protection from aggressive incarcerated persons. By showing strength through fighting with other families, women can demonstrate that they and their pseudo-family are not weak, thereby elevating their status within the prison.

In talking about pseudo-families, it is important to note that there are mixed results on this subject, with some research finding a decrease in the use of these family structures among incarcerated women (Collica, 2010). First, the idea of incarcerated women forming pseudo-families is something that is unique to female offenders in the United States; there is little evidence of this happening in other countries. Also, early research by Fox (1984) found that a decrease in participation in pseudo-families resulted in an increased participation in vocational and educational programs. This finding suggests that incarcerated persons who are participating in programs have less time to spend forming and maintaining family-like relationships. Further, Propper (1982) suggests that same-sex family relationships are sometimes misunderstood as romantic or sexual relationships, and that a distinction needs to be made between same-sex relationships and pseudo-families among both researchers and correctional staff. This is especially important for staff, as they assume that family-based relationships are automatically homosexual relationships, and research indicates that homosexual activities among pseudo-families are less important than platonic friendships (Kruttschnitt, 2000). Because of this misconception, staff may watch women in pseudo-families more closely, resulting in these women getting caught with minor institutional infractions, which can impact their incarceration experience (Collica, 2010). As a result of this increased scrutiny, females may avoid family-like relationships, which is why these types of relationships may be on the decline in prison.

Sexual Assault and Abuse Among Female Offenders

Women in the general population are also more likely to be victims of sexual assault and abuse, and that still holds true for incarcerated female populations. Several studies have looked at the sexual victimization history of incarcerated women. A recent meta-analysis by Karlsson & Zielinski (2020) reviewed studies on sexual victimization in childhood, teenage years, adult years, and since incarceration. There were 23 studies that reviewed childhood sexual abuse [CSA] rates, which ranged from a low of 10% to a high of 66%.

Six studies examined teenage sexual abuse [TSA], and the prevalence rate ranged from a low of 9% to a high of 36%. In 13 studies of adult sexual abuse [ASA], the prevalence rates ranged from 17%–68%. Additionally, six studies looked at revictimization after being incarcerated, and those rates ranged from 12% to 58% (Karlsson & Zielinski, 2020).

The reported high rates of victimization support the notion that there may be gender-specific pathways to incarceration (Salisbury & Van Vorhis, 2009). Karlsson and Zielinski (2020) also reported high rates of mental illness among incarcerated women, some of which was preceded by CSA & TSA. The link between sexual victimization and factors such as substance use disorders later in life suggests there is a greater need for psychological treatment and services for incarcerated women. Given the history of sexual violence, **trauma-focused treatment** is needed to best serve these populations (Carter, 2019; Karlsson et al., 2015; Roe-Sepowitz et al., 2014).

Misconduct and Prison Infractions

Much like incarcerated males, female offenders can engage in violent and aggressive acts that injure other incarcerated persons and prison staff (Reidy & Sorenson, 2018). Numerous studies indicate that incarcerated women are disciplined at a similar rate to incarcerated men for assaultive actions, but their actions are far less likely to lead to serious injury or death (Lahm, 2017; Reidy et al., 2012). Solinas-Sanders and Stacer (2012) researched a nationally representative sample of close to 3,000 incarcerated female offenders and found that they were less likely to engage in verbal or physical assaults on other incarcerated persons and staff (13%) when compared to men (20%). Another interesting finding from this study, which speaks to the power of maintaining connections with families while incarcerated, is the fact that violence was less likely for both males and females when the incarcerated person maintained telephone contact with friends and family outside of prison (Solinas-Sanders & Stacer, 2012). More research is needed to see if factors such as sentence length impact disciplinary patterns for incarcerated women (Reidy & Sorenson, 2018).

Incarcerated Mothers and Their Children

The increase in the number of incarcerated female offenders over the past few decades has resulted in an increase in incarcerated women with children and those who are expecting a child. Most incarcerated women, upwards of 80%, have a child at the time they enter prison, and three out of four of these children are under the age of 18 (Friestad, 2016; Vainik, 2008). Unlike incarcerated fathers, most incarcerated mothers were a single parent prior to incarceration, and were solely responsible for the care of their children (Glaze & Maruschak, 2009). This is not to say that children of incarcerated fathers are not impacted, but children with incarcerated mothers are more likely to experience guardianship and residency changes upon their mother's incarceration, resulting in a number of damaging, long-term consequences for these children (Friestad, 2016; Kjellstrand & Eddy, 2011).

While some mothers maintain contact with their children, almost half of all mothers report never having a personal visit with their children while they are incarcerated (Glaze & Maruschak, 2009). The reasons for the lack of visits vary. Many prisons are built in rural areas, requiring family members to travel in order to visit their incarcerated loved one, and some families simply do not have the resources to travel for visits. Some of the lack of visitation, though, is due to the mother's decision; some mothers believe the pains associated with visitation outweigh the benefits, and they do not want to take this risk. (Dixey & Woodall, 2012).

In addition to the number of incarcerated women who already have children, anywhere from 5%–10% of all women entering prison are pregnant upon admission, with more than 2,000 babies being born to incarcerated women annually (Vainik, 2008). Incarcerated women who are pregnant are considered high-risk due to the presence of some adverse factors, such as smoking while pregnant, alcohol and substance abuse, and the presence of STIs (Thomas & Lanterman, 2019). Despite the importance of **prenatal care** for these women, they often find that prenatal services are poor and inadequate, especially given that most state and federal facilities have limited policies regarding health care for pregnant incarcerated women (Weatherhead, 2003). Lack of prenatal care has become problematic for correctional officials, as some incarcerated women have sued over these issues. For example, in *West v. Mason* (1987), a class action suit was brought against the Connecticut Department of Corrections because of the lack of prenatal care, appropriate diet, medications, and vitamins for pregnant incarcerated women. As part of the settlement, correctional officials agreed to provide pregnant incarcerated women with a special diet and with access to nutritious food (Vainik, 2008). This is an important step in the right direction because failing to provide adequate prenatal care costs prisons and society as a whole more than the actual provision of the care, especially when lack of care results in costly medical complications that could have been avoided in the first place (Cardaci, 2013).

Another issue discussed in the literature on pregnant incarcerated women is the practice of **shackling** these women during their delivery. This occurs when mechanical restraints are used to limit the movement of pregnant women before, during, and after childbirth. Some of the devices used include handcuffs, zip ties, waist chains, and leg irons (Sichel, 2007). While the exact origins of shackling policies are not known, this practice became popular in the 1970s and 1980s (Thomas & Lanterman, 2019). Proponents of this practice justify it on the grounds that shackling protects those who come into contact with an incarcerated person when they leave the prison facility for a hospital facility, including correctional staff, medical personnel, and the general public (Mason et al., 2013). It is believed that shackling prevents escape, especially given the fact that over 90% of incarcerated people who escape report that they did not plan their escape in advance, but simply took advantage of the circumstances they found themselves in (Culp, 2005). Further, it has also been found that all incarcerated persons were equally likely to attempt escape regardless of characteristics such as gender (Culp & Bracco, 2005).

On the other hand, opponents of shackling pregnant women argue that these women need the ability to move freely, and that shackling places them at an increased risk of fall and injury. Further, the use of abdominal and leg shackles can impede medical staff's ability to provide care for pregnant women before, during, and after childbirth. Postpartum, the shackling of women puts them at an increased risk of blood clots and hemorrhaging due to restricted movement (Thomas & Lanterman, 2019). In addition to the potential harm to the mother, there is also risk to the fetus. The increased risk of falling, coupled with a decreased ability for the mother to break that fall if she is shackled, leaves the fetus at risk for injury. If an emergency C-section is needed, the time it takes to remove the restraints poses a threat to the unborn child, as even a delay of a few minutes can cause irreparable damages. Also, bonding between the mother and child immediately after birth is important for the child's development, and this can be hindered by shackles and restraints (Goshin et al., 2014). Despite these potential risks to mother and child, nine states currently allow the use of restraints during labor, and 28 states allow their use during the post-birth recovery (Thomas & Lanterman, 2019).

PROGRAMMING NEEDS OF INCARCERATED WOMEN

The goal of programming in prisons is to provide resources for incarcerated persons so that they can be successful during and after incarceration. As previously discussed, incarcerated women have different needs than incarcerated men do, and because of this, programming needs to be specifically tailored for incarcerated women. In reviewing programs for incarcerated women, there are three types of programs most frequently cited as important for reducing women's recidivism: substance abuse/mental health services, educational programming, and employment/vocational education (Spjeldnes & Goodkind, 2009). Additionally, programs that target parents are especially important given the large number of incarcerated women who have children. Therefore, programs created to strengthen family relationships before, during, and after incarceration are vital in the successful reintegration of incarcerated parents (Hairston, 1998).

Educational Programming

Carter (2019) suggests that programming focused on women's education, specifically on how it helps with successful reintegration post-incarceration, may be beneficial for incarcerated women. Women need to have a good education so they can get a good-paying job to acquire and maintain housing for themselves and their children. For some women, this may entail applying to college. Programs that assist women with things like the process of applying for college and financial aid, as well as exploration of careers and majors, may be of benefit to incarcerated women. At a minimum, basic courses needed to pass the general education development (GED) test should be available, as having this type of education in essential for a productive reentry. The importance of obtaining a GED cannot be understated, as research has shown that having a GED increases the likelihood of employment and higher earning potential. Further, obtaining a GED may have a trickle-down effect, as children with parents who graduate high school or obtain their GED are more likely to obtain their high school diploma, and are less likely to commit crimes (Laux et al., 2011). As discussed by Carter, "allowing inmates to complete educational programs and vocational training may increase their investment in conventional behavior and decrease opportunities for violating the law" (2019, p. 297). Given that the goal of any successful reentry program is that an offender does not recidivate, any opportunity to build social capital, such as through increased education, may be a step in the right direction.

Career and Vocational Education and Training

From a historical perspective, vocational training programs for incarcerated populations focused on men, and those programs that did focus on women often focused on traditional, gender-stereotyped roles for women (Young & Mattucci, 2006). Even though more programs are becoming available to incarcerated women, many women are not taking advantage of these programs. For example, in California, less than one third of incarcerated females take advantage of vocational and employment training programs; however, this is mainly attributed to the lack of program capacity for female offenders (Laux et al., 2011). Further, many programs focus on topics such as resume and cover letter writing, job search and interview skills, and how to dress for an interview. While all of these are important, they are not tailored to the unique needs of women returning to society after incarceration (Harley, 2014). To tailor programs, it is suggested that each offender should be to individually assessed on a variety of measures such as coping skills, stress management skills, and cultural context, in order to provide programming that addresses their specific needs (Snodgrass et al., 2017).

Parenting Programs

Most incarcerated mothers will resume their motherly roles upon release from prison, so maintaining and building relationships with their children while incarcerated is essential (Kennon et al., 2009). Much like parenting programs for non-incarcerated individuals, parenting interventions for incarcerated parents vary, depending on the desired treatment goal. For example, programs for short-term stays by jail offenders differ from programs meant for women with lengthy prison stays (Loper & Tuerk, 2011). Despite the desired outcome, parenting education programs for incarcerated females have historically been criticized for being inconsistent, often teaching ideals of parenting goals without giving parents the necessary tools they need to accomplish those goals in reality (Sandifer, 2008). For parental education to be effective, parents need to be taught the necessary skills they need to be an effective parent, and they need to be offered an interactional component where they can practice the skills they have learned. Unfortunately, very few prisons offer opportunities for both skill building and skill practice (Sandifer, 2008).

Research by Loper & Tuerk (2011) identified some potential treatment goals for parenting programs in prison. One potential goal is reduction of the stress that incarcerated parents face. It has been shown that reducing parenting stress and improving emotional regulation between parents and children results in improvements to both parents' mental health and problematic behaviors by children (Ortega et al., 2008). Another important goal of parenting programs is to improve the relationship between parents and their child's caregivers. Loper et al. (2009) found that incarcerated parents who had strong co-parenting relationships with their child's caregiver reported more frequent contact and better communication with their children. Increase in contact with their children can also be seen as a potential outcome goal of parenting programs (Gonzalez et al., 2007). Overall, especially in light of the challenges that incarcerated mothers face, they may best be serviced by a parental education program that "addresses ways of coping with stressful separation, mechanisms for achieving positive communication with children and caregivers, and recognition of the inmate's non-traditional role in her child's life" (Loper & Tuerk, 2011, pp. 90–91).

REENTRY NEEDS OF INCARCERATED WOMEN

As mentioned in this text, millions of people are incarcerated in the United States, and most of these individuals will eventually be released back into society. While there are more men reentering society than women, women face a number of unique issues that complicate their transition. For example, because of their higher rates of substance use and mental health issues, they may require additional treatment services to manage these issues (Bronson et al., 2017). They are also more likely than men to face economic issues such as unemployment (Staton et al., 2019). Also, as discussed, women are more likely to have children to take care of post-incarceration, and issues relating to parenting and custody can cause additional stress for these women (Koski & Constanza, 2015). These challenges ultimately affect the recidivism rates for women, with over 40% of women being reincarcerated within the first year of their release (Alper et al., 2018). Despite the challenges women face, the majority of research on reentry is focused on male reentry, and more research is needed on women in order to address the challenges they face after leaving jail and prison (Staton et al., 2019).

CONCLUSION

Although men make up the majority of incarcerated offenders in the United States, women are a fast-growing population in the corrections system. While the research on female offenders is limited compared to that focusing on male offenders, the research that does exist suggests that women face many unique challenges before, during, and after incarceration. It is important to understand and recognize these challenges, in order to inform correctional policies and create programs to best serve female offender populations. Almost all of the research on incarcerated women suggests that more inquiry is needed, in all areas regarding female incarceration, to better understand female offenders and the situations they face.

DISCUSSION QUESTIONS

- What are the experiences of women prior to incarceration? How might these experiences impact incarcerated female offenders?
- What are the typical characteristics of female offenders? What role do females play in specific types of crimes such as drug or sex offenses?
- How does incarceration impact women's mental and physical health? What can correctional officials do to promote the mental and physical wellness of female offenders?
- How do the programming needs of incarcerated women differ from those of incarcerated men? What types of programs are needed for the successful reentry of women?

APPLICATION EXERCISES

Exercise #1: Watch the Tutwiler Documentary

In 2020, PBS Frontline, in partnership with The Marshall Project, produced a short documentary called *Tutwiler* about a prison for women in Alabama. The video can be watched at the following link: https://www.pbs.org/wgbh/frontline/film/tutwiler/

As you watch the film, consider the following questions:

1. Who are the incarcerated women featured in the film? What challenges does each woman face?
2. What is the Alabama Prison Birth Project? What services does it offer to women at Tutwiler?
3. The film discusses how children are often searched when they come to the facility for a visit. What are the pros and cons of searching children prior to a visitation? What impact would this have on children?

4. In the film, women and their newborns are only together for 24 hours following the birth. What is the women's reaction to this? How long do you think women should be with their newborn children following their birth?
5. What is the Adullam House? How can it help the women who were incarcerated in this film?
6. What was happening at Tutwiler previously in terms of staff sexual abuse? What is being done to address these issues?
7. What is the breastfeeding program? How does this program benefit incarcerated mothers and their children?
8. What is the substance abuse program? What are some of the lessons the women learned through participation in the program?

Exercise #2: Explore Female Incarceration on the Prison Policy Initiative Website

For this exercise, you should visit the Prison Policy Initiative website at www.prisonpolicy. org. Do a search on their website for "Female Incarceration." A number of reports will appear. Some of the reports you might want to visit include:

- *Women's Mass Incarceration: The Whole Pie 2019* – https://www.prisonpolicy.org/reports/pie2019women.html
- *The Gender Divide: Tracking Women's State Prison Growth* – https://www.prisonpolicy.org/reports/women_overtime.html
- *State of Women's Incarceration: The Global Context 2018* – https://www.prisonpolicy.org/global/women/2018.html

You may choose one of these reports or any of the reports you find on the website. After you read the one you have chosen, you should be prepared to report back to your professor or to your classmates on what you read and learned. Some things to consider:

1. What report did you pick, and why did you pick that particular report?
2. What are the main issues facing incarcerated women that you can gather from the report you read?
3. What is being done to address the issues of the incarcerated women?
4. What are two or three main takeaways you are going to have after reading this report?

REFERENCES

Aday, R. H., & Dye, M. H. (2019). Examining predictors of depression among older incarcerated women. *Women & Criminal Justice, 29*(1), 32–51.

Aday, R. H., Dye, M., & Kaiser, A. (2014). Examining the traumatic effects of sexual victimization on the health of incarcerated women. *Women & Criminal Justice, 24*, 1–21.

Allsworth, J. E., Clarke, J., Peipert, J. F., Hebert, M. R., Cooper, A., & Boardman, L. A. (2007). The influence of stress on the menstrual cycle among newly incarcerated women. *Women's Health Issues, 17*, 202–209.

Alper, M., Durose, M. R., & Markman, J. (2018). *2018 update on prisoner recidivism: A 9-year follow-up period (2005–2014)*. U.S. Department of Justice, Office of Justice Programs, Bureau of Justice Statistics.

Alves, J., Maia, A., & Teixeira, F. (2016). Health conditions prior to imprisonment and the impact of prison on health: Views of detailed women. *Qualitative Health Research, 26*(6), 782–792.

Armour, C. (2012). Mental health in prison: A trauma perspective on importation and deprivation. *International Journal of Criminology and Sociological Theory, 5*, 886–894.

Atkinson, J. L. (1996). Female sex offenders: A literature review. *Forum on Corrections Research, 8*(2), 39-42.

Becker, L. (2020, May 7). *Special report: Women's prison nursery allows incarcerated mothers to keep their babies*. WBST 22. https://wsbt.com/news/local/special-report-womens-prison-nursery-allows-incarcerated-mothers-to-keep-their-babies

Becker, S., & McCorkel, J. A. (2011). The gender of criminal opportunity: The impact of male co-offenders on women's crime. *Feminist Criminology, 6*, 79–110.

Belknap, J. (2003). Responding to the needs of women prisoners. In S. F. Sharp & R. Muraskin (Eds.), *The incarcerated women: Rehabilitative programming in women's prisons* (pp. 93–106). Wadsworth Thomson Learning.

Binswanger, I. A., Krueger, P. M., & Steiner, J. F. (2009). Prevalence of chronic medical conditions among jail and prison inmates in the USA compared with the general population. *Journal of Epidemiology and Community Health, 63*(11), 912–919.

Blake, M. (2016, June 20). *How 'Orange Is the New Black' and other shows raise awareness of criminal justice and prison issues*. Los Angeles Times. https://www.latimes.com/entertainment/tv/la-et-st-orange-is-the-new-black-and-prison-awareness-20160616-snap-story.html

Bloom, B., & Covington, S. (2009). Addressing the mental health needs of women offenders. In R. L. Gido & L. Dalley (Eds.), *Women's mental health issues across the criminal justice system* (pp. 160–176). Pearson Prentice Hall.

Bloom, B., Owen, B., & Covington, S. (2004). Women offenders and the gendered effects of public policy. *Review of Policy Research, 21*(1), 31–48.

Bronson, J., Stroop, J., Zimmer, S., & Berzofsky, M. (2017). *Drug use, dependence, and abuse among state prisoners and jail inmates, 2007–2009*. U.S. Department of Justice, Office of Justice Programs, Bureau of Justice Statistics.

Budd, K. M., Bierie, D. M., & Williams, K. (2015). Deconstructing incidents of female perpetrated sex crimes: Comparing female sexual offender groupings. *Sexual Abuse: A Journal of Research and Treatment, 29*, 267–290.

Cardaci, R. (2013). Care of pregnant women in the criminal justice system: Implications for nursing practice, policy, and research. *The American Journal of Nursing, 113*, 40–48.

Carlen, P., & Tombs, J. (2006). Reconfigurations of penalty: The ongoing case of the women's imprisonment and reintegration industries. *Theoretical Criminology, 10*(3), 337–360.

Carson, E. A. (2020). *Prisoners in 2019* (Publication no. NCJ 255115). U.S. Department of Justice, Office of Justice Programs, Bureau of Justice Statistics. https://www.bjs.gov/content/pub/pdf/p19.pdf

Carson, E. A., & Anderson, E. (2016). *Prisoners in 2015* (Publication no. NCJ 250229). U.S. Department of Justice, Office of Justice Programs, Bureau of Justice Statistics. https://www.bjs.gov/content/pub/pdf/p15.pdf

Carter, L. M. (2019). "All they do is see the charge": Reentry barriers and correctional programming needs of women returning to society after incarceration. *Corrections: Policy, Practice, and Research, 4*(4), 272–301.

Chesney-Lind, M., & Rodriguez, N. (1983). Women under lock and key: A view from the inside. *The Prison Journal, 63*(2), 47–65.

Collica, K. (2010). Surviving incarceration: Two prison-based peer programs build communities of support for female offenders. *Deviant Behavior, 31*(4), 314–347.

Comartin, E. B., Burgess-Proctor, A., Kubiak, S., & Kernsmith, P. (2018). Factors related to co-offending and coerced offending among female sex offenders: The role of childhood and adult trauma histories. *Violence and Victims, 33*, 53–74.

Cortoni, F., Babchishin, K. M., & Rat, C. (2017). The proportion of sexual offenders who are female is higher than thought. *Criminal Justice & Behavior, 44*, 145–162.

Cook, S. L., Smith, S. G., Poster-Tusher, C., & Raiford, J. (2005). Self-reports of traumatic events in a random sample of incarcerated women. *Women & Criminal Justice, 16*, 107–126.

Culp, R. F. (2005). Frequency and characteristics of prison escapes in the United States: An analysis of national data. *The Prison Journal, 85*, 270–291.

Culp, R. F., & Bracco, E. (2005). Examining prison escapes and the routine activities theory. *Corrections Compendium, 30*(3), 1–27.

Curtice, M., Parker, J., Wismayer, F. S., & Tomison, A. (2003). The elderly offender: An 11-year survey of referrals to a regional forensic psychiatric service. *Journal of Forensic Psychiatry and Psychology, 14*, 253–265.

D'Alessio, S. J., & Stolzenberg, L. (2010). Do cities influence co-offending? *Journal of Criminal Justice, 38*, 711–719.

Daly, K. (1994). *Gender, Crime, and Punishment.* Yale University Press.

Dixey, R., & Woodall, J. (2012). The significance of "the visit" in an English category-B prison: Views from prisoners, prisoners' families and prison staff. *Community, Work, & Family, 15*(1), 29–47.

Dye, H. M., Aday, R. H., Farney, L., & Raley, J. (2014). "The rock I cling to": Religious engagement in the lives of life-sentences women. *The Prison Journal, 94*, 388–408.

Einat, T., & Chen, G. (2012). Gossip in a maximum security female prison: An exploratory study. *Women & Criminal Justice, 22*(2), 108–134.

Epstein, R., Blake, J. J., & Gonzalez, T. (2017). *Girlhood interrupted: The erasure of black girls' childhood.* Georgetown Law Center on Poverty and Inequality. https://endadultificationbias.org/wp-content/uploads/2019/05/girlhood-interrupted.pdf

Fedock, G. L. (2016). Women's psychological adjustment to prison: A review for future social work directions. *Social Work Research, 41*, 31–42.

Fox, J. (1984). Women's prison policy, prisoner activism, and the impact of the contemporary feminist movement: A case study. *The Prison Journal, 64*(2), 15–36.

Freeman, N. J., & Sandler, J. C. (2008). Female and male sex offenders: A comparison of recidivism patterns and risk factors. *Journal of Interpersonal Violence, 23*, 1394–1413.

Friestad, C. (2016). Mother-child contact during incarceration: A study based on a national survey of women prisoners. *Women & Criminal Justice, 26*(3), 199–211.

Gannon, T. A., & Rose, M. R. (2008). Female child sexual offenders: Towards integrating theory and practice. *Aggression and Violent Behavior, 13*, 442–461.

Gillespie, S. M., Williams, R., Elliott, I. A., Eldridge, H. J., Ashfield, S., & Beech, A. R. (2015). Characteristics of females who sexually offend: A comparison of solo and co-offenders. *Sexual Abuse: A Journal of Research & Treatment, 27*(3), 284–301.

Glaze, L. E., & Maruschak, L. M. (2009). *Parents in prison and their minor children.* U.S. Department of Justice, Office of Justice Programs, Bureau of Justice Statistics. https://www.bjs.gov/content/pub/pdf/pptmc.pdf

Goffman, I. (1961). *Asylums: Essays on the social situation of mental patients and other inmates.* Doubleday.

Gonzalez, P., Romero, T., & Cerbana, C. B. (2007). Parenting education for incarcerated mothers in Colorado. *Journal of Correctional Education, 58*, 357–373.

Goshin, L. S., Byrne, M. W., & Blanchard-Lewis, B. (2014). Preschool outcomes of children who lived in a prison nursery. *The Prison Journal, 94*, 139–158.

Hairston, C. F. (1998). The forgotten parent: Understanding the forces that influence incarcerated fathers' relationship with their children. *Child Welfare, 77*, 617–639.

Harley, D. A. (2014). Adult ex-offender population and employment: A synthesis of the literature on recommendations and best practices. *Journal of Applied Rehabilitation Counseling, 45*, 10–21.

Harner, H. M. (2004). Relationships between incarcerated women: Moving beyond stereotypes. *Journal of Psychosocial Nursing and Mental Health Services, 42*, 38–46.

Harner, H. M., & Riley, S. (2013). The impact of incarceration on women's mental health: Responses from women in a maximum-security prison. *Qualitative Health Research, 23*, 26–42.

Heimer, K., & DeCoster, S. (1999). The gendering of violent delinquency. *Criminology, 37*, 277–318.

James, D. J., & Glaze, L. E. (2006). Mental health problems of prison and jail inmates (NCJ 213600). U.S. Department of Justice, Office of Justice Programs, Bureau of Justice Statistics. https://www.bjs.gov/content/pub/pdf/mhppji.pdf

Jones, R. S. (1993). Coping with separation: Adaptive responses of women prisoners. *Women & Criminal Justice, 5*, 71–97.

Kajstura, A. (2019, Oct. 29). *Women's mass incarceration: The whole pie 2019.* Prison Policy Initiative. https://www.prisonpolicy.org/reports/pie2019women.html

Karlsson, M. E., Bridges, A. J., Bell, J., & Petretic, P. (2014). Sexual violence therapy group in a women's correctional facility: A preliminary evaluation. *Journal of Traumatic Stress, 27*, 361–364.

Karlsson, M. E., & Zielinski, M. J. (2020). Sexual victimization and mental illness prevalence rates among incarcerated women: A literature review. *Trauma, Violence, & Abuse, 21*(2), 326–349.

Kennon, S. S., Mackintosh, V. H., & Myers, B. J. (2009). Parenting education for incarcerated mothers. *Journal of Correctional Education, 60*(1), 10–30.

Kerman, P. (2011). *Orange is the new black: My year in a women's prison.* Random House.

Kjellsttrand, J. M., & Eddy, J. M. (2011). Parental incarceration during childhood, family context, and youth problem behavior across adolescence. *Journal of Offender Rehabilitation, 50*(1), 18–36.

Kolb, A., & Palys, T. (2018). Playing the part: Pseudo-families, wives, and the politics of relationships in women's prisons in California. *The Prison Journal, 98*(6), 678–699.

Koski, S. V., & Constanza, S. E. (2015). An examination of narratives from women offenders: Are gender-specific reentry efforts needed? *Qualitative Sociology Review, 11*(1), 70–89.

Kruttschnitt, C. (2000). Doing her own time? *Criminology, 38*(3), 681–718.

Lahm, K. F. (2017). Violent and nonviolent misconduct among female inmates: An exploration of competing theories. *Victims & Offenders, 12*, 175–204.

Laux, J. M., Clames, S., Moe, J. L., Dupuy, P. J., Cox, J. A., Ventura, L. A., Williamson, C., Benjamin, B. J., & Lambert, E. (2011). The career counseling needs of mothers in the criminal justice system. *Journal of Offender Rehabilitation, 50*(3), 159–173.

Leigey, M. E., & Hodge, J. F. (2012). Gray matters: Gender differences in the physical and mental health of older inmates. *Women & Criminal Justice, 22*, 289–308.

Leigey, M. E., & Reed, K. L. (2010). A woman's life before serving life: Examining the negative pre-incarceration life events of female life-sentenced inmates. *Women & Criminal Justice, 2*(4), 302–322.

Loper, A. B., Carlson, W., Levitt, L., & Scheffel, K. (2009). Parenting stress, alliance, child contact and adjustment of imprisoned mothers and fathers. *Journal of Offender Rehabilitation, 48*, 483–503.

Loper, A., & Tuerk, E. (2011). Improving the emotional adjustment and communication patterns of incarcerated mothers: Effectiveness of a prison parenting intervention. *Journal of Child & Family Studies, 20*(1), 89–101.

Lynch, S. M., DeHart, D. D., Belknap, B. L., Dass-Brailsford, P., Johnson, K. A., & Whaley, E. (2014). A multisite study of the prevalence of serious mental illness, PTSD, and substance use disorders of women in jail. *Psychiatric Services, 65,* 670–674.

Mason, C., Burke, T. W., & Owen, S. S. (2013). On the road again: The dangers of transporting ailing inmates. *Corrections Today, 75,* 77–82.

Mathews, R., Matthews, J., & Speltz, K. (1989). *Females who sexually offend.* Safer Society Press.

Mathews, R., Matthews, J., & Speltz, K. (1991). Females who sexually offend: A typology. In Q. Patton (Ed.), *Family sexual abuse: Frontline research and evaluation* (pp. 199–219). Sage.

McClellan, D. S., Farabee, D., & Couch, B. M. (1997). Early victimization, drug use, and criminality: A comparison of male and female prisoners. *Criminal Justice and Behavior, 24,* 455–476.

McPhail, M. E., Flavo, D. R., & Burker, E. J. (2012). Psychiatric disorders in incarcerated women: Treatment and rehabilitation needs for successful community reentry. *Journal of Applied Rehabilitation Counseling, 43*(1), 19–26.

Miller, H. A., & Marshall, E. A. (2019). Comparing solo- and co-offending female sex offenders on variables of pathology, offense characteristics, and recidivism. *Sexual Abuse: A Journal of Research & Treatment, 31*(8), 972–990.

Murdoch, N., Morris, P., & Holmes, C. (2008). Depression in elderly life sentence prisoners. *International Journal of Geriatric Psychiatry, 23,* 957–962.

Muskens, M., Bogaerts, S., VanCasteren, M., & Labrijn, S. (2011). Adult female sexual offending: A comparison between co-offenders and solo offenders in a Dutch sample. *Journal of Sexual Aggression, 17,* 46–60.

Nathan, P., & Ward, T. (2001). Females who sexually abuse children: Assessment and treatment issues. *Psychiatry, Psychology and Law, 8,* 44–55.

National Commission on Correctional Health Care. (2020). *Women's health care in correctional settings.* Retrieved from https://www.ncchc.org/womens-health-care

O'Keefe, M. (1998). Posttraumatic stress disorder among incarcerated battered women: A comparison of battered women who killed their abusers and those incarcerated for other offenses. *Journal of Traumatic Stress, 11*(1), 71–85.

Ortega, S., Beauchemin, A., Kaniskan, R. (2008). Building resiliency in families with young children exposed to violence: The Safe Start Initiative pilot study. *Best Practices in Mental Health, 4,* 48–64.

Owen, B., & Bloom, B. (1995). Profiling women prisoners: Findings from national surveys and a California sample. *The Prison Journal, 75,* 165–185.

Pettersson, T. (2005). Gendering delinquent networks: A gendered analysis of violent crimes and the structure of boys' and girls' co-offending networks. *Young: Nordic Journal of Youth Research*, *13*, 247–267.

Propper, A. (1982). Make-believe families and homosexuality among imprisoned girls. *Criminology*, *20*(1), 127–138.

Reidy, T. J., & Sorensen, J. R. (2018). The influence of sentence length on the commission of serious and violent prison infractions by female inmates. *Criminal Justice & Behavior*, *45*(9), 1420–1434.

Reidy, T. J., Sorensen, J. R., & Cunningham, M. D. (2012). Community violence to prison assault: A test of the behavioral continuity hypothesis. *Law and Human Behavior*, *36*, 356–363.

Richie, B. E. (1996). *Compelled to crime: The gendered entrapment of battered black women*. Routledge.

Roe-Sepowitz, D. E., Bedard, L. E., Pate, K. N., & Hedberg, E. C. (2014). Esuba: A psychoeducation group for incarcerated survivors of abuse. *International Journal of Offender Therapy and Comparative Criminology*, *58*, 190–208.

Salisbury, E. J., & Van Voorhis, P. (2009). Gendered pathways: A quantitative investigation of women probationers' paths to incarceration. *Criminal Justice & Behavior*, *36*, 541–566.

Sandifer, J. L. (2008). Evaluating the efficacy of a parenting program for incarcerated mothers. *The Prison Journal*, *88*(3), 423–445.

Saradjian, J., & Hanks, H. (1996). *Women who sexually abuse children*. John Wiley.

Severance, T. A. (2004). Concepts and coping strategies of women inmates concerning release: "It's going to take somebody in my corner." *Journal of Offender Rehabilitation*, *38*(4), 73–97.

Sichel, D. L. (2007). Giving birth in shackles: A constitutional and human rights violation. *American University Journal of Gender, Social Policy, & the Law*, *16*, 223–255.

Snodgrass, J. L., Jenkins, B. B., & Tate, K. F. (2017). More than a job club, sister: Career intervention for women following incarceration. *Career Development Quarterly*, *65*(1), 29–43.

Solinas-Saunders, M., & Stacer, M. (2012). Prison resources and physical/verbal assault in prison: A comparison of male and female inmates. *Victims & Offenders*, *7*, 279–311.

Spjeldnes, S., & Goodkind, S. (2009). Gender differences and offender reentry: A review of the literature. *Journal of Offender Rehabilitation*, *48*(4), 314–335.

Staton, M., Ciciurkaite, G., Oser, C., Tillson, M., Leukefeld, C., Webster, J. M., & Havens, J. R. (2018). Drug use and incarceration among rural Appalachian women: Findings from a jail sample. *Substance Use & Misuse*, *53*(6), 931–941.

Sterns, A. A., Law, G., Sed, C., Keohane, P., & Sterns, R. S. (2008). Growing wave of older prisoners: A national survey of older prisoners' health, mental health, and programming. *Corrections Today*, *70*(4), 70–72.

Strupp, H., & Wilmott, D. (2005). *Dignity denied: The price of imprisoning older women in California*. Legal Services for Prisoners with Children.

Sykes, G. M. (1958). *The society of captives: A study of maximum security prison*. Princeton University Press.

Terranova, V., & Vandiver, D. M. (2014). Does gender change things? Analysis of the difference between male and female violence crime for solo and co-offenders. *Violence & Gender, 1*(3), 124–130.

Terry, A. (2016). Surveying issues that arise in women's prisons: A content critique of *Orange Is the New Black. Sociology Compass, 10*(7), 553–566.

Thomas, S. Y., & Lanterman, J. L. (2019). A national analysis of shackling laws and policies as they relate to pregnant incarcerated women. *Feminist Criminology, 14*(2), 263–284.

Vainik, J. (2008). The reproductive and parental rights of incarcerated mothers. *Family Court Review, 46*(4), 670–694.

Vandiver, D. M. (2006). Females who sexually offend: A comparison of solo offenders and co-offenders. *Violence and Victims, 21*, 339–354.

VanMastrigt, S. B., & Farrington, D. P. (2010). Prevalence and characteristics of co-offending recruiters. *Justice Quarterly, 28*, 325–359.

Weatherhead, K. (2003). Cruel but not unusual punishment: The failure to provide adequate medical treatment to female prisoners in the United States. *Health Matrix, 13*, 429–472.

West v. Mason, H83-366 Conn. (1987)

Wijkman, M., Bijleveld, C., & Hendricks, J. (2010). Women don't do such things! Characteristics of female sex offenders and offender types. *Sexual Abuse: A Journal of Research & Treatment, 22*, 135–156.

Willers, D. M., Piepert, J. F., Allsworth, J. E., Stein, M. D., Rose, J. S., & Clarke, J. G. (2008). Prevalence and predictors of sexually transmitted infection among newly incarcerated females. *Sexually Transmitted Diseases, 35*, 68–72.

Williams, K. S., & Bierie, D. M. (2015). An incident-based comparison of female and male sexual offenders. *Sexual Abuse: A Journal of Research & Treatment, 27*, 235–257.

Williams, R., Gillespie, S. M., Elliott, I. A., & Eldridge, H. J. (2019). Characteristics of female solo and female co-offenders and male solo sexual offenders against children. *Sexual Abuse: A Journal of Research & Treatment, 31*(2), 151–172.

Young, D. S., & Mattucci, R. F. (2006). Enhancing the vocational skills of incarcerated women through a plumbing maintenance program. *Journal of Correctional Education, 57*(2), 126–140.

Zimmerman, G., & Messner, S. (2010). Neighborhood context and the gender gap in adolescent violent crime. *American Sociological Review, 75*, 958–980.

CHAPTER 10

Juvenile Populations

CHAPTER OBJECTIVES

After reading this chapter, you should be able to:

- Explain the history of the juvenile corrections system.
- Identify the different institutionalization options available for juvenile disposition and safety.
- Discuss the concept of community corrections and how it benefits offenders.

KEY WORDS

Aftercare

Attention homes

Boot camp

Community service

Continuum of sanctions

Detention centers

Diversion

Electronic monitoring

Forestry camps

Home confinement

Institutionalization

Office of Juvenile Justice and Delinquency
   Prevention (OJJDP)

Ranches

Reception and diagnostic center

Restitution

Shelter care facilities

Status offenses

Training school

CASE STUDY: OPERATION PEACEKEEPER

Operation Peacekeeper is a community- and problem-oriented policing program that was implemented in 1997 to address gun violence among youth gang members in Stockton, California. The goal of the program is to reduce gang involvement among urban youth aged 10 to 18 in the Stockton area, and to decrease gun-related violence among gang-involved youths. Modeled after the Ceasefire Initiative by the Boston Police Department, Operation Peacekeeper has been identified as a "model" program by the Office of Juvenile Justice and Delinquency Prevention.

Operation Peacekeeper relies on streetwise young men and women, called youth outreach workers, to communicate with at-risk youths about prosocial options for the future. These workers are trained in community organizing, mentoring, mediation, conflict resolution, and case management. They act as mentors for the youth and go to schools, parks, street corners, and apartment complexes to locate youth in need.

Questions for Discussion

1. In your opinion, what makes this a "model" program compared to other anti-gang initiatives?
2. Would this type of program be viable in other jurisdictions around the country? Why or why not?

INTRODUCTION

In 1825, the New York House of Refuge was opened by the Society for the Prevention of Juvenile Delinquency. Run mainly by religious leaders, this facility was identified as the first correctional facility for juveniles. One of the main objectives of the House of Refuge was to remove children from adult workhouses, as they could learn more lawbreaking behavior there. In addition, many youth were living in poverty on the streets, increasing fears that these poor youth, often from immigrant families, would be drawn in by corrupt politicians to help overthrow the government (Krisberg et al., 2019).

The New York House of Refuge and similar facilities opened in other states were not of the highest moral caliber. The staff of these refuges were taking youth off the streets and were not sympathetic to parents who demanded the return of their property (that is, their children). These facilities were run with religious teachings, forced labor, and discipline, and they often forced youth to serve as apprentices for the merchant marine.

Youth often revolted, based on the conditions of the facilities, with many running away and others initiating riots and fires.

In the early-to-mid-19th century, the group known as the "Child Savers" pushed for more humane treatment of juveniles in these facilities. However, the methods advocated by some of the members of these groups involved taking urban youth and shipping them to farms in the Midwest to work as laborers. Siblings and families were separated, and youth were given minimal food and shelter to compensate for their long days of back-breaking work.

As the juvenile corrections system moved into the 20th century, large training schools became popular. The accounts of abuse and harsh treatment were rampant in many of these schools, and in 1972, the state of Massachusetts closed all of their training schools and opened smaller, secure facilities. Demonstrating success and more humane treatment, Massachusetts created a wave of change across the United States, with multiple states changing their methods of juvenile corrections to model themselves after the Massachusetts method. In addition, the Juvenile Justice and Delinquency Prevention Act established the **Office of Juvenile Justice and Delinquency Prevention (OJJDP)**, a federal agency that has since provided guidelines for the development of successful juvenile programs.

All 50 states now have an established juvenile corrections system, built with the intention to provide rehabilitative resources to juvenile delinquents and at-risk youth so they may have the opportunity to divert away from the adult system. A range of options, or a **continuum of sanctions**, is available for juvenile disposition (Schmalleger & Marcum, 2019). These sanctions range in restriction based on the severity of the juvenile's criminal behavior, as well as the risks and needs associated for each juvenile. For example, the stability of home life and other environmental factors will affect the likelihood of placement of a child in a residential facility. This chapter will explore the correctional options available to juvenile court judges when considering disposition for those youth in the system, beginning with the most restrictive option: institutionalization. However, we will first explore the considerations the juvenile justice system faces when determining whether to treat the juvenile as a minor or adult.

TREATING JUVENILES AS MINORS OR ADULTS

One of the first decisions made in the juvenile court is whether to file a petition in juvenile jurisdiction (Clear et al., 2019). Cases that involve first-time offenders and/or are nonviolent may be eligible for **diversion** options, such as treatment programs, and charges may even be completely dropped based on the remorse demonstrated by the juvenile. **Status offenses** are often eligible for diversionary options. Behaviors categorized as status offenses are not criminal offenses, but are also not acceptable behavior for juveniles. There are a wide range of status offenses, such as underage drinking and consumption of tobacco products, truancy, and running away. Status offenses can even involve incorrigibility, acting immorally, and behavior that parents have been unable to control. Essentially, these behaviors are acts that are not considered "age appropriate" (Clear et al., 2019).

Other cases may be deemed appropriate for formal court management. In 2018, approximately 744,500 cases were handled by a delinquency court (Hockenberry & Puzzanchera, 2020). These courts were deemed to be the most appropriate venue to manage the juvenile and provide appropriate disposition to match their behaviors (disposition options are discussed in the following sections). Many offenses handled by juvenile courts are nonviolent behaviors.

Prosecutors may apply for a **waiver** to adult court by a judge, for juveniles who have committed more serious crimes (e.g., crimes exhibiting behavior often compared to that of adult offenders). In 2018, 1.5% of juvenile delinquency cases involving juveniles aged 16 years or older were waived to adult court. Only 0.2% of cases involving younger juveniles were waived. Offenses involving persons were likely to be waived, especially those involving African American juveniles (Hockenberry & Puzzanchera, 2020). Juveniles who are waived to adult court are more likely to receive dispositions akin to those given to adult offenders, such as forms of institutionalization.

While institutionalization of juveniles in adult facilities may seem like a logical reaction to serious and/or violent behavior, empirical studies have indicated the potential for negative behavioral and emotional consequences for the youth (Lane et al., 2002; Tie & Waugh, 2001). Juveniles incarcerated with adult offenders have a higher likelihood of being victimized by other inmates (Mulvey & Schubert, 2012), as well as increased recidivism rates (Myers, 2003). Lambie and Randell (2013) argued that less severe sanctions were more appropriate for juveniles, no matter the criminal behavior, due to the long-term effects of severe sanctioning.

In the past few decades, the Supreme Court of the United States has made several major rulings that have taken away serious sanctioning options for juveniles. *Roper v. Simmons* (2005) ruled it a violation of the Eighth Amendment to impose the death penalty on a person under the age of 18 years old. *Graham v. Florida* (2010) extended *Roper* and prohibited life-without-parole sentences for any crime other than homicide. Shortly after *Graham*, the *Miller v. Alabama* (2012) ruling determined that life without parole was not an option for juveniles who were convicted of homicide, and *Montgomery v. Louisiana* (2016) made this retroactive to all juveniles sentenced to life in prison without parole.

INSTITUTIONALIZATION

The state of Pennsylvania was an innovative force for the American corrections system of today. One of the first penitentiary systems, the Pennsylvania system (previously discussed in Chapter 1), was developed under the Quaker concepts of solitary meditation and hard work with the expectation of reforming offenders. When Eastern State Penitentiary was opened in 1829 in Philadelphia, incarcerated persons were placed in solitary confinement under the punitive and rehabilitative philosophy of punishment. Ultimately, the Pennsylvania system was found to be more expensive to construct compared to other systems, and to be ineffective as a rehabilitative method. Incarcerated persons suffered severe mental health repercussions due to the solitary confinement, indicating the need for prosocial interaction for rehabilitation. These findings from Pennsylvania helped shape further adult corrections practices, but also inspired the development of our juvenile corrections systems.

In 1903, the state of Pennsylvania ruled that juvenile proceedings would now be held separately from those of adult offenders, developing the state's juvenile court system. Following the model of the first juvenile court in Cook County, Illinois, the Pennsylvania court vowed to work in tandem with the juvenile corrections system to provide dispositions that would enact fair punishment, but also to act as a caregiver and guide to juveniles with a rehabilitative focus. In *Commonwealth v. Fisher* (1905), the Superior Court of Pennsylvania considered whether the juvenile boy, Fisher, had been given too long of a residential term at a juvenile school for delinquent boys for a minor offense. If the youth had been an adult, Fisher would have received a misdemeanor sanction. However, after consideration of his home life in conjunction with his behaviors, the Superior Court confirmed his sentence, stating that the juvenile system "is not for punishment of offenders but for the salvation of child … the duty of the state." The Court confirmed that a juvenile disposition is given based on the entirety of the life situation of the juvenile, with the system often acting as the parent figure and providing protection for the youth.

The most restrictive disposition option for juveniles is **institutionalization**, or the removal of the juvenile from the home and placement in a residential facility. A judge's decision to place a juvenile in an institution is not made lightly, and is the result of a careful weighing of all the facts in the case, the life circumstances of the juvenile, and the safety of the community. These institutional facilities range in the type and length of care provided and are separated into long-term and short-term care facilities. During any type of institutionalization, the state acts as the decision-making guardian for the juvenile, providing the supervision and care that serves the best interest of the minor.

As of October 2016, over 45,000 juveniles were held in 1,772 placement facilities in the United States (Hockenberry & Sladky, 2018). More than half of these facilities were publicly operated, and they supervised 71% of the juvenile offenders in a residential placement. Long-term institutions (e.g., training schools and boot camps) were more likely to be public facilities, while short-term shelters and group homes were more likely to be private facilities. These facilities were often at full capacity, with residents filling all bed spaces, and 22% of the facilities were marked as being over capacity.

Multiple types of screenings are performed on juveniles upon entry to any of these institutions. The purpose of these evaluations is to best evaluate the risks and needs of the juvenile so the best treatment can be provided. Hockenberry and Sladky (2018) evaluated all juvenile facilities in the United States in late 2016 and found a plethora of resources offered to youth during a stay. The majority of facilities screened for substance abuse issues, as substance abuse education was the most frequently provided service at juvenile facilities. In addition, drug testing was a routine procedure in most juvenile facilities in 2016.

Educational services are also in high demand at juvenile facilities. Eighty-eight percent of facilities reported they screened youth for grade level and educational needs, with the majority of them using previous educational records and many using interviews or screening devices (Hockenberry & Sladky, 2018). Many youth who are institutionalized are below scheduled grade-level attainment. For example, it is not unlikely for a 16-year-old who is categorized as a high school junior to have reading and math skills associated with a lower grade level. As a result, 87% of facilities offer high-school-level educational courses, and 80% offer middle-school-level courses. The majority of facilities also offer GED courses and special education classes. Less than 40% of facilities offer vocational training or college courses.

Mental health resources are also in high demand at juvenile facilities. According to Hockenberry and Sladky's (2018) study of juvenile facilities in the United States, all facilities provide some form of mental health resources. Approximately 65% of the facilities reported screening youth at intake for mental health issues with an in-house mental health professional, usually within the first week of placement. These screenings include an in-depth analysis for all potential mental health issues, ranging from mild depression to schizophrenic hallucinations. Almost all facilities also screened youth for suicide risk. These screenings help determine which therapies would be most beneficial and whether medication is recommended.

Figure 10.1 provides a summary view of the amount of each type of screenings provided by juvenile facilities in the United States (Hockenberry & Sladky, 2018). As can be seen from the chart below, the majority of facilities provide screenings for all youth in the following areas: educational needs, mental health needs, substance abuse risk, and suicide risk. A few of the facilities do not screen at all for educational needs, substance abuse, and suicide risks.

The next two sections will specifically examine two types of institutions available to juveniles, categorized by the length of stay available to the youth: long-term institutions and short-term institutions.

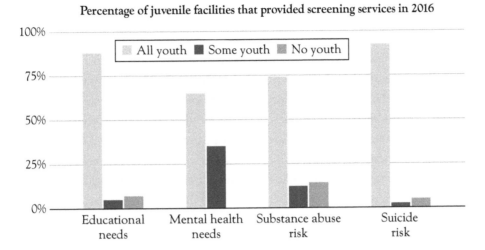

Image 10.1 Adapted from: *Juvenile Residential Facility Census, 2016: Selected Findings* (NCJ 251785), by S. Hockenberry & A. Sladky, 2018, U.S. Department of Justice, Office of Justice Programs, Office of Juvenile Justice and Delinquency Prevention (https://www.ojjdp.gov/pubs/251785.pdf).

Long-Term Institutions

Long-term institutions, or those that provide the opportunity for lengthier stays for juvenile offenders, are utilized after a judge has issued disposition. These institutions are utilized for a variety of categories of juvenile offenders: 1) juveniles who have not been receptive to short-term institutional stays or community correctional options; 2) juveniles who have demonstrated violent behavior and require institutionalization for their own safety and that of the entire community; and/or 3) juveniles who do not have a stable and safe home life and would benefit from a secure placement. Fortunately, there are several options available to judges and juvenile offenders that can be used for optimal safety and treatment of the youth.

Before any type of long-term confinement, juveniles are generally placed in a **reception and diagnostic center**. These facilities are used to initiate the classification process, in which the best treatment plan and placement for the juvenile is determined based on a variety of tests and assessments. Educational staff determine proper grade placement, identify educational deficiencies, and diagnose learning disabilities. A counselor or psychologist talks with the juvenile and identifies emotional and mental health issues. Physicians examine the youth to identify developmental achievement and needs, as well as potential physical health abnormalities. In addition, a social worker or case manager investigates family history (and potential abusive situations), while the center's living staff also makes note of adjustment and relationship behaviors. Finally, once a complete assessment is made, the juvenile is placed in one of the long-term options described below.

<u>Boot camps</u>, one long-term alternative, house a juvenile for 30 to 120 days and utilize strict discipline and physical programming. Often used for juveniles who have not responded positively to other sanctions, boot camps provide an extremely structured environment that is based on a regimen of educational programming, therapy, and physical training. Boot camps use the same strict routine implemented in military boot camps. While juvenile offenders are provided a prosocial environment at boot camp that is unlike the environments many of them come from, they often show high recidivism rates once released, for this same reason. Youth often return to the same disorganized, crime-ridden environments where they lived previously, which lack the rigorous structure and supervision found in a boot camp, and fall back into the same patterns and behaviors.

Forestry camps and **ranches** are long-term residential facilities that are used for minimum-security juvenile offenders. These have a more relaxed atmosphere, with youth performing conservation or animal-based work as a means of skill-building and therapy. As indicated in the name, these facilities are located in rural areas and allow youth to remove themselves from their places of origin, which are often crime-ridden urban areas. Juveniles are required to participate in educational programming and group therapy, but are also allowed to participate in field trips and other entertainment.

<u>Training schools</u> are secure environments managed under the *parens patriae* philosophy, or the government acting at the parent figure for these children, offering facilities that provide a range of security levels to fit all offenders. Originally constructed so juveniles could reside in cottages with "parents" (a couple providing a home atmosphere) as a way of experiencing a prosocial family environment, they are currently administered using dormitories that are supervised by staff members. Youth who are violent, and at risk for antisocial behaviors, are placed in more secure environments, while those who are nonviolent are placed in more relaxed, nurturing environments.

These training schools function much like an all-inclusive city for the residents. Juveniles live in dormitories and attend school during the day. They also participate in therapy, recreational activities (e.g., sports, art, or music), and vocational training. Staff provide supervision and guidance on building appropriate peer relationships, mediating conflict, and regulating behavior. The hope is that once a juvenile is released, whether back to the parents or to another home situation, they will have the skills available to successfully reintegrate and to handle the stress of life challenges.

A juvenile's right to treatment has been contested in the court system, with many courts ruling in favor of the juvenile's right to treatment during residency in a training school. In the District of Columbia, *White v. Reid* (1954) ruled that juveniles could not be held in an institution without programming (e.g., therapy, education, and medical treatment), and this ruling was later supported by cases in Rhode Island, Indiana, and Texas. However, juveniles do have the right to deny treatment, as long it does not affect their safety and health. For example, a juvenile can refuse medicine for a headache or upset stomach, but not medication that could have tragic effects if not taken, such as seizure medication. In addition, juveniles cannot refuse to participate in educational programming.

It is important to note that the safety of the juvenile and the community is also vital. Juveniles in long-term care facilities, as well as some short-term facilities, have confinement restrictions; they are not allowed to roam as they please. These facilities use staff supervision, locked doors, and external fencing to regulate the movement of offenders during the day. At bedtime, youth are generally locked in their rooms. Table 10.1 outlines the number of facilities that used more than one confinement method in the United States in 2016.

Table 10.1 Juvenile Facilities With More Than One Confinement Method.

FACILITY TYPE	NUMBER	PERCENTAGE
Detention center	638	97
Ranch/wilderness camp	13	43
Reception/diagnostic center	45	78
Residential treatment center	316	48
Shelter	35	27
Treatment center	179	95

Note. Adapted from *Juvenile Residential Facility Census, 2016: Selected Findings* (NCJ 251785), by S. Hockenberry & A. Sladky, 2018, U.S. Department of Justice, Office of Justice Programs, Office of Juvenile Justice and Delinquency Prevention (*https://www.ojjdp.gov/pubs/251785.pdf*).

Short-Term Institutions

There are less time-invasive choices available for juvenile disposition that still involve spending time in a facility. Short-term institutional options for juveniles are used with the intention of temporary placement. Some youth may be given an abbreviated stay in a short-term facility as their disposition. These facilities may also be used for safe housing of a juvenile if the home is deemed unfit during the adjudication process, or for the security of the community if the juvenile is considered potentially violent during court proceedings. Once a disposition is determined by the juvenile court judge, the minor moves to either a long-term housing option or a form of community corrections. However, until that occurs, the state has a variety of short-term options that may be chosen.

Detention centers (aka juvenile halls) are common short-term housing facilities, used solely as a means of control and supervision. In addition, they do not utilize any rehabilitative emphasis (Hockenberry et al., 2016). While educational programming is provided, it is not conducted in a therapeutic environment. Punishment is administered for infractions, with physical restraints as a potential sanction. Individuals in a detention center are juveniles who are awaiting their adjudicatory hearing, or have been given a short stay as a disposition.

Jails, generally used for adult offenders, can also be used to detain juvenile offenders, especially in situations of severe overcrowding at the detention center or when the juvenile is accused of a violent crime. Due to the transitional nature of jails, very few resources, if any, are available to youth while they are there. In addition, due to overcrowding, they may be exposed to violent behavior and victimization. Passed in 1974, the Juvenile Justice and Delinquency Act (JJDPA) created restrictions on juvenile confinement in adult jail, with a 1980 amendment calling for the removal of youth from jails (OJJDP, 2021). In addition, the JJDPA required that even during temporary custody in adult jails, youth are to have no contact with the adult offenders. Some states have completely stopped placing youth in adult jails, while others use this practice on a limited basis, especially with the judicial waiver system (Schwartz et al., 1988; Steinhart, 1988).

It is important to note that detention center staff cannot use any method of control they choose for unruly offenders. The Eighth Amendment protects all offenders, juvenile and adult, against cruel and unusual punishment. Use of certain methods of control is inappropriate for juveniles. For instance, in *Pena v. New York State Division for Youth* (1976), the court ruled that the use of tranquilizers, restraints, and isolation was a violation of the Eighth Amendment. Other states followed suit, with similar rulings against abusive and brutal behavior.

Attention homes and **shelter care facilities** are less severe and restrictive options for juveniles (Bartollas & Miller, 2017). Both homes are non-secure, not using locks or fences to restrict movement of the residents. The JJDPA provided funding for these facilities, advocating for their use over the placement of youth in adult jails (Coalition for Juvenile Justice, 2017). These facilities focus more on encouragement and safety, giving juveniles the option to hopefully make positive choices and form good relationships. However, due to the leniency of the environment, it can be difficult to manage runaways and keep contraband out of the homes.

Disparity in Juvenile Institutions

When discussing juvenile institutions, it is important to note that there are disparities in the representation of youth populations in juvenile institutions. In regard to racial disparity, African American youth and youth of Hispanic/Latino origin are more likely to be confined in juvenile institutions. In addition, these youth are more likely to have official interaction with the juvenile court. In 2013, the OJJDP estimated that African American youth were 340% more likely to be referred to juvenile court and 490% more likely to be waived to adult court compared to White youth (Krisberg et al., 2019; Sickmund & Puzzanchera, 2014). Once waived to court, African American youth were 20% more likely to be formally charged and 30% more likely to be placed out of the home. Hispanic/Latino youth were also more likely than White youth to be referred to juvenile court (20%), but were as likely as White youth to receive probation, rather than receiving more severe sanctions.

Female juvenile offenders also have a notable presence in institutions. Approximately 14% of institutionalized juveniles are females. Some states have actually experienced a decline in male offenders, but an increase in the institutionalization of female offenders. Females are more likely to be placed in facilities for status offenses, such as curfew violations, running away, and truancy from school. In addition, young women who commit probation violations or minor offenses are more likely to be placed in a residential facility compared to male offenders.

COMMUNITY CORRECTIONS

Juveniles who are placed in any form of institution have limited freedoms and liberties, with the government acting as their supervisory guardian. However, this type of sanction is not necessary for most youth. The majority of juvenile offenders are sentenced to sanctions that are categorized as a form of **community corrections**. These options range in restriction and requirement but allow a juvenile delinquent to serve his or her disposition while still living in the community. Juvenile dispositions that fall under the community corrections category are meant to be rehabilitative for the offender. The hope is that prosocial bonds can be maintained (and formed) in community corrections, while the juvenile continues with productive behaviors like attending school, learning a vocational trade, or maintaining gainful employment. In addition, community corrections are a more cost-effective option for the juvenile justice system, as full-time room and board do not have to be provided by the state. The following sections discuss the multiple forms of community corrections available to juvenile offenders.

Probation

Probation is the most frequently administered form of community corrections for both juveniles and adults. Juveniles on probation live in the community, most often with parents or appointed guardians, and are supervised by a probation officer. Every juvenile who is given probation is required to meet a set of conditions. Standard conditions are those given to all individuals on probation, such as regular meetings with a probation officer.

The remaining two types of conditions are individualized based on the risks and needs of the offender. Punitive conditions, such as community service or a fine, are meant to act as punishment for the offense. Treatment conditions are those used to address a need of the juvenile offender, such as drug treatment or anger management (White, 2019). As not all juveniles are the most willing participants in probationary programs, it is often the responsibility of the probation officer to act as a motivator for the juvenile to comply with the conditions, with the hopes of successful completion (Schwartz et al., 2017).

The probation officer is an integral part of the disposition, involved from the beginning to end of the process (Clear et al., 2019). At intake, a probation officer screens all juveniles referred to the court. This process includes interviewing the juvenile, the affiliated parents or guardians, and sometimes other important individuals in the child's life. This helps to determine if detention is necessary for the safety of the juvenile and the community, and to identify other potential risks and needs affiliated with the youth.

Once the disposition of probation is given by a juvenile court judge, the probation officer acts as both a social worker and a law enforcement officer (Nijnatten & Elk, 2015; Schwartz, et al., 2017). In the social work role, the probation officer meets regularly with the juvenile, more frequently with youth with higher security levels. During the meetings, the probation officer discusses the success of the juvenile in meeting the conditions discussed above, their performance in school, and their other therapeutic needs. In the law enforcement role, the probation officer performs surveillance of the behavior of the juvenile in the community and administers consequences for youth who violate their conditions or break the law. However, as juvenile probation officers often have large caseloads, it is difficult for them to provide the individualized attention each juvenile needs.

Probation officers are also responsible for reporting to the court (Gale-Bentz et al., 2019). Before disposition, probation officers prepare a social study report with the offending and personal history of the youth, as well as a recommendation for disposition (and institutionalization if needed). If probation is part of the sanction, the probation officer reports to the court regarding the progress of the youth, successes and setbacks, and recommendations of revocation if applicable.

Juveniles who are accused of a technical violation, or of breaking one of the conditions of probation, are entitled to the same due process rights as adults regarding revocation, based on the rulings of two Supreme Court cases. In *Mempa v. Rhay* (1968) and *Gagnon v. Scarpelli* (1973), the Court determined that juveniles have the right to a hearing, along with a 5-day notification of the hearing, and the right to counsel at this hearing. Juveniles are also allowed to confront their accusers and examine the evidence of the violation. When making a decision regarding the revocation and how to handle the additional sanction, judges often use the "reasonable efforts" standard. If the juvenile court is found to have provided all reasonable resources for the juvenile, and that juvenile still failed to meet the requirements for probation, a judge can decide to revoke.

Intermediate Sanctions

There are other dispositional options available to juvenile court judges that provide more stringent supervision for the youth but still allow them to remain in the community. Otherwise known as intermediate sanctions, these options are more restrictive for juveniles but hopefully allow them to successfully reintegrate back into society. In addition, these sanctions are more cost effective for the juvenile justice system, compared to institutionalization. An example of an intermediate sanction is a disposition of **restitution**, to compensate the victim for the damage caused by the crime. The juvenile may be asked to pay a fine, to pay to replace something that was stolen or destroyed, or to repair property that was damaged. Restitution can also be paid in the form of **community service**. A juvenile may be asked to wash police cars, clean graffiti off of a building, or pick up trash.

Juveniles may be given intensive supervised probation (ISP), which is a stricter version of the probation discussed earlier. Often given to youth who were not successful with probation, ISP requires the juvenile to have increased contact with the probation officer. In addition, the conditions of ISP are stricter and have more requirements for successful completion (Griffin & Torbet, 2002). Although the supervisory requirements are more stringent, this can often result in more probation violations for the offender.

Another option for juveniles is **house arrest**, generally combined with **electronic monitoring**. This is an especially viable option if the youth comes from a stable home with responsible parents or guardians. Juvenile offenders are required to spend the majority of their time in their home, wearing an electronic monitoring device that has GPS tracking. Youth are preapproved to leave the home at designated times for school, employment, religious services, and other legitimate activities. The monitoring device notifies the probation officer if the youth is away from the home at an unapproved time, or visits a location not noted as appropriate. Violating these requirements may result in revocation of the house arrest or increased restrictions during the house arrest (Martin et al., 2009).

AFTERCARE

One of the main goals of the juvenile justice system is to provide safety and care for youth during detention and/or supervision. Another goal is to assist with the reintegration of the over 100,000 juveniles who are released from institutionalization each year. A large percentage of these youth have a history of abuse, addiction, educational deficiencies, and/or physical and mental health problems (OJJDP, 2010). While juvenile facilities offer resources related to these issues, they are often overwhelmed with need and do not have enough for all the offenders. In addition, many youth do not have supportive and stable homes to continue the care. As a result, many youth are given aftercare conditions.

Aftercare, another term for parole, should ideally start during the disposition phase and follow the youth throughout the entire time period under supervision (National Juvenile Defender Center, 2017). However, the methods of aftercare and institutional release are dependent on the jurisdiction. The majority of states use the executive branch to make decisions regarding release. If the youth lives in a state with determinate sentencing policies, release decisions are made upon entry to the training school. Other states use a structured sentencing guideline to determine release and aftercare options. This can include use of an assessment tool to determine the risks and needs of an offender. A popular assessment tool is the Level of Service Inventory-Revised, or LSI-R, which weighs a multitude of factors to predict success during release (Andrews & Bonta, 2017).

FACTORS CONSIDERED IN THE LSI-R TO PREDICT SUCCESS AFTER RELEASE

Accommodation	Employment status
Addiction	Family environment
Attitude	Financial patterns
Criminal history	Peer groups
Educational achievement	Recreational activities
Emotional stability	

During the aftercare phase, youth are given a set of supervisory and treatment conditions (much like during probation). A caseworker monitors the successes and failures of the youth with the conditions, providing resources to help with success and discouraging affiliation with individuals who participate in criminal enterprises. For individuals who are affiliated with gangs, caseworkers try to provide prosocial activities to divert the youth. In addition, if the juvenile is in an abusive situation at home, the caseworker can place them in protective custody.

CONCLUSION

Our juvenile justice system was created to provide protection and rehabilitation to young offenders with the hope of steering them away from an adulthood of criminality. While originating from a flawed past and still working on establishing best practices, the current juvenile corrections system aims to provide solace and help to those in need. As can be seen from this chapter, a multitude of options are available to juveniles, with the goal of meeting their needs while addressing the risks presented in each case.

While the maturation process "ages out" many youth from deviant behavior, there are still thousands who become entrenched in the system. This book mainly focuses on the adult aspect of the corrections system, but adult offenders often have long histories of criminality, beginning at a young age. It is important for academics, practitioners, and legislators to continue to work towards developing proactive and reactive programming to meet the needs of our youth, so that their experience with the corrections system ends early.

DISCUSSION QUESTIONS

1. The state of New Hampshire has had pay-to-stay laws as part of its statutes for years. While these laws do not apply to all offenders, the families of juveniles can be charged for a portion of their institutionalization, based on an income ratio. Do you believe parents should be responsible for payment of the institutionalization fees for their child? Why or why not?

2. Which of the correctional sanctions for juveniles do you feel are the least stigmatizing? Most stigmatizing?

3. Do you believe it is constitutional to institutionalize a juvenile based on a lack of stability and safety in their home environment? Is there a better alternative option if their offense does not warrant that type of sanction?

APPLICATION EXERCISES

Exercise #1: Solitary Confinement

The constitutionality of the extended use of solitary confinement has long been debated for adult offenders, considering the potential lasting mental health repercussions of the isolation. This is especially true for juveniles, which prompted President Barack Obama to call for a ban on solitary confinement practices for juveniles in 2016. As a result, many states have banned the use of solitary confinement for juveniles for punitive purposes and rely on it solely for temporary protective measures, while other states have chosen to limit its use for punitive purposes for a maximum of 3–5 days. However, some states have no limitations on the use of solitary confinement for juveniles and base restrictions on administrative discretion. Choose two states and compare their policies on the use of solitary confinement for juveniles. Which state do you feel best applies President Obama's recommendation? In your opinion, which state is implementing the best practices for punitive measures for juvenile punishment?

Exercise #2: *In re Ricardo P.*

In the case *In re Ricardo P.* (2015), the court ruled on the constitutionality of electronic searches of juveniles on probation. As we are now in the age of reliance on technology, it has infiltrated our court systems as well. Find online and read the details of the case of *In re Ricardo P.* Do you agree with the court's ruling? Secondly, do you feel as if we give up certain rights to privacy when we post information and pictures online?

REFERENCES

Andrews, D., & Bonta, J. (2017). *LSI-R: Level of security inventory-revised. MHS Beyond Assessments.* https://storefront.mhs.com/collections/lsi-r

Bartollas, C., & Miller, S. (2017). *Juvenile justice in America* (8th ed.). Pearson Education.

Clear, T., Reisig, M., & Cole, G. (2019). *American corrections* (12th ed.). Cengage Publishing.

Coalition for Juvenile Justice. (2017). *Juvenile justice and delinquency prevention act.* http://www.juvjustice.org/federal-policy/juvenile-justice-and-delinquency-prevention-act

Commonwealth v. Fisher, 27 Pa. Super. 175 (1905)

Gagnon v. Scarpelli, 411 U.S. 778 (1973)

Gale-Bentz, E., Goldstein, N., Cole, L., & Durham, K. (2019). Impact of community-based provider reports on juvenile probation officers' recommendations: Effects of positive and negative framing on decision making. *Law & Human Behavior, 43*(2), 193–204.

Graham v. Florida, 560 U.S. 48 (2010)

Griffin, P., & Torbet, P. (2002). *Desktop guide to good juvenile probation practice: Mission-driven, performance-based and outcome-focused.* National Center for Juvenile Justice.

Hockenberry, S., & Puzzanchera, C. (2020). *Juvenile court statistics 2018.* National Center for Juvenile Justice. https://www.ojjdp.gov/ojstatbb/njcda/pdf/jcs2018.pdf

Hockenberry, S., & Sladky, A. (2018). *Juvenile residential facility census, 2016: Selected findings* (NCJ 251785). U.S. Department of Justice, Office of Justice Programs, Office of Juvenile Justice and Delinquency Prevention. https://www.ojjdp.gov/pubs/251785.pdf

Hockenberry, S., Wachter, A., & Sladky, A. (2016, September). *Juvenile residential facility census, 2014: Selected findings* (NCJ 250123). U.S. Department of Justice, Office of Justice Programs, Office of Juvenile Justice and Delinquency Prevention. https://www.ojjdp.gov/pubs/250123.pdf

In re Ricardo P., 193 Cal. Rptr., 3d 883, 887 (Ct. App. 2015)

Kraner, N., Barrowclough, N., Weiss, C., & Fisch, J. (2016, July). *Jurisdiction survey of juvenile solitary confinement rules in justice systems.* Lowenstein Center for the Public Interest. https://www.lowenstein.com/files/upload/51-jurisdiction%20survey%20of%20juvenile%20solitary%20confinement%20rules.pdf

Krisberg, B., Marchionna, S., & Hartney, C. (2019). *American corrections: Concepts and controversies* (2nd ed.). Sage Publications.

Lambie, I., & Randell, I. (2013). The impact of incarceration on juvenile offenders. *Clinical Psychology Review, 33*, 448–459.

Lane, J., Lanza-Kaduce, L., Frazier, C. E., & Bishop, D. M. (2002). Adult versus juvenile sanctions: Voices of incarcerated youths. *Crime & Delinquency, 48*(3), 431–455. http://dx.doi.org/10.1177/0011128702048003004

Martin, J., Hanrahan, K., & Bowers, J. Offenders' perception of house arrest and electronic monitoring. *Journal of Offender Rehabilitation, 48*(6), 547–570.

Mempa v. Rhay, 339 U.S. 128, 2d Cir. 3023 (1968)

Miller v. Alabama, 567 U.S. 460 (2012)

Montgomery v. Louisiana, 577 U.S. _____ (2016)

Mulvey, E. P., & Schubert, C. A. (2012). *Transfer of juveniles to adult court: Effects of a broad policy in one court.* Juvenile Justice Bulletin. U. S. Department of Justice, Office of Juvenile Justice and Delinquency Prevention.

Myers, D. L. (2003). The recidivism of violent youths in juvenile and adult court: A consideration of selection bias. *Youth Violence and Juvenile Justice, 1*(1), 79–101. http://dx.doi.org/10.1177/1541204002238365

National Juvenile Defender Center. (2017). *Juvenile court terminology.* http://njdc.info/juvenile-court-terminology/

Nijnatten, C., & Elk, E. (2015). Communicating care and coercion in juvenile probation. *British Journal of Social Work, 45*(3), 825–841.

Office of Juvenile Justice and Delinquency Prevention. (2010). *Federal advisory committee on juvenile justice annual report 2010* (NCJ 231620). https://ojjdp.ojp.gov/library/publications/federal-advisory-committee-juvenile-justice-annual-report-2010

Office of Juvenile Justice and Delinquency Prevention. (2021). *Legislation.* Available at https://ojjdp.ojp.gov/about/legislation

Pena v. New York State Division for Youth, 419 F. Supp. 203 (S.D.N.Y. 1976)

Roper v. Simmons, 543 U.S. 551 (2005)

Schwartz, K., Alexander, A., Lau, K., Holloway, E., & Aalsma, M. (2017). Motivating compliance: Juvenile probation officer strategies and skills. *Journal of Offender Rehabilitation, 56*(1), 20–37.

Schwartz, I., Harris, L., & Levi, L. (1988). The jailing of juveniles in Minnesota: A case study. *Crime & Delinquency, 34*, 146.

Sickmund, M., & Puzzanchera, C. (2014). *Juvenile offenders and victims: 2014 national report.* National Center for Juvenile Justice. https://www.ojjdp.gov/ojstatbb/nr2014/downloads/nr2014.pdf

Steinhart, D. (1988). California's legislature ends the jailing of children: The story of policy reversal. *Crime & Delinquency, 34*, 169–170.

Tie, D., & Waugh, E. (2001). *Prison youth vulnerability scale: Administration and technical manual.* Department of Corrections Psychological Service.

White, C. (2019). Treatment services in the juvenile justice system: Examining the use and funding of services by youth on probation. *Youth Violence & Juvenile Justice, 17*(1), 62–87.

White v. Reid, 125 F. Supp. 647 (D.D.C. 1954)

CHAPTER 11

Vulnerable Populations

CHAPTER OBJECTIVES

After reading this chapter, you should be able to:

- Understand what is meant by the term "vulnerable populations" and identify key vulnerable populations in the U.S. corrections system.
- Recognize the key struggles facing vulnerable LGBTQ, elderly, medically ill, and mentally ill incarcerated populations.
- Discuss key policies related to the management of vulnerable prison populations, and give suggestions for how practitioners can best serve these populations.

KEY WORDS

Accelerated aging

Classification

Compassionate release

Co-occurring conditions

Dementia

Deinstitutionalization

Elderly offenders

Hormone replacement therapy (HRT)

Intergenerational relationships

LGBTQ populations

Mental illness

Segregation

Prison Rape Elimination Act (PREA) of 2003

Vulnerable populations

CASE STUDY: THE NEED FOR HOSPICE CARE FOR INCARCERATED POPULATIONS

This chapter discusses the aging of the U.S. prison population over the past several decades. The number of incarcerated elderly persons has grown exponentially and is projected to continue to grow. In fact, some experts predict that one third of the U.S. prison population will be age 55 or older by the year 2030 (Prison Fellowship, n.d.). With these populations being more likely to suffer from chronic illness and disease, this statistic means that more people are dying while incarcerated. Elderly persons who are not incarcerated often turn to hospice care as a place for support and comfort when dealing with terminal illness. Unfortunately, hospice care is not available for many elderly inmates who are facing their final days behind bars. It is estimated that only 3.5% of prisons in the United States have on-site hospice programs available for incarcerated offenders.

One facility that does have an on-site hospice program is at the California Medical Facility in Vacaville. This is a medium-security prison located near San Francisco. It was established in the 1990s as the first licensed prison hospice in the United States. This was especially important at the time it was established because the AIDS crisis was exploding in U.S. prisons. Today the Vacaville program has 17 beds available for incarcerated terminally ill persons, with staff who help with basic care and pain management for these offenders. Other hospice programs include those at the Oak Park Heights prison in Minnesota and at Louisiana State Penitentiary. In these particular programs, family are allowed to visit their incarcerated loved ones, much as they would in a traditional hospice program. In addition to these programs being beneficial for the terminally ill offender, research suggests that incarcerated volunteers in prison hospice programs report gaining a sense of purpose and undergoing psychological rehabilitation by being an end-of-life caregiver (Neumann, 2016). With the number of incarcerated elderly persons steadily rising in the United States, it will be of interest to see whether prison-based hospice programs gain more traction in the future.

Questions for Discussion

1. In your opinion, should prison facilities have hospice-based programs? What are the potential benefits of doing this? What are the drawbacks of doing this?
2. Do you think family members should be allowed to come in and visit incarcerated persons who are in hospice programs? Do you see any potential drawbacks of allowing this practice?

INTRODUCTION

In 2020, the emergence of COVID-19 in the United States had a drastic impact on all aspects of American life, including the corrections system. Across the country, jail and prison officials released tens of thousands of incarcerated persons to help stop the spread of COVID-19 among incarcerated populations. In California, a number of attorneys who represented incarcerated persons appealed to Governor Gavin Newsom for targeted release of incarcerated elderly persons and those with chronic medical conditions. On March 31, 2020, the state of California granted early release to 3,500 prisoners, representing 3% of the total prison population at that time. In addition, counties across California released an additional 67,000 persons incarcerated in jails (Kreidler, 2020). Similar tactics were seen in other states, including Michigan, Colorado, and New Mexico. The release of so many incarcerated elderly and medically ill persons shined a spotlight on these populations, their unique needs, and the correctional responses to these needs. If an elderly offender is not a danger to themselves or the community, should they be released from prison? How can incarcerated persons with chronic mental illnesses best be served by the corrections system? These questions and more will be explored in this chapter.

The purpose of this chapter is to discuss vulnerable populations in the U.S. corrections system. In this text, a **vulnerable population** is defined as those who experience barriers to resources or face limitations due to illness, age, and social status (Institute of Medicine and National Research Council, 2013). While there are many populations in the corrections system that can be deemed as vulnerable, this chapter discusses the impact of incarceration on LGBTQ, elderly, and mentally ill populations. It explores the issues that face each population, and the response of the corrections system to the specific needs of each population. It is also important to note that while each population area will be explored individually, many incarcerated persons are facing **co-occurring conditions**, meaning they have more than one condition happening at a time. An example of a co-occurring condition would be an elderly offender or LGBTQ offender who suffers from two or more medical or mental health disorders. The presence of co-occurring conditions is more prevalent for incarcerated populations than for the general population (Koons-Witt & Crittenden, 2018; Peters et al., 2015). The co-occurrence of these vulnerabilities only makes the adequate care of these individuals that much more difficult, and also that much more important to study and understand.

LGBTQ OFFENDERS

Lesbian, Gay, Bisexual, Transgender, and Questioning/Queer (LGBTQ) populations in the U.S. prison system have been growing, and there is reason to believe that these individuals have been disproportionately impacted by practices of mass incarceration. An example of this can be seen in the incarcerated transgender population. Approximately 2.7% of the total U.S. adult population has been incarcerated, compared to 16% of the total transgender population (Marksamer & Tobin, 2014). The same can be seen in the incarcerated juvenile population, where LGBTQ youth make up 4%–8% of the total youth population and 13%–15% of the juvenile detention population (Irvine, 2010). A looming question is, what has caused this disproportionality?

There are a number of potential reasons for the disproportionate incarceration of LGBTQ populations. One reason may be that these populations are at an increased risk of police profiling, and may be subject to discrimination by the police based on their sexual orientation or gender identity (Marksamer & Tobin, 2014). Also, these populations are more likely to experience poverty and homelessness, and the enforcement of laws that affect poor and homeless populations may also adversely affect LGBTQ populations (Peek, 2004). Regardless of the reason, the disproportionate rates of incarceration are clear, and it is of interest to explore the unique issues that face incarcerated LGBTQ populations. Areas of focus in this discussion will include problems related to the classification of incarcerated persons and housing of LGBTQ offenders, the use of segregation and protective custody for this population, and policies regarding hormone replacement therapy for incarcerated transgender persons.

Classification and Housing of Incarcerated LGBTQ Populations

Before discussing how **classification** decisions for incarcerated persons are made for LGBTQ populations, it is important to discuss how gender is defined in an incarceration setting. Historically, gender was seen as being the same as biological sex (i.e., either male or female) for incarcerated persons, and this view can be especially troublesome when the system is classifying incarcerated transgender persons (Sumner & Jenness, 2014). According to Malkin and DeJong (2018), even the earliest understanding of incarcerated transgender persons was defined in a dualistic manner, with transgender individuals being seen as "either boys who wanted to be girls, or girls who wanted to be boys" (p. 2). Those who study gender, on the other hand, tend to view it as a continuum, with many identities falling between the poles of "masculinity" and "femininity." While gender is viewed as a continuum from a modern perspective, recognizing it as a continuum is nearly impossible in a correctional setting, where the entire system is based on the dichotomy between "men" and "women." Classification of individuals who do not fit perfectly into either of these two categories becomes problematic for correctional officials (Sumner & Jenness, 2014).

Historically, people in the U.S. corrections system were placed in either men's or women's facilities based on their genitalia (Marksamer & Tobin, 2014; Peek, 2004; Sumner & Jenness, 2014). However, it is important to consider the consequences of housing an incarcerated person based on genitalia, rather than based on their own gender identity.

One potential negative consequence of housing someone based on their genitalia may be increased risks for that person because of the placement. For example, if an incarcerated transgender person who identifies as female but has male sex organs is placed in a male facility, that individual is at an increased risk of physical injury, sexual assault, harassment, or even death (Peek, 2004). Further, transgender and gender nonconforming persons might not be able to access gender-appropriate clothing or grooming items, and staff may punish them for expressing their gender identity (Marksamer & Tobin, 2014).

On the other hand, there are certainly still risks associated with classification based on self-identified gender identity. For example, if an incarcerated transgender person who identifies as male but has female genitalia is placed in a male facility, they too have an increased risk of sexual victimization, and the facility runs the risk of incidents such as unwanted pregnancies. Also, in classifying incarcerated persons based on self-identified gender identity, there is an underlying assumption that the individual wants to disclose this information on intake, and there are many reasons why they may not want to disclose. Issues such as homophobia and transphobia are as prevalent in prison as they are out of prison, and might even be worse in an incarcerated environment. Incarcerated LGBTQ persons may fear that disclosing their sexual orientation or gender identity could subject them to discrimination or victimization (Gorczynski, 2016). Adding to this, incarcerated individuals still face the fear of how their relationships with family members, friends, and the community will be impacted by the revelation of their LGBTQ status (Dunn, 2013). All things considered, one can certainly declare that the classification and housing of incarcerated LGBTQ persons is a complex issue, and one that has serious implications for all parties involved. In order for this issue to be handled successfully, a delicate balance has to be struck between maintaining individual rights and maintaining the safety and security of a correctional facility.

The Use of Segregation and Protective Custody for Incarcerated LGBTQ Populations

One solution that has historically been implemented to handle the problems associated with classification of incarcerated LGBTQ persons has been to segregate these individuals from the general prison population (Malkin & DeJong, 2018; Marksamer & Tobin, 2014). Those who are in favor of **segregation** would argue that segregating an incarcerated person removes them from danger and protects them from victimization. Those who oppose it argue that segregating an incarcerated person limits their access to programs, recreation, education, and vocational opportunities. Also, the act of segregating someone is typically used as a punishment in prison facilities, so segregating an incarcerated person because they are LGBTQ essentially punishes them for their gender or sexuality. One might even argue that prolonged stays in segregation are a violation of an incarcerated person's right to be protected from cruel and unusual punishment (Marksamer & Tobin, 2014). What is the right answer here?

In reference to the segregation of incarcerated LGBTQ populations, the **Prison Rape Elimination Act (PREA) of 2003** has set clear standards regarding segregated housing. Incarcerated persons should not be placed in segregated housing unless all other housing options have been deemed unsuitable to protect them from their abuser (National PREA Resource Center, 2018). In cases where an incarcerated person has to be segregated for their own protection, the PREA standard is that the segregation should not last more than 24 hours (Malkin & DeJong, 2018). If an incarcerated person does need to be segregated for more than 24 hours, they should have access to programs, education, and vocational opportunities, to the extent this is possible. PREA clearly states that segregation stays should not last longer than 30 days, and that those 30 days should be spent finding alternative housing to keep the incarcerated person safe. Stays beyond 30 days have to be reviewed every 30 days to determine if there is still a need for separation (National PREA Resource Center, 2018). Overall, the PREA guidelines are clear; segregation of incarcerated LBGTQ persons should only be done in extreme circumstances in which no alternate housing options are available, and should be done for the least amount of time possible.

Hormone Replacement Therapy Policies

Another area of debate involving incarcerated transgender persons is whether they should continue on, or in some cases even begin, **hormone replacement therapy (HRT)** while incarcerated. States are very divided on policies related to HRT. Some states make blanket policies against HRT, while others provide for the initiation and continuation of HRT (Marksamer & Tobin, 2014). As of 2014 there were 20 states that allowed for the continuation of HRT, 13 that allowed for initiation upon incarceration, and 20 states that had specific policies against its use (Routh et al., 2015).

Arguments against the use of HRT are based primarily on monetary considerations; as stated by Routh et al. (2015), "the greater the cost for treatment, the greater the likelihood that treatment will be denied" (p. 18). Also, HRT is not the only treatment for gender dysphoria. Alternatives such as psychotherapy are considerably more cost effective than HRT (Routh et al., 2015). Opponents of HRT argue that they are not opposed to incarcerated transgender persons, but rather are supportive of providing adequate care in the most cost-effective manner possible.

Proponents of HRT initiation and continuation argue that this is not just something an incarcerated person wants; rather, it is a medical need. One must also consider what an incarcerated person has to go through to even request HRT. This requires the person to reveal their transgender status to authorities, something that they may be hesitant to do for a number of reasons, including the fear of being housed in administrative segregation. Further, to get the HRT, they will have to be strip-searched and patted down when entering and leaving the medical wing of the facility (Routh et al., 2015). There are some incarcerated persons who do not want to experience the hassle, embarrassment, or risks associated with these hurdles and will therefore forgo the treatments they need (Scott, 2013). One must also consider that, depending on where an incarcerated person is in their transition, abruptly stopping HRT can have potential negative consequences. Without treatment for their symptoms, some incarcerated persons resort to self-harm, suicide, and even autocastration (Routh et al., 2015). Overall, the future of HRT as a viable treatment option for incarcerated transgender persons is still not known. While some states have adopted policies regarding HRT, there are still some states that have not adopted any policies, which demonstrates that there is more work to be done in this particular area of correctional administration (Routh et al., 2015).

ELDERLY OFFENDERS

Elderly offenders are proportionately the fastest-growing age group in the U.S. prison system and around the world (Aday & Krabill, 2012; DiLorito et al., 2018; Skarupski et al., 2018). In 2017 there were approximately 200,000 incarcerated persons aged 55 and older in the United States (Reese, 2019). This number is astounding, especially when compared to the same statistic 50 years earlier in the 1970s, where there were just 6,500 incarcerated persons aged 55 or older in U.S. prisons (Sabol et al., 2007). As discussed by Blowers and Blevins (2015), the shift towards a more punitive justice system beginning in the 1970s resulted in harsher, lengthier sentences for incarcerated persons. The 1980s and 1990s saw the creation of "get tough" sentencing laws, as previously discussed in Chapters 1–3. The War on Drugs, Three Strikes laws, and truth-in-sentencing all resulted in increased rates and lengths of sentences (Blowers et al., 2014). By 2000, the number of incarcerated elderly persons swelled to 50,000, representing a near 750% increase in just 30 years (Sabol et al., 2007). The number continues to grow, and the number of incarcerated elderly persons is expected to reach upwards of 400,000 by 2030, representing a 4,000% increase since 1981 (Reese, 2019).

Regarding the challenges that incarcerated elderly offenders face, they are more likely than younger prisoners to suffer from disease and disability, which is burdensome on the system. Due in large part to their high health needs, they are a major reason for the rising prison health-care costs (Yarnell et al., 2017). The price tag for caring for incarcerated elderly persons is well over $16 billion annually (Reese, 2019). Maschi et al. (2013) estimate that it costs two to three times more money to incarcerate an older person than to incarcerate a younger person. Given the often limited resources in prisons and jails, it is important that sufficient and cost-effective treatments are implemented (Merkt et al., 2020). While this certainly sounds straightforward, investigation quickly reveals that data on the health care needs of incarcerated elderly persons is very limited, and that the existing literature often shows disagreement between researchers (DiLorito et al., 2018). The following section of this chapter explores this scarce research and discusses some of the key issues facing incarcerated elderly persons.

Before exploring the issues related to incarcerated elderly persons, it is important to define who is referred to by the term "elderly offender." As discussed by Merkt and colleagues (2020), research in the field of gerontology typically uses the age of 65 as a cut-off for designating someone as an "older person." Things get a little more complicated in the case of older offenders, though. Definitions of these offenders are usually based on chronological age, with a cut-off age ranging from 45 to 65 years of age (Yorston & Taylor, 2006; Aday & Krabill, 2012). In a review of studies on elderly age cut-off for incarcerated persons, Merkt et al. (2020) found that the cut-off age of 50 was most commonly used. One reason why offenders have a younger age cut-off may be that prisoners are subject to premature aging, what Cipriani and colleagues call "**accelerated aging**" (2017). As discussed by Merkt and colleagues (2020), coming to a shared understanding of who qualifies as an incarcerated elderly person might help advance research on prisoner health, which would assist in planning health services, programming, housing, and transition planning for these individuals.

Characteristics and Needs of Incarcerated Elderly Persons

As discussed by Gross (2007), the elderly population, whether incarcerated or not, will experience the aging process and all that comes with advanced age. The elderly are more likely to suffer from sensory deficits, as well as declines in balance and stamina. They are at an increased risk of choking and often lose weight with age. Their bones are more likely to break, and they are more likely to experience immobility. They may experience issues of incontinence and frequent urination, in additional to being more vulnerable to communicable diseases.

While all elderly persons experience the pains associated with aging, there is reason to believe that the prison environment has long-term, negative effects on the physical health of incarcerated elderly persons. As discussed by Gross (2007), "an inadequate or unbalanced diet, a sedentary lifestyle, and insufficient preventative health care are features of long-term incarceration that may have negative effects on the physical health of older and long-term [incarcerated persons]" (p. 60). This is further exacerbated by the fact that many who enter prison later in life are more likely to have lived in less-than-ideal conditions prior to incarceration, characterized by factors such as poor diet, limited access to health care, and alcohol and drug abuse (Gross, 2007). So, while all elderly persons are affected by aging, long-term incarceration and pre-incarceration lifestyles may leave incarcerated elderly persons at greater risk of negative health complications.

Incarcerated Elderly Persons and Dementia

One condition that explicitly affects incarcerated elderly offenders is **dementia**. As discussed by Cipriani et al. (2017), dementia is "one of the most feared and devastating disorders that can occur in the later phases of life" (p. 40). Those who suffer from dementia experience cognitive impairment and diminished social skills, as well as changes in mood and behavior, sometimes including bizarre behavior (Cipriani et al., 2017). With the graying incarcerated population in the United States, it is only expected that cases of dementia will become increasingly common. Some estimates suggest that the prevalence of dementia among incarcerated persons will double in the coming decades (Blowers & Blevins, 2015). Research also indicates that dementia is two to three times more frequent among incarcerated elderly populations than among community-dwelling elderly populations (Wilson & Barboza, 2010). Further, co-occurring disorders are found in upwards of 85% of incarcerated elderly persons, only complicating the care of those with dementia (Loeb & AbuDagga, 2006).

Another aspect of dementia to consider is how it impacts prison rule violation. As discussed by Blowers & Blevins (2015), incarcerated persons with dementia might have problem following basic instructions, making them more likely to violate prison rules, sometimes without even knowing they are doing so. This is supported by research suggesting that incarcerated persons who are mentally ill are more likely to have prison misconduct violations (Houser et al., 2012; Steiner & Wooldredge, 2009). Further, incarcerated elderly persons with dementia may not like the routine of prison life, finding the continuous noise and distraction of other incarcerated persons aggravating, which makes them more likely to act out and face an infraction (Blowers & Blevins, 2015).

In looking at policies and practices related to the detention of people with dementia, Cipriani and colleagues (2017) argue for a proactive rather than a reactive approach to dealing with these populations. They suggest that healthcare workers in the correctional field need to treat all incarcerated persons with basic human dignity, regardless of their past or present behaviors. It is also suggested that incarcerated younger persons could be trained to notice the subtle changes that often occur among elderly persons when dementia is setting in, so they can alert prison staff. Those who are just starting to show symptoms or are newly diagnosed should be given the opportunity to contribute to their advanced care plan while they still have the mental capacity to participate. If possible, prisons may want to consider having separate housing units for offenders with dementia. One such unit was created at Fishkill, a medium-security prison outside of New York City, and it has had good results for the incarcerated persons (Cipriani et al., 2017). In conclusion, while assimilation into prison culture can be difficult for any incarcerated elderly person, those with dementia face additional barriers into a safe transition into prison life. Understanding these barriers is essential for the health, safety, and well-being of these individuals.

Intergenerational Relationships Among Elderly Offenders

In response to the growing number of incarcerated elderly persons, many facilities have chosen to implement age-segregated facilities, as well as programs specifically for elderly offenders. These practices are based on a belief that separating incarcerated older persons from incarcerated younger persons is better for the older persons, and that an intergenerational environment is harmful to elderly offenders (Filinson & Ciambrone, 2019). There is, however, a growing body of research that argues for the maintenance of **intergenerational relationships** for elderly offenders, including their relationships with children and grandchildren outside the prison and with incarcerated younger persons inside the prison (Ehlman et al., 2014; Underwood & Dorfman, 2006).

Filinson & Ciambrone (2019) examined intergenerational relationships among incarcerated elderly offenders, their children and grandchildren, and incarcerated younger persons to uncover whether these relationships are harmful or helpful to elderly offenders. They recruited 100 incarcerated elderly persons (aged 55 or older) from a medium-security prison facility in the northeastern United States. In regard to intergenerational relationships with children and grandchildren, while most participants (85%) had children and grandchildren, less than one quarter received any visits from them. Of those who did receive visits, they did not report that these visits enhanced their prison life. In fact, some incarcerated elderly persons found the visitation to be an unpleasant experience for their children and avoided it altogether to protect them. In terms of their intergenerational relationships with incarcerated younger persons, older offenders reported that they did have bonds with younger offenders, and that these often revolved around the younger offenders assisting them in some manner. Many incarcerated elderly persons took on the role of mentor, seeing reflections of their younger selves in the younger offenders. Unlike other studies on this topic, this study highlighted the importance of intergenerational relationships for elderly offenders, suggesting that separation of elderly offenders from younger offenders might not be in the best interest of either group, as both had something to gain from their continued relationship (Filinson & Ciambrone, 2019).

Compassionate Release of Elderly Offenders

Given the large number of elderly offenders in the prison population, some policy makers are calling for "**compassionate release**," which allows incarcerated sick and elderly persons an opportunity to live out their final days outside of prison. These types of programs were first implemented in the 1970s, and today 49 states have laws related to compassionate release, though some laws distinguish between geriatric release for the elderly and compassionate release for the ill (Reese, 2019). Most compassionate release programs require an applicant to have reached a minimum age, usually ranging from 45–65. Some states require that an incarcerated person serve a minimum number of years before being eligible for the program, some upwards of 25 years. Many states have a requirement in place that excludes persons who are incarcerated for certain types of felonies, such as murder or sexual assault. Given that many of the older persons are serving long sentences for these types of violent crimes, geriatric release programs might not apply to a majority of elderly offenders (Parks, 2018). For officials, it is a matter of striking a balance between maintaining public safety and allowing people to live out the end of their lives in comfort and dignity.

OFFENDERS WITH MENTAL ILLNESS

While the rate varies from source to source, a good estimate of the prevalence of incarcerated persons with **mental illness** is 15%–20% (Adams & Ferrandino, 2008; Brandt, 2012; Hanson, 2017; Karlsson & Zielinski, 2020). Bronson and Berzofsky (2017) report that approximately one in seven persons incarcerated in state and federal prison, and one in four persons incarcerated in jail, reported experiencing severe psychological distress in the 30 days leading up to being surveyed. Additionally, 37% of those incarcerated in prison and 44% of offenders in jail had been told in the past by medical providers that they had a mental illness. The most common mental illnesses among incarcerated persons include depression (38%), schizophrenia (29%), anxiety disorders (8%), and bipolar disorder (8%) (Adams & Ferrandino, 2008; Brandt, 2012).

It is of interest to note the higher rate of mental illness in jails, as symptoms of these diseases are much more prevalent in jails when compared to prisons. One reason for this might be that people are in jail for a shorter period of time (typically less than one year), and some of the people in jail are persons with mental illness who are waiting to be transferred to mental health facilities. Spending less time in jail means that many will have less time to adjust, thus presenting with more symptoms of mental illness (Brandt, 2012). Regardless of the distinction between jail and prison, the vast number of people affected by mental health issues creates problems for the corrections system because, in short, the corrections system was not designed to be able to handle this many offenders with mental illness.

Causes for the Dramatic Increase in Incarcerated Offenders With Mental Illness

In order to understand what has led to the high numbers of incarcerated offenders with mental illness, it is necessary to examine the relationship between **deinstitutionalization** and the corrections system. The deinstitutionalization of mental health hospitals began after World War II, "fueled by media accounts of patient abuse, the development of drugs that treat severe mental illness, and federal funding of community-based treatment facilities" (Brandt, 2012, p. 545). The goal was to release patients from mental hospitals into community-based treatment programs, but this goal was not met without problems. Many community-based facilities could not help those with limited finances, and the services offered were often inadequate (Lurigio et al., 2004). Those who were medicated while in mental hospitals were suddenly off their medications, and many ended up on the streets because of a lack of affordable housing options for those with mental illness. This increased their chances of making contact with the police (Soderstrom, 2007). Because of deinstitutionalization, the population of state mental hospitals decreased from a high of 550,000 in the 1950s to approximately 70,000 in 2010 (Brandt, 2012). This also accompanied the swelling prison populations seen in the same period of time.

While deinstitutionalization certainly played a role in the increase of incarcerated persons with mental illness, there are some other ongoing potential causes for this increase as well. One secondary cause is legal restrictions, for example changes in mental health laws that make it more difficult to involuntarily commit a person to a psychiatric hospital (Lurigio et al., 2004). When laws regarding the rights of patients were strengthened in recent decades, it led to situations in which only the most severely mentally ill people are hospitalized, leaving many potentially dangerous mentally ill offenders in the community with the opportunity to offend (Brandt, 2012). Further, the fragmentation of the mental health system also causes offenders who are mentally ill to get trapped in the criminal justice system. As discussed by Lurigio and colleagues (2004), the mental health system in the United States is highly compartmentalized; for example, those who treat mental health typically do not also treat chemical dependency, and vice versa. If a mental health program requires abstinence from a substance for participation, those with co-occurring disorders are not able to participate. The War on Drugs has brought more drug users into the criminal justice system, and this also includes many who have both substance use and mental health problems (Brandt, 2012).

Treatment for Incarcerated Offenders With Mental Illness

Due to the lack of resources such as time, space, and money, the most common form of treatment for incarcerated persons who suffer from mental illness is medication (Adams & Ferrandino, 2008). As discussed by Brandt (2012), "we cannot be sure whether medication is used to treat the mental illness or to control the symptoms of the illness to make it easier for correctional staff and administrators" (p. 547). Most correctional staff are not trained specifically to handle offenders who are mentally ill or to watch for symptoms of their illness, which poses additional problems for their treatment. While correctional staff may take part in providing medication, they are not necessarily trained to do so, and many experience role conflict between the need to maintain safety and the need to provide treatment (Adams & Ferrandino, 2008; Turner, 2007). One might assume that not having the training to deal with these dual roles would result in correctional staff defaulting to safety, potentially missing an opportunity to provide treatment to incarcerated persons (Brandt, 2012).

Unfortunately, the correctional environment itself can be difficult for incarcerated persons who are mentally ill, especially in regard to following the rules and regulations of a facility. Offenders with mental illness have higher rates of disciplinary actions than the general population (O'Keefe, 2007). This may be because some offenders with mental illness are simply not able to understand the rules of the facility (Turner, 2007). Regardless of this factor, though, they still suffer the consequences of not following the rules. Incarcerated persons who are mentally ill are also 1.7 times more likely to be physically injured while incarcerated, when compared to incarcerated persons without mental illness (Blitz et al., 2008).

Another way incarcerated persons with mental illness are handled in prison is through the use of administrative segregation. This is used to control behaviors that are the manifestation of the mental illness because there is not space to control these behaviors in psychiatric correctional facilities (Rhodes, 2005). Despite being a relatively inexpensive way to deal with these persons, the use of administrative segregations can lead to increased risk of suicide by isolated, mentally ill offenders (Brandt, 2012). Isolation for exhibiting behaviors related to mental health can come to be seen as a punishment by these offenders, leading them to keep their suicidal thoughts and ideations hidden from correctional staff (Adams & Ferrandino, 2009). Further, when these offenders are isolated, they lose their access to services and programs that are available to the general population, which is especially problematic given that offenders with mental illness have greater needs for academic, vocational, substance abuse, and anger management programming (O'Keefe & Schnell, 2007).

In addition to medication, other treatment methods are also used for incarcerated offenders who are mentally ill; in 2005, 22% of those incarcerated in prison and 7% of those incarcerated in jail received counseling, and 5% of those incarcerated in prison and 2% of those incarcerated in jail reported an overnight hospital stay in a psychiatric facility (James & Glaze, 2006). While those numbers increased starting in the 1990s, they continued to be quite low compared to the prevalence of mental illness in prisons and jails. Also, the high prevalence of offenders who are mentally ill means that each mental health provider has to handle more patients, which ultimately decreases their effectiveness (O'Keefe & Schnell, 2007). Further, Bewley and Morgan (2011) interviewed mental health service providers in state prison facilities and found that 57% had no specific training in correctional or forensic psychology. As far as the effectiveness of their treatment, the professionals rated themselves between "neutral" and "mildly effective." While 50% of the participants felt that rehabilitation was an important goal of incarceration, 65% did not believe there was adequate funding for care for incarcerated persons (Bewley & Morgan, 2011). While incarcerated offenders with mental illness are receiving some treatment, it is clear that more needs to be done in order to meet the unique needs of these populations. Medication and counseling seem to be a step in the right direction, but more resources and funding are needed to make these measures fully effective.

CONCLUSION

What is clear from a review of the available information on vulnerable prison populations is that, among people who are incarcerated, a large number are considered vulnerable for one or more reasons. These individuals create challenges for correctional administrators, as their unique needs often require accommodations that can be difficult for facilities to undertake. Correctional facilities have to strike a gentle balance between maintaining the safety and security of a facility and upholding the basic rights and meeting the needs of the vulnerable populations they serve.

Faced with difficult situations and inadequate training, correctional officers and administrators often fall short of meeting the correctional needs of vulnerable populations. It is important to address and remedy these shortcomings, as it is unavoidable that most of those who are vulnerable and incarcerated will leave prison and jail and return to society, and they will need the skills and tools necessary to survive in the outside world. At the very least, no offender who leaves incarceration should be more dangerous than they were before incarceration. More research is needed on how to best serve vulnerable incarcerated populations in the future.

DISCUSSION QUESTIONS

1. Do you think incarcerated transgender persons should be housed based on their own self-identified gender identity, or based on the biological sex listed on their birth certificate? What are some arguments you see for and against each policy?
2. What age do you think we should view as the "cut-off" age for elderly offenders? 50? 55? 60? What are the pros and cons of having a younger or older age cut-off?
3. What effect did deinstitutionalization have on offenders with mental illness in the United States? What do you think we should do to help these offenders moving forward?

APPLICATION EXERCISES

Exercise #1: Exploring the Transgender Offender Manual

For this exercise, you should access the Transgender Offender Manual put out by the Federal Bureau of Prisons (https://www.bop.gov/policy/progstat/5200-04-cn-1.pdf). While you are exploring this manual, consider the following questions:

1. How will the Transgender Executive Council (TEC) make the initial designation of an offender? What factors will be included in making this decision? What factors do you think should be included?

2. What criteria will the TEC use to make an assessment about the housing and programming assignment of incarcerated transgender persons? What are your thoughts on this criteria?

3. What does the manual say about HRT and necessary medical treatment? What are your thoughts on these guidelines?

4. What does the manual say about staff use of pronouns and names for transgendered individuals? What do you think staff should do in terms of use of pronouns?

5. What does the manual say about pat and visual searches of incarcerated persons?

6. What does the manual say about clothing and commissary items for incarcerated transgender persons? Do you think incarcerated persons should have access to undergarments of their identified gender?

Exercise #2: Designing Programs for Vulnerable Populations

For this exercise, you should work in small groups to further explore one of the vulnerable populations discussed in this chapter, or another population that you deem to be vulnerable. In doing this, you should think about programming, and what type of programs, either prison- or community-based, could be beneficial for the population you explore. Some questions to consider while doing this exercise:

1. What are the top three problems facing this vulnerable population? What makes them considerably vulnerable?

2. If you could design a program to assist the vulnerable population you explored, what would this program look like? What would the name of the program be? What supplies/facility needs would you have to make this program work? Give as much detail about the workings of the program as possible.

3. What role would the community play in your program? Can you think of any key stakeholders or community members you would reach out to specifically?

4. How would you know if your program was successful? That is, how is success measured in your program?

REFERENCES

Adams, K., & Ferrandino, J. (2008). Managing mentally ill inmates in prisons. *Criminal Justice and Behavior, 35,* 913–927.

Aday, R. H., & Krabill, J. J. (2012). Older and geriatric offenders: Critical issues for the 21st century. In L. Gideon (ed.), *Special needs offenders in correctional institutions*. Sage Publications.

Bewley, M. T., & Morgan, R. D. (2011). A national survey of mental health services available to offenders with mental illness: Who is doing what? *Law and Human Behavior, 35*(5), 351–363.

Blitz, C. L., Wolff, N., & Shi, J. (2008). Physical victimization if prison: The role of mental illness. *International Journal of Law and Psychiatry, 31*(5), 385–393.

Blowers, A. N., & Blevins, K. R. (2015). An examination of prison misconduct among older inmates. *Journal of Crime & Justice, 38*(1), 96–112.

Blowers, A. N., Jolley, J. M., & Kerbs, J. J. (2014). The age segregation debate. In J. J. Kerbs and J. M. Jolley (Eds.), *Senior citizens behind bars: Challenges for the criminal justice system* (pp. 133–156). Lynne Rienner Publishers.

Brandt, A. L. S. (2012). Treatment of persons with mental illness in the criminal justice system: A literature review. *Journal of Offender Rehabilitation, 51*(8), 541–558.

Bronson, J., & Berzofsky, M. (2017). *Indicators of mental health problems reported by prisoners and jail inmates, 2011–12* (NCJ 250612). U.S. Department of Justice.

Cipriani, G., Danti, S., Carlesi, C., & DiFiorino, M. (2017). Old and dangerous: Prison and dementia. *Journal of Forensic & Legal Medicine, 51*, 40–44.

DiLorito, C., Vilm, B., & Dening, T. (2018). Psychiatric disorders among older prisoners: A systematic review and comparison study against older people in the community. *Aging & Mental Health, 22*(1), 1–10.

Dunn, P. (2013). Slipping off the equalities agenda? Work with LGBT prisoners. *Prison Service Journal, 206*, 3–10.

Ehlman, K., Ligon, M., & Moriello, G. (2014). The impact of intergenerational oral history on perceived generativity in older adults. *Journal of Intergenerational Relationships, 12*(1), 40–53.

Filinson, R., & Ciambrone, D. (2019). "Trying to blend in, what else can we do?": Intergenerational relationships among aged inmates. *Journal of Intergenerational Relationships, 17*(1), 74–92.

Gorczynski, P. F. (2016). LGBT prisoners. *Psychologist, 29*(5), 327.

Gross, B. (2007). Elderly offenders: Implications for corrections personnel. *Forensic Examiner, 16*(1), 56–61.

Hanson, A. (2017). Will anything break the jail to hospital logjam? *American Jails, 31*(5), 23–28.

Houser, K. A., Bleneko, S., & Brennan, P. K. (2012). The effects of mental health and substance abuse disorders on institutional misconduct among female inmates. *Justice Quarterly, 29*(6), 799–828.

Institute of Medicine and National Research Council. (2013). *Health and incarceration: A workshop summary*. National Academic Press. https://doi.org/10.17226/18372

Irvine, A. (2010). We've had three of them: Addressing the invisibility of lesbian, gay, bisexual, and gender nonconforming youths in the juvenile justice system. *Columbia Journal of Gender and Law, 19*(3), 675–701.

James, D. J., & Glaze, L. E. (2006). *Mental health problems of prison and jail inmates* (NCJ 213600). U.S. Department of Justice, Office of Justice Programs, Bureau of Justice Statistics.

Karlsson, M. E, & Zielinski, M. J. (2020). Sexual victimization and mental illness prevalence rates among incarcerated women: A literature review. *Trauma, Violence & Abuse, 21*(2), 326–349.

Koons-Witt, B., & Crittenden, C. (2018). Gender differences and program participation among prisoners with co-occurring substance abuse and mental health disorders. *Journal of Offender Rehabilitation, 57*(7), 431–458.

Kreidler, M. (2020, April 16). *Jails and prisons spring thousands of inmates to prevent COVID-19 outbreaks.* U.S. News & World Report. https://www.usnews.com/news/healthiest-communities/articles/2020-04-16/jails-and-prisons-spring-inmates-to-prevent-coronavirus-outbreaks

Loeb, S. J., & AbuDagga, A. (2006). Health-related research on older inmates: An integrative review. *Research in Nursing & Health, 29*(6), 556–565.

Lurigio, A. J., Rollins, A., & Fallon, J. (2004). The effects of serious mental illness on offender reentry. *Federal Probation, 68*(2), 45–52.

Malkin, M. L., & DeJong, C. (2018). Protections for transgender inmates under PREA: A comparison of state correctional policies in the United States. *Sexuality Research and Social Policy, 15*, 1–15.

Marksamer, J., & Tobin, H. J. (2014). *Standing with LGBT prisoners: An advocate's guide to ending abuse and combating imprisonment.* National Center for Transgender Equality. http://www.transequality.org/sites/default/files/docs/resources/JailPrisons_Resource_FINAL.pdf

Maschi, T., Viola, D., & Sun, F. (2013). The high cost of the international aging prisoner crisis: Well-being as the common denominator for action. *The Gerontologist, 53*(4), 543–554.

Merkt, H., Haesen, S., Meyer, L., Kressig, R. W., Elger, B. S., & Wangmo, T. (2020). Defining an age cut-off for older offenders: A systematic review of literature. *International Journal of Prisoner Health, 16*(2), 95–116.

National PREA Resource Center. (2018). *Prison and jail standards.* https://www.prearesourcecenter.org/training-technical-assistance/prea-101/prisons-and-jail-standards

Neumann, A. (2016, February 16). *What dying looks like in America's prisons.* The Atlantic. https://www.theatlantic.com/health/archive/2016/02/hospice-care-in-prison/462660/

O'Keefe, M. I. (2007). Administrative segregation for mentally ill inmates. *Journal of Offender Rehabilitation, 45*(1–2), 149–165.

O'Keefe, M. I., & Schnell, M. J. (2007). Offenders with mental illness in the correctional system. *Journal of Offender Rehabilitations, 45*(1–2), 81–104.

Parks, E. A. (2018). Elderly and incarcerated: Preventing the medical deaths of older people in Texas prisons. *Texas Journal on Civil Liberties & Civil Rights, 23*, 145–164.

Peek, C. (2004). Breaking out of the prison hierarchy: Transgender prisoners, rape, and the Eighth Amendment. *Santa Clara Law Review, 44*, 1211–1248.

Peters, R. H., Wexler, H. K., & Lurigio, A. J. (2015). Co-occurring substance use and mental disorders in the criminal justice system: A new frontier of clinical practice and research. *Psychiatric Rehabilitation Journal, 38*(1), 1–6.

Prison Fellowship (n.d.). *Hospice: The prison's forgotten corner.* Retrieved March 21, 2021 from https://www.prisonfellowship.org/2019/10/hospice-the-prisons-forgotten-corner/

Prison Rape Elimination Act of 2003. S. 1435, 108th Congress. (2003).

Reese, H. (2019, July 17). *What should we do about our aging prison population?* JSTOR Daily. https://daily.jstor.org/what-should-we-do-about-our-aging-prison-population/

Rhodes, L. A. (2005). Pathological effects of the supermaximum prison. *American Journal of Public Health, 95*(10), 1692–1695.

Routh, D., Abess, G., Makin, D., Stohr, M. K., Hemmens, C., & Yoo, J. (2015). Transgender inmates in prisons: A review of applicable statutes and policies. *International Journal of Offender Therapy & Comparative Criminology, 59*, 1–22.

Sabol, W. J., Couture, H., & Harrison, P. M. (2007). *Prisoners in 2006* (NCJ 219416). U.S. Department of Justice, Office of Justice Programs, Bureau of Justice Statistics.

Scott, S. (2013). "One is not born, but becomes a woman": A fourteenth amendment argument in support of housing male-to-female transgender inmates in female facilities. *University of Pennsylvania Journal of Constitutional Law, 15*, 1259–1297.

Skarupski, K. A., Gross, A., Schrack, J. A., Deal, J. A., & Eber, G. B. (2018). The health of America's aging prison population. *Epidemiological Reviews, 40*(1), 157–165.

Soderstrom, I. A. (2007). Mental illness in offender populations: Prevalence, duty, and implications. *Journal of Offender Rehabilitation, 45*(1–2), 1–17.

Steiner, B., & Wooldredge, J. (2009). Individual and environmental effects on assaults and nonviolent rule breaking by women in prison. *Journal of Research in Crime and Delinquency, 46*(4), 437–467.

Sumner, J., & Jenness, V. (2014). Gender integration in sex-segregated U.S. prisons: The paradox of transgender correctional policy. In D. Peterson & V. R. Panfil (Eds.), *Handbook of LGBT communities, crime, and justice* (pp. 229–259). Springer.

Turner, C. (2007). Ethical issues in criminal justice administration. *American Jails, 20*, 49–53.

Underwood, H. L., & Dorfman, L. T. (2006). A view from the other side: Elders' reactions to intergenerational service-learning. *Journal of Intergenerational Relationships, 4*(2), 43–60.

Wilson J., & Barboza, S. (2010). The looming challenge of dementia in corrections. *Correct Care, 24*(2), 12–14.

Yarnell, S. C., Kirwin, P. D., & Zonana, H. V. (2017). Geriatrics and the legal system. *Journal of the American Academy of Psychiatry and the Law, 45*(2), 208–217.

Yorston, G. A., & Taylor, P. J. (2006). Commentary: Older offenders – no place to go? *Journal of the American Academy of Psychiatry and the Law, 34*(3), 333–337.

Correctional Controversies

CHAPTER 12

Racial Equity in Corrections

CHAPTER OBJECTIVES

After reading this chapter, you should be able to:

- Discuss the history of racially discriminatory practices in corrections in the United States.
- Identify indirect punishments of offenders, even after formal sanctions are served.
- Explain the current state of racial inequality in the U.S. corrections system.

KEY WORDS

100-to-1 ratio

Accumulated disadvantage

Black Codes

Chain gang

Convict leasing program

Disparity

Felony disenfranchisement

Law Enforcement Assistance Administration

Prison farms

School-to-prison pipeline

War on Drugs

CASE STUDY: BAN THE BOX

As previously discussed in Chapter 5, thirty-five states and the federal government have attempted to reconcile some of these problems through legislative actions like "ban the box" and "fair chance" laws, which no longer allow employers to inquire about a person's criminal record on the application (Avery & Lu, 2019). In 2015, President Barack Obama endorsed ban the box policy at the federal level by announcing a change in the hiring practices of the federal Office of Personnel Management. The Fair Chance to Compete for Jobs Act of 2019 passed Congress 4 years later. Effective December 2021, the law prohibits most federal agencies from requesting information about a job applicant's conviction record until after making a conditional offer of employment to the applicant. Ban the box laws have also been adopted in over 35 states and 150 cities and counties around the United States, significantly affecting Black and Hispanic/Latino individuals as they seek employment after incarceration, as these groups are overrepresented among those who were previously incarcerated.

Questions for Discussion

1. In your opinion, will ban the box laws decrease the effect of felony disenfranchisement on racial minorities in the United States?
2. Should similar initiatives be applied for certain categories of sex offenders when it comes to housing opportunities?

INTRODUCTION

Although the era of mass incarceration caused severe disparities in the U.S. corrections population, there was already a long history of racial inequity in our criminal justice system prior to that era. A **disparity** is the overrepresentation of a population compared to its presence in the general population. As applied to this topic, there are large racial disparities in our corrections system. In the United States, Black people are incarcerated at 5.1 times the rate of White people, and Hispanic/Latino people are incarcerated at 1.4 times the rate of White people (Nellis, 2016). Research has attributed these disparities to **accumulated disadvantage**, or the incremental differences in the management of individuals during each step of the criminal justice process that creates cumulative discriminatory treatment (Bushway & Piehl, 2007). This difference in the treatment of different racial groups is a result of multiple factors, including conscious and unconscious biases.

The purpose of this chapter is to explore the history of racial inequity in the corrections system, as well as its current state. This chapter investigates practices dating back to the Civil War, as well as current trends. The effects of sentencing practices from the late 20th century are explored. In addition, current statistics describing racial disparities in the United States are discussed.

HISTORY OF RACIAL DISCRIMINATION IN CORRECTIONS

The year 1865 marked the end of the bloody American Civil War and the passage of the 13th Amendment, abolishing slavery across the United States. However, not all Americans supported the decision, and many White Americans were anxious about what the new freedom of Black Americans would mean for the country. Racist attitudes were still firmly rooted in many American households, especially in the South. In addition, the free labor that was previously available through slavery was no longer afforded to landowners, and the War had caused an economic depression. Government leaders in the South used the criminal justice system as a way of quelling public fears by rerouting many free Black Americans into correctional facilities. Multiple methods were used to funnel disproportionate numbers of Black people into jails and prisons. For example, **Black Codes** were passed in Southern states that outlawed behaviors common to Black people, such as "walking at night" and settling on public land (Muhammed, 2011).

As a result of law enforcement targeting newly freed Black Americans in the South, approximately 95% of individuals under correctional custody were Black in the 1870s. After the Civil War ended and the nation entered Reconstruction, there was economic depression. As a result, Southern states tried new strategies to rebuild, but also to debilitate Black Americans. State correctional authorities leased out individuals in the **convict leasing program** to help rebuild agricultural farms (Pisciotta, 1983). In other words, private landowners paid the corrections systems for the use of incarcerated persons (typically Black) for hard labor. These individuals were never paid for their work, essentially working as slaves once again.

In 1928, the convict leasing program ended as a result of a variety of political, industrial, and economic changes in the United States (Mancini, 1978). However, other forms of slavery were introduced that involved predominantly Black offenders. The 13th Amendment forbade slavery and indentured labor except as punishment for those who had been convicted of a crime, allowing the corrections system to serve as a conduit for slave labor. Incarcerated persons on a **chain gang** were forced to perform hard labor, such as building roads and clearing land, without pay and in grueling conditions (Goluboff, 2001). **Prison farms** were also prevalent in the Southern states and in Texas. These farms were large correctional facilities that used inmate manual labor to perform agricultural tasks, mining, and other responsibilities for economic benefit.

In the early 20th century, the North saw a huge influx in population due to the industry boom and increased employment opportunities. Free African Americans and European immigrants flooded cities like New York and Philadelphia, looking for a better life and financial stability. In addition, Black Americans hoped to live in a place without racial targeting and torture. However, with the spike in violent crime in the 1920s, both immigrants and Black Americans were the target of public fear and suspicion. Prison populations grew substantially into the mid-20th century, often with high rates of Black Americans being incarcerated (Delaney et al., 2019). Prisons, including their education and treatment programs, were also racially segregated (Krisberg et al., 2018).

It was also during this time that U.S. penitentiaries used incarcerated persons as free labor. Much like the industries that were booming on the outside, the prison system was itself an industry that produced goods for cheaper cost than private companies did (as discussed in depth in Chapter 8). Incarcerated persons were often not compensated for this rigorous labor. The 1930s and early 1940s brought several pieces of federal and state legislation that limited or stopped inmate-made goods, due to pressure from private organizations (Fields, 2005). As also discussed in Chapters 8 and 15, it was not until the Nixon administration that the prison industry began a series of regulations that changed the cycle of corruption and abuse. Congress lifted the ban on interstate sale of prison-made goods and encouraged the improvement of the prison industry in 1979, and the **Law Enforcement Assistance Administration (LEAA)** allotted funding for seven states to develop industry programs in their prison facilities. The LEAA was established by the Omnibus Crime Control and Safe Streets Act of 1968 and funded research, planning, and programs until it was abolished in 1982. The LEAA also required standards and implementation of components in prison labor that required reasonable wages for the incarcerated persons and productivity standards akin to those of the private industry (National Archives, 2016).

During the Civil Rights movement of the 1960s, a huge influx of racial tension and violence occurred even as new social and political freedoms were afforded to Black Americans. The mass incarceration era began, and prisons and jails became severely overcrowded, with severe and continuing racial disparities in the makeup of incarcerated populations (Chase, 2015). Prisons were generally located in rural areas, where there were often racial conflicts and deep prejudicial feelings toward racial minorities. Until the 1960s, there were very few employees of correctional facilities who were not White.

As a result of these tensions, protests and riots erupted in correctional facilities. Inmates rallied for the right to practice the religion of their choice, hold political meetings, and practice free speech. These protests were not unlike those occurring between racial groups outside the prison walls. One of the most infamous riots, which as some have noted was the bloodiest one-day encounter since the Civil War, was the Attica Prison Riot in New York. In summer 1971, frustrated incarcerated men held 39 guards and employees hostage for 4 days. On September 13, 1971, prison officials organized a raid on the group, which resulted in the death of 10 hostages and 29 incarcerated persons due to a hail of bullets. In January 2000, the state of New York settled with approximately 500 formerly and currently incarcerated men for an amount of $8 million (divided unevenly, based on their damages) (History.com, 2018).

There was also sentencing legislation in the late 20th century that had a disproportionate effect on racial minorities (as seen in Chapters 1 and 4). The Anti-Drug Abuse Acts of 1986 and 1988 were two pieces of federal legislation that created harsher punishments for drug offenders during the infamous time period known as the **War on Drugs** (discussed in Chapter 4). One of the contributions of these Acts was the establishment of the **100-to-1 ratio**, a sentencing policy that mandated the same minimum sentence for drug offenders possessing 1 gram of crack cocaine as that mandated for an offender possessing 100 grams of powder cocaine (as discussed in Chapter 1). The 100-to-1 rule had a disproportionate effect on racial minorities, especially young Black men, compared to White offenders, creating huge racial disparities in the numbers of offenders sent to prison for long sentences (American Civil Liberties Union [ACLU], 2007).

The ACLU filed a brief noting that while judges should consult the federal sentencing guidelines, the law requires sentences to be imposed that are "sufficient, but not greater than necessary" so that there is a fair sentencing scheme (ACLU, 2007). In *United States v. Booker* (2005), the Supreme Court confirmed that the federal sentencing guidelines are not mandatory but advisory. Furthermore, *Rita v. United States* (2007) instructed all sentencing courts to consider whether the federal sentencing guidelines "reflected an unsound judgment."

The push to change the unfair application of the 100-to-1 rule continued in 2010 with the passage of the Fair Sentencing Act (FSA) (USSC, 2015). Signed into law by President Barack Obama, the FSA changed the ratio from 100-to-1 to 18-to-1 in the sentencing of offenses related to the possession, manufacture, or distribution of powder cocaine and crack cocaine. A year later, the United States Sentencing Commission retroactively applied the FSA to cases sentenced before 2010, opening up the opportunity for thousands of cases to be reviewed and possibly resentenced (ACLU, 2019). The United States Sentencing Commission (2014) reported that over 7,700 federal incarcerated persons had received sentencing reductions as a result of the retroactive FSA. More recently, in December 2018, former President Donald Trump signed into law the First Step Act, continuing the retroactive application of a reduction in sentences of crack cocaine offenses. Since that time, over 1,000 incarcerated persons have had their crack-related sentences reduced (United States Sentencing Commission, 2019).

Punishment After the Sanction: Felony Disenfranchisement

As described above, there were several legislative and government efforts against racial equality in the corrections system during the 19th and 20th centuries. The practice of **felony disenfranchisement** also became a popular method of restricting the constitutional rights of the formerly incarcerated, specifically targeting newly freed Black Americans. In this practice, termed "civil death" by early English colonists, individuals who committed certain crimes that were "egregious violations of moral code" had their right to vote revoked after release from a penitentiary (Chung, 2018). After the American Revolution, several states began codifying this practice and applying it as a penalty for all felony offenses. By 1869, 29 of the 37 states in the Union had adopted felony disenfranchisement policies barring released offenders from voting. After the passage of the 13th Amendment, Southern states started tailoring these laws so they would be most likely to affect Black men and therefore restrict the entire racial group's voting power. States targeted crimes that were committed more often by Black men, such as burglary, arson, and domestic violence, but not more serious crimes like murder (Chung, 2018; Muhammed, 2011).

During the Civil Rights era, when voter rights expanded, the rate of felony disenfranchisement decreased between 1960 and 1976 (Chung, 2018). However, from 1976 to 2016, the disenfranchisement rate grew dramatically with the mass incarceration era. As of 2016, the overall disenfranchisement rate was noted at 6.1 million offenders, with the majority of this number composed of racial minorities. Fortunately, public opinion has shifted, and almost half the states in the United States have passed new legislation to amend or repeal disenfranchisement laws in order to restore voting rights to released offenders. Close to one million released offenders have regained the right to vote as a result of these legislative changes (Chung, 2018).

CURRENT RACIAL DISPARITIES IN CORRECTIONS

Despite efforts to improve equal treatment of all races in the criminal justice system, there are still lingering effects of the years of biased behaviors in our correctional facilities. Men compose 93% of the incarcerated population in the U.S. corrections system. However, as discussed in Chapter 4, there are large racial disparities in the male population. In 2016, the rate of imprisonment for White men was 400 per 100,000 compared to 2,415 per 100,000 for Black men (Carson, 2018). In other words, Black men were five times as likely to be incarcerated compared to White men. Hispanic/Latino men were imprisoned at a rate of 1,092 men per 100,000. Bonczar (2003) projected that for males born in 2001, Black men had a 32% chance and Hispanic/Latino men had a 17% chance of incarceration in their lifetime, compared to a 6% chance for White men.

Despite the small percentage of women who are incarcerated compared to men, there are also issues of racial disparity demonstrated via imprisonment rates. In 2016, the rate of imprisonment for White women was 49 per 100,000 compared to 96 per 100,000 for Black women (nearly double). Hispanic/Latina women were imprisoned at a rate of 67 per 100,000 (Carson, 2018). Much like men, Black and Hispanic/Latina women had a higher likelihood of incarceration compared to White women (Bonczar, 2003).

According to Nellis (2016), multiple states have notable racial disparities in their correctional populations. Twelve states, including Georgia, Michigan, and North Carolina, have prison populations in which over half the inmates are Black. At the time of the study, approximately 72% of Maryland's prison population was composed of Black inmates. States such as Massachusetts, New York, and Pennsylvania have high disparity rates for incarcerated Hispanic/Latino individuals compared to incarcerated White individuals.

Racial disparities in our corrections system are particularly an issue for younger people who are incarcerated, as discussed in Chapter 10. Nationally, Black juveniles are five times more likely to be held in juvenile placement, and Latino youth are 65% more likely to be held in placement, compared to White youth (Hockenberry et al., 2016; Sickmund et al., 2017). While overall juvenile placements decreased by 54% between 2001 and 2015 in the United States, White juvenile placements have decreased more quickly than Black juvenile placements. There is also differences that can be seen between the states. For instance, six states report at least 10 times more likelihood of placement for Black youth compared to White youth, including Connecticut, New Jersey, and Wisconsin. However, New Hampshire, Vermont, and West Virginia decreased racial disparity between Black and White juveniles in placement by at least half. In regard to Hispanic/Latino youth, eight states were at least three times as likely to hold a juvenile in placement compared to White youth, including Pennsylvania, South Carolina, and Utah (Hockenberry et al., 2016; Puzzanchera et al., 2016; Sickmund et al., 2017).

As discussed in Chapter 7, prison gang formation in the mid-20th century was based on racial segregation, and this pattern continues today without facility encouragement. This racial divide organizes the promotion of the gang agenda, such as drug sales, prostitution, gambling, and protection of turf. Incarcerated men often join racially segregated gangs for protection against sexual assault and violence, so membership in an Aryan Nation or Latin Kings sect may not occur until incarceration. While *Johnson v. California* (2005) ruled against segregation of inmates based solely on race, gang members tend to group by race during social or recreational hours. Correctional facilities have used multiple methods of attempting to combat gang violence, from separating gang members to housing individual gangs together. Some officers make deals with incarcerated persons, essentially giving gang leaders more control in exchange for better behavior of the members.

Another minority group often managed by our corrections system is immigrants, as discussed in Chapter 4. These individuals are currently housed in federal detention centers operated by Immigration and Customs Enforcement (ICE). Housed under the United States Department of Homeland Security, ICE enforces federal legislation that criminalizes undocumented persons and detains and deports illegal immigrants. Secure Communities, a program used for ICE raids of United States citizens and noncitizens, utilizes local law enforcement agencies and the Federal Bureau of Investigation to apprehend suspects accused of illegal residency. In 2014, President Obama discontinued use of Secure Communities, but it was reinstated by President Trump in 2017 (Krisberg et al., 2018). In the fiscal year 2018, over 158,000 illegal immigrants were arrested by ICE, with 90% of those already possessing criminal convictions. This was an 11% increase from 2017. Over 256,000 individuals were removed from the United States by ICE in 2018, a 9% increase from the previous year. Of those individuals removed, approximately 5,900 were known or suspected gang members.

School-to-Prison Pipeline

Multiple factors have been linked to the great increases in incarcerated populations and overcrowding rates in numerous facilities and the racial disparities they contain. One of these influential factors is a connection between the demographics of incarcerated populations and the elementary and secondary education systems (Fader et al., 2014; Halkovic, 2014; Mallett, 2014). The punishment policies in public schools, especially those located in urban areas, have been correlated with the racial and economic disparities seen in incarcerated populations in multiple studies (Goss, 2015; Halkovic, 2014). In other words, students of color and low-income adolescents receive disproportionate discipline in middle and high school for behavioral offenses and then become adult offenders. Meiners (2011) called this the **school-to-prison pipeline**, describing it as a "complex network of relations that naturalize the movement of youth of color from our schools and communities into permanent detention" (pp. 550). The severe treatment and management of students when they violate school policy can facilitate the transition to incarceration.

As a result of increased physical violence in schools, weapons use, and drugs, schools are changing the ways students are monitored. For instance, schools are more likely to utilize metal detectors, drug detection dogs, and backpack searches, likening the school experience for some to that experienced in detention. In addition, these policies increase the likelihood of suspension or expulsion for offenses that are categorized as "zero tolerance" behaviors, as well as relying on formal law enforcement intervention. However, suspension and expulsion practices can cause a student to feel ostracized and isolated from school and peers, influencing decisions to drop out and to participate in criminal behavior. All of these factors are attributed to the origin of the school-to-prison pipeline (Cregor & Hewitt, 2011; Snapp et al., 2015).

Studies have indicated that stringent punishment policies are used more frequently in urban schools, resulting in disproportionate numbers of students of color and low-income students receiving these penalties (Meiners, 2011; Simmons, 2017). Students who receive these penalties are also linked to incompletion of a high school diploma, unemployment, and incarceration (Meiners, 2011), traits often shared by adult offenders. The connections between these traits and the increased likelihood of going from the classroom to the prison cell demonstrate the need for change.

Recent research has produced several options to diminish the effect of the school-to-prison pipeline. For example, Cregor and Hewitt (2011) and Meiners (2011) suggested the implementation of restorative justice practices in high school as an alternative to harsh disciplinary infractions. As discussed in Chapter 1, restorative justice practices emphasize the use of mediation and communication to manage conflict and inappropriate behavior, while strengthening the bonds between the offending student, victims, faculty, and staff. Students are able to receive a punishment for their behavior, but one that is reintegrative rather than isolating. For example, a juvenile who spray-paints graffiti on a school could receive community service for the offense, issue an apology to the school, and be accepted back into the community without further shaming or punishment. Studies have shown that school districts who utilize these practices have decreased student suspensions (Cregor & Hewitt, 2011). Another suggestion to combat the school-to-prison pipeline is the use of education in correctional facilities. Offenders who participate in and complete correctional education programs are less likely to recidivate and return to prison (Barringer-Brown, 2015; Larson, 2015; Meiners, 2011; Scott, 2016).

CONCLUSION

The United States has a long history of racial discrimination, including institutionalized actions that have affected our criminal justice system. Silton (2002) argued that the Fourteenth Amendment was "lifeless" in combating racial disparities resulting from the crack cocaine versus powder cocaine distinction. Further, Silton asserted that the amendment does not allow racially motivated evidence to be suppressed. The passage of Title VI of the Civil Rights Act of 1964 prohibited discrimination on the grounds of race via federal programming, and this legislation appeared to have more impact compared to the Fourteenth Amendment (Silton, 2002). However, Title VI only allows claims to be filed against entities, not individuals.

While this nation has a long history of racial discrimination, that is not to say the future is as bleak. Our criminal justice system, and the corrections system specifically, is diligently working to delete institutionalized racism. The key is to provide education and programming for staff, administration, and inmates; not surprisingly, financial resources are necessary in order for this effort to be successful. As we continue to work toward equality, we will continue to improve our system as a whole.

DISCUSSION QUESTIONS

1. Of the government-supported policies discussed in this chapter, which one do you believe most increased racial disparities in corrections and why?
2. In what other ways do we see offenders being disenfranchised after release from incarceration? Do you see these as constitutional violations?
3. What are some proactive measures the corrections system can now take to combat the years of institutionalized racism?

APPLICATION EXERCISES

Exercise #1: Racial Profiling

The law enforcement practice of racial profiling was introduced in the early 1990s to target young African American men suspected of transporting drugs between states. This practice continued directly after the September 11th terrorist attacks, with the profiling of individuals of Arabic descent at airports and major ports. New York City's "stop and frisk" policy ceased after a decade, as opponents argued it was a violation of constitutional rights and wrongly targeted minority populations. All of these practices have affected correctional disparities. Explain your opinion of these practices and how they have affected the corrections system, also discussing the application of these profiling practices in your geographic area.

Exercise #2: Felony Disenfranchisement

Each state has different policies on felony disenfranchisement. For example, some states deny offenders the right to vote only during incarceration, while others include this restriction after sentence completion. Using internet research, compare your home state and another state of your choice regarding felony disenfranchisement policies. Which state do you believe handles this issue most appropriately? What is your personal opinion on disenfranchisement?

REFERENCES

American Civil Liberties Union. (2007, October 2). *U.S. Supreme Court weighs 100-to-1 disparity in crack/powder cocaine sentencing.* https://www.aclu.org/press-releases/us-supreme-court-weighs-100-1-disparity-crackpowder-cocaine-sentencing

American Civil Liberties Union. (2019). *Fair Sentencing Act.* https://www.aclu.org/issues/criminal-law-reform/drug-law-reform/fair-sentencing-act

Avery, B. & Lu, H. (2019). *Ban the box: U.S. cities, counties, and states adopt fair hiring policies.* National Employment Law Project. https://www.nelp.org/publication/ban-the-box-fair-chance-hiring-state-and-local-guide/

Barringer-Brown, C. (2015). Teaching college courses in selected correctional facilities in the Commonwealth of Virginia. *Journal of Education & Social Policy, 2*(2), 47–52.

Bonczar, T. (2003). *Prevalence of imprisonment in the U.S. Population, 1974–2007* (NCJ 197976). U.S. Department of Justice, Office of Justice Programs, Bureau of Justice Statistics. https://www.bjs.gov/content/pub/pdf/piusp01.pdf

Bushway, S., & Piehl, A. (2007). The inextricable link between age and criminal history in sentencing. *Crime & Delinquency, 53*(1), 156–183.

Carson, E. (2018). *Prisoners in 2016* (NCJ 251149). U.S. Department of Justice, Office of Justice Programs, Bureau of Justice Statistics. https://www.bjs.gov/content/pub/pdf/p16.pdf

Chase, R. (2015). We are not slaves: Rethinking the rise of carceral states through the lens of the prisoners' rights movement. *Journal of American History, 102*(1), 73–86.

Chung, J. (2018). *Felony disenfranchisement: A primer.* The Sentencing Project. https://www.sentencingproject.org/publications/felony-disenfranchisement-a-primer/

Cregor, M. & Hewitt, D. (2011). Dismantling the school-to-prison pipeline: A survey from the field. *Poverty & Race, 20*(1), 5–7.

Delaney, R., Subramanian, R., Shames, A., & Turner, N. (2019). *American history, race, and prison.* Vera Institute of Justice. https://www.vera.org/reimagining-prison-web-report/american-history-race-and-prison

Fader, J. J., Lockwood, B., Schall, V., & Stokes, B. (2014). A promising approach to narrowing the school-to-prison pipeline: The WISE arrest diversion program. *Youth Violence and Juvenile Justice, 13*(2), 123–142.

Fields, C. (2005). Hawes-Cooper Act 1929. In M. Bosworth (Ed.), *Encyclopedia of prisons and correctional facilities.* Sage Publishers.

Goluboff, R. (2001). The Thirteenth Amendment and the lost origins of civil rights. *Duke Law Journal, 50*(6), 1609–1685.

Goss, A. (2015). Toward a village consciousness: Organizing in the African American cultural tradition. *Journal of Black Studies, 46*(8), 797–816.

Halkovic, A. (2014). Defining possible: Re-visioning the prison-to-college pipeline. *Equity & Excellence in Education, 47*(4), 494–512.

History.com. (2018). *Riot at Attica Prison.* https://www.history.com/this-day-in-history/riot-at-attica-prison

Hockenberry, S., Wachter, A., & Sladky, A. (2016, September). *Juvenile residential facility census, 2014: Selected findings* (NCJ 250123). U.S. Department of Justice, Office of Justice

Programs, Office of Juvenile Justice and Delinquency Prevention. https://www.ojjdp.gov/pubs/250123.pdf

Johnson v. California, 543 US 499 (2005)

Krisberg, B., Marchionna, S., & Hartney, C. (2018). *American corrections: Concepts and controversies* (2nd ed.). Sage Publishing.

Larson, D. (2015). Localizing prison higher education. *New Directions for Community Colleges, 2015*(170), 9–17.

Mallet, C. (2014). The "learning disabilities to juvenile detention" pipeline: A case study. *Children & Schools, 36*(3), 147–154.

Mancini, M. (1978). Race, economics, and the abandonment of convict leasing. *Journal of Negro History, 63*(4), 339–352.

Meiners, E. (2011). Ending the school-to-prison pipeline/building abolition futures. *Urban Review, 43*(4), 547–565.

Muhammed, K. (2011). Where did all the white criminals go? Reconfiguring race and crime on the road to mass incarceration. *Souls, 13*(1), 72–90.

National Archives. (2016). *Records from the Law Enforcement Assistance Administration.* https://www.archives.gov/research/guide-fed-records/groups/423.html

Nellis, A. (2016). *The color of justice: Racial and ethnic disparity in state prisons.* The Sentencing Project. https://www.sentencingproject.org/publications/color-of-justice-racial-and-ethnic-disparity-in-state-prisons/

Pisciotta, A. (1983). Scientific reform: The new penology at Elmira. *Crime & Delinquency, 29*(4), 619–630.

Puzzanchera, C., Sladky, A., & Kang, W. (2016). *Easy access to juvenile populations: 1990–2015.* http://www.ojjdp.gov/ojstatbb/ezapop

Rita v. United States, 551 U.S. 338 (2007)

Scott, K. (2016). Corrections and education: The relationship between education and recidivism. *Journal of Intercultural Disciplines, 15,* 147–169.

Sickmund, M., Sladky, T., Kang, W., & Puzzanchera, C. (2017). *Easy access to the census of juveniles in residential placement.* http://www.ojjdp.gov/ojstatbb/ezacjrp/

Silton, D. J. (2002). U.S. prisons and racial profiling: A covertly racist nation rides a vicious cycle. *Law & Inequality: A Journal of Theory and Practice, 20*(1), 53–90.

Simmons, L. (2017). *The prison school: Educational inequality and school discipline in the age of mass incarceration.* University of California Press.

Snapp, D., Hoenig, J., Fields, A., & Russell, S. (2015). Messy, butch, and queer: LGBTQ youth and the school-to-prison pipeline. *Journal of Adolescent Research, 30*(1), 57–82.

United States Sentencing Commission. (2014, December). *U.S. Sentencing Commission final crack retroactivity report.* https://www.ussc.gov/research/congressional-reports/2015-report-congress-impact-fair-sentencing-act-2010

United States Sentencing Commission. (2015). *Impact of the Fair Sentencing Act 2010.* https://www. ussc.gov/sites/default/files/pdf/research-and-publications/retroactivity-analyses/fair-sentenc- ing-act/Final_USSC_Crack_Retro_Data_Report_FSA.pdf

United States Sentencing Commission. (2019, June). *U.S. Sentencing Commission First Step Act of 2018 resentencing provisions retroactivity data report.* https://www.ussc.gov/sites/default/files/ pdf/research-and-publications/retroactivity-analyses/first-step-act/201900607-First-Step-Act- Retro.pdf

United States v. Booker, 543 U.S. 220 (2005)

CHAPTER 13

Wrongful Conviction

CHAPTER OBJECTIVES

After reading this chapter, you should be able to:

- Identify and discuss the factors associated with wrongful conviction.
- Recognize the social and political pressure that contributed to wrongful conviction.
- Discuss necessary changes to legislation, court processes, and investigative practices that are needed to prevent wrongful conviction.

KEY WORDS

Wrongful conviction
Exoneration
Capital case
National Registry on Exonerations
Innocence Project
Forensic science
      CSI effect
      Criminalist
Eyewitness identification
System variables
Estimator variables

Show-ups
Live lineups
Photo arrays
Single-blind administration
Double-blind administration
False confession
      Central Park Five
      Miranda v. Arizona (1966)
Official misconduct
      Exculpatory evidence
      Prosecutorial misconduct
      Immunity

Inadequate defense

    Indigent defense

    Strickland v. Washington (1984)

    Conviction integrity units

Informants

    Jailhouse informants

CASE STUDY: ROSA JIMENEZ

Rosa Jimenez immigrated to the United States in 1999 at the age of 17. In 2003, she was charged with the murder of a 21-month-old infant whom she had been babysitting. By 2005, she was convicted and sentenced to 99 years in prison. After six short years, Rosa Jimenez went from being a new and expectant mother to her 1-year-old daughter and soon-to-be baby boy, to a convicted murderer who would likely never get to raise either of those children. Ms. Jimenez's case was, from the beginning, both unique and highly troubling.

The young boy Ms. Jimenez was convicted of murdering had swallowed a "wad of paper towels the size of an egg." For the four medical professionals testifying against her, it was unfathomable that the child could have choked by accident. This was the only evidence logged against Ms. Jimenez. The trial included no presentation of evidence related to motive or any other sort of abuse against the child. Rosa Jimenez would languish in prison for an additional 14 years, even developing a severe kidney disease, before a United States District Court overturned her conviction. In October of 2019, the court overturned Ms. Jimenez's conviction based on new and recanted testimony by medical experts which debunked the theory that the child's death could not have been an accident.

Ms. Jimenez spent an additional year in prison after this decision, but was finally released on January 27, 2021. On the day of her release, she was immediately detained by U.S. Immigration and Customs Enforcement (ICE) officers due to her status as an illegal immigrant at the time of her arrest in 2005. ICE, however, would reverse their decision to deport her that very same day, eventually releasing her into the custody of her attorneys and her children, with whom she had not had physical contact since she was imprisoned.

Questions for Discussion

1. How do you think the intersectional issues of race, gender, and immigration status impact a person's likelihood of wrongful conviction?
2. How should we hold expert witnesses accountable when their testimony is falsified or based on invalid research?

INTRODUCTION

The criminal justice system is often discussed as being one large body, but this view fails to recognize that justice often comes from numerous individual, but interconnected, systems. As important as the processes themselves are the individual actors within the system who must carry out justice accurately and without bias. When mistakes are made in the criminal justice system, or when individual actors like police officers, criminalists, judges, prosecutors, and witnesses knowingly commit acts of misconduct, innocent people can be found guilty of crimes they did not commit, landing them in prison for often extremely long sentences. **Wrongful conviction** is the conviction of an individual for a crime they did not commit.

Each year there are numerous cases of exoneration throughout the country. **Exoneration** occurs when a person has their conviction overturned and they are cleared of wrongdoing. The **National Registry of Exonerations** (2019) keeps a running total of the number of exonerations that have occurred in the United States since 1989. As of December 2019, 2,529 exonerations have been recorded over the course of the last 4 decades. This number includes 151 exonerations in 2018 alone. One of the concerning facts about these numbers is that many of the exonerated individuals had either served their complete sentences of incarceration or were serving their sentences at the time of their exoneration. The total number of years spent incarcerated by individuals who have been exonerated has recently exceeded 20,000 (National Registry of Exonerations, 2019). With an average life expectancy in the United States of 78.5 years, over 250 lifetimes have been served by just those individuals who have been identified as wrongfully convicted (World Bank, 2019).

Wrongful convictions can happen in relation to any crime. However, because the burden of proof that must be met to overturn a criminal conviction is so high, the cases that typically have the most resources devoted toward them are serious criminal cases carrying longer prison sentences, such as murder and rape (Loeffler et al., 2019). This means that numerous other wrongful convictions, for minor crimes like drug possession or theft, could be going unnoticed by the system every year and adding to the years of unjust imprisonment. This also makes determining the total number of wrongful convictions each year extremely difficult. Best estimates for wrongful convictions in **capital cases**, or cases that carry the possibility of a death sentence, range from 1%–6%. While very little research has been done on wrongful convictions in non-capital cases, current estimates range from 2%–40%, depending on the type of crime committed (Loeffler et al., 2019).

Wrongful conviction is a complex problem; even the seemingly simple and routine tasks that occur, from investigation all the way through a criminal trial, can be cause for errors in the finding of guilt. There is considerable debate over what causes, and what is simply correlated with, wrongful conviction (LaPorte, 2017). The intricacies and interconnectedness of the system prevent criminologists from determining causality in cases of wrongful conviction. It is clear, however, that a number of factors are correlated with the conviction of innocent persons. The National Registry of Exonerations and the **Innocence Project**, an organization aimed at reducing the number of wrongfully convicted individuals through DNA testing and criminal justice reform, have studied the cases and "causes" of wrongful conviction extensively. While the National Registry of Exonerations focuses on exonerations in any case, and the Innocence Project focuses on convictions overturned through the use of DNA evidence, both organizations agree that the following factors contribute to wrongful convictions:

- Faulty forensic science;
- Eyewitness misidentification;
- False confession;
- Official misconduct; and
- Informants.

Additional factors that have been identified by at least one of these organizations include:

- Race;
- Inadequate defense;
- Mistaken identification; and
- Perjury/false accusation.

With the presence of any one of the above factors in a criminal case, the potential for a wrongful conviction increases. It is common to see not just one but several of these factors playing a role in cases that are eventually overturned. What is evident from this list is that not all wrongful convictions are made in error. Sometimes, an actor within the criminal justice system knowingly violates their duty by committing acts of misconduct, resulting in the conviction of an innocent person.

Wrongful conviction is arguably one of the most serious mistakes that can be made in the search for justice. The lives of innocent people are turned upside down. If a wrongfully convicted person is lucky enough to have their criminal conviction overturned, the damage done to them by a trial and incarceration—socially, mentally, and even physically—can be irreparable. A wrongful conviction also means that the person who is legally responsible for committing the crime is likely still roaming free and may feel empowered to continue victimizing others. In addition to the harm caused to the wrongfully convicted, and to the potential victims of the person who should have been convicted, the credibility of the criminal justice system is diminished by each case of exoneration. This chapter explores the reality of wrongful convictions, including the associated factors, the impact to individuals and to society, and the ways in which the criminal justice system is trying to combat this problem.

THE FACTORS

Forensic Science

Forensic science, or the use of scientific methods to study the evidence of a crime, has become the gold standard in both the real world of criminal justice and the fictional world of criminal justice entertainment. There are numerous techniques employed by professionals that fall under the heading of forensic science, including but not limited to: DNA, hair, and blood splatter analysis; ballistics testing; and bite mark identification (lesser known). Some of these undoubtedly represent the most sophisticated existing methods of fighting crime. Methods like DNA analysis have been used to solve decades-old cold cases, and to exonerate hundreds of wrongfully convicted persons, some of whom were on death row at the time their conviction was overturned. Ironically, the concerns over forensic science come more from its "successes" than from its failures.

The criminal justice system sees DNA analysis as the poster child for advancements in forensic science. This is primarily because of the decades of scientific testing that have gone into producing the levels of sophisticated analysis that we see today. While we know that DNA analysis is imperfect, the popular belief is that it is an infallible science. Throughout popular entertainment media, DNA analysis has become synonymous with forensic science as a whole. When DNA analysis was appropriated by entertainment media to fit the narrative of criminal identification, it created a misconception that all the other forms of forensic science presented across those same shows are as valid and reliable as DNA analysis.

Methods of forensic science have since become the centerpieces of crime scene investigation shows. The techniques themselves, and the reliability of their outcomes, are often molded to fit the narrow storyline demanded by primetime programming. These manipulated perceptions of the abilities of forensic science are then shown to viewers on a nightly basis. Specifically, viewers are led to believe that anything the actors do on television is able to be replicated in real-world criminal scenarios. It is those same viewers who could someday find themselves as the arbitrators of guilt or innocence on a criminal trial jury. Thus, television shows and movies that have replicated the popularity of the trendsetting franchise *Crime Scene Investigation* (CSI) may have contributed to what has been coined the CSI effect (Cole & Dioso-Villa, 2009).

The **CSI effect** is the perceived cause-and-effect relationship between the viewing habits of the general public and their understanding and expectations of evidence in criminal trials. The belief is that the popularity of the television show CSI, as well as its spinoff programs and the other shows that have duplicated its heavy reliance on forensic science as the key to criminal investigation, are influencing the way jurors view evidence during a trial (Cole & Dioso-Villa, 2009; Cole, 2015). While the CSI effect has become a popular term, the research concerning its actual impact on jurors in the courtroom is far from conclusive (Cole, 2015). Furthermore, the focus on the CSI effect by the media, and subsequently by criminologists, may have masked the crisis of validity that is being uncovered with regard to multiple forensic science techniques (Bell et al., 2018).

The lack of scientific validity in forensic science, particularly in its application to criminal investigations, has been discussed regularly since the Committee on Identifying the Needs of the Forensic Sciences Community of the National Research Council (2009) issued its report entitled *Strengthening Forensic Science in the United States: A Path Forward.* The report details the issues inherent in nearly every method of forensic science outside of DNA analysis (although it is also discussed as problematic). Specifically, the committee questioned the *science* behind methods of forensic science and argued that the broad application of forensics to criminal investigations has occurred without the proper research to support its validity. The committee stated that:

> A body of research is required to establish the limits and measures of performance and to address the impact sources of variability and potential bias. Such research is sorely needed, but it seems to be lacking matching characteristics. These disciplines need to develop rigorous protocols to guide these subjective interpretations and pursue equally rigorous research and evaluation programs. (p. 8)

A decade later, there have been advancements, but many of these same issues still plague the field. As Bell et al. (2018) discuss, the termination of the National Commission for Forensic Science in 2017 is a sign that the federal government is no longer willing to address the concerns of the scientific community. They also note that when science has to live up to an already-established reputation, which is the case for most methods of forensic investigation built on "historical precedent ... [and not] meaningful empirical validation," the consequences can be disastrous (p. 4541).

An example of relying on precedent over empirical validation comes from bite mark comparison. Bite mark comparison is part of the field of forensic odontology and has been used in the identification of criminal suspects. However, as Souviron and Haller (2017) point out, the use of bite mark comparison, where suspects are matched to the marks left on victims, has been coopted by dentists who lack the requisite training and skill necessary to effectively present the accuracy of the comparison to a jury. While bite mark analysis can be beneficial to the justice process, the courts, rather than the scientific community, have determined the validity and reliability of bite mark comparison (Souviron, & Haller, 2017). Similar questions have been raised about techniques such as hair comparison, arson analysis, and certain forms of ballistics analysis, among others (Innocence Project, 2019).

Another important issue, which will be examined in more detail below, is official misconduct committed by criminal justice professionals. **Criminalists** are the professionals who utilize scientific techniques of criminal investigation and testify in court regarding their findings. There have been cases where criminalists have lied on the stand, contaminated evidence, and/or overstated the validity of their scientific analysis. This contributes to the belief that the applicability of forensic science to criminal investigations, and the validity of forensic science techniques in general, have been exaggerated and are in dire need of reexamination.

Eyewitness Identification

On September 21, 2011, Troy Davis was put to death by lethal injection by the state of Georgia. Davis's case hinged on the testimony of multiple eyewitnesses who claimed they had seen Davis shoot and kill an off-duty police officer. For many people, this case is the perfect example of the problems inherent in eyewitness identification, as seven of the nine eyewitnesses eventually recanted their testimony (Sturgis, 2011). **Eyewitness identification** is the identification of a suspect by a person who witnessed an event or crime. This includes witnesses who may have, for example, seen someone enter a home or a place of business. The eyewitness may have not seen the crime in question take place, but their testimony can help place a suspect at the scene of a crime.

The importance of appropriate identification of a perpetrator by eyewitnesses in influencing an eventual verdict should not be understated. Like forensic evidence, the presentation of eyewitness testimony is often regarded as highly trustworthy by jurors. Thus, a similar misunderstanding exists, as jurors are not well educated on the flaws that are persistent in testimony obtained from eyewitnesses. Eyewitness *misidentification* has been determined to be one of the leading factors in cases of wrongful conviction. Inaccurate eyewitness accounts have been present in over 70% of the cases overturned by DNA evidence (Innocence Project, 2019).

The National Research Council (2014) produced one of the most extensive examinations into eyewitness identification to date. They identify research on two types of variables that impact eyewitness identification: system variables and estimator variables. **System variables** include procedural issues with the way law enforcement officers obtain an identification from an eyewitness. This can occur at the scene of the crime or at later points during the investigation. System variables are seen as controllable by law enforcement. **Estimator variables** are the contextual factors related to the witnessing of an event and can include everything from the physical proximity of the witness to the event, to the level of stress experienced by the eyewitness. Estimator variables are variables that are outside the control of law enforcement (National Research Council, 2014).

The inaccuracy of a person's ability to perceive what they see, and of the retrieval of memories both immediately and over time, have been extensively examined (Wixted et al., 2018). The high-stress nature of a criminal event, the anxiety of loss, the lag time between the criminal event and questioning, and dozens, if not hundreds, of other variables impact the way a person experiences, and ultimately remembers, the event. Traditionally, the conditions that affect one's memory have been seen as unchangeable. Most of the research has instead focused on the procedural issues that officers can change, and there is current research suggesting that officers can increase the reliability of a witness's memory through the development of better methods of interviewing (Wixted et al., 2018).

The Police Executive Research Forum (2013) identified five primary police procedures related to the identification of criminal perpetrators. In a national survey of law enforcement agencies, the most common identification procedures included photo lineups (94.1%), show-ups (61.8%), composites (sketches, etc.) (35.5%), mugshot searches (28.8%), and live lineups (21.4%). The three primary areas believed to cause the most inaccuracies are show-ups and two forms of lineups: live lineups and photo arrays. The term **show-ups** refers to the questioning of eyewitnesses at or near the scene of a crime, and could go as far as having an eyewitness point out the suspect who is being detained at the scene. **Live lineups** use actual suspects and stand-ins or "non-suspect fillers" to present to eyewitnesses. **Photo arrays** are collections of photos that witnesses can examine to identify a perpetrator. Photo arrays and live lineups often occur at the police station at a later date (National Research Council, 2014; Police Executive Research Forum, 2013).

The common belief regarding police procedures is that they are always backed by a well-articulated set of guidelines that leave little room for error. Unfortunately, exhaustive policies regarding what the police can and cannot do, or rather what is legal or illegal when questioning witnesses, do not exist in many police departments (Police Executive Research Forum, 2013). Therefore, all of these procedural methods have the potential to be misused by police officers, either deliberately or unknowingly. One of the greatest concerns, from a wrongful conviction standpoint, is that of police officers coercing or pressuring eyewitnesses into identifying a person whom they have already deemed a suspect.

During a show-up, police officers present a photo of a suspect in custody, or, if the suspect is caught near the crime, officers can present the detained suspect to the witness for identification. This puts a great deal of pressure on the eyewitness to corroborate the beliefs of the police on the spot. The same holds true in photo arrays and live lineups. During photo arrays, officers present the eyewitness with a number of hand-selected pictures which often include the suspect that the police have been investigating. Live lineups occur the same way, except that in live lineups, non-suspect "fillers" are used alongside actual suspects. Most of the concern about the reliability of photo arrays and live lineups has to do with the use of single-blind administration.

Single-blind administration means that the officer who is presenting the array or lineup to the eyewitness is aware of who the suspect is in the case (Kovera & Evelo, 2017). The officer can knowingly or unknowingly provide confidence cues to the eyewitness through their verbal agreement and/or their nonverbal movements. Some departments have begun to develop the needed policy changes in the administration of arrays and lineups by moving to a model of double-blind administration. **Double-blind administration** occurs when neither the eyewitness nor the officer administering the photo array or live lineup knows who the suspect is. This small procedural change can help negate the cues of confidence that officers relay to witnesses.

The implementation of double-blind administration is one of the primary procedural changes that has been agreed upon as necessary for the protection of a suspect's due process rights. Innocence Project and the National Resource Council both outline a number of other changes that can be made to increase the reliability of eyewitness identification, including better instructions to witnesses, better lineup composition, and documentation of all array and lineup procedures, among others. Only 24 states have adopted the necessary procedural changes identified by Innocence Project (Innocence Project, 2019). As these procedures are some of the most widely used by police officers, the need for oversight has become more apparent.

False Confessions

One of the hardest things for people outside the field of criminal justice to comprehend is how any person could confess to a crime they did not commit. Intuition and conviction would have us believe that there are no circumstances under which we would admit to doing something we did not do. Make that crime a rape or murder, and in many people's minds, the likelihood of confessing to that crime changes from an improbability to an impossibility. **False confession** occurs when a suspect wrongfully, and illegally, admits to a crime they did not commit. The importance of a confession to a criminal conviction cannot be understated. The common belief in the impossibility of a wrongful confession adds to the likelihood that it will be accepted as the truth by law enforcement, and eventually by a jury. Even when a person recants their confession, and even where there is overwhelming evidence suggesting it was fabricated, many people will still believe in its truthfulness (Kassin, 2017).

Despite persistent skepticism, the fact that false confessions are a significant factor in wrongful convictions is supported by the number of people who confessed to their crimes but were later exonerated through DNA evidence. Innocence Project (2019) reports that 25% of exonerations through DNA evidence included a false confession. Finding an exact rate of false confessions would be nearly impossible, due to the number of cases nationwide each year and the time it would take to analyze each one. However, it is likely that the percentage cited above (25%) only represents a small portion of the total number of false confessions that exist, as guilty pleas, minor crimes, and crimes committed by juveniles, among others, are not included in that number (Kassin et al., 2010).

There is a long and storied history of high-profile cases being used to sensationalize false confessions. One of the most widely publicized cases was that of the Central Park Five in 1989. The **Central Park Five** case, also known as the Central Park Jogger case, hinged on the separate confessions of five young African American boys, ages 14–16. Each child admitted to playing a role in the rape of a 28-year-old White woman who had been exercising in the park (Stratton, 2015; Kassin, 2017). From the beginning, questions of racial bias, police misconduct, and moral panic prompted advocates to question the legality of the young boys' confessions. The belief in the infallibility of videotaped admissions of guilt was too much for the juries to overlook, and the boys were all convicted. Their confessions, trials, and eventual imprisonment were broadcast around the world. The youth served between 5 and 12 years of incarceration in juvenile and adult facilities and were all released *prior to* their eventual exoneration in 2002 (Stratton, 2015). In 2002, Matias Reyes was linked to the crime through DNA evidence and his own confession (Stratton, 2015). The case, and the exoneration of all five men, has since been popularized in documentaries and Hollywood movies and can be considered one of the most serious acts of wrongdoing in the modern history of the criminal justice system.

As with eyewitness identification, much of the research on false confessions comes from the field of psychology. Accordingly, variables internal to the suspect, as well as system and procedural variables relevant to the investigation and interrogation of suspects, are examined for their contributions to false confessions. **Interrogation** refers to the law enforcement practice of questioning suspects. This can include everything from the questions asked of suspects by arresting officers at the scene of a crime to the hours-long questioning that is conducted by trained interrogators at police stations.

False confessions seem relatively simplistic in how they occur: A person simply admits to something they did not do. That admission of guilt tends to conceal the complex processes of human psychology, and the impact of interrogation on those processes, which both force that admission. Furthermore, "the practices of interrogation and the elicitation of confessions are subject to historical, cultural, political, legal, and other contextual influences" (Kassin et al., 2010, p. 5). Much of the blame has been placed squarely on law enforcement, as they are truly the gatekeepers of confessions. They are typically the first to elicit a confession, and the first to determine its credibility. They also prepare that confession to withstand legal scrutiny in the courts. Law enforcement officers ensure the legality of a confession by having the suspect sign a written statement, or by videotaping their admission to the crime. Because the only product of a confession is often that written or videotaped statement, the methods of interrogation that led to that confession continually occur without scrutiny.

The goal of an interrogation, in the most basic sense, is to obtain information about the suspect's whereabouts at the time of a crime, their knowledge and relationship to the victim, and any potential motive they may have had. More precisely, interrogation is about obtaining a confession. The pressure to obtain a confession from their superiors, the public, and victims can lead officers to use tactics of physical and psychological coercion on suspects (Chapman, 2013). In the past, the methods used in acquiring that information amounted to physical and psychological torture. Methods commonly known as the "third degree" included:

> … physical violence (e.g., beating, kicking, or mauling suspects); torture (e.g., simulating suffocation by holding a suspect's head in water, putting lighted cigars or pokers against a suspect's body); hitting suspects with a rubber hose (which seldom left marks); prolonged incommunicado confinement; deprivations of sleep, food, and other needs; extreme sensory discomfort (e.g., forcing a suspect to stand for hours on end, shining a bright, blinding light on the suspect); and explicit threats of physical harm. (Kassin et al., p. 6)

Some suggest that methods like these are virtually non-existent in practice today, but the research suggests otherwise. Bang et al. (2018) point out that police officers in the United States are legally permitted to lie to suspects in order to get them to confess, a practice that has been banned in other countries. This means police officers can present multiple forms of fabricated evidence to the suspect, and can even use victim-blaming tactics in their interrogations (Bang et al., 2018). Every exoneration brings increased concern over the frequency of physically and mentally coercive interrogations.

As with all of the contributing factors to wrongful convictions, the courts and lawmakers have narrowed the scope of acceptable police behavior during the questioning of suspects. The landmark case of **Miranda v. Arizona (1966)** gave individuals being questioned by the police the right to be notified of specific due process safeguards such as the right against self-incrimination and the right to the presence of an attorney. This was seen as a necessary first step in reining in coercive interrogative practices, but it failed to address the more formal practices of interrogation that take place at police stations, behind closed doors.

Law enforcement agencies across all jurisdictions are also looking toward technology to better control officer behavior, and to add reliability to their procedures, but the change has been slow. One of the primary methods of controlling what happens during an interrogation is through audio and visual recording. Recording an interrogation allows for a more transparent process that can better withstand legal challenges (Bang et al., 2018).

Recordings also provide for a more thorough review of both police officer behavior and the mental stability of suspects during the time of their confession. Unfortunately, very few states have made the recording of all interrogations mandatory, and those states that do have defined recording procedures often only list them as recommended rather than required (Norris et al., 2019).

False confessions are particularly problematic because they are an admission of guilt by someone who is accused of a crime. Prosecutors using these confessions in the courtroom are far removed from the tactics employed in an interrogation and must simply show that a defendant made the admission of guilt voluntarily and of sound mind. What constitutes a voluntary confession is increasingly fluid, and this has become a point of contention in the U.S. justice system. There is even increasing evidence to suggest that those with a mental handicap, and juveniles whose mental capacity is not fully developed, are particularly susceptible to coercion during interrogation (Kassin, 2017). At any rate, the system of interrogation, and the legal processes needed to safeguard against false confessions, are failing suspects and defendants, compromising justice for victims, and causing innocent people to, in some cases, believe in their own false guilt (Chapman, 2013).

Official Misconduct

The factors discussed so far—forensic science, eyewitness identification, and false confessions—have included mentions of official misconduct, but are largely driven by criminal justice system actors carrying out their duties without malicious intention. This means that the criminalists, eyewitnesses, law enforcement officers, and prosecutors who play a role in those cases are not deliberately avoiding their ethical responsibilities in the search for justice. **Official misconduct**, on the other hand, refers to the intentional actions of criminal justice officials that circumvent their professional and ethical responsibilities.

The officials who gain the most attention for their inappropriate actions, or in some cases their inaction, are police officers and prosecutors. In 2018, the National Registry of Exonerations reported their highest numbers ever for exonerations that included police and prosecutorial misconduct. Out of 151 exonerations in 2018, 107 included misconduct by police officers or prosecutors. The misconduct most often included the withholding of exculpatory evidence. **Exculpatory evidence** is evidence that helps to prove the innocence of the accused person. Police officers and prosecutors are bound by their ethical duties to either report that evidence or present it to the court and the defense team.

Police officers must continuously make the decision to either adhere to their sworn duties or take justice into their own hands. There are a wide range of behaviors that could be labeled as police misconduct, and all of them can play a part in the wrongful conviction of an innocent person. Dozens, if not hundreds, of opportunities for police officers to commit misconduct present themselves every day. Potential misconduct by officers can range from racially profiling a citizen during a traffic stop, to planting evidence on suspects, to perjuring themselves on the stand. What is certain is that the vast majority of police officers carry out their duties for their entire careers without issue. In instances where this is not the case, the consequences to the criminal justice system, and to those who are wrongfully convicted, can be devastating.

One of the most infamous cases of police misconduct leading to wrongful conviction involved the Los Angeles Police Department (LAPD) and is known as the Rampart Scandal. The Rampart Community Resources Against Street Hoodlums (CRASH) unit of the LAPD was an anti-gang unit that became notorious for their egregious acts of misconduct. Their misconduct ranged from planting drugs on suspects to bank robbery and attempted murder. Once the breadth of their misconduct was uncovered, and following the arrest of several officers, over 150 convicted persons were exonerated. While some of these individuals may have been convicted of crimes they legitimately committed, many were not, and the credibility of any arrest made by Rampart officers was brought into question (Covey, 2013).

When police officers commit acts of misconduct, one of the few groups of people who can recognize it and help to hold them accountable are prosecutors. This assumes that prosecutors themselves are cognizant enough to recognize police misconduct and brave enough to confront police officers in their jurisdiction. Many prosecutors are in a unique position that requires them to balance the will of the constituents who elected them with the due-process protections of criminal defendants. Even when the public thinks someone is guilty, an ethical prosecutor would drop the charges against a defendant before compromising their integrity and putting an innocent person on trial. However, the pressure of being judged on verdicts of guilt is too much to overcome for some, and prosecutors step over the line of what is legally acceptable behavior.

Prosecutors are some of the most powerful, if not the most powerful, actors in the criminal justice system. They determine what charges will be brought against a person, and they are ultimately responsible for making sure that those charges are turned into convictions. They also have a great deal of trust placed in them, both by the public, who trust that prosecutors will help keep them safe, and by juries, who believe prosecutors to be ethical actors who would only present a legitimate case. **Prosecutorial misconduct** refers to behaviors by prosecutors that include direct and negligent violations of the law, abuses of discretion, and breaches of public trust (Green & Yaroshefsky, 2016). Withholding exculpatory evidence, fabricating charges and evidence, and targeting suspects because of race or ethnicity are just some examples of acts considered to be prosecutorial misconduct.

Historically, misconduct by prosecutors was seen as happening only on rare occasions (Green & Yaroshefsky, 2016). Recently, calls for reform have grown more abundant, as defendants, judges, and even prosecutors themselves have joined in the fight to address what some believe has now become a systemic problem (Block, 2018; Green & Yaroshefsky, 2016). One of the primary concerns is that the only accountability for prosecutors comes in the form of professional reprimands, which rarely (if ever) result in their removal from office. Prosecutorial misconduct also does not warrant criminal charges, and if defendants would like to bring a civil case against a prosecutor, they are protected by immunity. **Immunity** refers to the fact that prosecutors cannot be held civilly liable for their actions in a criminal case. The lack of mechanisms for prosecutorial accountability creates another set of actors in the system (in addition to police officers) who are only policed by themselves, which is why even judges are calling for an end to immunity (Block, 2016).

Police officers and prosecutors bear the brunt of public scrutiny for their misconduct because of their elevated status and popularity in the community. However, there are numerous other actors who can commit official acts of misconduct that could contribute to a wrongful conviction. Criminalists, judges, correctional officers, probation and parole officers, and defense attorneys must all adhere to the ethical codes that come with their positions. The criminal justice system has a responsibility to vet, hire, train, and hold accountable the officials who take others' lives into their hands on a regular basis.

Inadequate Defense

Inadequate defense arises when defense attorneys do not provide the best legal representation they are capable of giving to their clients. In general, defense attorneys are not typically classified as officials within the criminal justice system, as they may not be employed by a local or state government like police officers and prosecutors are. Inadequate defense is therefore seen as a separate variable contributing to wrongful convictions and is not counted toward official records of misconduct. This is also due to the fact that there may be no malicious intent on the part of the defense attorney to have their client convicted, but their lack of action contributes to the conviction nonetheless. This chapter includes inadequate defense as a form of official misconduct because many states and counties, and the Federal Government, employ attorneys for the purposes of indigent defense.

Indigent defense is the defense of persons who cannot afford a private attorney and has been deemed a constitutional protection under the 6th Amendment. Indigent defense is one of the variables most heavily correlated with inadequate defense, as defendants are left to the mercy of public defenders or court-appointed attorneys who may not have the time, resources, or level of passion necessary to produce an adequate legal defense. According to the Bureau of Justice Statistics (BJS), there are a variety of methods of indigent defense (Strong, 2016). Public defenders who are employed by government entities, as well as assigned and contracted private attorneys, can all represent indigent clients in court. Several issues within the indigent system of defense limit the abilities of attorneys in this area. Baćak et al. (2019) identify five specific issues that contribute to inadequate indigent defense:

- High caseloads;
- Inadequate compensation;
- Lack of resources;
- Perceived legitimacy (internal & public); and
- Risk of secondary trauma.

All of these issues are important in recognizing the challenges defense attorneys face in providing appropriate defense representation, but two in particular stand out in cases of wrongful conviction: high caseloads and a lack of resources.

Public defenders, unlike appointed or contracted counsel, do not have as much, if any, discretion in determining the number of cases they take on each year. In 2013, the range of state caseloads was between 50 and 590 per public defender (Strong, 2016). A caseload of 590 in a single year would leave enough time, assuming 40-hour work weeks, for 3.5 hours to be spent on each case. This is consistent with research by Farole and Langton (2010) that found average caseloads of 370, which equated to 5 to 6 hours being spent on each case. The lack of time spent on cases makes for an easy indicator of the type of representation that is being given to indigent clients. It can be assumed that the amounts of time spent on preparing the case, scrutinizing the legality of arrest, filing motions, and searching for exculpatory evidence are all compromised, at the expense of the accused. Caseload size is also a direct result of the lack of resources available to expand the number of attorneys working in public defense.

For public defenders who are able to manage their caseloads, the lack of resources accessible to them becomes the next hurdle to clear. While an abundance of cases can lead to limited time spent on each, limited resources can halt the processes of public defense all together, leaving suspects who have not been convicted of any crime to languish in jail indefinitely. The city of New Orleans, Louisiana presents the perfect example of what a lack of resources can do to systems of indigent defense. New Orleans has been embroiled in controversy for the last several years, as the city currently faces multiple lawsuits targeting its lack of remedy for indigent defendants (Sledge, 2019). Many of the city's problems stem from a reduction in indigent defense funding. It was reported that, beginning in 2012, the public defender's office budget was reduced exponentially, and by 2016, the budget had fallen by $3.5 million (Hager, 2016). The cuts continued, and the office eventually announced that it would no longer take many new felony cases, as "caseloads [had] become so onerous that the lawyers can only spend seven minutes preparing for each of their cases" (Hager, 2016, para. 2).

Unfortunately, what is happening in New Orleans is not an exception, and we may quickly be approaching a constitutional crisis. Jurisdictions all over the country continue to grapple with issues of resource allocation and their inability to uphold the right to effective counsel for indigent defendants. This will continue to leave jurisdictions vulnerable to lawsuits. Fortunately, as Hager (2016) points out, lawsuits may be the only thing that can save these offices, as the suits bring increased national attention and public scrutiny to issues of indigent defense and force state legislatures to respond.

Indigent defense may represent the largest concern related to inadequate defense, but it is by no means the only concern. Even when public defenders and private attorneys have every available resource and ample time to dedicate toward a case, their behavior can be cause for claims of ineffective counsel. Some of the behaviors that could be displayed by a lawyer, private or public, include: failing to investigate alibis, call witnesses, or file motions and appeals in time; sleeping in court; and showing up drunk. The Supreme Court has provided the guidelines for appealing a conviction due to ineffective counsel. In the case of **Strickland v. Washington (1984)**, the court developed a two-pronged test prove that one's right to effective counsel had been violated. The first prong requires a defendant to show that their lawyer's performance was deficient in some way. The second prong requires them to show that had it not been for the deficient performance, the outcome of the case would have been different.

Inadequate defense is seemingly one of the variables causing wrongful conviction that can most easily be avoided. Federal, state, and local governments must provide public defenders with adequate tools to uphold the constitutional rights of the people they defend. Private attorneys who are hired directly by clients, or who are contracted and assigned by the courts, must be held accountable for acts of misrepresentation that compromise the integrity of the criminal defense. One way this is already happening is through the use of conviction integrity units. **Conviction Integrity Units** (CIU) are units within prosecutors' offices that review, and help prevent, cases where wrongful conviction has occurred or may occur. The number of these units continues to grow, as states are beginning to understand the costs, both fiscal and social, of wrongful convictions (National Registry of Exonerations, 2016).

Informants

Informants are used widely throughout the criminal justice system to provide needed information. Police officers may rely on them for street-level information, such as identifying drug dealers or making controlled buys of illegal substances that can be tracked. One point of contention, from the perspective of wrongful conviction, is the use of jailhouse informants to implicate suspects in crime. **Jailhouse informants** are individuals who are already incarcerated and are induced into providing information with the expectation that they will receive a benefit from their cooperation. It is not difficult to then establish a link to falsified information on the part of informants, as they stand to directly benefit from any information they can provide. Additionally, the more useful to a criminal conviction the information is, the greater the potential reward to the informant.

Unreliable informant testimony has been a contributing factor in 8% of the exonerations reported by the National Registry of Exonerations. The effects of jailhouse informants on the outcome of a case may not be as apparent because there is a belief that a jury will be able to discern false information provided by an informant from true information. However, just as juries believe false confessions, they are also likely to accept informant testimony as true, even when informant testimony is not provided the level of scrutiny necessary to accurately determine its validity (Neuschatz et al., 2008). Juries, in some cases, are also not given any indication of the inducements used by prosecutors to gain information from the informant. Couple this with a lack of punishment for jailhouse informants who do fabricate their testimony, and it becomes easy to see why the use of informant testimony in criminal cases is being questioned (Neuschatz et al., 2008).

One of the most apparent protective factors to the unreliability of jailhouse informants is allowing juries to know the specific details of any incentives offered to the informant. States are currently taking up these efforts by strengthening the legislation regarding the use of jailhouse informants. Some states, like Connecticut, are now developing legislation to formally track the use of jailhouse informants and the inducements they receive (Collins, 2019). Another step would be to disclose those incentives, and the research on the unreliability of jailhouse informants, to juries. This would allow jurors to make a more informed decision on the credibility of the testimony, and would add another layer of protection for defendants standing trial.

EFFECTS OF WRONGFUL CONVICTION

The effects of wrongful conviction are widespread. Wrongfully convicted persons not only may lose their lives on the outside, but also must assimilate to the prison subculture, as discussed in Chapter 7. Birthdays, holidays, births, and deaths are all moments that wrongfully convicted persons can never get back. In the most unfortunate cases of wrongful conviction, kids become adults in prison, and the formative years of their adolescence are ripped away from them. The mental and physical anguish that accompany this transition can make their eventual release, assuming there is one, all the more difficult.

From a criminal justice system perspective, wrongful convictions bring into question every conviction that is handed down. Wrongful convictions also cost the taxpayers money, as they are ones who must pay the bill in cases where restitution is handed out. In 2015, Silbert et al. reported that the state of California had spent nearly $221 million between 1989 and 2012 on the prosecution, and eventual exoneration, of criminal defendants. This included nearly 700 wrongfully prosecuted and convicted individuals, who collectively spent over 2,000 years incarcerated.

Innocence Project (2019) reports that 35 states currently have provisions to compensate the wrongfully convicted. Within many states, the compensation exceeds $50,000; in some cases, like those handled by the federal government, each year spent in prison can add to the restitution that is paid. Other restitution can come in the form of tuition assistance, medical expenses, and job/housing assistance (Innocence Project, 2019).

The residual effects of wrongful conviction are felt in other places as well. One of the concerns that is often overlooked in the discussion of wrongful conviction is the impact on the victims in cases where their perpetrator is not the one put behind bars. Irazola et al. (2014) describe what it can be like for victims in cases of wrongful conviction. The authors note that the victim is re-victimized by the system, and that "the impact of the wrongful conviction may be comparable to—or even worse than—that of their original victimization" (p. 34). What is even more problematic is that the person who committed the crime against them may still be out there, adding a renewed fear for victims who thought their cases had been closed. A new fear also manifests itself, the fear that the exonerated person will want to harm the victim for their role in the wrongful conviction (Irazola et al., 2014).

CONCLUSION

Convicting someone of a heinous crime, and potentially punishing them with death or with life in prison, is the ultimate form of retribution. For cases that end with a sentence of death, that decision, once carried out, is irreversible. From a public standpoint, wrongful convictions should concern even the most law-abiding citizen, as anyone could find themselves on the wrong end of a criminal conviction. While it may be the case that anyone could fall victim to wrongful conviction, there are certain individuals who need to be protected more than others, particularly those who belong to the racial groups that are disproportionately incarcerated.

It has been reported that almost 50% of exonerations involve African Americans, while they represent only 13% of the U.S. population (Gross et al., 2017). What is more disturbing is that, as charges get more serious, the likelihood of a person who is Black being wrongfully convicted increases. Based on exonerations, innocent Black individuals are three-and-a-half times more likely to be convicted of sexual assault, and seven times more likely to be convicted of murder, when compared to innocent white individuals (Gross et al., 2017). This may come as no surprise to many, as the racial bias inherent in the system is well documented, but it adds urgency to the need for reform.

Wrongful conviction is a problem that will not go away easily. The search for justice can make even the most ethical person compromise their beliefs. As this chapter has shown, the system-wide efforts that need to take place are just beginning. As a criminal justice system and a society built upon the ideals of due process, we all have a duty in preventing, recognizing, and counteracting wrongful convictions.

DISCUSSION QUESTIONS

1. What are the short- and long-term consequences of wrongful conviction to the criminal justice system?
2. Who is responsible for addressing the causes of wrongful conviction?
3. Can wrongful convictions ever be completely avoided by the criminal justice system?

APPLICATION EXERCISES

Exercise #1: Getting Involved in the Fight to End Wrongful Convictions

The Innocence Project has representative network members across the country. Start by finding the affiliated network closest to you at https://innocencenetwork.org/members/#map. Explore the ways you can get involved in the fight to end wrongful conviction. Draft a plan of action to get involved in ways that you feel comfortable with. The Pennsylvania Innocence Project outlines several ways to advocate, including:

- Providing social media support;
- Developing a community event or fundraiser;
- Building relationships with your elected representatives; and
- Reaching out to the media.

Exercise #2: What We Owe to the Wrongfully Convicted

Start by providing your opinion on the compensation of those who have been exonerated. Should people who are exonerated be compensated for the criminal justice system's mistake? Next, identify what harm is done in cases of wrongful conviction. Include your thoughts on harm done to the wrongfully convicted, harm done to the criminal justice system, harm done to society, and harm done to both direct and indirect victims of the crime. As difficult as it is to quantify suffering, think about what is necessary to repair some of the harm done by wrongful convictions. Think about the following concerns:

1. How does the amount of compensation change based on the crime for which the person was wrongfully convicted?
2. What impact does the number of years incarcerated have on compensation?

3. What role do the contributing factors of wrongful conviction play? Do official acts of misconduct deserve higher amounts of restitution?

4. Is it enough to provide monetary restitution? What other types of restitution should be made to the wrongfully convicted?

REFERENCES

Baćak, V., Lageson, S. E., & Powell, K. (2020). "Fighting the good fight": Why do public defenders remain on the job? *Criminal Justice Police Review, 31*(6), 939–961.

Bang, B. L., Stanton, D., Hemmens, C., & Stohr, M. K. (2018). Police recording of custodial interrogations: A state-by-state legal inquiry. *International Journal of Police Science & Management, 20*(1), 3–18.

Bell, S., Sah, S., Albright, T. D., Gates, S. J., Jr., Denton, M. B., & Casadevall, A. (2018). A call for more science in forensic science. *Proceedings of the National Academy of Sciences of the United States of America, 115*(18), 4541–4544.

Block, F. (2016). *Let's put an end to prosecutorial misconduct.* The Marshall Project. https://www.themarshallproject.org/2018/03/13/let-s-put-an-end-to-prosecutorial-immunity

Chapman, F. E. (2013). Coerced internalized false confessions and police interrogations: The power of coercion. *Law and Psychology Review, 37,* 159–192.

Cole, S. A. (2015). A surfeit of science: The "CSI effect" and the media appropriation of the public understanding of science. *Public Understanding of Science, 24*(2), 130–146.

Cole, S. A., & Dioso-Villa, R. (2009) Investigating the 'CSI Effect' effect: Media and litigation crisis in criminal law. *Stanford Law Review, 61*(6), 1335–1373.

Collins, D. (2019, September 14). *Lying prisoners: New laws crack down on jailhouse informants.* AP News. https://apnews.com/9f8858ef3fbf4965874d314ce41ec69c

Covey, R. (2013). Police misconduct as a cause of wrongful convictions. *Washington University Law Review, 90*(4), 1133–1189.

Farole, D. J., Jr., & Langton, L. (2010). A national assessment of public defender office caseloads. *Judicature, 94*(2), 87–90.

Green, B., & Yaroshefsky, E. (2016). Prosecutorial accountability 2.0. *Notre Dame Law Review, 92*(1), 51–116.

Gross, S. R., Possley, M., & Stephens, K. (2017, March 7). *Race and wrongful convictions in the United States.* National Registry of Exonerations, Newkirk Center for Science and Society.

Hager, E. (2016, January 28). *Why getting sued could be the best thing to happen to New Orleans public defenders.* The Marshall Project. https://www.themarshallproject.org/2016/01/28/why-getting-sued-could-be-the-best-thing-to-happen-to-new-orleans-public-defenders

Irazola, S., Williamson, E., Sticker, J., & Niedzwiecki, E. (2014). Addressing the impact of wrongful convictions on crime victims. *NIJ Journal, 274,* 34–38.

Kassin, S. M., Drizin, S. A., Grisso, T., Gudjonsson, G. H., Leo, R. A., & Redlich, A. D. (2010). Police-induced confessions: Risk factors and recommendations. *Law and Human Behavior, 34*(1), 3–38.

Kassin, S. M. (2017). False confessions: How can psychology so basic be so counterintuitive? *American Psychologist, 72*(9), 951–964.

Kovera, M. B., & Evelo, A. J. (2017). The case for double-blind lineup administration. *Psychology, Public Policy, and Law, 23*(4), 421–437.

LaPorte, G. (2017, September 7). Wrongful convictions and DNA exonerations: Understanding the role of forensic science. *NIJ Journal, 279*, April 2018, 1–16.

Loeffler, C. E., Hyatt, J., & Ridgeway, G. (2019). Measuring self-reported wrongful convictions among prisoners. *Journal of Quantitative Criminology, 35*, 259–286.

Miranda v. Arizona, 384 U.S. 436 (1966)

National Registry of Exonerations. (2016). *Conviction integrity units.* https://www.law.umich.edu/special/exoneration/Documents/2.2016_Newsletter_Art2.pdf

National Registry of Exonerations. (2019). *Exonerations in 2018.* https://www.law.umich.edu/special/exoneration/Documents/2018_Exonerations_Report.pdf

National Research Council. (2009). *Strengthening forensic science in the United States: A path forward.* National Academies Press.

National Research Council. (2014). *Identifying the culprit: Assessing eyewitness identification.* National Academies Press.

Neuschatz, J. S., Lawson, D. S., Swanner, J. K., Meissner, C. A., & Neuschatz, J. S. (2008). The effects of accomplice witnesses and jailhouse informants on jury decision making. *Law and Human Behavior, 32*(2), 137–149.

Norris, R. J., Bonventre, C. L., Redlich, A. D., Acker, J. R., & Lowe, C. (2019). Preventing wrongful convictions: An analysis of state investigation reforms. *Criminal Justice Policy Review, 30*(4), 597–626.

Silbert, R., Hollway, J., & Larizadeh, D. (2015). *Criminal (in)justice: A cost analysis of wrongful convictions, errors, and failed prosecutions in California's criminal justice system* (U of Penn Law School, Public Law Research Paper No. 16-12). Chief Justice Earl Warren Institute on Law and Society.

Police Executive Research Forum. (2013). *A national survey of eyewitness identification procedures in law enforcement agencies.* https://www.policeforum.org/assets/docs/Free_Online_Documents/Eyewitness_Identification/a%20national%20survey%20of%20eyewitness%20identification%20procedures%20in%20law%20enforcement%20agencies%202013.pdf

Sledge, M. (2019, May 5). *Orleans public defenders to cut services, freeze hiring in face of revenue shortfall.* The Times-Picayune. https://www.nola.com/news/courts/article_6e6bbaf3-2bff-5dfd-8701-91a9c7cee9fb.html

Souviron, R., & Haller, L. (2017). Bite mark evidence: Bite mark analysis is not the same as bite mark comparison or matching or identification. *Journal of Law and Biosciences, 4*(3), 617–622.

Stratton, G. (2015). Transforming the Central Park jogger into the Central Park Five: Shifting narratives of innocence and changing media discourse in the attack on the Central Park jogger, 1989–2014. *Crime Media Culture, 11*(3), 281–297.

Strickland v. Washington, 466 US 668 (1984)

Strong, S. M. (2016). *State-administered indigent defense systems, 2013* (NCJ 250249). U.S. Department of Justice,Office of Justice Programs, Bureau of Justice Statistics. https://www.bjs.gov/content/pub/pdf/saids13.pdf

Sturgis, S. (2011, September 22). *Troy Davis case shows need for eyewitness identification reform.* Facing South. https://www.facingsouth.org/2011/09/troy-davis-case-shows-need-for-eyewitness-identification-reform.html

The World Bank. (2019). *Life expectancy at birth, total (years)—United States.* World Bank Group. https://data.worldbank.org/indicator/SP.DYN.LE00.IN?locations=US.

Wikted, J. T, Mickes, L., & Fisher, R. P. (2018). Rethinking the reliability of eyewitness memory. *Perspectives on Psychological Science, 13*(3), 324–335.

CHAPTER 14

The Death Penalty

CHAPTER OBJECTIVES

After reading this chapter, you should be able to:

- Explain the purpose of capital punishment, its methods, and its impact on criminal justice decision-making and sentencing policies.
- Identify court cases and historical events that helped to shape modern death penalty laws.
- Critically evaluate the arguments for and against the death penalty.
- Identify contemporary issues that challenge the use of capital punishment.

KEY WORDS

Aggravating factor

Bifurcated trial

Botched execution

Clemency

Coker v. Georgia

Death row phenomenon

Death row syndrome

Electrocution

Execution

Execution warrant

Firing squad

Furman v. Georgia

Gas chamber

Godfrey v. Georgia

Gregg v. Georgia

Habeus corpus

Hanging

Kennedy v. Louisiana

Lethal injection

McCleskey v. Kemp

Mitigating factor

Moratorium

Proportionality review

Retribution

Roper v. Simmons

Stay of execution

Writ of certiorari

CASE STUDY: LISA MONTGOMERY

On January 13, 2021, 52-year-old Lisa Montgomery was executed by the federal government for kidnapping and killing an expectant mother in Melvern, Kansas in 2004. The victim, Bobbie Jo Stinnett, 23, was strangled by Montgomery, 36, and she bled to death after the baby was cut from her womb. The baby, who had survived, was later recovered by police, and returned to the father. Lisa Montgomery was sentenced to death for the offense in 2004. Prior to her execution in 2021, Lisa Montgomery was the only female on death row at the federal prison complex in Terre Haute, Indiana. In late December 2020, Montgomery's legal team submitted a petition to former President Donald Trump, arguing that she was too mentally ill to be executed. Her mental illness, they maintained, was the result of physical, sexual, and emotional abuse that she experienced during childhood. Lisa's mother was the source of many of her issues; Montgomery was born with fetal alcohol syndrome after her mother drank during her pregnancy, and her mother beat her regularly and utilized cruel forms of punishment. It was also revealed that Montgomery's stepfather built a shed near the family's home where he and his friends raped and beat her. Lisa's mother also trafficked her, allowing handymen like electricians and plumbers to sexually abuse Montgomery in exchange for work on the house.

Lisa Montgomery became the first female federal inmate in 67 years to be executed by the United States federal government, and the fourth overall. Her death, which was administered via lethal injection, resulted in heavy criticism, with her defense team maintaining that at the time of her crime, Montgomery was psychotic and out of touch with reality. That opinion is supported by current and former lawyers, as well as human rights groups like the Inter-American Commission on Human Rights. Still, regardless of her mental health, the victim's family and friends argue that the execution was justified due to the heinous nature of the crime.

Questions for Discussion

1. Do you believe Lisa Montgomery's execution was justified? Why or why not?
2. Mental illness, childhood abuse, and brain injuries affect a large share of those who face the death penalty. What implications does this case have for future convictions?

INTRODUCTION

Perhaps one of the most controversial issues in corrections is the death penalty. This practice, which is often referred to as capital punishment, is the most extreme punishment utilized in the American criminal justice system (Pojman & Reiman, 1998; Mandery, 2005). To receive capital punishment, citizens must be convicted of committing a capital offense, or a government-sanctioned crime deemed punishable by death. The capital offenses that lead to a person's eligibility for the death penalty are defined by state or federal capital statutes that outline which procedures are used in capital cases, including the implementation of the punishment. Historically, the death penalty has generated much discussion and controversy, given the serious nature and finality of this type of punishment.

The following chapter gives a detailed overview of the death penalty. This chapter begins by outlining the history of capital punishment in the United States, including the major pieces of legislation and landmark court cases that have shaped its utilization over the past several decades. Specific elements of capital offenses such as sentencing and conviction, incarceration on death row, and execution methods are discussed. In addition, this chapter presents arguments both in support of, and in opposition to, the death penalty to give a balanced perspective of each viewpoint. The chapter concludes with insight into several contemporary issues that continue to challenge America's use of the death penalty, including human rights concerns, mass incarceration, and cost effectiveness.

CAPITAL PUNISHMENT IN THE UNITED STATES

A capital offense is defined by the Bureau of Justice Statistics (BJS) as an offense that is eligible for a death sentence that is defined by statute in each jurisdiction that authorizes capital punishment. The Federal Death Penalty Act of 1994 expanded the number of eligible capital offenses to 60 offenses; however, by year-end 2018, the government had reduced this number to 41 offenses that warrant the death penalty including murder, treason, espionage, war crimes, crimes against humanity, and genocide. First-degree murder is the most common capital offense accompanied by at least one aggravating factor (Snell, 2020). Currently, no offenses impose a mandatory death sentence because the Supreme Court held that mandatory death sentences violated both the Eighth and the Fourteenth Amendments to the Constitution (Davis & Snell, 2018; Death Penalty Information Center, 2019a; Kronenwetter, 2001). A list of federal capital offenses is outlined in Table 14.1.

Capital crimes are deeply ingrained in the criminal justice system, and several Constitutional developments relate directly to the death penalty. For example, the Fifth Amendment to the Bill of Rights reads that the death penalty can be utilized with a grand jury indictment for a capital crime. The Fourteenth Amendment also relates to capital

Table 14.1 Federal Capital Offenses (2018).

FEDERAL OFFENSES
Murder related to the smuggling of aliens.
Destruction of an aircraft, motor vehicles, or related facilities, resulting in death.
Murder committed during a drug-related drive-by-shooting.
Murder committed at an airport serving international civil aviation.
Retaliatory murder of a member of the immediate family of a law enforcement official.
Civil-rights offenses resulting in death.
Murder of a member of Congress, an important executive official, or U.S. Supreme Court justice.
Espionage.
Death resulting from offenses involving transportation of explosives, destruction of government property, or destruction of property related to foreign or interstate commerce.
Murder committed using a firearm during a crime of violence or a drug-trafficking crime.
Murder committed in a federal government facility.
Genocide.
First-degree murder.
Murder of a federal judge or law enforcement official.
Murder of a foreign official.
Murder by a federal prisoner.
Murder of a U.S. national in a foreign country.
Murder by an escaped federal prisoner already sentenced to life imprisonment.
Murder of a state or local law enforcement official or other person aiding in a federal investigation; or murder of a state correctional officer.
Murder during a kidnapping.
Murder during a hostage-taking.
Murder of a court officer or juror.
Murder with the intent of preventing testimony by a witness, a victim, or an informant.
Retaliatory murder of a witness, a victim, or an informant.
Mailing of injurious articles with intent to kill or resulting in death.
Assassination or kidnapping resulting in the death of the U.S. president or U.S. vice president.
Murder for hire.
Murder involved in a racketeering offense.
Willful wrecking of a train resulting in death.
Murder or kidnapping related to bank robbery.
Murder relating to a carjacking.
Murder related to rape or child molestation.
Murder related to sexual exploitation of children.
Murder committed during an offense against maritime navigation.
Murder committed during an offense against a maritime fixed platform.

(continued)

Table 14.1 Federal Capital Offenses (2018).   *(continued)*

FEDERAL OFFENSES

Murder involving torture.
Treason.
Murder relating to a continuing criminal enterprise, or related murder of a federal, state, or local law enforcement officer.
Death resulting from aircraft hijacking.

Total Offenses: 41

Note. Adapted from *Capital Punishment, 2018—Statistical Tables*, by T. J. Snell, 2020, U.S. Department of Justice, Office of Justice Programs, Bureau of Justice Statistics (https://www.bjs.gov/content/pub/pdf/cp18st.pdf).

punishment because due process of law is required if the government is to deprive citizens of their life or liberties. The Amendment that receives the most attention in relation to the death penalty, however, is the Eighth Amendment, which prohibits the government from inflicting cruel and unusual punishments on citizens. Since it was espoused, the Eighth Amendment has served as a cornerstone to arguments made by opponents of capital punishment who maintain that the death penalty violates a person's constitutional rights and should therefore be abolished (American Civil Liberties Union [ACLU], 2012).

Capital Punishment in an International Context

In 2007, the United Nations voted to condemn the death penalty through a global moratorium, with 104 nations supporting the decision, 54 opposing it, and 29 abstaining. The United States was one of the countries that opposed the vote, as were China, Iran, Syria, India, and North Korea (McGowen, 2011). At present, most of the world's countries (106) have abolished the death penalty in law for all crimes. Comparatively, 142 countries (more than two thirds of the nations in the world) have abolished the death penalty in law or practice (Amnesty International, 2018). In 2020, there were 54 countries that utilized capital punishment, employing a variety of methods including hanging, shooting, lethal injection, electrocution, and beheading. In 2019, 20 countries executed their citizens as a sanction for a criminal offense. It is estimated that most executions in the world took place in China; however, the country does not actively report their numbers, which makes it difficult to know for sure. Most of all known executions in 2019, by order, occurred in China, Iran, Saudi Arabia, Iraq, Egypt, and the United States (Amnesty International, 2020).

The United States is the only Western country that utilizes capital punishment, although every state maintains different standards, which have evolved over time (Bienen, 2010). Currently, 22 states and the District of Columbia have abolished the death penalty,

Table 14.2 U.S. States Without the Death Penalty (2021).

Alaska (1957)	Minnesota (1911)
Colorado (2020)	New Hampshire (2019)
Connecticut (2012)	New Jersey (2007)
Delaware (2016)	New Mexico (2009)
Hawaii (1957)	New York (2007)
Illinois (2011)	North Dakota (1973)
Iowa (1965)	Rhode Island (1984)
Maine (1887)	Vermont (1972)
Maryland (2013)	Washington (2018)
Massachusetts (1984)	West Virginia (1965)
Michigan (1847)	Wisconsin (1853)

Total states: 22

Note. Adapted from *State by State,* by the Death Penalty Information Center, 2020c (https://deathpenaltyinfo.org/state-and-federal-info/state-by-state).

with Colorado being the most recent state to do so. In addition, three states have established gubernatorial moratoria: California (2019), Oregon (2011), and Pennsylvania (2015) (Amnesty International, 2020). Table 14.2 lists the non-death-penalty states in the United States.

It is also important to note that some death penalty states use capital punishment more actively than others. For example, in 2019, 22 executions occurred in: Texas (9), Alabama (3), Georgia (3), Tennessee (3), Florida (2), Missouri (1), and South Dakota (1) (Amnesty International, 2020). In comparison, 12 states, including Utah, North Carolina, and Kansas, have not executed anyone in more than a decade (Death Penalty Information Center, 2020e). Table 14.3 lists the states in the United States that currently utilize the death penalty.

The Bureau of Justice Statistics reports that the number of people on death row has decreased annually since 1991, so states have not been relying on capital punishment as much as they did in the past (Davis & Snell, 2018). Despite this downward trend, the death penalty remains deeply entrenched in the American criminal justice system, as approximately 20,000 court-ordered executions have taken place in the United States, particularly during the 20th century (Acker, 2003; Banner, 2002).

Table 14.3 U.S. States With the Death Penalty (2021).

Alabama	Nebraska
Arizona	Nevada
Arkansas	North Carolina
California	Ohio
Florida	Oklahoma
Georgia	Oregon
Idaho	Pennsylvania
Indiana	South Carolina
Kansas	South Dakota
Kentucky	Tennessee
Louisiana	Texas
Mississippi	Utah
Missouri	Virginia
Montana	Wyoming

Total states: 28

Note. Adapted from *State by State*, by the Death Penalty Information Center, 2020c (https://deathpenaltyinfo.org/state-and-federal-info/state-by-state).

THE HISTORY OF THE DEATH PENALTY

Capital punishment has been utilized by societies around the world for centuries as a means of maintaining social control and sanctioning society's worst offenders (Banner, 2002). The very first death penalty laws were written into code in the 18th century BCE in the Code of Hammurabi of Babylon and were pronounced again during the seventh century BCE in the Draconian Code of Athens, and in the fifth century BCE in the Roman Law of the Twelve Tables. American settlers who used the death penalty were influenced by Britain and European settlers, who had utilized it once early colonies were formed. Since prisons had not been erected in the United States prior to the 18th century, fines, corporal punishment, and short-term incarceration in jail were the predominantly used forms of criminal sanctions. Historically, repeat offenders and individuals who engaged in murder, rape, adultery, sodomy, bestiality, and some property crimes were most often targeted by death penalty convictions (Acker, 2002; Rothman, 1971). While several of these offenses are still recognized by both state and federal governments, there is evidence to suggest that capital punishment has also been used as a tool to suppress vulnerable and marginalized populations of citizens, including poor people and racial minorities (Amnesty International, n.d.; Banner, 2002).

In early America, many settlers held the belief that people possessed their own free will to make rational, calculated decisions, which meant that they were quick to blame wrongdoers and demand government intercession when an offense occurred. Many viewed the death penalty as a quick, cheap way to purge the community of criminals (Banner, 2002). The death penalty was also seen as being useful for dissuading future criminal acts. Many executions occurred in public settings so that people were made aware of the consequences of crime. The first recorded execution took place in 1608 when a man was executed by firing squad after being accused of espionage. Conversely, the first female was hanged in 1632 for killing her baby, followed by scores of other women during the 17th and early 18th centuries because of convictions for infanticide or witchcraft (Baker, 2016; Karlsen, 1998). The first juvenile execution took place in 1642 in Massachusetts when a teenage boy was convicted of bestiality. Since this time, hundreds of juveniles have been executed, although the practice has since been abolished in the United States (Eleftherious-Smith, 2014).

An abolitionist movement began in the late 1700s when citizens began to question the need for capital punishment, especially for property crimes (e.g., theft, counterfeiting, and burglary), and it continued throughout the 19th century. At the time, many people were influenced by reformers' speeches and writings, including Cesare Beccaria's *Essay on Crimes and Punishments* (1764), which denounced the death penalty and emphasized the disproportionality of capital punishment for certain offenses (Banner, 2002). The abolitionist movement led many states to reduce the number of capital cases across the Unites States, and during the early 1800s many states began to construct penitentiaries to house individuals convicted for life terms, since execution was no longer a viable solution. In 1834, Pennsylvania became one of the first states to charge individuals with first-degree murder and move them into correctional facilities. Several years later in 1847, Michigan became the first state to abolish the death penalty for all offenses other than treason. Michigan has since banned the practice altogether (Acker, 2003; Death Penalty Information Center, 2019a).

The 1900s ushered in the beginning of the Progressive Period of criminal reform in the United States. Between 1907 and 1917, nine states had eliminated capital punishment from criminal statutes, or they had placed strict limitations on its use. Public attitudes soon shifted between the 1920s and 1940s, however, and new execution methods, including the use of cyanide gas, were introduced. Use of the death penalty peaked in the 1930s when executions reached the highest levels in American history. Several years later, in

1948, the United Nations adopted the Universal Declaration of Human Rights, which decreed an individual's right to life, thereby denouncing the death penalty. Soon after, states began to move away from capital punishment, which they continue to do to this day (Death Penalty Information Center, n.d.).

In 1956, a Gallup poll found that for the first time, more American citizens opposed the death penalty than supported it. The declining crime rates, softened attitudes about punishment, and civil rights campaigns are possible explanations for the weakened support of capital punishment (Acker, 2003). By the end of the 1960s, a record 14 states, all of which were outside the South, had either abolished capital punishment altogether or were using it only in cases of specific homicides, such as the murder of a law enforcement officer or a death as the result of aircraft piracy (Banner, 2002).

In 1972, the Supreme Court implemented a nationwide moratorium and suspended the death penalty in the United States. The Court was inspired to do so after the Justices reviewed the case of *Furman v. Georgia* (1972) and questioned how the states and federal government processed capital offenders. Justices Brennan and Marshall argued that imposing the death penalty on someone convicted of murder or rape was in and of itself cruel and unusual punishment. Justices Douglas, Stewart, and White maintained that the death penalty was being administered in an arbitrary and capricious manner. Ultimately, the Court ruled in a 5-4 decision that the death penalty constituted cruel and unusual punishment. As a result of the decision, all pending death sentences were reduced to life terms. The Court also called for states to establish consistency in the process of determining if an offender convicted of a capital crime would be sentenced to death or life without parole (Marciniak, 2016). Finally, the Court required states to ensure that capital cases were not arbitrary or discriminatory in nature (Banner, 2002).

Following *Furman*, Georgia established a list of aggravating factors to guide jurors' decisions as to whether to impose a life sentence or the death penalty. The death penalty moratorium ended in 1977 following the Supreme Court's review of *Gregg v. Georgia* (1976), when guided discriminatory statutes were approved, and in a 7-2 decision, the Court ruled that the death penalty is not in and out itself cruel and unusual (Death Penalty Information Center, 2019a; Marciniak, 2016). Support for the death penalty was later evidenced by the fact that at least 35 states enacted new statutes providing for the death penalty in the four years following the *Furman* decision (Marciniak, 2016).

CAPITAL PUNISHMENT IN THE MODERN ERA

The modern era of capital punishment began in 1977 when the death penalty was reinstated and new laws were enacted to address the problems that were identified in *Furman v. Georgia* (1972) and *Gregg v. Georgia* (1976), respectively (Acker, 2003; Banner, 2002). The first person was executed by lethal injection in Oklahoma in 1982. Two years later in 1984, the first woman was executed since the death penalty had been reinstated (Death Penalty Information Center, n.d.). Although males comprise most of the population convicted of capital offenses, there have been several issues with the death penalty that relate directly to the protection of females and serve as precedent today. For example, pursuant to the Universal Declaration of Human Rights, the federal death penalty cannot be executed upon a pregnant woman (Amnesty International, 2011).

International law also protects mentally ill populations from execution (Amnesty International, 2011). In the United States, the issue has been visited in the Supreme Court's review of the case *Ford v. Wainwright* (1986), in which it was decided that people who were classified as insane by the state could not be executed. Based on this case, petitioners now have the right to an evaluation and evidentiary hearing to examine whether they are competent to be executed; however, it is up to each state to determine the defendant's sanity (Amnesty International, 2011; Banner, 2002). In another landmark decision, *Atkins v. Virginia* (2002), the Supreme Court ruled that executing an individual with intellectual disabilities violates their Eighth Amendment rights. As in the *Ford* ruling, the Court decided that states could define who has an intellectual disability (*Atkins v. Virginia*, 2002). Regardless of this issue, it is estimated that 5%–10% of people on death row have serious mental illness, including schizophrenia, and it is documented that mentally ill individuals have been executed (Amnesty International, 2011).

The death penalty has also been challenged in relation to race and racial bias. In the landmark case *McCleskey v. Kemp* (1987), the court upheld the death penalty sentence for a man who was arguing on appeal that capital punishment was racially discriminatory, and that it violated his right to an equal protection of law under the Fourteenth Amendment. To argue the case, the defense referenced a statistical study that showed racial disparities in Georgia death penalty cases. Despite the empirical evidence that showed racial bias, the court decided that general disparities in a state's administration of the death penalty did not sufficiently demonstrate the presence of unconstitutional discrimination in an individual defendant's case (Lewis, 1987; Neklason, 2019). The contentious 5-4 decision was criticized because the court was within one vote of eliminating capital punishment in Georgia. Moreover, critics of the decision blasted the Supreme Court for being blatantly racist and for allowing racial bias to become an aspect of the law. The decision made in *McCleskey* created a precedent that is still being challenged to this day (Neklason, 2019).

During the same time, President Ronald Reagan signed the Anti-Drug Abuse Act (1988), which was previously discussed in Chapters 1 and 12 in relation to the 100-to-1 ratio. This Act authorized the death penalty for individuals who were convicted of killing or ordering a killing during the commission of a drug-related felony. The legislation, which was a part of the larger War on Drugs effort, not only represented a shift from a rehabilitative federal system to a more punitive one but also helped to establish racially oppressive laws that targeted people of color who were involved with the production, distribution, and trafficking of illegal substances (Banner, 2002). Several years later in 1994, President Bill Clinton signed the Federal Death Penalty Act and the Violent Crime Control and Law Enforcement Act, both of which expanded the use of the federal death penalty to make 60 crimes capital offenses. Clinton also signed the Anti-Terrorism and Effective Death Penalty Act (1996), which restricted the reviews of death penalty cases in federal courts (Death Penalty Information Center, 2019a). The first federal execution post-*Furman* occurred in 2001, when Timothy McVeigh was executed at the U.S. federal penitentiary in Terre Haute, Indiana for killing 163 people in the Oklahoma City bombing in 1992 (Jeffery, 2001; May, 1988).

The 2000s ushered in a time of reform for capital punishment. In 2005, the United States Supreme Court decided in the case of *Roper v. Simmons* (2005) that it was unconstitutional to execute offenders who were under the age of 18 at the time of their crime. Prior to the ruling, the prevailing jurisprudence for the capital convictions of youth was *Stanford v. Kentucky* (1989), which set the minimum age for death penalty eligibility at 16. Prior to *Stanford*, the United States had historically sentenced 365 juveniles to death, with the youngest being a 14-year-old Black male from South Carolina in 1944 (Eleftherious-Smith, 2014). The last juvenile execution to take place in United States occurred in Maryland in 1959 (Streib, 1987).

According to data from the Death Penalty Information Center (2019a), there has been a decline in the use of the death penalty at the state level over the past 25 years. Specifically, there has been a 75% decline in the number of executions carried out in the United States since their use peaked in 1999. Since 2000, states have moved away from capital punishment, and capital criminal statutes have been reexamined. For example, in 2007 New Jersey became the first state to abolish the death penalty since it was reinstated with the *Furman* decision. One year later, the Supreme Court decided in *Kennedy v. Louisiana* (2008) that crimes committed against persons that do not result in death, including child rape, are not punishable by death (Banner, 2002). Indeed, the United States has witnessed significant changes in death penalty legislation throughout history.

CAPITAL OFFENSES

There are several stages in a capital case, although some states and the federal government follow different procedures. The legal administration typically involves a prosecutorial decision to seek the death penalty, sentencing, direct review, state collateral review, and federal *habeas corpus*. Initially, each jurisdiction determines the offense for which the death penalty can be imposed if it is an option in that jurisdiction. Generally, death penalty states implement procedural safeguards that manifest from state- and federal-level decisions to help identify and eliminate disparities. For example, courts mandate the use of sentencing guidelines, automatic appellate reviews of convictions, proportionality reviews, and bifurcated proceedings.

Bifurcated trials have two separate parts in the trial process: the former to determine a defendant's guilt, and the latter to determine if capital punishment is warranted (Davis & Snell, 2018; Kamin & Pokorak, 2005). Conversely, **proportionality reviews** occur when a state appellate court compares the sentences of similar cases to eliminate sentencing disparities, although several states have moved away from this practice (Kaufman-Osborn, 2008). During a sentencing hearing, a jury considers whether aggravating and/or mitigating factors played a role in the crime. An **aggravating factor**, also called an aggravating circumstance, involves the specific elements of a crime that are defined by a statute. To sentence an offender to death, the jury must find that at least one aggravating factor was present and was not outweighed by any **mitigating factors**, or circumstances that weigh in the defendant's favor, such as intellectual disability or their mental state at the time of the crime (Davis & Snell, 2018). This procedure is pursuant to the U.S. Supreme Court case *Godfrey V. Georgia* (1980), in which it was decided that murder is punishable by death if the case involves a narrowly defined, specific aggravating factor.

Once an individual is convicted of a crime, they have the right to directly appeal the decision at both state and federal levels; however, they must prove that a procedural mistake was made during their trial. For example, they can make a claim about insufficient or newly discovered evidence or about jury misconduct. In addition, appeals regarding the individual's conviction and sentence can be made to the state's highest criminal court or to the U.S. Court of Appeals in which the case was tried. Defendants can also ask the high courts to review the constitutionality of their case (Death Penalty Information Center, 2019a). This petition, however, known formally as a **writ of certiorari**, rarely works in the defendant's favor. For example, the Supreme Court only reviews about 1% of the case review requests they receive annually (United States Courts, n.d.). Once a person is found guilty in a capital case, the jury is given an option to impose a death sentence, or a sentence of life imprisonment without the possibility of parole (ACLU, 2012).

Post-conviction reviews can also include petitions in which defendants can raise concerns about ineffective counsel or prosecutorial or juror misconduct. A defendant can request a state or federal *habeas corpus* (previously discussed in Chapter 6), a lengthy process that involves a court deciding whether an individual's imprisonment is illegal. During an evidentiary hearing, if a judge decides to hear a case, they then determine whether there is support for the statement made in the *habeas corpus* petition. If the defendant loses the trial, they may appeal the court ruling to the U.S. Court of Appeals. The next phase, the clemency stage, takes place when a pardon board decides to grant **clemency**, or a reduction in the punishment imposed on the individual by the courts (Knight, 2016). At the federal level, the President of the United States is the only one who can grant clemency to individuals serving time on death row (Death Penalty Information Center, 2019c). All other cases move on to the **execution** stage, in which a sentence of death is legally carried out on a condemned person (Knight, 2016).

STATE AND FEDERAL EXECUTIONS

While the future of the death penalty is difficult to predict, data reveals that fewer states are relying on this method as a form of punishment. In 1976, 30 states utilized the death penalty, whereas 20 did not. In comparison, 28 states currently have death penalty statutes, and 22 do not utilize capital punishment. Rather than facing execution, individuals convicted in states without the death penalty are serving life terms for their crimes, which means that the convicted person will remain incarcerated for the remainder of their life rather than being executed. According to the Bureau of Justice Statistics, in 2018, eight out of 34 states that utilized capital punishment executed a total of 25 people, with Texas accounting for more than half (13) of the executions that year. Of those individuals who were housed on death row in state institutions at year-end 2018, 56% were White, 42% were Black, and 15% were Hispanic/Latino. The majority (98%) of individuals housed on death row at the state level were male, while females made up a small portion (2%) of the population (Snell, 2020).

Notably, the federal death penalty applies in all 50 states; however, executions at the federal level are much rarer than state executions. Prior to 2020, 62 people (61 males and 1 female) were held on death row in federal institutions since the reinstatement of the federal death penalty in 1988, and nearly half of the federal death sentences emerged from Texas, Virginia, and Missouri. The population of people serving time on federal death row in 2018 was made up of mostly White (43.6%) and Black males (41.9%), though there were also men on death row who identified as Latino (11.3%), Asian (1.6%), and Native American (1.6%) (Death Penalty Information Center, 2019c). The only female who was on federal death row in 2018 was a White woman who was convicted and sentenced to death in 2007 for killing a woman and seizing her unborn baby from her womb (Marshall, 2008).

However, in late 2019, the Trump Administration announced that that the federal government would resume federal executions beginning in December 2019, after having not done so for 17 years (Higgins, 2019). Before Trump's term was over, 13 federal executions were carried out; the move was unprecedented and had concluded just five days before the inauguration of President-elect Joe Biden. No president in more than 120 years had overseen that number of executions at the federal level (Tarm & Kunzelman, 2021). President Joe Biden is the first sitting president to openly oppose the death penalty, and he has discussed the possibility of instructing the Department of Justice to stop scheduling new executions; however, at the time of this writing, he has not taken any action to end the practice, despite pledging during his presidential campaign to pass legislation to eliminate the death penalty at the federal level and to incentivize states to follow the federal government's example (Tarm, 2021).

Death Row

Prior to executions, or while awaiting decisions from the court, individuals who have been convicted of capital crimes are housed on death row. There are only three federal correctional institutions that house incarcerated individuals on death row. Males convicted of capital cases are held at either the United States Penitentiary in Terre Haute, Indiana (Federal Bureau of Prisons, n.d.b), or ADX, a supermax facility in Florence, Colorado (Federal Bureau of Prisons, n.d.a). Females on death row are housed at the Federal Medical Center in Fort Worth, Texas (Death Penalty Information Center, 2019c). According to the Bureau of Justice Statistics, 2,628 incarcerated individuals were held on death row in state institutions in 2018, with more than half (49%) being held in California (28%), Florida (13%), and Texas (8%) (Snell, 2020).

The conditions on death row are quite different from those in other areas of the prison. For example, individuals on death row do not have access to programming, and they are isolated from others by being confined to their cells for 23 hours a day. In addition, individuals on death row spend more than a decade awaiting their executions, and they are constantly uncertain of when they will be executed. This uncertain period of isolation, known as the **death row phenomenon**, often results in individuals experiencing serious psychological effects including depression and suicidal ideation; these effects are known more commonly among psychologists and lawyers as **death row syndrome** (Death Penalty Information Center, 2019c; Smith, 2008).

Although the courts have recognized the dire consequences that the lengthy time between sentencing and execution has for taxpayers, victims, and families, as well as for the incarcerated individuals themselves, policy reforms now include appellate review, which has extended the process significantly (*Medley*, 1890; *Foster v. Florida*, 2002). The process is slowed further due to mandatory minimum sentences and changes in laws and technology (Death Penalty Information Center, 2019c). In all, it has been estimated that a person serving time on death row will have approximately 15 years of time between their sentencing and an actual execution (Snell, 2011). About a quarter of the incarcerated individuals on death row end up dying naturally before their execution, or because of starvation, torture, dehydration, or illness (Hillman, 1993). So far, there have not been any cases reviewed by the Supreme Court regarding the length of time an individual spends on death row; however, its constitutionality has been questioned before, so it may be only a matter of time before the issue comes up again (Death Penalty Information Center, 2019c).

When an execution occurs in the United States, the government agency charged with carrying out the procedure (e.g., the state Department of Corrections or the Federal

Bureau of Prisons) signs an **execution warrant** containing the date of execution. Typically, as the execution draws nearer, the condemned person is placed in a cell that is closer to the area in which the execution will take place, and they are put under a suicide watch. In addition, the individual is given an opportunity to prepare their final words and to meet with several people, including family members, legal representatives, and spiritual advisers. Some correctional institutions also allow the incarcerated person to choose their last meal, both with and without restrictions (Jacobs, 2017). During this period, an official notice to stop an execution, known as a **stay of execution**, can be ordered at either the state or the federal level at any time, including when the individual is being prepared for execution in the execution chamber (Death Penalty Information Center, 2019c). Execution chambers, when utilized, are typically very sparse and clinical, with a gurney, a mirror, a microphone, and a clock, as well as a witness gallery, which houses the families of both the offender and the victim or victims, lawyers, and members of the press who are present to view the execution (Kirby, 2014).

Methods of Execution

Executions take various forms including hanging, electrocution, the gas chamber, the firing squad, and lethal injection, although stoning and beheading are used in other nations as well, including Saudi Arabia, Sudan, and Yemen (Hillman, 1993). In the modern era, lethal injection is the most used method of execution in the United States. Up to the point of this writing, the Supreme Court has not ruled any methods to be unconstitutional; however, some states have limited their executions to lethal injections because this method is viewed as the most humane option (Death Penalty Information Center, 2019b). Lethal injection has not always been the preferred method of execution among death penalty states, however. Historically, death by hanging was the primary method used in the United States until the 1890s (Death Penalty Information Center, n.d.).

A **hanging** occurs when a convicted individual is blindfolded, secured, and hung by a noose around their neck and dropped through a trapdoor (Hillman, 1993). Once that individual falls through the trapdoor, their weight causes a quick neck fracture, and they die shortly after. It is estimated that an individual's heart may beat for up to 20 minutes after the drop through the trapdoor (Hillman, 1993). Notably, however, death by hanging is not usually instantaneous and can present several challenges when considering the strength of an individual's neck muscles, the depth of the drop, or incorrect positioning of the noose, which can lead to slow asphyxia or suffocation. Individuals who die by hanging often display an engorged face with their tongue hanging out. Further, the individual can display violent body movements due to reflexes in the spinal cord (Hillman, 1993). With the adoption of other means to execute people, states began to move away from hangings. The last execution by hanging in the United States occurred in Delaware in 1996, and even that hanging was only the third to have taken place since the nationwide death penalty moratorium was lifted in 1976 (Tuchman, 1996). By the end of 2018, the only state that allowed hanging as an alternative method to lethal injection was New Hampshire; this state recently declared a statewide moratorium on the death penalty, which implies that hangings will soon no longer occur there (Death Penalty Information Center, 2019b; Krupa, 2019).

Electrocution, which was first introduced in New York in 1888, became an alternative to hangings throughout the United States during the 19th century but is no longer a primary method of execution today (Death Penalty Information Center, 2019b). When a person is electrocuted, their hair is shaved off, they are blindfolded, and they are strapped several times to a chair, with a skullcap-shaped electrode attached to their scalp and forehead that is moistened with a sponge and conductive jelly to help aid the electric current. The execution team then returns to the observation room, where the executioner begins the electrocution with a power supply of between 500 and 2,000 volts. If the initial shock does not kill the person, another volt of power is given, until their heart stops beating. Reports of the aftermath of electrocutions describe the presence of various bodily fluids, including urine, vomit, and feces, as well as dislocated limbs, swelled body tissue, gouged eyeballs, and the smell of burning flesh (Hillman, 1993; Weisberg, 1991).

The **gas chamber** as a method of execution for incarcerated individuals was first introduced in Nevada in 1924. This method, which utilizes cyanide gas, involves a person being strapped to a chair in an airtight chamber that is sealed prior to the release of the lethal gas. Although this method of execution was first introduced as a humane alternative to hanging and the electric chair, there have still been many concerns. For example, there is evidence to suggest that people experience extreme pain and anxiety during the process and that the experience is similar to a heart attack. In addition, a person's skin changes color, and their eyes protrude from their head. Individuals who are executed by this means die due to a lack of oxygen to the brain (Hillman, 1993; Weisberg, 1991).

Currently, the only states to allow lethal gas as an option secondary to lethal injection are Alabama, Arizona, Mississippi, Missouri, Oklahoma, and Wyoming. California used to be among the states that permitted death by gas; however, at the time of this writing, there is currently a governor-imposed moratorium on the state (Death Penalty Information Center, 2020b). There are also several cases of individuals on death row challenging the method that will be used to execute them. For example, a recent report indicates that a quarter of individuals on death row in Alabama (51 out of 180) have chosen to die by gas rather than by lethal injection or the electric chair (Chandler, 2018). In addition, an individual on death row in Missouri recently petitioned the Supreme Court to be executed by lethal gas, but the court did not rule in his favor because he did not have sufficient evidence to prove that the state's use of lethal gas would cause him exceptional suffering due to a medical condition, and because there was no proof to support an alternative method of execution (Barnes, 2019).

The **firing squad** as a method of execution consists of a person being executed by either a single shooter or a policeman who fires from close range. Most of the time, the individual is hooded and bound to a chair that is surrounded by sandbags (to absorb blood). The range of the person's heart is identified and marked to provide a target for five shooters who are in an enclosure in proximity to the execution chair. From their position, each shooter—most of them armed with blanks—aims at the target. People who are executed by the firing squad die because of blood loss or tearing to the lungs (Hillman, 1993; Weisberg, 1991). Currently, the three states that utilize the firing squad as an alternative to lethal injection are Mississippi, Oklahoma, and Utah (Death Penalty Information Center, 2019b).

Lethal Injection

Lethal injection was introduced in Oklahoma in 1977 as a peaceful medical procedure that was less brutal than its predecessors (Crair, 2014). Since 1977, all states that utilize capital punishment have adopted lethal injection as the primary means of executing people, although some death penalty states allow secondary options such as lethal gas or electrocution. Regulations also require that federal executions utilize lethal injection as the means of execution (Death Penalty Information Center, 2019b). The process of executing an individual by this manner consists of binding them to a gurney and injecting them, usually in the arms, with two needles that dispense a chemical cocktail (Weisberg, 1991). Lethal injection causes immediate death once the person becomes unconscious, stops breathing, and experiences a heart arrhythmia from ingesting the chemicals—typically sodium thiopental (an anesthetic that causes sleep), pancuronium bromide (to paralyze muscles), and potassium chloride (to stop the heart) (Weisberg, 1991).

The process of executing someone through lethal injections is wrought with issues. For example, jurisdictions that rely on lethal injection have recently been met with the challenge of accessing the drugs needed to carry out an execution because the pharmaceutical companies that make them are becoming increasingly reluctant to provide correctional facilities with the chemicals needed to initiate death (Vivian, 2013). As a result, corrections officials have resorted to exploring nontraditional means. For example, Oklahoma, Alabama, and Mississippi have authorized nitrogen for executions despite there being no scientific data on executing people in this manner (Grady & Hoffman, 2018). In addition, Nevada recently proposed the use of fentanyl, becoming the first state to do so. The move is certainly controversial, given the opioid epidemic that is occurring in the United States (McGreal, 2018). Alcoven, the pharmaceutical company that produces the drug, filed a lawsuit against the Nevada Department of Corrections after stating that they do not condone the use of its products in state-sponsored executions (Kennedy, 2018). The case is still pending litigation, and the first execution to be implemented in this manner has been halted twice already (Ferrara, 2018).

In addition, medical doctors are not active participants in government executions because it violates their code of ethics to never do harm, which leaves correctional staff responsible. Errors often occur during lethal injections because many times, correctional staff who carry out executions are not well-trained, which can result in a botched execution. A **botched execution** occurs when an execution departs from standard protocol (Death Penalty Information Center, 2018; Sarat, 2014). Botched executions can cause the condemned individual serious pain and discomfort and can prolong the eventual death. For example, in 2006, the state of Florida executed Angel Diaz using two doses of the lethal drugs, which caused the death to take twice as long. Prior to the execution, the execution team had forcefully pushed several catheters through his veins and underlying tissue, which created large, red chemical burns on his flesh (Crair, 2014). While botched executions are rare, some states, including Florida after Diaz's botched execution, have called moratoriums on executions because of them. However, botched executions have not significantly dissuaded death penalty states because lethal injections continue to be used at both the state and federal levels (Crair, 2014). Overall, it is estimated that 3% of executions (276 out of 8,776) that took place in the United States between 1890 and 2010 resulted in botched executions, especially in cases where lethal injection was the method of execution (Sarat, 2014). Despite the challenges presented by lethal injection, some people believe that the need for capital punishment outweighs the risks.

SUPPORT FOR THE DEATH PENALTY

Public support for the death penalty has fluctuated over time, although support for capital punishment is lower at the time of this writing than it has been in recent decades (Ellsworth & Gross, 1994; McCarthy, 2018; Oliphant, 2018; Warr, 1995). The most recent Gallup Poll regarding the death penalty found that 49% of Americans believed that capital punishment was generally applied unfairly. Additionally, 29% of respondents reported that the death penalty was imposed too often (McCarthy, 2018). Still, public support for the death penalty remains high; according to the Pew Research Center, 54% of Americans favor the death penalty for people convicted of murder (Oliphant, 2018). In fact, multiple studies have found that most Americans have supported capital punishment for more than 40 years (Sethuraju et al., 2016).

Research indicates that the most common reasons why someone might support the death penalty include deterrence, retribution, crime control, incapacitation, and cost.

Retribution is the most common reason why people support capital punishment. Under this view, individuals convicted of capital offenses are viewed as deserving death because of the harm they knowingly caused with their crime (Banner, 2002; Sethuraju et al., 2016). Supporters of retribution often point to the death penalty as giving victims, families, and communities justice by condemning the offender's actions (Berns, 1979). Supporters also argue that a convicted individual's punishment should be proportionate to the harm they inflicted. This concept, **just deserts** (previously discussed in Chapter 1), suggests that death is an appropriate consequence when someone has willfully taken the life of another. Proponents also note that the death penalty is effective at deterring others from committing future crimes and that execution is a more effective deterrent than life imprisonment (Ellsworth & Gross, 1994; Whitehead & Blankenship, 2000).

Supporters of capital punishment also maintain that the death penalty is an effective way to rid society of criminals because individuals who are executed can no longer pose harm to others. Some people also argue that the only way to stop a person from murdering again is to execute them (Whitehead & Blankenship, 2000). Certainly, **incapacitation** prevents individuals who are convicted of capital offenses from committing future crimes because they are physically prevented from doing so. However, some people believe that not everyone who is sentenced to life imprisonment will serve their full sentence, which, to supporters, warrants death further (Ellsworth & Gross, 1994).

More recently, it has been suggested that capital punishment be utilized more often as an option for punishment because it can be useful in plea bargaining and help to speed up the administration of justice (Blecker, 2013, 2014). Overall, it is estimated that 90% of defendants in felony cases plead guilty to a lesser charge after waiving their right to trail and accepting a plea bargain (Ehrhard, 2008). To death penalty supporters, the plea-bargaining process benefits society in terms of cost, efficiency, and certainty of punishment, all of which serve as a foundation to the criminal justice system's crime control model (Bibas, 2003; Packer, 1968).

OPPOSITION TO THE DEATH PENALTY

Like their counterparts, opponents of capital punishment list various reasons why they do not agree with this practice. While the criminal justice system historically used the death penalty to protect communities, the advances in the management of correctional institutions in the United States undermine the argument that capital punishment controls offenders in that manner (Acker, 2003). Additionally, several studies suggest that the death penalty is not any more effective at deterring crime than other punishments (Acker, 2003; Bailey & Peterson, 1994; Bohm, 1999; Peterson & Bailey, 1998). In addition, FBI data indicates that death penalty states have had homicide rates at, or slightly below, the national rate (Amnesty International, 2011).

Opponents of the death penalty also argue that many crimes, including murder, are committed impulsively, meaning that not all offenses are the result of a rational thought process. Given the significant finality and exuberant cost of the death penalty, opponents uphold that there must be a clear reason why capital punishment is a better alternative than life imprisonment (Acker, 2003; Zeisel, 1977). Relatedly, opponents note that capital punishment can never be consensual or voluntary because mental illness, the barbaric conditions of isolated confinement, and the bleak prospects of appeals or parole can lead people to drop their right to appeal or overturn their own death sentence. Overall, it is estimated that 11% of all executions since 1977 were "voluntary" (Amnesty International, 2011; *Whitmore v. Arkansas*, 1990).

Human rights violations are considered primary reasons why the death penalty should be condemned and abolished. During the 1980s, the abolitionist movement gained momentum when international treaties were drafted to cease the use of capital punishment. Since then, countries have moved to abolish the practice because it violates an individual's right to life as outlined in the Universal Declaration of Human Rights and because it is inhumane and irreversible (Anckar, 2014; National Research Council, 2012; United Nations, 2015). Morality has also been a prevalent reason why some oppose capital punishment. That is, many people view the death penalty as immoral or wrong and do not believe that the state is justified in killing a person and/or believe that a higher power overrides the state's authority to do so (Ellsworth & Gross, 1994; Sethuraju et al., 2016). Opponents also argue that the federal death penalty is arbitrary and overreaching because it can be used in any U.S. state or territory (Amnesty International, 2011).

Capital punishment has also been met with much criticism regarding discriminatory treatment toward people of color and the poor, and regarding how the practice may encourage a culture of violence (ACLU, 2012; Amnesty International, 2011). A large amount of research indicates that historically, the death penalty in the United States, particularly in Southern states, is connected to racial oppression and has been used disproportionately with people of color (Acker, 2003; Baldus & Woodworth, 1998; Cohen & Smith, 2010; Pierce & Radelet, 2002; Sorensen et al., 2001). For example, studies have found that of the 771 executions of people convicted for rape between 1870 and 1950, of those with a known race, 701 people were Black. In addition, since 1977, most individuals who have been executed have been convicted for killing White victims, even though African Americans comprise about half of homicide victims. A non-partisan report written in 1990 also concluded that a defendant was more likely to be sentenced to death if the victim was White. Since this report, several additional reports have been published that also conclude that the death penalty is racially biased. Unsurprisingly, capital punishment is viewed by opponents as a systemic way of maintaining social control over people of color (Amnesty International, 2011; Banner, 2002).

Opponents of capital punishment also express concern about innocent people being executed (Sethuraju et al., 2016). Their apprehension warrants notice, as innocent people have been executed in the past. One study found that between the years 1900 and 1985, 350 innocent people were sentenced to death in the United States, and 23 were executed (Bedau & Radelet, 1987). Additional research found that between 1973 and 2014, more than 155 people were exonerated and released from death row because of doubts about their guilt (Sethuraju et al., 2016).

CONTEMPORARY ISSUES IN CAPITAL PUNISHMENT

Without doubt, the use of the death penalty in the United States has been presented with a plethora of challenges, and it will continue to be challenged in the future. One of the major present concerns is the cost of executing someone (ACLU of Northern California, 2009). Contrary to popular belief, it is more costly to execute a person than it is to incarcerate them for the rest of their life (Ellsworth & Ross, 1983; Lambert & Clarke, 2004; Roman et al., 2008). The greatest cost of death penalty cases is accrued prior to and during trial, not necessarily in post-conviction proceedings, so even if appeals were eliminated, capital cases would still be more expensive than alternative sentences. California, which currently has a governor-imposed moratorium on the death penalty, is saving the state millions of dollars by not utilizing capital punishment. In 2008, it was estimated that the criminal justice system nationwide was spending $137 million per year, whereas a system without the death penalty would cost around $11.5 million. Accordingly, death penalty opponents believe that resources should be allocated to crime prevention, education, rehabilitation, mental health and drug treatment, and victim compensation rather than to capital punishment (Amnesty International, 2011).

America's death row population is pointedly aging. In 2005, a record number of people who were over the age of 60 were incarcerated on death row. As such, criminal justice reformers have begun to challenge capital proceedings for geriatric individuals who are awaiting executions for crimes that were committed much earlier in their lives (Death Penalty Information Center, 2019c). Ultimately, it is the lengthy appeals process that contributes significantly to the length of time between a conviction and an eventual execution (Rapaport, 2012). In one case in 2004, Alabama executed the oldest person in decades, 74-year-old J. B. Hubbard, an alarming 27 years after his conviction for homicide. Leading up to the execution, Hubbard was very frail, and he suffered from several ailments including dementia, hepatitis, and emphysema. Many people argue that the sentence itself was cruel because it had taken so long to execute

Hubbard, due to many appeals that had taken place over the years (Roig-Franzia, 2004). Certainly, these issues are worth noting, so that this type of harm is prevented and alleviated.

CONCLUSION

As this chapter has discussed, capital punishment presents unique challenges for society. Indeed, citizens are emotionally invested in the issue, and the issue continues to present unexpected developments (McGowen, 2011). Accordingly, the death penalty has given cause to both proponents and opponents alike. Historically, the death penalty has gone through various renditions and challenges, each shedding light on areas in need of reform or elimination. Time will tell whether the United States will continue to utilize capital punishment; however, considering the obvious issues of cost-ineffectiveness, access to lethal injection drugs, and human rights violations, the death penalty will likely continue to be at the forefront of controversial issues in the criminal justice system for the foreseeable future.

DISCUSSION QUESTIONS

1. Do you support the death penalty? Why or why not?
2. In your opinion, can the death penalty be implemented humanely? What methods would you suggest for achieving this ideal?
3. Do you predict that states and the Federal Government will continue to utilize capital punishment in the future? Explain your reasoning.

APPLICATION EXERCISES

Exercise #1: State Utilization of the Death Penalty

Using Tables 14.3. select one death penalty state from the list. Then, conduct state-specific research that addresses the following information:

- When was the death penalty first reinstated?
- How many people are on death row?
- How many men are on death row? How many women are on death row?
- How many executions have occurred in the state during the past ten years?
- What is the total number of executions that have occurred in the state since the death penalty was reinstated?
- What is the racial breakdown for those currently on the state's death row? What about those who have been executed?
- What is(are) the state's method(s) of execution?

Then, compare your state findings to others in the class. What patterns have you observed in your data? What sources did you use to find this information?

Exercise #2: Utilizing Death Penalty Websites

Various websites offer a wealth of knowledge regarding the death penalty. Utilize these sources to organize supplemental activities, including data analytics, presentations, debates, and research projects:

- Death Penalty Information Center (www.deathpenaltyinfo.org) — The DPIC is a non-profit organization that disseminates studies and reports about the death penalty and analyzes annual trends and developments in relation to U.S. policy and the use of capital punishment.
- The Marshall Project's *The Next to Die: Watching Death Row* (www.themarshallproject. org/next-to-die.com) — The Marshall Project, which takes an impartial stance on the death penalty, uses live tracking of scheduled executions in the United States. In addition, *The Next to Die* features recent updates of death penalty news and includes a history and past and scheduled executions for death penalty states.
- The Innocence Project (www.innocenceproject.org/) — The Innocence Project aims to exonerate the wrongly convicted through DNA testing and pass laws and implement policies to reform the criminal justice system. To help combat future injustices, this organization offers legal representation to the wrongly convicted and provides support for exonerees post-release. The organization's website also features an interactive map of innocence network member organizations from around the world.

REFERENCES

Acker, J. (2002). Capital crimes. In D. Levinson (Ed.), *Encyclopedia of crime and punishment* (Vol. 1, pp. 152–158). Sage Publications.

Acker, J. (2003). The death penalty: An American history. *Contemporary Justice Review, 6*(2), 169–186.

American Civil Liberties Union. (2012). *The case against the death penalty.* https://www.aclu.org/other/case-against-death-penalty

American Civil Liberties Union of Northern California. (2009). *The hidden death tax: The secret cost of seeking execution in California.* https://www.aclunc.org/sites/default/files/asset_upload_file358_8069.pdf

Amnesty International. (2018). *Amnesty International global report: Death sentences and executions 2017.* https://www.amnesty.org/download/Documents/ACT5079552018ENGLISH.PDF

Amnesty International. (2020). *Amnesty International global report: Death sentences and executions 2019*. https://www.amnesty.org/download/Documents/ACT5018472020ENGLISH.PDF

Amnesty International. (n.d.). *Death Penalty*. https://www.amnesty.org/en/what-we-do/death-penalty/

Anckar, C. (2014). Why countries choose the death penalty. *Brown Journal of World Affairs, 21*(1), 7–25.

Atkins v. Virginia, 536 U.S. 304 (2002)

Bailey, W. C., & Peterson, R. (1994). Murder, capital punishment and deterrence: A review of the evidence and an examination of police killings. *Journal of Social Issues, 50,* 53–74.

Baker, D. V. (2016). *Women and capital punishment in the United States: An analytical history.* MacFarland.

Baldus, D. C., & Woodworth, G. (1998). Race discrimination and the death penalty: An empirical and legal overview. In J. R. Acker, R. M. Bohm, and C. S. Lanier (Eds.), *America's experiment with capital punishment: Reflections on the past, present, and future of the ultimate penal sanction* (pp. 385–415). Carolina Academic Press.

Banner, S. (2002). *The death penalty: An American history.* Harvard University Press.

Barnes, R. (2019, April 1). *Divided Supreme Court rules against death-row inmate with rare condition.* Washington Post. https://www.washingtonpost.com/politics/courts_law/divided-supreme-court-rules-against-death-row-inmate-with-rare-condition/2019/04/01/ff523f-dc-5489-11e9-8ef3-fbd41a2ce4d5_story.html?utm_term=.60b5cdaeb000

Beccaria, C. (1764). *Essay on crimes and punishments.*

Bedau, H. A., & Radelet, M. L. (1987). Miscarriages of justice in potentially capital cases. *Stanford Law Review, 40,* 21–173.

Berns, W. (1979). *For capital punishment: Crime and the morality of the death penalty.* Basic Books.

Bibas, S. (2003). Harmonizing substantive-criminal-law values and criminal procedure: The case of Alford and Nolo Contendere pleas. *Cornell Law Review, 88,* 1361.

Bienen, L. B. (2010). *Murder and its consequences: Essays on capital punishment.* Northwestern University Press.

Blecker, R. (2013). *The death of punishment: Searching for justice among the worst of the worst.* Palgrave Macmillan.

Blecker, R. (2014, April 6). *The death penalty needs to be an option for punishment.* The New York Times. https://www.nytimes.com/roomfordebate/2014/04/06/what-it-means-if-the-death-penalty-is-dying/the-death-penalty-needs-to-be-an-option-for-punishment

Bohm, R. M. (1999). *Deathquest: An introduction to the theory and practice of capital punishment in the United States.* Anderson Publishing Co.

Bye, R. T. (1926). Recent history and present status of capital punishment in the United States. *Journal of Criminal Law and Criminology, 17,* 234–245.

Chandler, K. (2018, August 25). *Lethal injection or gas? Alabama inmates choose.* Associated Press. https://www.al.com/news/2018/08/lethal_injection_or_gas_alabam.html

Cohen, G. B., & Smith, R. J. (2010). The racial geography of the federal death penalty. *Washington Law Review, 85*(425), 425–492.

Crair, B. (2014, May 29). *Photos from a botched lethal injection.* The New Republic. https://newrepublic.com/article/117898/lethal-injection-photos-angel-diazs-botched-execution-florida

Davis, E., & Snell, T. J. (2018). *Capital punishment, 2016—statistical tables.* U.S. Department of Justice, Office of Justice Programs, Bureau of Justice Statistics. https://www.bjs.gov/index.cfm?ty=pbdetail&iid=6246

Death Penalty Information Center. (n.d.). *Lethal injection.* https://deathpenaltyinfo.org/lethal-injection

Death Penalty Information Center. (n.d.). *The history of the death penalty: A timeline.* https://deathpenaltyinfo.org/stories/history-of-the-death-penalty-timeline

Death Penalty Information Center. (2018). *Botched executions.* https://deathpenaltyinfo.org/some-examples-post-furman-botched-executions

Death Penalty Information Center. (2019a). *Federal death penalty.* https://deathpenaltyinfo.org/federal-death-penalty

Death Penalty Information Center. (2019b). *Methods of execution.* https://deathpenaltyinfo.org/methods-execution

Death Penalty Information Center. (2019c). *Time on death row.* https://deathpenaltyinfo.org/time-death-row

Death Penalty Information Center. (2020a). *Colorado becomes 22nd state to abolish death penalty.* https://deathpenaltyinfo.org/news/colorado-becomes-22nd-state-to-abolish-death-penalty

Death Penalty Information Center. (2020b). *Facts about the death penalty.* https://deathpenaltyinfo.org/documents/FactSheet.pdf

Death Penalty Information Center. (2020c). *State by state.* https://deathpenaltyinfo.org/state-and-federal-info/state-by-state

Death Penalty Information Center. (2020d). *States with and without the death penalty - 2020.* https://deathpenaltyinfo.org/states-and-without-death-penalty

Death Penalty Information Center. (2020e). *Utah reaches ten years with no executions.* https://deathpenaltyinfo.org/news/utah-reaches-ten-years-with-no-executions

Ehrhard, S. (2008). Plea bargaining and the death penalty: An exploratory study. *The Justice System Journal, 29*(3), 313–325.

Eleftherious-Smith, L. (2014, December 18). *George Stinney Jr: Black 14-year-old boy exonerated 70 years after he was executed.* Independent. https://www.independent.co.uk/news/world/americas/george-stinney-jr-black-14-year-old-boy-exonerated-70-years-after-he-was-executed-9932429.html

Ellsworth, P. C., & Gross, S. R. (1994). Hardening of the attitudes: Americans' views on the death penalty. *Journal of Social Issues, 50,* 19–52.

Ellsworth, P. C., & Ross, L. (1983). Public opinion and capital punishment: A close examination of the views of abolitionists and retentionists. *Crime & Delinquency, 29*, 116–169.

Federal Bureau of Prisons. (n.d.a). *USP Florence Admax.* U.S. Department of Justice. https://www.bop.gov/locations/institutions/flm/

Federal Bureau of Prisons. (n.d.b). *USP Terre Haute.* U.S. Department of Justice. https://www.bop.gov/locations/institutions/thp/

Ferrara, D. (2018, September 28). *Judge stops Nevada from using drug in execution.* Las Vegas Review-Journal. https://www.reviewjournal.com/crime/courts/judge-stops-nevada-from-using-drug-in-execution/

Ford v. Wainwright, 477 U.S. 399, (1986)

Foster v. Florida, 537 U.S. 990, (2002)

Furman v. Georgia, 408 U.S. 238, (1972)

Godfrey V. Georgia, 446 U.S. 420 (1980)

Grady, D., & Hoffman, J. (2018, May 7). *States turn to an unproven method of execution: Nitrogen gas.* New York Times. https://www.nytimes.com/2018/05/07/health/death-penalty-nitrogen-executions.html

Gregg v. Georgia, 428 U.S. 153 (1976)

Higgins, T. (2019, July 25). *Attorney General William Barr orders first federal executions in nearly two decades.* CNBC. https://www.cnbc.com/2019/07/25/william-barr-orders-first-federal-executions-in-nearly-two-decades.html

Hillman, H. (1993). The possible pain experienced during executions by different methods. *Perception, 22*(6), 745–753.

H.R. 5582—100th Congress: Anti-Drug Abuse Act of 1988.

Jacobs, S. (2017, January 11). *What 17 death-row inmates requested for their last meal.* Business Insider. https://www.businessinsider.com/the-last-meals-of-17-death-row-inmates-2017-1

Jeffrey, S. (2001, June 11). *McVeigh executed.* The Guardian. https://www.theguardian.com/world/2001/jun/11/mcveigh.usa

Kamin, S., & Pokorak, J. J. (2005). Death qualification and true bifurcation: Building on the Massachusetts governor's council's work. *Indiana Law Journal, 80*(1), 131–152.

Karlsen, C. F. (1998). *The devil in the shape of a woman: Witchcraft in colonial New England.* W.W. Norton & Company.

Kaufman-Osborn, T. V. (2008). Proportionality review and the death penalty. *The Justice System Journal, 29*(3), 257–272.

Kennedy, M. (2018). *Nevada postpones planned execution using fentanyl.* National Public Radio, Inc. https://www.npr.org/2018/07/11/628050984/nevada-postpones-planned-execution-using-fentanyl

Kennedy v. Louisiana, 554 U.S. 407 (2008)

Kirby, J. (2014, May 16). *Photos: A haunting look at America's execution chambers.* New York Magazine. http://nymag.com/intelligencer/2014/05/haunting-photos-of-us-death-chambers.html

Knight, M. (2016, October 15). *Capital punishment—procedures and appeals for death penalty cases.* Sidebar Saturdays. https://www.sidebarsaturdays.com/2016/10/15/httpwp-mep7vddb-mo/

Kronenwetter, M. (2001). *Capital punishment: A reference handbook* (2nd ed.). ABC-CLIO.

Krupa, C. (2019, May 30). *New Hampshire abolishes the death penalty as lawmakers override governor's veto.* National Public Radio. https://www.npr.org/2019/05/30/728288240/new-hampshire-abolishes-death-penalty-as-lawmakers-override-governors-veto

Lambert, E., & Clarke, A. (2004). Crime, capital punishment, and knowledge: Are criminal justice majors better informed than other majors about crime and capital punishment? *The Social Science Journal, 4,* 53–66.

Lewis, A. (1987, April 28). *Abroad at home; Bowing to racism.* The New York Times. https://www.nytimes.com/1987/04/28/opinion/abroad-at-home-bowing-to-racism.html

Mandery, E. J. (2005). *Capital punishment: A balanced examination.* Jones and Bartlett.

Marciniak, L. M. (2016). *Sentencing and modern reform: The process of punishment.* Carolina Academic Press.

Marshall, J. (2008, April 4). *Lisa Montgomery gets death penalty for killing pregnant woman.* Southeast Missourian. https://www.semissourian.com/story/1323151.html

May, K. (1988, November 19). *Reagan signs broad 'sword and shield' anti-drug law: Casual users face stiff fines; kingpins could get the death penalty.* Los Angeles Times. https://www.latimes.com/archives/la-xpm-1988-11-19-mn-388-story.html

McCarthy, J. (2018). *New low of 49% in U.S. say death penalty applied fairly.* Gallup. https://news.gallup.com/poll/243794/new-low-say-death-penalty-applied-fairly.aspx

McCleskey v. Kemp, 481 U.S. 279 (1987)

McGowen, R. (2011). Getting the question right? Ways of thinking about the death penalty. In D. Garland, R. McGowen, and M. Meranze (Eds.), *America's death penalty: Between past and present* (pp. 1–29). New York University Press.

McGreal, C. (2018). *Nevada to become first state to execute inmate with fentanyl.* The Guardian. https://www.theguardian.com/us-news/2018/jul/10/nevada-fentanyl-execution-opioid-crisis-drug-death-row

Medley, Petitioner, 134 U.S. 160 (1890)

National Research Council. (2012). *Deterrence and the death penalty.* The National Academies Press.

Neklason, A. (2019, June 14). *The 'Death Penalty's Dred Scott' lives on.* The Atlantic. https://www.theatlantic.com/politics/archive/2019/06/legacy-mccleskey-v-kemp/591424/

Oliphant, J. B. (2018). *Public support for the death penalty ticks up.* Pew Research Center. https://www.pewresearch.org/fact-tank/2018/06/11/us-support-for-death-penalty-ticks-up-2018/

Packer, H. (1968). *The limits of the criminal sanction.* Stanford University Press.

Peterson, R., & Bailey, W. C. (1998). Is capital punishment an effective deterrent for murder? In J. R. Acker, R. M. Bohm, & C. S. Lanier (Eds.), *America's experiment with capital punishment:*

Reflections on the past, present, and future of the ultimate penal sanction (pp. 157–182). Carolina Academic Press.

Pierce, G. L., & Radelet, M. L. (2002). Race, region, and death sentencing in Illinois 1988–1997. *Oregon Law Review, 81*, 39–96.

Pojman, L., & Reiman, J. (1995). *The death penalty: For and against.* Rowman & Littlefield.

Rapaport, E. (2012). A modest proposal: The aged of death row should be deemed too old to execute. *Brooklyn Law Review, 77*(3), 1089–1132.

Roig-Franzia, M. (2004, August 6). *Execution of man who was sick, frail sets off controversy: At 74, he was oldest put to death in decades.* SF Gate. https://www.sfgate.com/news/article/Execution-of-man-who-was-sick-frail-sets-off-2703558.php

Roman, J., Chalfin, A., Sundquist, A., Knight, C., & Darmenov, A. (2008). *The cost of the death penalty in Maryland.* Urban Institute Justice Policy Center.

Roper v. Simmons, 543 U.S. 551 (2005)

Rothman, D. J. (1971). *The discovery of the asylum: Social order and disorder in the new republic.* Little, Brown and Co.

Sarat, A. (2014). *Gruesome spectacles: Botched executions and America's death penalty.* Stanford University Press.

Sethuraju, R., Sole, J., & Oliver, B. E. (2016). Understanding death penalty support and opposition among criminal justice and law enforcement students. *SAGE Open*, 1–5.

Smith, A. (2008). The anatomy of death row syndrome and volunteering for execution. *Boston University Public Interest Law Journal, 17*(237), 1–20.

Snell, T. J. (2011). *Capital punishment, 2010—statistical tables.* U.S. Department of Justice, Office of Justice Programs, Bureau of Justice Statistics. https://www.bjs.gov/content/pub/pdf/cp10st.pdf

Snell, T. J. (2020). *Capital punishment, 2018—statistical tables.* U.S. Department of Justice, Office of Justice Programs, Bureau of Justice Statistics. https://www.bjs.gov/content/pub/pdf/cp18st.pdf

Sorensen, J., Wallace, D. H., & Pilgrim, R. L. (2001). Empirical studies on race and death penalty sentencing: A decade after the GAO report. *Criminal Law Bulletin, 37*, 395–408.

Stanford v. Kentucky, 492 U.S. 361 (1989)

Stiles, B. (2015, March 25). *Judge: Triple killer Edwards of Fayette County ineligible for death penalty.* Tribune Review. https://archive.triblive.com/news/judge-triple-killer-edwards-of-fayette-county-ineligible-for-death-penalty/

Streib, V. L. (1987). *Death penalty for juveniles.* Indiana University Press.

Tarm, M. (2021, February 7). *Big challenge: Biden is pressed to end federal death penalty.* AP News. https://apnews.com/article/joe-biden-us-news-pandemics-health-coronavirus-pandemic-ad-6b1681aaf4128aa5e3ca0e94672e45

Tarm, M., & Kunzelman, M. (2021, January 15). *Trump administration carries out 13th and final execution.* AP News. https://apnews.com/article/donald-trump-wildlife-coronavirus-pandemic-crime-terre-haute-28e44cc5c026dc16472751bbde0ead50

Tuchman, G. (1996, January 25). *Delaware holds first hanging since 1946.* CNN. http://www.cnn.com/US/9601/hanging/

United States Courts. (n.d.). *Supreme Court procedures.* https://www.uscourts.gov/about-federal-courts/educational-resources/about-educational-outreach/activity-resources/supreme-1

United Nations. (2015). *Universal declaration of human rights.* https://www.un.org/en/udhrbook/pdf/udhr_booklet_en_web.pdf

Vivian, J. C. (2013, October 18). *Lethal injections, drug shortages, and pharmacy ethics.* U.S. Pharmacist. https://www.uspharmacist.com/article/lethal-injections-drug-shortages-and-pharmacy-ethics-44470

Warr, M. (1995). Poll trends: Public opinion on crime and punishment. *The Public Opinion Quarterly, 59*(2), 296–310.

Weisberg, J. (1991). This is your death. *The New Republic,* 23–27.

Whitehead, J. T., & Blankenship, M. B. (2000). The gender gap in capital punishment attitudes: An analysis of support and opposition. *American Journal of Criminal Justice, 26,* 1245–1270.

Whitmore v. Arkansas, 495 U.S. 149 (1990)

Zeisel, H. (1977). The deterrent effect of the death penalty: Facts v. faith. In P. B. Kurland (Ed.), *The Supreme Court review, 1976* (pp. 317–343). The University of Chicago Press.

CHAPTER 15

The Prison Industrial Complex and Corrections Privatization

CHAPTER OBJECTIVES

After reading this chapter, you should be able to:

- Describe the historical and modern development of corrections privatization.
- Define the prison industrial complex and explain how it operates.
- Discuss the ethical and practical issues related to corrections privatization.

KEY WORDS

Public corrections

Prison privatization

Corrections privatization

Indenturing

Prison industrial complex

Non-governmental organizations (NGOs)

Reconstruction Era (1865–1877)

Convict leasing

Jim Crow laws

CoreCivic

GEO Group

Management and Training Corporation

The Day 1 Alliance

CASE STUDY: GLOBAL TEL LINK

Global Tel Link, now known as GTL, is the nation's largest provider of telecommunication systems inside prisons and jails throughout the country (Wagner, 2017). Aside from covering the technical aspects of telephone and tablet communication, GTL also reportedly serves the moral good by giving "incarcerated individuals the ability to stay engaged with their support networks by making meaningful connections through our products and services" (GTL, 2021). The need for individuals who are incarcerated to maintain contact with their support networks, as suggested by GTL, is arguably one of the most important factors related to a person's ability to serve time well, and to remain free of criminality once they reenter society.

While GTL's stated mission may be admirable, there is concern over how the company has delivered on that mission. GTL has been the target of numerous lawsuits by incarcerated persons claiming that the prices charged for calls are predatory in nature. In 2016, a federal judge approved a settlement in a class-action lawsuit filed by individuals incarcerated in the state of New Jersey from 2006–2016. GTL was ordered to pay $25 million in the settlement, as "the court found GTL guilty of receiving kickbacks from overly inflated prices, charging its prisoner customers as much as 100 times the going rate for a call" (Prison Legal News, 2021). As of April 2021, GTL is facing another class action lawsuit from inmates in Georgia prisons alleging similar treatment (Prison Legal News, 2021).

Questions for Discussion

1. Why do you think communicating with loved ones and having support networks are such an important part of a person's rehabilitation?
2. Should services like telephone calls or virtual visitations be paid for by taxpayer dollars or by individuals who are incarcerated? Please explain your answer.

INTRODUCTION

The responsibility of correcting criminal behavior has traditionally fallen upon formal governmental institutions. **Public corrections** refers to systems in which local, state, and federal governmental agencies are granted custodial authority over individuals who are convicted of crimes. The system of public corrections most notably includes the use of public prisons, which are funded and staffed using taxpayer dollars. Throughout America's history, public prisons have been the dominant model of institutions used for the incapacitation of individuals accused or convicted of a crime. However, the reliance on incarceration as a primary form of punishment would inevitably allow for the expansion of the private sector into correctional systems.

The system of **prison privatization**, in which private or publicly traded companies are given custodial authority over individuals and services within a prison system, is not exactly a new system, but it has seen a resurgence since the 1980s. The increasing usage of private prisons over the last 4 decades, and the push for institutional reform at all levels of the criminal justice system, have catapulted private correctional facilities into the national spotlight in recent years. Questions have arisen regarding the legality of private institutions and the ethical implications of privatizing correctional systems that take control over human beings and their freedom. Prison privatization has become the catch-all phrase for any element of correctional privatization. This singular focus on for-profit prisons has let other forms of privatization operate without the same level of scrutiny (Mears & Montes, 2019).

There are really two main issues that arise in attempts to understand the privatization of corrections. The first is the scope of privatization at all levels of corrections. Members of the public, and even criminal justice researchers, often have a very narrow view of what privatization means in the correctional system and therefore limit their discussions to private prisons owned by large corporations. The second issue is the ethical concerns that present themselves when corporations, or even private individuals, profit off of crime and criminals by privatizing their punishment and rehabilitation. These two issues prevent the American public, and subsequently legislators, from making informed and accurate decisions as to the appropriateness of utilizing privatized services and facilities within corrections.

This chapter examines the meaning of corrections privatization, the incorporation of privatization into every aspect of correctional operations, the historical development and modern forms of privatization, and the ethical and practical implications that drive the continued debate about privatization. This chapter also explores how major corporations have become some of the most powerful voices in the arena of correctional policy and practice.

CORRECTIONS PRIVATIZATION AND THE PRISON INDUSTRIAL COMPLEX

Corrections privatization encompasses not only prisons that are privately owned and operated, but also any element of the correctional system that is transferred to private control. For example, food, communication, mental health, healthcare, rehabilitative services or programs, and community corrections services like probation and parole are just some of the fundamental aspects of correctional operations that may be handled partly or entirely by private, often for-profit, entities. When a correctional system is examined holistically, private industry can be found in every aspect of it, from the building of a facility to the release of a person into private care and everywhere in between.

The push for privatization has been driven by the idea that the privatization of corrective services, and entire correctional facilities, should be taken from the clunky, bureaucratically tied hands of governments and given to private entities who can streamline processes and increase efficiency, all while decreasing cost to taxpayers (Morris, 2007; Mumford et al., 2016). This is also where much of the debate about corrections privatization comes from: for-profit companies claiming cost-saving efficiency measures. The argument itself seems counterintuitive, but it has made states and the Federal Government buy in, at least in part, to the sales pitch of the private sector.

Possibly the most recognizable form of corrections privatization is the labor that is performed by incarcerated individuals for large corporations, and for pennies on the dollar. These corporate schemes are examples of **indenturing**, or the act of binding laborers—in this case, individuals convicted of crimes—to jobs with little to no pay. This is also the type of privatization that has been popularized by entertainment media for decades and has more recently been shown in series like *Orange Is the New Black*. Therefore, even public prisons and jails can have a variety of privatized elements within them without being fully owned or leased by a private company.

Over time, correctional systems across the country have begun to privatize a number of their services including "Health care, education, mental health, supervision, transportation, and training" (Latessa & Brusman Lovins, 2019, p. 324). Thousands of companies, both public and private, maintain active contracts with criminal justice systems throughout all levels of government (Worth Rises, 2020b). The thread that connects them all is the profit gained from one of society's most vulnerable populations. Consequently, the merging of corporate interests from the private sector, and public safety and policy in the public sector, create what has become popularly known as the **"prison industrial complex"** (Davis, 1998; Schlosser, 1998).

The prison industrial complex (PIC) is a concept introduced by Angela Davis, famed political activist and scholar, in the late 1990s to describe the relationship that exists between the private sector and criminal justice policy-making, which Davis compared to the relationship seen in the military industrial complex. Davis (1998) notes that the "dividends [profit] that accrue from investment in the punishment industry, like those that accrue from investment in weapons production, only amount to social destruction" (para. 3). Davis (1998) was one of the first to identify the pitfalls of corrections privatization and the impact of America's infatuation with incarceration on the social fabric of society. She argued that the penal system as a whole "devours the social wealth" that could be used to provide crucial services to the public like education and free drug rehabilitation programs (para. 17). More importantly, she recognized early on that this was a concerted effort to further engrain racism within our structural systems.

Davis's concept of the PIC was taken up and further detailed by prominent American journalist Eric Schlosser in an article for *The Atlantic* written later the same year. Schlosser (1998) begins by examining the rapid expansion and eventual privatization of California's Department of Corrections, or what he referred to at the time as "the biggest prison system in the Western industrialized world" (para. 3). He then describes how the PIC supports the interests of both dominant political parties and how its proponents enlist the fear of crime to strengthen political support and economic gain, particularly in poverty-stricken, rural America:

> Three decades after the war on crime began, the United States has developed a prison-industrial complex—a set of bureaucratic, political, and economic interests that encourage increased spending on imprisonment, regardless of the actual need. The prison-industrial complex is not a conspiracy, guiding the nation's criminal-justice policy behind closed doors. It is a confluence of special interests that has given prison construction in the United States a seemingly unstoppable momentum. It is composed of politicians, both liberal and conservative, who have used the fear of crime to gain votes; impoverished rural areas where prisons have become a cornerstone of economic development; private companies that regard the roughly $35 billion spent each year on corrections not as a burden on American taxpayers but as a lucrative market; and government officials whose fiefdoms have expanded along with the inmate population. (para. 7)

The realities of a move toward privatization laid out in these early accounts of the PIC proved to be correct. Davis (1998) and Schlosser (1998) believed that this was just the beginning of a movement that would see increasing reliance on the private sector as a means of public control. As we moved into the 21st century and began to see the fallout from decades of the War on Drugs, privatization became, and continues to be, a means to an end. Rather than relying on the government to control punishment and rehabilitation, we have allowed private expansion into the public sector of corrections with limited oversight. Currently, only a small portion of convicted individuals are housed at privately run prison facilities, yet the reaches of corrections privatization, and the PIC, are far and wide.

The Vast Reaches of Corrections Privatization

Private prisons and private prison labor can conjure mental images of greed-driven corporations who will do anything to ensure the profitability of their companies. This may be true for some prisons that are being run privately; however, corporations are not the only ones benefitting from the business of warehousing and indenturing criminal offenders. Criminal warehousing is propelled by increasingly longer sentence lengths. Local jails also contract with their state or federal counterparts to warehouse percentages of their inmate populations, thereby creating a direct budget line that is dependent upon the income gained by keeping jail beds full (Wagner, 2016). As Wagner points out:

> Nationally in 2014, 5.2% of those sentenced to prison were placed in county jails under contracts between state prison officials and local jails (compared to 8.4% with private prisons) … In 2014, a whopping 51% of Louisiana's state prison population was imprisoned in local jails. Or to say it another way, 75% of the jail cells in Louisiana parish (county) jails are used not for people serving jail sentences but are instead rented out to the state. (2016, para. 2)

What makes this a form of privatization is the profit gained by local jails entering into these contracts. Many jails would not be able to maintain their operations without the added revenue from state and federal inmates.

Making things more complicated are non-profit organizations, or **non-governmental organizations (NGOs)**, which have long been a part of the privatization of corrections as well. As their designation suggests, these organizations have no governmental affiliation and are typically not funded directly through taxpayers. NGOs provide services within correctional facilities like rehabilitation and drug and alcohol programs, among many others. Similar to privatized juvenile facilities or halfway houses, these NGOs are generally not the types of privatized services that catch the attention of progressive prison reform efforts. While they are unlike for-profit companies in that the *goal* of NGOs may not be to generate profit, even a non-profit organization needs to create revenue in order to continue providing their services and to remain in business, raising similar ethical concerns to those that arise with fully privatized services (Latessa & Brusman Lovins, 2019).

Prominent among the most recent and visible forms of corrections privatization are privatized immigration detention facilities. These facilities, which are owned and operated by many of the same companies that run private prison facilities, have gained the attention of the national media and criminal justice reform advocates alike. In 2019, the U.S. Immigration and Customs Enforcement (ICE) agency had an average daily population of 50,165. This figure "measures the number of individuals in ICE custody on an average day during the fiscal year" and shows "an increase of 19 percent compared to [Fiscal Year] 2018" (ICE, 2019, p. 5). Approximately 70% of those held by the federal government in immigration detention facilities at that time were in facilities run by private companies (Kassie, 2019). These facilities have come under fire, as federal immigration policy under former President Trump made extensive use of detention, including the separation of migrant children from their parents.

Juvenile facilities and services constitute another area of privatization that has largely been ignored in criminological research. Privatized juvenile corrections mirror much of what is seen in the adult system. Private companies, in some cases the same companies that own and operate adult facilities and services, provide custodial authority, rehabilitative programming, and other needed services for adjudicated delinquents. As of 2017, a total of 43,580 juveniles were being housed in residential facilities; however, less than 10% of juveniles (or 4,242) were detained in private residential facilities across the United States (Sickmund et al., 2019). Juvenile facilities pose unique challenges for privatization. Rehabilitative services and treatment are core functions of the juvenile justice system, and it is possible that those systems of care are harder to maintain without direct governmental oversight.

As discussed in Chapter 3, the majority of Americans under correctional supervision are not those who are in prisons or jails, but those who are within the system of community corrections. Privatization has permeated every community correctional option there is, which can include everything from coordinating the physical custody of a person to securing mental, behavioral, and emotional support services that aid in the prevention of recidivism. With over 4.5 million Americans under some form of community supervision, there seems to be more consensus, and less concern, about the privatization of these services that operate privately outside of prisons and jails (Latessa & Brusman Lovins, 2019).

What is clear is that corrections privatization comes in various shapes and sizes and that understanding the true scope of privatization is nearly an impossible task. This contributes to concerns that the full extent of privatized corrections is, as a whole, escaping the public scrutiny that could keep these systems safe, accountable, and effective in their attempts to reduce criminality. Criminal justice systems at every level have determined the privatization that is appropriate for them, based on their collective need. Although practical constraints such as prison capacity and budgeting can be the deciding factors in choosing to privatize some or all parts of a system, the ideological and economic motivations that have led to privatization over time cannot be ignored.

Historical Roots of Privatization

Describing the emergence of the private prison industry as beginning in the mid-1980s would be much less difficult and painful than examining its historical roots. This more recent date is generally what scholars acknowledge as the starting point of correctional privatization, with the founding of the nation's first private corrections company, the Corrections Corporation of America (Corrections Corporation of America, n.d.; Gaes, 2019; Kim & Price, 2014). This specific type of privatization, which comes with corporate stock holdings and filings with the New York Stock Exchange, did begin in the mid-1980s, but the roots of privatization in the United States stretch all the way back to pre-colonial America (Harding et al., 2019).

Private control over individuals convicted of crimes was a longstanding practice in many parts of the world prior to colonists setting foot on Indigenous soils in what would become the United States. The monarchy of England regularly saw the king taking private control over those deemed guilty of a crime. Included in this system of justice was the ability for the monarchy to remove the convicted individual from British soil by selling that person to the private sector for the purposes of labor in the colonies (Harding et al., 2019). As previously discussed in Chapter 1, beginning in 1717 convicted persons were regularly indentured, a practice that lasted until the American Revolution. During this time "approximately 50,000 British convicts were transported post-trial to America" (Grubb, 2001; Harding et al., 2019, p. 244).

Slavery, in and of itself, could be considered a form of privatization. However, the enslavement of African & African American people, which lasted from the colonization of America until the ratification of the Thirteenth Amendment, was not precipitated by any sort of criminal offense. Slavery, along with the British model of selling convicted criminals into private servitude, provided a template for governmental control over a person as a tool for economic gain. Following the ratification of the Thirteenth Amendment in December of 1865, advocates of slavery were forced to consider how their wealth, built on the literal backs of enslaved persons, would remain intact without forced labor (Alexander, 2020; DuVernay, 2016). Unfortunately, those proponents of slavery found consolation in the very same amendment that was supposed to prevent the continued enslavement of human bodies for the purposes of economic gain.

The Thirteenth Amendment to the U.S. Constitution in its entirety states that "Neither slavery nor involuntary servitude, except as punishment for crime whereof the party shall have been duly convicted, shall exist in the United States, or any place subject to their jurisdiction" (U.S. Const. amend. XIII). Specifically, scholars have recognized that both slavery and involuntary servitude were in effect not abolished at all, but rather codified and supported by, this amendment (Alexander, 2020; DuVernay, 2016; Gilmore, 2001). As previously discussed in Chapters 4 and 12, the phrasing "except as punishment for crime whereof the party shall have been duly convicted" left the door open for continued slavery and servitude via criminal conviction.

At first glance, this may seem like a glaring oversight on the part of President Lincoln and the Republican Party (now the current Democratic Party), but it should be noted that this phrasing of the amendment was specifically designed to protect the systems of convict leasing that existed in those states considered to be free (Fraser & Freeman, 2012). **Convict leasing** was a form of corrections privatization that allowed states to lease convicted persons to the private sector for the purposes of labor and production. The states, in turn, would reap the benefits of increased revenue generated by these leases. As Fraser & Freeman (2012) discuss:

the leasing out of prisoners was originally known as a "Yankee invention" The reason the Thirteenth Amendment, abolishing slavery, made an exception for penal servitude is precisely because it had long since become the dominant form of punishment throughout free states. (pp. 94–95)

Therefore, in order to maintain the economic systems propped up by slave labor, and to keep pace with the economic output of convict leasing in the North, state governments had to find ways to expand criminal convictions to newly "freed" individuals (Alexander, 2020; DuVernay, 2016; Fraser & Freeman, 2012; Gilmore, 2001). States now understood that they could use the justice system as a tool to force laborers into their fields and eventually into their factories (Fraser & Freeman, 2012).

The years that would follow the emancipation of individuals who had been enslaved are known as the **Reconstruction Era (1865–1877)**. The period of Reconstruction was an attempt by the Federal Government "to promote a future characterized by racial harmony and economic advancement" through the reintroduction of Confederate states to the Union (Huston, 2005, p. 403). The intentions may have been noble, but as Huston (2005) points out, "the ferocious racism of Southern whites" that precipitated Reconstruction was all but impossible to overcome (p. 403). This is particularly noticeable in the successful attempts by Southern states to begin/expand upon on the practice of convict leasing through the extension of what would come to be infamously known as "Black Codes."

Black Codes, as discussed in Chapter 12, were laws—again, particularly in the South but also present in the North—that criminalized the movement and behavior of predominantly Black former slaves during Reconstruction. This included acts of vagrancy or not holding a job, both of which were nearly impossible standards to adhere to due to the lack of education, capital, and opportunity for newly freed peoples (DuVernay, 2016). Historians and scholars have long since recognized that these laws were an attempt at filling the labor void left by the dismantling of slavery, and were a continuation of the same beliefs of racial superiority that underpinned it (DuBois, 1910; DuVernay, 2016; Gilmore, 2000; Mancini, 1978). As DuBois (1910) notes, "The Codes spoke for themselves. They have often been printed and quoted. No open-minded student can read them without being convinced that they mean nothing more nor less than slavery in daily toil" (p. 784). Not all scholars are convinced that Black Codes and convict leasing were a direct replacement for the agricultural labor that characterized slavery, as many leased persons worked in industry as well, but there is consensus on the use of these policies as tools of racial oppression (Muller, 2018).

Black Codes signaled formalized and broader versions of corrections privatization than were already taking place throughout the country. Following the end of the Civil War and throughout the early part of the next century, persons convicted under the Black

Codes were leased to coal mining companies, railroad companies, clothing factories, and numerous other manufacturers (Mancini, 1978; Muller, 2018). The result of these policies, which were codified into state law, was a transformation of the penal system that included large jumps in the number of inmates and in the lengths of time they were serving. Inmates were now also beginning their sentences at a much younger age and ending them as old men (Mancini, 1978). Mancini addresses the shifting demographics of the prison population in both the rural and urban South during this time:

> North Carolina's state convict population was 121 in 1870, 1,302 in 1890. Florida, with 125 convicts in its care in 1881, had 1,071 by 1904. Mississippi's prison population quadrupled in the eight years between 1871 and 1879, from 234 to 997. Alabama's population—374 in 1869—swelled to 1,183 in 1892, 1,878 in 1903, 2,453 in 1919. (1978, p. 343)

Black Codes and convict leasing would prove to be just the precursors to a much larger strategy of oppression and commodification that would take place following Reconstruction.

The limited freedoms and protections offered in other areas of life under the Black Codes were not enough to maintain them. The Codes had a blatant disregard for a person's basic humanity, and they eventually fell out of favor. Unfortunately, more subtle and covert methods of undermining and criminalizing the behavior of Black individuals were already taking place in the "Jim Crow" South. **Jim Crow laws** (1877–1965) were an attempt to segregate, control, and criminalize the Black population. Every aspect of their behavior, including their etiquette with White individuals, was set up in a system of total "racial control" (Thompson-Miller et al., 2014). Alexander (2020) argues that a close correlation exists between what occurred under Jim Crow and the current system of mass incarceration in the United States, in that they both operate "as a tightly networked system of laws, policies, customs and institutions that … collectively … ensure the subordinate status of a group defined largely by race" (p. 16).

Jim Crow laws lasted for nearly 100 years. During this time privatization fell out of favor, due in part to the abhorrent working conditions of convict laborers and the abuses that were taking place within private facilities. Facilities like San Quentin in California, which originally opened in 1854 and was the first fully privatized correctional facility, eventually returned to the public domain. Additionally, several major federal acts drastically diminished the reliance on private prison labor and private correctional facilities. According to Harding et al. (2019), "By the commencement of World War II, private involvement in corrections became a thing of the past" (p. 246). As discussed in Chapter 12, arduous inmate labor was redirected inward during this time, with chain gangs and prison farms being used to cut costs, generate profit, and expand correctional operations.

Modern Development of Privatization

There is an unmistakable link between the boom in the prison population and the modern development of corrections privatization. The need for expanded and additional prison facilities has been driven predominantly by the simultaneous wars on drugs and crime, as previously discussed in Chapter 2. The "get tough on crime" and "law and order" mantras have characterized political campaigns from Democrats and Republicans alike, at all levels of government, for the last 5 decades. Nixon made good on his 1968 campaign promises of "law and order" when he declared the War on Drugs in 1971. We know now that the Nixon administration set out to specifically target the Black populace that would vote against him in the 1972 election, just as slavery, convict leasing, Black Codes, and Jim Crow laws had specifically targeted Black people (Baum, 2016). John Ehrlichman, President Nixon's right-hand man and Assistant to the President for Domestic Affairs, has admitted to the racially charged motivation of the War on Drugs:

> The Nixon campaign in 1968, and the Nixon White House after that, had two enemies: the antiwar left and black people. You understand what I'm saying? We knew we couldn't make it illegal to be either against the war or black, but by getting the public to associate the hippies with marijuana and blacks with heroin, and then criminalizing both heavily, we could disrupt those communities. We could arrest their leaders, raid their homes, break up their meetings, and vilify them night after night on the evening news. Did we know we were lying about the drugs? Of course we did. (Baum, 2016, para. 2)

As the War on Drugs progressed into the 1980s, correctional systems were pushed to their limits. According to The Sentencing Project (2021), between 1985 and 2017, the correctional population in the United States increased by 500% and state expenditures on corrections ballooned to nearly $60 billion. These massive increases in both infrastructure and public expenditure, as well as the growing concern over the state of decay that many of our nation's correctional facilities were operating under, opened the door for private correctional companies to enter into the public detention domain (Harding et al., 2019). The growth in the private correctional industry beginning in the mid-1980s was swift, as companies first entered into federal contracts to detain migrants and then moved into the private detention of prisoners. As Harding et al. (2019) note, "By 1999, 5.3% of U.S. state and federal prisoners were being held in privately operated facilities" (p. 249). With the continued growth of the private prison industry, and with companies taking control of individual services within correctional systems, the movement toward ever-increasing privatization seemed inevitable.

The Current Scope of Corrections Privatization

Privatized prisons exist all over the world, as other countries have taken the resurgent ideas of privatization seen in the United States and made them their own. Within the United States, it would be nearly impossible to determine an exact number of people incarcerated under some form of private correctional supervision, or receiving privatized services. Beyond that, it is also difficult to accurately count the services that are privatized in correctional systems across the country. This is due in part to the unstandardized and limited record-keeping and reporting structures of correctional services used across local, state, and federal jurisdictions. When this limitation is paired with the revolving door of criminal justice discussed in Chapter 5, and the natural business cycle of corrections privatization in which contracts can be signed, renewed, or allowed to expire, this number becomes even more problematic to estimate.

As mentioned, our foremost understanding of the scope of corrections privatization only comes from our knowledge of those individuals who are being held in privately owned or operated correctional facilities across the country. Currently, of the 2.3 million people incarcerated in the United States, the number of people being held in private facilities is less than 9% (Sawyer & Wagner, 2020). This includes those held in private local, state, and federal institutions. At first glance, it is easy to see this as a much smaller portion of the total incarcerated population than expected. However, in a country like the United States, which houses 25% of the world's entire prison population, less than 9% of 2.3 million represents approximately 200,000 individuals. Consequently, the private prison population alone in the United States is higher than the *total prison populations* of 185 other countries (World Prison Brief, 2020).

Who Benefits From Privatization?

It is important to recognize who benefits from the privatization of correctional systems in order to evaluate them as a practical and ethical alternative to maintaining public control over those systems. The most complete models of privatization, again, occur inside the prison system. Three of the nation's most prominent privatized corrections corporations are **CoreCivic** (formerly Corrections Corporation of America), **The GEO Group** (formerly Wackenhut Corrections Corporation), and **Management & Training Corporation**. Core-Civic and GEO Group are both publicly traded on the New York Stock Exchange. In 2015, The GEO Group and CoreCivic alone made $3.5 billion in revenue from their correctional industry businesses, including their private prisons (The Sentencing Project, 2018). These companies, which are currently both valued in the billions, have also begun to corner the private corrections market.

Like any other major corporation, these companies have started to diversify, moving into all areas of correctional service including rehabilitation, juvenile justice, community corrections, and even prisoner transportation. According to The Sentencing Project (2018):

> Since 2005, GEO Group and Core Civic have spent $2.2 billion to acquire smaller companies in order to branch out to new industries beyond incarceration. For instance, in 2011, GEO Group acquired BI Incorporated, an ankle bracelet monitoring company. The companies also provide prison healthcare services and have established residential reentry centers. (p. 12)

However, these are not the only companies profiting from crime and criminals. The non-profit organization Worth Rises (2020b) has made it their mission to keep track of the taxpayer and inmate dollars/labor that companies profit from. The list includes everything from small single-owner companies that provide commissary items, to personnel management companies, to data collection and management agencies, and quite literally everything in between, as there is almost no portion of the corrections system that has not been privatized in some manner. Their report from 2020 details over 4,000 companies who profit from the $80 billion America spends on incarceration every year (Worth Rises, 2020b). These profit margins are driven by the extremely low wages that are paid to persons who are incarcerated to do the work, and the high costs and fees associated with inmate services and necessities (Sawyer, 2017). The Prison Policy Initiative addressed the wage disparity for incarcerated workers:

> The average of the minimum daily wages paid to incarcerated workers for non-industry prison jobs is now 86 cents, down from 93 cents reported in 2001. The average maximum daily wage for the same prison jobs has declined more significantly, from $4.73 in 2001 to $3.45 today. Incarcerated people assigned to work for state-owned businesses earn between 33 cents and $1.41 per hour on average—roughly twice as much as people assigned to regular prison jobs. (para. 3)

The list of companies profiting from incarcerated labor includes well-known names like ACE Hardware, Barnes and Noble, Chevrolet, GEICO, and General Electric, to name a few (Worth Rises, 2020b). This list, however, represents only a small fraction of the companies that have benefitted from prison labor, as some companies have made millions in this market and then swiftly exited. Companies like J. C. Penney and Victoria's Secret, amid pressure from reform advocates, have moved away from using prison labor systems, but not before profiting exponentially (Yahr, 2015).

The private service sector has fared similarly, except that their profit is driven by the consumers themselves—inmates and/or the family members who support them financially. Telecommunications has been an area of increased attention as the "correctional telecom sector rakes in an estimated $1.4 billion annually in just phone call revenue, with three corporations controlling 91 percent of the market" (Worth Rises, 2020a, p. 49). The cost of communication for those incarcerated continues to be an issue, as correctional systems have expanded the use of electronic messaging, video conferencing, and personal tablets. These same issues are repeated and exacerbated in other areas of privatized service inside correctional facilities, including food and commissary, healthcare, and financial services (Worth Rises, 2020a).

Public pressure has managed to reach some private sector businesses, as the exorbitant costs of privatized service inside correctional facilities have decreased (Worth Rises, 2020a). That same pressure reached the federal government, and in 2016, President Obama declared that the federal government would move away from of the use of private prisons. His vision was not realized, and the decision was later reversed under President Trump, but subsequently reinstated under President Biden (Armstrong, 2019; Ahmed, 2019; Madhani, 2021).

The Ethical and Practical Issues with Privatization

ETHICAL ISSUES

With the Federal Government providing some of the largest contracts for these companies, it is no surprise that the companies deliver regular donations to the campaigns of politicians who are privatization's most fervent supporters. Recently, the three major players in private corrections, CoreCivic, The GEO Group, and Management and Training Corporation, created **The Day 1 Alliance**. The Day 1 Alliance is "a trade association representing private sector contractors helping address corrections and detention challenges in the United States" (The Day 1 Alliance, 2020). The alliance suggests that it does not lobby "for or against" anything that would "impact the basis for or duration of an individual's incarceration or detention" (The Day 1 Alliance, 2020). This brings to light two intertwined ethical concerns of privatization: the pursuit of profit over inmate needs, and the opposition to correctional reform/oversight.

The continued use of private federal corrections contracts in recent years has renewed the debate over whether companies, whose bottom line is always profit, should control the freedoms and labor capacity of people convicted of even minor crimes (Burkhardt & Connor, 2016). The question really becomes: Will profit drive their business decisions, or will what is best for inmates be the deciding factor? Some believe that question has already been answered and point to those companies offering specific services inside correctional facilities. Companies can, and do, charge excessive amounts of money for even the smallest of services or necessities, often placing profit over a person's basic needs. A report complied in 2019 showed that 15-minute phone calls from a jail in Arkansas can cost nearly $25. State averages for 15-minute phone calls made from jails range from $1.26 to $14.49. With many inmates already living in poverty prior to their incarceration, the financial burden placed on them and their families to simply keep in touch can be crippling (Wagner & Jones, 2019).

There is also concern that companies who profit from keeping beds full will do everything in their power to lobby for policies and practices that incarcerate people at higher rates, and for longer periods of time. As can be seen from The Day 1 Alliance above, the major private corporations have tried to publicly distance themselves from lobbying efforts that push such policies. However, because at least two of these corporations are publicly traded on the stock market, they have a responsibility to profit for their shareholders. Thus, CoreCivic makes it clear in their 2018 annual filings that the first and primary "Risk Related to Our Business and Industry" is that "decreases in occupancy levels [amount of prisoners/detainees] could cause a decrease in revenues and profitability" (CoreCivic, 2018, p. 32). So, while the companies themselves may not directly advocate for harsher laws, it is clear to their stockholders which politicians and bills they should support: those that increase bed capacity and length of time incarcerated. Many people see this as an ethical conflict of interest that should automatically preclude private expansion into public corrections systems.

PRACTICAL ISSUES

Beyond the issues of profit and ethics are the practical impacts of private versus public corrections. This brings into question the philosophies of punishment that are discussed in Chapter 1. If our collective correctional ideology is simply incapacitation, then maybe for-profit prisons can do the job at a lower cost. However, if our punishment ideology is rehabilitation, what role does privatization have in this process? Are private companies able to meet the rehabilitative standards that are expected of correctional institutions? Do they run programs that are evidence-based and effective in reducing recidivism? Do the operational standards of for-profit facilities differ from public facilities, and how are the rights of prisoners upheld? Who is accountable when violence or human rights violations occur? There has been some attempt to answer these questions, but the research on privatization needs to be expanded greatly before making definitive conclusions.

In 2016, the Office of Inspector General (OIG) commissioned what was essentially a performance review of the contracts that were handed out to private correctional companies by the Bureau of Prisons between 2011 and 2014. The prisons were measured on eight specific metrics:

- Contraband;
- Reports of incidents;

- Lockdowns;
- Inmate discipline;
- Telephone monitoring;
- Selected grievances;
- Urinalysis drug testing; and
- Sexual misconduct.

The OIG found, on six of eight metrics, that contract prisons had more incidents per capita than the other federal public institutions with the exception of positive drug tests and sexual misconduct (both of which could be driven by lax testing or underreporting) (OIG, 2016). The OIG made a number of recommendations that sought to increase oversight and ensure the safety and security of inmates in contract prisons; however, at the time of this writing it remains to be seen if there has been widespread compliance with these measures.

One of the major motivations for states and the federal governments to privatize has been the allure of cost savings. If governments can pay companies to do the same job they do, at a lower cost to taxpayers, do they have a responsibility to privatize? A comprehensive analysis by Gaes (2019) details a number of outcomes regarding privatization research. Regarding the cost savings of privatization, it was found that the savings were minimal at the very best, and that more often, the cost of public versus private institutions was the same. Other studies have found that any realization of cost savings often comes through paying correctional personnel less and through hiring less officers (Mumford et al., 2016). Thus, it has been found that "Private prisons do not currently offer a clear advantage over their public-sector counterparts in terms of cost or quality" (Mumford et al., 2016, p. 6). Research also indicates the necessity for more comprehensive evaluation of prison privatization, from continued cost savings analysis to outcome evaluations of private programming (Gaes, 2019).

CONCLUSION

The topic of corrections privatization spans a number of disciplines, not just criminal justice. Ethics, philosophy, business, economics, public policy, and many more fields come into play. For some thinkers, any form of corrections privatization constitutes a clear violation of the trust that the public places in the criminal justice system. For others, there is still belief that, when handled properly, privatization can produce better outcomes at a more cost-effective rate. There is also belief that the system of privatization is waning and could soon become a thing of the past.

Part of the concern over privatization is the lack of extensive research that has been done. Companies have not been sufficiently scrutinized on their abilities to deliver effective and cost-efficient results. Juvenile justice systems, community corrections, and even inmate transportation are all areas of corrections privatization that have not received sufficient attention from researchers. This is especially concerning in regard to the juvenile system, which is undoubtedly centered on rehabilitation rather than simple incapacitation. What happens to youth who do not receive adequate rehabilitative services? Do they end up in adult institutions owned by the very same companies who cut their programming? These are questions that are worth asking and researching as the decision to privatize is being made.

There are inextricable links between corrections privatization and the forced labor of slavery. Trying to separate these two concepts as distinct events misrepresents how much the past guides the present, and the future, of the criminal justice system. We also cannot ignore the recent historical events that have taken place in 2020 with regard to policing. With calls for extreme police reform, there are undoubtedly changes on the horizon for correctional systems throughout the United States as well. How will governments and companies respond in the face of public pressure to de-institutionalize prisons?

DISCUSSION QUESTIONS

1. What other ethical and practical issues do you think can develop when correctional systems privatize?
2. Are there differences in the way we should examine privatization in the juvenile system versus the adult system?
3. How do you think people inside prisons should be paid for their labor?

APPLICATION EXERCISES

Exercise #1: Start Local

Contact your local prison or elected officials and ask them to provide you with information regarding the contracts they have with private companies. Gather the data, all of which should be available to you as a member of the public. Think about the services they offer and the cost to inmates. Are there ways to reduce those costs? Are there ways to provide the same services for free? Start a local program or campaign that educates people on the for-profit industry of corrections, and ask for their help in changing your local policies to reflect the changes you think are necessary.

Exercise #2: Take a Stance

Examine the list of companies that profit from corrections privatization compiled by Worth Rises (see https://worthrises.org/theprisonindustry2020). Which companies do you recognize, or use personally? Worth Rises also indicates a *harm score*:

The harm score measures the engagement of each corporation in human rights violations along three criteria: the salience or gravity of the violation, their responsibility for the violation, and their responsiveness to advocacy engagement. Each criterion was measure[d] on a scale from 1 to 5, making the overall harm score range 3 to 15.

If you believe that no longer supporting these companies is appropriate, take the personal action to stop using them. Ask others to join you by posting on social media that you will no longer be shopping at, or using the services of, companies that profit from corrections privatization. These seemingly small actions can have a tremendous impact on public policy and practice.

REFERENCES

Ahmed, H. (2019). *How private prisons are profiting under the Trump administration.* Center for American Progress. https://www.americanprogress.org/issues/democracy/reports/2019/08/30/473966/private-prisons-profiting-trump-administration/

Alexander, M. (2020). *The new Jim Crow: Mass incarceration in the age of colorblindness.* The New Press.

Armstrong, M. (2019). *Here's why abolishing private prisons isn't a silver bullet.* The Marshall Project. https://www.themarshallproject.org/2019/09/12/here-s-why-abolishing-private-prisons-isn-t-a-silver-bullet

Baum, D. (2016). *Legalize it all: How to win the war on drugs.* Harper's Magazine. https://harpers.org/archive/2016/04/legalize-it-all/

Burkhardt, B. C., & Connor, B. T. (2016). Durkheim, punishment, and prison privatization. *Social Currents, 3*(1), 84–99.

CoreCivic. (2018). *Annual report pursuant to section 13 or 159d) of the Securities and Exchange Act of 1934* [Form 10-K]. http://ir.corecivic.com/static-files/f289bea9-086c-4540-82b2-114dbfb95e4e

Corrections Corporation of America. (n.d.). *Our history.* http://www.correctionscorp.com/our-history

Davis, A. Y. (1998, September 10). *Masked racism: Reflections on the prison industrial complex.* Colorlines. https://www.colorlines.com/articles/masked-racism-reflections-prison-industrial-complex.

The Day 1 Alliance. (2020). *Who we are.* https://day1alliance.org/

DuBois, W. E. B. (1910). Reconstruction and its benefits. *The American Historical Review, 15*(4), 781–799.

DuVernay, A. (Director). (2016). *13th* [Film]. Kandoo Films; Netflix.

Fraser, S., & Freeman, J. B. (2012). In the rearview mirror: Barbarism and progress: The story of convict labor. *New Labor Forum, 21*(3), 94–98.

Gaes, G. G. (2019). Current status of prison privatization research on American prisons and jails. *Criminology & Public Policy, 18*(2), 269-293.

Gilmore, K. (2000). Slavery and prison: Understanding the connections. *Social Justice, 27*(3), 195–205.

Grubb, F. (2001). The market evaluation of criminality: Evidence from the auction of British convict labor in America, 1767–1775. *American Economic Review, 91*(1), 295–304.

GTL. (2021). *Our Mission.* https://www.gtl.net/about-us/our-mission/

Harding, R. W., Rynne, J., & Thomsen, L. (2019). History of privatized corrections. *Criminology & Public Policy, 18*(2), 241–267.

Huston, J. L. (2005). An alternative to the tragic era: Applying the virtues of bureaucracy to the Reconstruction dilemma. *Civil War History, 51*(4), 403–415.

Kaeble, D. (2018). *Probation and parole in the United States, 2016* (NCJ 251148). U.S. Department of Justice, Office of Justice Programs, Bureau of Justice Statistics. https://www.bjs.gov/content/pub/pdf/ppus16.pdf#page=15

Kassie, E. (2019, September 24). *Detained: How the US built the world's largest immigrant detention system.* The Guardian. https://www.theguardian.com/us-news/2019/sep/24/detained-us-largest-immigrant-detention-trump

Kim, Y., & Price, B. (2014). Revisiting prison privatization: An examination of the magnitude of prison privatization. *Administration & Society, 46*(3), 255–275.

Latessa, E. J., & Brusman Lovins, L. (2019). Privatization of community corrections. *Criminology & Public Policy, 18*(2), 323–341.

Madhani, A. (2021, January 26). *Biden orders Justice Dept. to end use of private prisons.* AP News. https://apnews.com/article/joe-biden-race-and-ethnicity-prisons-coronavirus-pandemic-c8c246f00695f37ef2afb1dd3a5f115e

Mancini, M. J. (1978). Race, economics, and the abandonment of convict leasing. *The Journal of Negro History, 63*(4), 339–352.

Mears, D., & Montes, A. (2019). Introduction to the special issue on privatized corrections. *Criminology & Public Policy, 18*(2), 457–476.

Morris, J. C. (2007). Government and market pathologies of privatization: The case of prison privatization. *Politics & Policy, 35*(2), 318–341.

Muller, C. (2018). Freedom and convict leasing in the Postbellum South. *Journal of Sociology, 124*(2), 367–405.

Mumford, M., Whitmore Schanzenbach, D., & Nunn, R. (2016). *The economics of private prisons.* The Hamilton Project. https://www.hamiltonproject.org/assets/files/economics_of_private_prisons.pdf

Office of the Inspector General. (2016). *Review of the Federal Bureau of Prisons' monitoring of contract prisons.* https://oig.justice.gov/reports/2016/e1606.pdf

Prison Legal News (2021, February 1). Federal judge in Georgia grants class action status to prisoners' suit against Global Tel*Link. *Prison Legal News*. https://www.prisonlegalnews.org/faq/#faq-12

Sawyer, W. (2017). *How much do incarcerated people earn in each state?* The Prison Policy Initiative. https://www.prisonpolicy.org/blog/2017/04/10/wages/

Sawyer, W., & Wagner, P. (2020). *Mass incarceration: The whole pie 2020*. The Prison Policy Initiative. https://www.prisonpolicy.org/reports/pie2020.html

Schlosser, E. (1998, December). *The prison-industrial complex*. The Atlantic. https://www.theatlantic.com/magazine/archive/1998/12/the-prison-industrial-complex/304669/

Sentencing Project. (2021). *Trends in U.S. corrections*. https://www.sentencingproject.org/wp-content/uploads/2016/01/Trends-in-US-Corrections.pdf

Sickmund, M., Sladky, T. J., Kang, W., & Puzzanchera, C. (2019). *Easy access to the census of juveniles in residential placement: 1997–2017*. National Center for Juvenile Justice. https://www.ojjdp.gov/ojstatbb/ezacjrp/

Thompson-Miller, R., Feagin, J. R., & Picca, L. H. (2014). *Jim Crow's legacy: The lasting impact of segregation*. Rowan & Littlefield.

U.S. Const. amend. XIII.

U.S. Immigration and Customs Enforcement. (2019). *Fiscal year 2019 enforcement and removal operations report*. https://www.ice.gov/sites/default/files/documents/Document/2019/eroReportFY2019.pdf

U.S. Immigration and Customs Enforcement. (2020). *Currently detained population by arresting agency* [Infographic]. https://www.ice.gov/detention-management

Wagner, P. (2016). *Some private prisons are, um, public*. Prison Policy Initiative. https://www.prisonpolicy.org/blog/2016/06/09/privatejails/

Wagner, P. (2017, August 28). *Prison phone giant GTL gets bigger, again*. Prison Policy Initiative. https://www.prisonpolicy.org/blog/2017/08/28/merger/

Wagner, P., & Jones, A. (2019). *State of phone justice: Local jails, state prisons and private phone providers*. Prison Policy Initiative. https://www.prisonpolicy.org/phones/state_of_phone_justice.html

World Prison Brief. (2020). *Highest to lowest - prison population total*. https://www.prisonstudies.org/highest-to-lowest/prison-population-total?field_region_taxonomy_tid=All

Worth Rises. (2020a). *The prison industry: How it started. How it works. How it warms*. https://static1.squarespace.com/static/58e127cb1b10e31ed45b20f4/t/5ff2bbe-318d44937a922e754/1609743335995/The+Prison+Industry+-+How+It+Started%2C+How+It+Works%2C+and+How+It+Harms+%28December+2020%29.pdf

Worth Rises. (2020b). *The prison industry: Mapping private sector players.* https://static1.squarespace.com/static/58e127cb1b10e31ed45b20f4/t/5eb26cb17cc82c67c6254da6/1588751538880/The+Prison+Industry+-+2020.pdf

Yahr, E. (2015, June 17). *Yes, prisoners used to sew lingerie for Victoria's Secret—just like in 'Orange is the New Black' Season 3.* The Washington Post. https://www.washingtonpost.com/news/arts-and-entertainment/wp/2015/06/17/yes-prisoners-used-to-sew-lingerie-for-victorias-secret-just-like-in-orange-is-the-new-black-season-3/

Index

9 781516 596119